The New Pilgrims

YOUTH PROTEST IN TRANSITION

Edited by

PHILIP G. ALTBACH
The University of Wisconsin—Madison

ROBERT S. LAUFER
The State University of New York at Albany

DAVID McKAY COMPANY, INC.
NEW YORK

THE NEW PILGRIMS: YOUTH
PROTEST IN TRANSITION

Acknowledgements

ALL OF the essays in this volume, except those noted below, first appeared in the *Annals of the American Academy of Political and Social Science*, volume 395 (May 1971). They are reprinted with the kind permission of the *Annals* and its editor, Dr. Richard Lambert.

Essays reprinted from other sources are as follows:

Vern L. Bengtson, "The Generation Gap: A Review and Typology of Social-Psychological Perspectives," *Youth and Society*, vol. 2, number 1 (September 1970): 7–32, by permission of the publisher, Sage Publications, Inc.

Richard Flacks, "On the New Working Class and Strategies for Social Change," reprinted from *Social Policy*, vol. 1, number 6 (March-April 1971): 7–15, with some revisions by the author.

Karl Mannheim, "The Problem of Generations," from Karl Mannheim, *Essays in the Sociology of Knowledge* (New York: Oxford University Press, 1952), pp. 286–322, by permission of the publisher, Oxford University Press.

Seymour Martin Lipset and Everett Carll Ladd, Jr., "The Political Future of Activist Generations," is printed in this volume for the first time. An earlier and substantially different version of this essay appeared in *The Public Interest*, 25 (Fall 1971): 99–113.

Robert J. Lifton, "The New History," from *Boundaries* (New York: Random House, 1969), pp. 95–113, by permission of the publisher.

iv   *Acknowledgements*

Philip E. Slater, "Women and Children First," from *The Pursuit of Loneliness* (Boston: Beacon Press, 1970), pp. 53–80, by permission of the author and publisher.

Biographical Notes

Philip G. Altbach is associate professor of Educational Policy Studies and Indian Studies at the University of Wisconsin. He has been lecturer in Education and fellow of the Center for International Affairs at Harvard University, and was Fulbright Visiting Professor in the Department of Sociology at the University of Bombay, India, in 1968. He is author of *Student Politics in Bombay*, editor of *Turmoil and Transition: Higher Education and Student Politics in India*, and co-editor, with Seymour Martin Lipset, of *Students in Revolt*. He is also a member of the editorial board of the *Comparative Education Review*. He received his Ph.D. in Comparative Education from the University of Chicago in 1966.

Vern L. Bengtson is associate professor of Sociology at the University of Southern California, Los Angeles. He is principal investigator of the Study on Generations and Mental Health, and is on the staff of the Gerontology Center of the University of Southern California.

Raymond Boudon is professor of Sociology at the University of Paris (Sorbonne) and director of the Centre d'Études Sociologiques (Centre National de la Recherche Scientifique). He is the author of several books and many articles in the field of sociological methodology, social mobility, and sociology of education, including *L'analyse mathematique des faits sociaux* (1967), and *La notion de structure dans les sciences humaines* (1968), both of which are to be published in English.

Shmuel N. Eisenstadt is professor of Sociology at the Hebrew

University, Jerusalem, Israel. He has also been visiting professor at the London School of Economics, the University of Chicago, Harvard University, and the University of Michigan, as well as Carnegie visiting professor at the Massachusetts Institute of Technology. He is the author of *From Generation to Generation*, (1956), *The Political Systems of Empires* (1963), *Modernization, Protest, and Change* (1966), *Israeli Society* (1968), and other books and articles. He has edited, among other books, *The Protestant Ethic and Modernization* (1968), and, most recently, *Political Sociology* (1970).

Richard Flacks has been associate professor of Sociology at the University of California at Santa Barbara since 1969. His studies of the social backgrounds of student activists, conducted in the mid-sixties, contributed heavily to the "portrait" of the young radical which this article brings up to date. He is the author of many articles on student protest.

Edgar Z. Friedenberg is professor of Education at Dalhousie University in Halifax, Nova Scotia. The author of *The Vanishing Adolescent* and *Coming of Age in America*, he was awarded the B.S. degree in Chemistry at Centenary College, the M.A., also in Chemistry, at Stanford University, and the Ph.D. in Education at the University of Chicago and landed immigrant status in Canada in 1970.

Kenneth Keniston is professor of Psychology and director of the Behavioral Sciences Study Center, Yale Medical School. He is the author of *The Uncommitted* (1965), *Young Radicals* (1968), and *Youth and Dissent* (1971), as well as numerous articles on student disaffection.

Everett Carll Ladd, Jr. is professor of Political Science at the University of Connecticut. He has written widely on the politics of American higher education, and is working, with Seymour Martin Lipset, on a study of the American professoriate funded by the Carnegie Commission on Higher Education.

Robert S. Laufer is an assistant professor of Sociology at the State University of New York, Albany. In 1970 he was a visiting lecturer in the departments of Educational Policy Studies and Sociology at the University of Wisconsin. He has recently completed a book on the University of Wisconsin, in collaboration with Philip Altbach and Sheila McVey.

Michael Lerner is assistant professor of Political Science at Yale University, with a joint appointment in the Behavioral Sciences Study Center at the Yale Medical School. He has written on academic bigotry, anarchism and the American counter-culture, political biography, and other topics.

Robert J. Lifton is Foundation's Fund professor for research in Psychiatry at Yale University. He did research at Harvard from 1956 to 1961, where he was associated with the East Asian Research Center as well as with the Department of Psychiatry. He is the author of *History and Human Survival, Death in Life; Survivors of Hiroshima, Thought Reform and the Psychology of Totalism: A Study of "Brainwashing" in China*, and other books. Professor Lifton has been particularly concerned with the problems of youth in the modern age in both America and in Asia.

Seymour Martin Lipset is professor of Sociology and Government and a member of the Center for International Affairs at Harvard University. He is author of *Political Man, Revolution and Counter-Revolution*, editor of *Student Politics*, and co-editor (with Philip G. Altbach) of *Students in Revolt*, as well as numerous other books and articles.

Milton Mankoff has been assistant professor of Sociology at the University of California at Santa Barbara since 1969. The study reported here is based upon his doctoral research at the University of Wisconsin. He is currently working on a book based upon some of the central themes of this article and an anthology on American institutions from an historical and sociological perspective. He has written articles on Marxist and elitist critiques of pluralist theory and social deviance.

Karl Mannheim (1893–1947) was professor of Sociology at the University of Frankfurt until 1933, when he assumed faculty position at the University of London, where he served until his death in 1947. He is author of *Ideology and Utopia* and many other books. The essay reprinted in this volume is from his *Essays in the Sociology of Knowledge*.

Barbara G. Myerhoff is associate professor of Anthropology at the University of Southern California, Los Angeles. She served as research associate at the Youth Studies Center at the university from 1960 until 1967. Her writings include "Family Integration and Police Contact," in *Juvenile Gangs in Context*, Malcolm W. Klein and W. R. Larson, eds. (1967), reprinted in C. A. Bersani, *Crime and Delinquency* (1970); also "New Styles of Humanism: American Youth," in *Youth and Society*, December, 1969, and in *Era of Dissent*, R. A. Rosenstone and Joseph Boskin, eds. (1971).

James P. O'Brien holds a Ph.D. degree in American History from the University of Wisconsin, Madison. His *History of the New Left, 1960–1968*, published as a pamphlet by the New England Free Press, is the only general narrative history of the New Left. He is completing a full scale study of the New Left.

Patti McGill Peterson is a doctoral candidate in the Department of Educational Policy studies at the University of Wisconsin. She has been a lecturer at Schiller College in Kleiningersheim, Germany, and is now engaged in research on the relationship of the student pacifist movement to radical student politics.

Frank A. Pinner has been teaching in the Department of Political Science of Michigan State University since 1955. His Ph.D. degree is from the University of California, Berkeley. He is a former fellow of the Social Sciences Research Council, the Center for Advanced Study in the Behavioral Sciences, and a former Fulbright research fellow in Belgium. His published research includes several studies of political socialization and of student activism and movements.

John R. Seeley, professor of Cultural Studies at the California Institute of the Arts, was, from 1963 to 1966, the dean of the Center for the Study of Democratic Institutions in Santa Barbara. Previous to this, he was for three years a sociologist with the medical department at the Massachusetts Institute of Technology, and was research director of, and later consultant to, the Alcoholism Research Foundation of Ontario, also for three years. He was professor and chairman of the Department of Sociology at both Brandeis University and York University, Ontario. He is the author of *The Americanization of the Unconscious* and *The Alcohol Language* (with Mark Heller, and *Crestwood Heights* (with others).

Philip E. Slater received his A.B. in Government in 1950 from Harvard University and his Ph.D. in Sociology in 1955, also from Harvard University. His doctoral thesis was on psychological factors in role specialization. His publications include *The Glory of Hera: Greek Mythology and the Greek Family*, *Microcosm*, and *The Pursuit of Loneliness*, from which the excerpt in this volume is drawn.

Contents

Introduction

PHILIP G. ALTBACH and ROBERT S. LAUFER

It is hard to believe that student protest and generational conflict became a topic of concern only in the past decade. Although young people have been involved in politics for many years in foreign countries, it is only recently that American youth and students have played an important political role in society and the university.* It is the purpose of this book to place the revolt of youth into its contemporary perspective, and to add some historical background to what has become a major social issue in advanced industrial societies. While some attention is given to other advanced industrial societies, the primary focus is on the United States.

Much of the analysis of the "youth movement" has referred to student activism and campus unrest for the simple reason that it has been primarily college youth who have been involved in activist movements and demonstrations. This volume also deals with students but it considers as well the broader, non-student, aspects of the youth revolt. The volume goes beyond the university context to explore the roots of generational conflict which exists as a more general malaise among other segments of the youth population in some modernized societies. In this volume, we have sought to integrate these two approaches in order to achieve a better understanding of the relation-

*For bibliographical sources of materials on student activism, see Philip G. Altbach, *A Select Bibliography on Students, Politics, and Higher Education*, revised edition (Cambridge, Mass.: Harvard Center for International Affairs, 1970), and Philip G. Altbach, *Students, Politics and Higher Education in the United States: A Select Bibliography* (Cambridge, Mass.: Harvard Center for International Affairs, 1968).

1

ship between young people and social conflict. This book does not, however, present a clear "theoretical" perspective because, in our view, there are still many unanswered questions concerning both student activism and generational conflict.

Student protest and generational conflict are different but complementary ways of analyzing the unrest among young people which has manifested itself so dramatically in recent years. The student protest approach looks at the immediate causes as well as at sociological, political, and cultural issues which relate to student activism. Focus is placed on organizations and movements, as well as on the institutional context of student activism, the universities. Generational conflict, as an approach to activism, goes beyond the student protest approach in that it is concerned with an analysis of the cultural and political discontinuities between age groups which result from the difference in societal and historical experiences. Rather than focusing on specific acts of protest, the generational conflict approach views student unrest as a series of events which stem from a growing opposition of the young to the values and institutions of society. The antagonism between young and old is not merely a product of political disagreement; it is caused by basic differences in perceptions of society which result in the formation of antithetical and culturally distinct groups. The generational approach frames broad questions about the nature of advanced industrial society, the processes of social change within it, and the impact of such societies upon youth.

The volume is divided into three parts: a description and analysis of the American student movement from several different perspectives; an examination and analysis of generational consciousness and the sources and patterns of generational conflict; and a comparative analysis of student protest as a product of the marginal elite positions of students. The first two sections deal almost exclusively with the development of student protest and generational conflict in America. The final section places the American experience in a cross-national perspective.

AMERICAN STUDENT ACTIVISM

Both the historical background of the American student movement and its current manifestations are discussed in the chapters in this section. Such factors as the social class base of the student movement, its historical origins, the organizations which were instrumental in establishing a New Left, and the impact of the university on student activism are considered.

The history of student protest in America during the twentieth century demonstrates the continuity of issues which have drawn the attention of student activists. Civil rights, civil liberties, war and disarmament have been central to each phase of the student movement since the 1920s. However it is only during the 1960s that political protest and cultural radicalism are decisvely joined in a student protest movement. The growth of the American student movement from a relatively small, isolated group of intellectuals to a broad-based student movement at the end of the decade is, in large part, attributable to the impact of the civil rights movement and the Vietnam War. Students' perceptions of the unresponsiveness of the political system to the protest movement provided a foundation upon which cultural radicalism could grow. Also important in the growth of cultural radicalism is the dissatisfaction of students with their academic condition and the growing importance of degrees, together with the haphazard growth of educational institutions and their involvement in the life of the society.

The importance of the relationship between higher education and socio-economic development is debated in this volume. Two positions emerge: everyone agrees that the most important source of student disaffection is related to the major social and political issues of the day, rather than to the internal workings of academic institutions; however, there is disagreement over the importance of the interpenetration between higher education and political, economic, and social institutions, and the extent of that interpenetration. Those authors who view the relationship as significant often relate student protest directed against the university to this tendency in advanced industrial societies. If the authors see the relationship between higher education and other institutions as less significant, then they are unlikely to see this as a source of student protest.

The isolation of the student movement from adult organizations is unique to the 1960s. It is a product of the alienation which developed between the student and adult organizations during the civil rights and antiwar movements, and the generally hostile response of adults to cultural radicalism. Certain structural features of contemporary society also fostered the isolation of the student movement. The existence of a semi-autonomous youth subculture encourages the isolation of the young from adult society. The role of the campus as the center of the protest movement, and the increasing number of young people in and around academic communities, accentuated this isolation. Faculty and other adults are only segmentally involved with campus life and student culture. Also, the conflict between student and adult organizations aids the development of subcultures.

Academic institutions expose young people to the ideas of the intelligentsia, who professionally and critically examine the quality of life in the society. On the other hand, the student is expected to acquire those skills which will allow him to find a position. In the past decade, students, and especially activists, have demanded that the university become a base for political activism and social change. Experiences in the protest movement, failure to effect basic social change, and isolation on the campuses have created a frustrating situation for many students. At the same time, the campus environment and the impact of the critical intelligentisia, based in the universities, contributes to the social base of what may emerge into a significant social movement.

GENERATIONAL CONFLICT

Although there is general agreement about the sources of unrest, there is significant disagreement about the size, social base and implications of student protest. There are two basic positions which are developed in this book. Position one argues that the size of the movement has grown dramatically, and this growth is a product of the penetration of the movement into social strata beyond its initial upper-middle-class base in prestigous universities. Position two argues that the movement has indeed expanded, but not very much, and that on the evidence available, the major strength of the movement is to be found is those places where it began. Position one moves from its analysis of the growth of the movement to argue that a broadly based movement is emerging among young people that is antithetical to the dominant ethos and institutions of American society. The source of this animosity was initially the disaffection with the Vietnam War and the failure of the civil rights movement. Position two is skeptical of the notion that the protest movement of the sixties is the vanguard of a widespread radical upsurge. Most students and a large majority of the non-student youth remain committed to basic American social institutions and values.

These two positions naturally have quite different predictions about the future. Position one sees a growing period of unrest, based on large scale dissatisfaction and the emergence of conflict along generational lines. Position two predicts that while student activism may from time to time play an important role, it does not provide the basis of a future revolutionary movement.

Many of the authors in this volume suggest that position one is a more accurate analysis of the present situation than position two, and predict the emergence of more widespread generational conflict. The editors agree, at least in part, that the student movement has indeed moved from a rather clear issue orientation in the early 1960s to a generational protest movement. However, it is not clear that these manifestations of generational conflict will result in effective radical political movements among young people. By and large, although the scope of the student movement has grown and has included the less prestigous colleges for the first time, youth protest remains on the campus. Furthermore, the class nature of the student movement has changed somewhat and now includes some students from lower-middle-class and working-class backgrounds.

However, despite the growth of "the movement," the majority of young people in America, are basically loyal to the "establishment." There are two kinds of minorities which are of importance to a discussion of generalitonal conflict; that small group of students who play an active role in protest and who constitute the leadership of the "movement," and those students who can be mobilized for specific demonstrations and who share many of the anti-establishment attitudes of the leaders. As has been shown, for example, in the massive demonstrations which followed the Cambodian incursions in May 1970, these minorities can have a major impact on the campuses. Consideration of the degree of action and commitment on the part of all members of a given population reveals that sizeable minorities— 30–35 percent—are able to become *de facto* majorities. In university protests, as well as in presidential elections, 35–40 percent of the population fail to enter the political arena. A majority of the remaining, 60–65 percent, therefore, constitutes a *de facto* majority. A recent study of a demonstration at the University of Wisconsin (Lyons 1971) shows that 42 percent of the respondents supported the demonstration, while only 24 percent were opposed. Thus, the 42 percent, although only a minority of the total student population, constituted a *de facto* minority.

If this pattern is characteristic of youth protest, then we can argue that it represents the dominant impulse among young people in the United States, and, as such, represents the basis of a movement for a radical reconstruction of society. The size potential of such a movement is dependent on both the proportion of the population that is permanently mobilized, and that proportion which can be recruited for specific activities such as demonstrations. Identification of the permanently mobilized members of a group is a fairly simple matter: identification of those who are active only sporadically—most usually during crises—is a far more difficult but nonetheless critical task. For only by accurately assessing this segment of the population can we realistically predict the strength of a social movement.

Attitude surveys are generally inadequate instruments for prediction of the strength of a movement for radical reconstruction unless they include a test for potential activists. In other words, information about dynamics of conflict is as important as information concerning the general attitude structure of a given population. Social revolutionary movements usually represent distinct minorities that are capable of generating a critical mass which lays claim to power in the name of the people but which, in fact, constitutes only a *de facto* majority. The French, Russian and American revolutions are illustrative cases. These insurgent minorities develop into political and cultural forces that have a deeper faith in their values and their critiques of society than the general population has in the established values and institutional systems. Their commitment is a decided asset, especially when they face established elites who reveal their lack of faith and confidence in the existing system through self-destructive, or inconsistent and arbitrary actions.

Finally, it is crucial to recognize that the centers of generational protest and student activism will play a disproportionate role in defining issues, patterns of action and, more generally, the consciousness of the younger generation. Whatever one's political attitude toward this type of leading role for these minorities, it seems rather clear that the dispersion of ideas and patterns of behavior from the centers to the general constitutency of youth is in no way different from the patterns of dispersion of politics, economics and culture, characteristic of the establishment. In fact, one could argue that there is more openness and diversification, and less centralization in the generational protest movement than is characteristic of the establishment culture.

The intraclass nature of generational conflict raises several questions: What are the consequences of divisions within the dominant social strata? What constitutes the critical mass such a movement must mobilize, both within its own social strata and among others?

The second section of this volume explores these questions. The sequence of articles moves from a general consideration of the basis and process of generational differentiation to specific issues and particular sources of conflict between generations. The reader must keep in mind the fact that generational discontinuity is developed over time and expresses the differing images of man and society held by generations engaged in conflict. There is no neat break which defines the different generations, but there are general age cohorts which are likely to share a common experience and social location. Many people fall into a transitionary category, but generally ally themselves with either the younger or older generational perspective rather than forming a separate generational consciousness.

CROSS-CULTURAL PERSPECTIVES

The major focus of this volume is on the United States, but we feel that it is also important to add a comparative dimension, since student movements are world wide in scope. We are not postulating that there is any ready international "theory" of student activism. Indeed, we are impressed by the importance of national variations in student movements, although common elements are also discernable, particularly among the advanced industrialized countries. For this final section of the book, Frank Pinner's theoretical article on students as a marginal elite is used as a framework for viewing student protest in several different areas. As the following articles show, the marginal elite position of students is an important factor in each case. Pinner differentiates student organizations from religious and military organizations, which are also marginal elites, because student groups lack a well-defined hierarchical structure as well as an independent source of social and political power. These factors effectively limit the political power of student activists and are critical elements which make student movements especially vlunerable to repression. Few student movements, as this section indicates, have been able to take power and hold it. They have, in most cases, been catalysts for social change but have lost initiative once the revolutionary impetus is lost.

There are, however, significant differences in the marginal condition of students in societies which are various stages in the development process. The more advanced the stage of industrial development, the larger the proportion of youth to be found in the student category. The expansion of the student population increases the numbers available for protest, but decreases the value of studenthood as a stage on the road to elite membership. Advanced industrial societies, therefore, loosen the direct tie between students and the elite. Developing societies, on the other hand, maintain a close relation between student and elite status.

In the post-independence period, the events which activated students in developing societies tend to center around specific political issues. These issues can be related to the prerogatives of the student community and their future elite status, or they can be related to broader social issues for which the students act as a "vanguard" for the rest of society. It should be noted that prior to World War II, students in developing areas, then under colonial rule for the most part, were intensively involved in nationalist movements and often played a leading role in them. Thus, the differences between pre- and post-independence student movements in developing countries is quite important.

Student movements, in both advanced and developing countries, have been something of a barometer of the political situation in their countries. The student unrest that characterized France and West Germany in 1968 was an indication of more widespread discontent with internal politics in those countries. In developing areas, student movements have accurately reflected national moods, and have, in many cases, led successful movements against repressive or corrupt governments. Students have also been involved with activism concerning university related questions, such as poor conditions, unemployment of graduates, or repression of students by police or other authorities.

The comparative perspective developed in this section may add some insights into the American situation. It seems clear that the generational conflicts, reported in this volume, concerning the United States, have not occurred, in any substantial degree, in developing countries and are only now growing to major proportions in other advanced industrial nations. In this sense, perhaps the United States is providing a "model" for other nations. American students, however, have a lot to learn from their compeers in other countries in terms of the effectiveness of student movements on political issues.

This volume deals with several key aspects of students activism and generational conflict. In a sense, it raises as many questions as it answers, but at the same time, it links two pressing problems of modern society. It is clear that the "problem" of youth, in modern societies at least, is not a passing phenomenon and that it can have major political, social, and educational consequences. If this volume has placed some of the issues and their possible effects in perspective, then it has served a useful purpose.

Part I

Perspectives on American Student Activism

.1. *Before Berkeley: Historical Perspectives on American Student Activism*

PHILIP G. ALTBACH and PATTI M. PETERSON

AMERICAN STUDENT activism has a long history, although it was only in the sixties that it received national attention and serious analysis. In 1823, half the Harvard senior class was expelled shortly before graduation for participating in disruptive activity, and students were involved in anti-conscription campaigns during the Civil War.[1] Student activism before 1960, however, had no major impact on national policy, and prior to 1900, no organized student activist groups emerged. Yet there is a tradition of student involvement in politics in the United States, and many of the concerns of the activists of the sixties are reflected in the past.

This essay provides a broad historical picture of American student activism from 1900 to 1960. We have concentrated on organizations and movements, and have omitted a more detailed sociological analysis. Although religious student movements, pacifist groups, and conservative organizations were important during this period, it was liberal and radical student activity which exerted greater impact on the campus—hence our emphasis.

The American student movement prior to 1960 closely followed political trends in society. Members of the Intercollegiate Socialist Society (ISS), founded in 1905, were a "vanguard" among university students. But until major political crises mobilized large numbers of students, such groups remained small. The student movements which

[1]See S. M. Lipset and G. Schaflander, *Passion and Politics: Student Activism in America* (Boston: Little, Brown, 1971), pp. 124–196 for a detailed description of the early origins of American student activism.

flourished prior to 1960 were generally linked closely with adult movements and no "generation gap" is readily discernible among activists. In fact, the independence of the current student movement might well be one of its strengths, since it is not necessarily bound by the organizational or ideological limitations of adult movements.

The student activism which developed in the early twentieth century took place in a context different from that of the modern American university. The colleges were much less in the mainstream of American life and the academic community was much smaller than at present. In 1912, for example, there were approximately 400,000 students in American universities. Activism, even of the moderate type reported here, was confined to a very small proportion of the student community and to a relatively few institutions. Yet, the student "movement," if it can be called that, set the political tone of a basically apathetic campus community and influenced a small number of students who later played important roles in American public life. The foundations for student political activity on the campus were formed in the early years of this century.

EARLY ACTIVIST GROUPS

As the earliest major leftist student political organization, the ISS included among its early active members Upton Sinclair, Morris Hillquit, Jack London, Charlotte Perkins Gilman, Clarence Darrow, Walter Lippmann, and others later prominent in reformist and radical movements. Interestingly, most of the ISS founders were not students. From the beginning, the ISS was an educational organization, formed to "promote an intelligent interest in socialism among college men and women."[2] While the major strength of the ISS was in the prestige colleges of the eastern seaboard, from 1910 until the outbreak of World War I it spread across the country, and by 1917 claimed sixty chapters with 2,200 members.[3]

The major thrust of ISS activity was educational. The organization's journal, the *Intercollegiate Socialist*, was published regularly from 1913 until 1919 and featured articles on aspects of Socialist thought as well as on university-related issues and public affairs. ISS affiliates sponsored radical speakers on campus and often caused

[2]Harold Lewack, *Campus Rebels: A Brief History of the Student League for Industrial Democracy* (New York: Student League for Industrial Democracy, 1953), p. 4.
[3]*Ibid.*, p. 5.

local crises over free speech. These speakers were the main educational thrust of ISS activity.

A number of themes emerged from ISS campus activities in the early 1900s, and also in its national conventions and summer conferences. The debate over American rearmament and entry into World War I caused substantial disagreement among members, and was a constant topic of discussion. Other popular topics were free speech on campus, immigration, a World Court, and various aspects of socialism.[4] In this period, there was relatively little attention paid to foreign affairs and, surprisingly, only slight emphasis given to internal university problems and academic reform. The ISS convention of 1916, however, voted to oppose the introduction of military training on campus.

The society did not take the complexities of ideological politics very seriously. In 1913, a questionnaire of 450 ISS members indicated that a third of the membership was non-Socialist, and a few members were even anti-Socialist.[5] If the *Intercollegiate Socialist* is any indication, the factional disputes over Socialist doctrine which characterized the 1930s and later periods were rare in the ISS.

As the Intercollegiate Socialist Society became more concerned with the creation of a broader movement, it began to shift its emphasis from the campus. In 1919, it changed its name to the League for Industrial Democracy, and its journal became the *Socialist Review*.[6] Although this was done to broaden the movement, the organization remained more intellectual than activist and most of its strength stayed on the campus.

Another organization which attempted to build a broad-based youth movement but which had some strength on campus was the Young People's Socialist League (YPSL). Organized in 1907 as the youth affiliate of the Socialist party, the YPSL claimed 4,200 members in 112 chapters by 1913.[7] Much of YPSL's membership was,

[4]Harry Laidler's editorial accounts in the *Intercollegiate Socialist* offer some idea of what ISS concerns were. A good example of convention discussion topics can be found in vol. 4 (October-November 1916).

[5]*Intercollegiate Socialist* 1 (February-March 1913): 13.

[6]Some members were concerned that the society's name might exclude non-collegian members and some expressed concern that it might give the impression that the ISS was affiliated with the Socialist party.

[7]"Report of the Young Peoples Department of the Socialist Party of the U.S. to the International Young Socialist Congress," *Young Socialist Magazine* (June, 1914): 12.

however, off the campus. The YPSL tended to engage in more direct political campaigns, usually in support of Socialist candidates and other struggles, although it also carried on an active educational program.

Less obviously political than the ISS or the YPSL, the Student Christian Volunteer Movement (SCVM) played an active and important role on the campuses. Founded in 1886, the SCVM was a federation of various Protestant religious youth organizations, among which the YMCAs and YWCAs were perhaps the most active. The SCVM exhibited a strong sense of social concern, although prior to 1920 its main emphasis was on foreign missionary work. The SCVM's journal, the *North American Student*, was concerned with foreign missionary activity but also featured articles on problems at home. Some of the earliest articles supporting educational reform and women's liberation appeared in the *North American Student*. During both the pre–World War I period and the twenties, religious student organizations played a key role in bringing social concerns to the campuses and particularly to those colleges somewhat out of the mainstream of academic life, in which religious groups were the only source of social concern.

World War I and the postwar Red Scare of 1918–1919 inhibited the student movement as it did the adult radical movement. Many liberal and radical intellectuals were perplexed by the war issue, and this question split the radical movement. The ISS did not support the war, but maintained a position which neither condoned nor condemned it and in the process lost much of its membership. The YPSL, which strongly opposed the war, was also decimated during the war.

THE MOVEMENT IN THE TWENTIES

The Issues

The twenties were a curious period in the history of the student movement, as they were for American society generally. The period was characterized by political apathy on and off campus, but at the same time exhibited some significant political and social currents. For example, the student movement strongly criticized the universities for the first time, and devoted itself to some extent to educational issues. A study conducted in 1926 showed that a majority of the 1,026 students responding opposed ROTC. In addition, college students were involved in a minor "cultural revolution." It can be argued that the "new" cultural patterns of the twenties which were stimulated largely by youth were in a sense similar to the hippie and other counter-cultural developments of the 1960s and 1970s. While the data are somewhat rudimentary, they seem to indicate that college students of the twenties were substantially freer in their sexual and religious attitudes and were in general more tolerant than their elders. Articles in student journals as well as commentary in intellectual magazines indicate that many socially conscious students felt that adult society was hypocritical, base, and anti-intellectual. Indeed, many of the charges sound very similar to those made at present by radical students.

The organized student movement of the previous decade was destroyed by the war and repression, and never regained its strength in the twenties. Much of the student activity which took place had no organizational roots and little continuity. The *New Student*, a journal founded in 1922, reported extensively on student events and tried to provide a communications link between disparate local groups. Despite the lack of organization, there was a good deal of ferment taking place during the twenties. The period was characterized by substantial repression; students with radical inclinations were often expelled from colleges, student newspapers were censored, and administrators often acted in a heavy-handed manner. Much of the thrust of student activism was aimed at establishing and protecting free speech on the campus. Campus newspaper editors protested censorship, and student groups attempted to bring radical speakers on campus.

Students criticized "giganticism" in universities, and many of their criticisms have a very modern ring to them. Students complained that professors were boring and that there was too little contact with them, that academic bureaucracy was overwhelming the campus, and that they generally were alienated from their colleges. Articles reprinted in the *New Student* from college newspapers indicate that these kinds of criticisms were very strong. The twenties were a period of rapid expansion of higher education—the proportion of youth attending college rose from 4 percent in 1900 to 12 percent at the end of the twenties. This period was also one of rapid social change, and college curricula did not often keep up with currents in society.

The Groups

A number of student groups emerged in the 1920s which have been generally ignored because of the more dramatic events of the following decade. Strong student sentiment in favor of the League of Nations and for disarmament sparked the organization of the National Student Committee for the Limitation of Armaments. This group sent antiwar speakers to college campuses. In 1922, it merged with the Intercollegiate Liberal League to form the National Student Forum (NSF), and the new group claimed a thousand student members and several hundred graduate and faculty members. The NSF avoided general social reform issues, and its leadership tried to prevent it from getting a "radical" image. The *New Student* was the official organ of the NSF, and both the organization and the journal saw their image as stimulating thought and social concern among American college students.[8]

The National Student Forum was not the only group to emerge during the twenties. Organizations such as the National Student Federation of America (NSFA), the Student League for Industrial Democracy (SLID), and various Christian groups were attempting to unite students on social and, to some extent, political issues. The SCVM convention of 1923 considered a number of social action issues, and a number of radical speakers pressed for social change. Many Christian youth organizations passed strong antiwar statements at their meetings and, in 1924, a group of 700 Christian students at an SCVM convention took a strong pacifist stand under the leadership of the Fellowship of Youth for Peace, an affiliate of the Fellowship of Reconciliation, a prominent pacifist organization.

The SLID claimed seventy-five student chapters and about 2,000 student members in 1927. Its major activities included campaigns against ROTC on campus, organizing student committees to defend Sacco and Vanzetti, and campaigning against American intervention in Nicaragua and Mexico.[9] Among the SLID's active members in the late 1920s were Walter Reuther, Sidney Hook, and Max Lerner. Indeed, one observer in the 1950s stated that one of the SLID's main functions in the twenties was to train leaders for the labor, Socialist, and other reform movements.

A forerunner of the present-day National Student Association, the NSFA was founded in 1925. The NSFA was a loose federation of student governments, and was interested mainly in international cooperation and understanding among student groups. Other efforts at student involvement in the twenties were issue-oriented.

[8]*New Student* 1 (May 3 1922): 1.
[9]Lewack, *Campus Rebels*, pp. 9–10.

Single-issue conferences were common. For example, students gathered at Bear Mountain, New York, in 1924 to discuss "Youth's Standard of Living." Among the sponsors of this meeting—foreshadowing the coalitions of student groups in the 1930s—were the YPSL, YM and YWCAs, Young Workers' League (the youth group of the Communist party), Rand Students League (Socialist), and the Ethical Culture Society. In 1927, the first conference of the American Federation of Youth, representing fifty youth organizations, met and went on record favoring a nationwide campaign against compulsory military training, militarism, imperialism, and child labor. Conventions of religious students were addressed by SLID speakers, and often took radical or reformist stands.

THE THIRTIES

The 1930s saw the growth of the first mass student movement in American history. The most important campus issue was the antiwar question; thousands of students were involved in many American colleges. For the first time, the student movement engaged in a political campaign which, although ultimately unsuccessful, aroused substantial public support on and off the campus. Despite its size—the American Student Union claimed 20,000 members in 1938, and several hundred thousand students participated in peace strikes during the decade—the impact of the student movement should not be overestimated. For the most part, the activities of radical students were a reflection of other, more significant, social movements and organizations.

The generation gap, so much a part of the political rhetoric of the sixties, was absent during the thirties. Politically active students were generally affiliated with adult political groups and usually took their cues from the adult movement. Even the antiwar movement was stimulated as much by conservative isolationists as by radical students. Finally, the activism of the thirties was mainly confined to metropolitan centers, most notably New York City, and to the more cosmopolitan campuses. The majority of colleges was unaffected by the political ferment taking place. Despite these limitations, the student movement of the thirties was one of the most significant in American history, and in terms of proportions of students involved in activism, perhaps more significant than the New Left of the 1960s.

The student movement of the thirties had a number of key foci. It was not generally interested in issues of academic reform. In fact, the continuing criticisms of the educational system which were made in the twenties generally stopped in the thirties. Students fought battles over ROTC and over free speech on campus, and occasionally defended academic freedom, but in general their concerns were more political. The antiwar issue was the most volatile campus question of the thirties despite the Depression and other domestic crises, perhaps reflecting the overwhelmingly middle-class student population. The more ideologically sophisticated students were also involved in labor organizing, and in the internal politics of the significant left-wing movements of the period.

The Radical Trend

The early thirties saw the radicalizing of existing student groups and the formation of new leftist organizations. The Student League for Industrial Democracy, perhaps the most important left-wing campus group with an historical tradition, moved substantially to the Left although it maintained its Social Democratic orientation. The Socialist and Communist parties, which had been unenthusiastic about campus organizing in the early thirties, became active in the universities by 1933. In 1931, the National Student League was organized with Communist support and eventual domination. While the NSL was more radical than SLID—its program included an effort to "promote student participation in the revolutionary movement against capitalism"—it tried to appeal to a range of student opinion. NSL received national publicity when its members went to Harlan County, Kentucky in 1932 to support striking coal miners. SLID and NSL did work together, however, in organizing "united front" antiwar campaigns on campus in 1931 and 1932 and in the American Student Union.

The thirties also radicalized the Christian student movement. The Council of Christian Associations, the organization uniting the YM and YWCAs, published a pamphlet in 1931 entitled "Toward a New Economic Society" in which collective ownership of natural resources and public utilities was advocated.[10] Older national leaders of the Ys became disturbed at the Council's publication and disavowed its Socialist position. The SCVM placed less stress on overseas missionary work and paid more attention to domestic problems. Resolutions passed at the first National Assembly of Student Christian

---

[10]"Student Radicalism," *World Tomorrow* 14 (June 1931): 181.

Groups in 1938 indicated religious students had become more radical. One resolution, passed by a substantial majority, stated that capitalism and fascism were unacceptable and that the goals of the Cooperative Movement and of Marxian socialism were preferred.[11]

The Peace Issue

The most dramatic campus issue of the period was peace and disarmament. A poll conducted by the Intercollegiate Disarmament Council in 1931 indicated that 39 percent of the 22,627 students polled at seventy colleges would not participate in any war and 33 percent stated that they would fight only if the United States were invaded.[12] The Brown University *Daily Herald* polled approximately 22,000 students in sixty-five colleges; and of the 15,636 students who responded, around 50 percent stated they would bear arms only in case of an invasion of the United States. Students also fought over civil liberties and academic freedom, and with somewhat more success than they had had in the twenties. The most dramatic case involved the editor of the Columbia University *Spectator*, who was expelled from the university in 1932 for publishing "misrepresentations." One of the first successful campus student strikes took place over this issue.

Events in Europe and a continuing domestic crisis greatly increased the constituency for radical student activism in the United States. By 1935, the most active student groups were the SLID (Social Democratic), the National Student League (Communist), religious pacifist groups such as the Fellowship of Reconciliation, social-action-minded religious groups like the Ys, and the National Student Federation of America (Liberal). Attempts at unity among progressive students were made during the early thirties, such as the National Conference of Students in Politics in 1933, but the major united-front student group was the American Student Union (ASU), which functioned from 1935 to 1939.

Like many of the other campus trends of the period, the formation of the ASU reflected broader events in society. The Communist International's stress on the formation of "united fronts" provided

---

[11]Jeffrey Campbell, "Youth, Religion, and Peace," *Socialist Review* 6-7 (July-August 1938): 12.

[12]George Rawick, "The New Deal and Youth," doctoral dissertation (University of Wisconsin, 1957):282.

the major impetus for the ASU and other similar groups among other constituencies. The ASU was basically a union of the Communist NSL, the Socialist SLID, and various unaffiliated liberals.[13] From 1935 until 1937, there was an effective sharing of power between Socialists and Communists, due in part to Liberal support of the Socialist position. By 1937, however, the Communists were able to take control of the ASU and from that time until the ASU's demise it slavishly followed the turns of Communist policy.

The Oxford Pledge was a center of controversy in the ASU, and a key issue in the student movement as a whole. In 1933, the Oxford Union adopted a resolution that stated that under no circumstances should one fight for "King and Country." The ASU adopted an American version of the pledge in 1936 and it became the center of campus organizing by both the ASU and various liberal and pacifist groups. National student peace strikes were organized from 1935 until 1939, and these attracted great public attention. Among the most successful strikes, one took place in April, 1935 which involved more than 150,000 students and had the support of a number of liberal college presidents, and another in 1938 involved more than 500,000 students. On many campuses these "strikes" involved only a one-hour work stoppage, however. The campus peace movement lost support as groups like the ASU closely followed Communist policy in supporting collective security, and as war in Europe looked increasingly possible.

Despite the fact that in 1938 the ASU claimed 20,000 members in 150 colleges and 100 high schools, all was not well with the organization. ASU's reversal of its antiwar stand and its increasingly clear Communist domination disillusioned many students. Vocal Socialist and pacifist groups also took away some ASU supporters. The final blow to the organization came when collective security was abandoned by the ASU at the time Stalin signed the Nazi-Soviet non-aggression pact. ASU membership dropped to 2,000 in 1940, and the organization soon went out of existence.

The "Active Left"

At the same time that mass "united front" student groups were functioning, the political parties and sects of the Left were also ac-

---

[13]The best account of the American Student Union is Hal Draper, "The Student Movement of the Thirties: A Political History," in R. J. Simon, ed., *As We Saw the Thirties* (Urbana: University of Illinois Press, 1967), pp. 151–89. Draper's account reflects the Socialist faction of the radical student movement.

tive on the campuses. The Young Communist League, clearly the largest of the political groups, claimed 22,000 members in 1939, both student and non-student. The Young People's Socialist League continued to function during this period, and although it took more of an interest in students than it previously did, its effectiveness was limited by internecine factional disputes. Smaller political student groups affiliated with Trotskyist, pacifist, and other tendencies on the Left also existed, although it is unlikely that their combined membership was more than 3,000 nationally, with a major segment concentrated in New York City. One of the political trends of the thirties, on the campus as well as more broadly, was a splintering of the radical movement. Student groups spent much of their time fighting each other. The major thrust of the student movement was leftist during the 1930s, but there are indications that not all politically conscious students were radicals. The liberal National Student Federation of America continued to function throughout this period. Furthermore, students were involved in a number of anti-strike activities in the thirties, indicating that conservative activism also existed. Right-wing Berkeley students helped to break the San Francisco general strike, and some radical students were thrown into the lake at the University of Wisconsin in 1937. There are no indications of a major right-wing organizational thrust on the campus at this period, but sentiment did exist.

The student movement of the 1930s involved large numbers of students in impressive demonstrations and in large organizations. But in the last analysis it failed to build a viable movement. Its lack of interest in campus issues and its deep involvement in the factional politics of the Left cut it off from many students. The adult movement allowed the students little autonomy, and when political difficulties emerged on the adult level, the student movement immediately collapsed. Yet, the student movement of the thirties involved impressive numbers of individuals, many of whom received their political education in the movement, and many are the parents of today's generation of activists.[14]

THE FORTIES

The contrast between the thirties and the following two decades is dramatic. With the onset of World War II, the American student

[14]See Richard Flacks, "The Liberated Generation: An Exploration of the Roots of Student Protest," *Journal of Social Issues* 23 (July 1967): 52–75.

movement simply collapsed. Radicals who opposed the war were disillusioned and confused by the splits in the adult radical movement concerning the war and related foreign policy issues. Other radicals and liberals threw themselves behind moves for collective security and supported the Allied cause. And with American involvement in 1941, many students volunteered or were drafted into the armed forces and campus activism came to an end. The most active groups on campus were such organizations as the Student Defenders of Democracy.

The immediate postwar period saw a number of efforts to revive the student movement, but none of these was very successful. The first postwar convention of SLID, held in 1946, was attended by only forty delegates from twelve schools. Communist activists organized the American Youth for Democracy (AYD) in 1943, which sought to combine campus-oriented issues with opposition to the beginning of the Cold War. While AYD had a respectable membership, it did not inspire major student support, nor was it a force on the campus. Perhaps the most successful postwar student groups were those related directly to the desire for a durable peace; among these students, many were returning veterans anxious to complete their studies and settle down to a job. The United World Federalists had a short period of support on the campus, and engaged in various kinds of educational programs aimed at convincing Americans to give up their national sovereignty and join in a world government.

The liberal movement also was reflected in a number of student groups which were formed around 1948. These organizations reflected in part a growing anti-communism, both on and off the campus, and a desire to counter groups like the AYD, as well as large numbers of students who supported Henry Wallace's presidential campaign in 1948. The Students for Democratic Action (SDA), founded in 1947, was an affiliate of the liberal, anti-Communist Americans for Democratic Action. It attracted substantial support on the campus but did not engage in major campus-oriented campaigns. There was a brief upsurge of student political activism during the 1948 presidential election campaign. The Young Progressives of America, formed largely with AYD initiative, provided strong campus support for Wallace's election campaign, and involved thousands of students under Communist direction. When the Wallace forces were roundly defeated, many of those who were active became disillusioned and left the political scene altogether.

Efforts at reviving the student movement in the late 1940s faced substantial odds. The mood of the campus, as of the country at large, was decidedly apolitical. As previously mentioned, many veterans returned to their studies and were anxious to finish their academic work quickly. The student movement itself was unable to shift its attention to campus issues, such as overcrowding in universities, poor housing conditions, and other problems created by the returning veterans. The adult Left was in substantial disarray and could provide no guidance, and no independent student groups existed which could strike out on their own. But perhaps the major reason was the general political climate in the country, which was confused in the immediate postwar period, and increasingly anti-Communist and conservative during the 1950s. The Korean War, the development of the Cold War, the Communist coup in Czechoslovakia, and the increasingly anti-Communist foreign and domestic stance of the American government, combined to make radical or even liberal student organizing difficult.

THE FIFTIES

The one major national student organization founded in the late 1940s reflected many of the trends which have been noted. The U.S. National Student Association was founded in 1948 in the flush of international student unity and cooperation. It was not long before the NSA became involved in the Cold War, and its stand became strongly anti-Communist.[15] The NSA's early support was impressive—some 1,000 student leaders representing 1,100,000 students and more than twenty national student organizations attended the founding convention of the NSA—but the organization never achieved major active support on the campus. It was from the outset a federation of student governments without grass-roots support. Although there was a small minority of Communists in NSA, and a rather substantial minority of conservative Catholics, the NSA's policies were from the outset "mainline Liberal." Recent disclosures of the CIA's involvement in NSA's financial affairs are not so surprising, considering the political climate in the early 1950s and the strong anti-

---

[15]The most adequate account of the early period of the NSA can be found in Martin McLaughlin, "Political Processes in American National Student Organizations," doctoral thesis (Notre Dame University, 1948). The author writes from a strongly anti-Communist viewpoint and was himself involved in the founding of the NSA.

Communist position of NSA's liberal leadership during this period.[16] Although clearly the largest and probably externally the most influential student organization of the 1950s, the National Student Association made very little impact on its more than one million student "members."

The 1950s were also a period of direct political repression and general apathy. Investigations by Senator Joseph McCarthy and various congressional committees instilled fear in many liberals and radicals. Faculty members were forced from their jobs in some cases because of their political views, and loyalty oaths became common. Journals like *The Nation* and *The New Republic* chronicled the silent generation, and the liberal press decried the apathy of the young. Right-wing student groups gained some prominence on the campuses for the first time in years. The pro-McCarthy Students for America, founded in 1951, had a short period of strength in the early 1950s; and other conservative groups were founded, often with substantial outside financial support, later in the decade. The Students for America was a blatant arm of McCarthyism with a national security division that maintained direct liaison with anti-subversive government agencies. The Intercollegiate Society for Individualists, founded in 1957, reflected an intellectual concern for right-wing libertarianism, while the Young Americans for Freedom (YAF), founded in 1960, is a more activist-oriented, conservative student organization.

It is a curious paradox that although antiwar feelings among students in the 1930s and the 1960s helped to sustain active radical student movements, similar tendencies among students in the 1950s had no organizational effect. The Korean War was never very popular on the campuses. A poll taken in 1953 indicated that 26 percent of those responding were strongly opposed to the war while 36 percent had strong reservations.[17] No groups emerged to mobilize this feeling, and as a result the campus was virtually silent on the subject of the Korean conflict.

Despite pervading apathy and repression, left-wing student groups did survive the 1950s, providing some organizational continuity which kept radical thought alive in the United States during a

---

[16]For an assessment of the NSA-CIA affair, see Sol Stern, "NSA-CIA," *Ramparts* 5 (March 1967): 29–39.

[17]Edward Suchman, Rose K. Goldsen, and Robin Williams, Jr., "Attitudes Toward the Korean War," *Public Opinion Quarterly* 17 (1953): 173, 182.

rather difficult period. The Communists changed the name of their student group from American Youth for Democracy to Labor Youth League, to reflect shifts in party policy. The LYL maintained a small number of chapters during the fifties, mainly in New York and a few major campus centers, and it was subjected to substantial repression by campus authorities and others. The pacifist Fellowship of Reconciliation maintained a presence on the campus and was especially active among seminarians. The Young People's Socialist League and the SLID both continued to function, although with memberships varying around two hundred each. As in the twenties, religious student organizations kept the spark of social reform and political concern alive on many of the less politically active campuses. Groups like the YM-YWCA were especially active in this area, and they provided a forum of radical speakers, and engaged in some mild social action campaigns.

THE SIXTIES AND THE "NEW LEFT"

The end of this narrative brings us to the beginnings of the New Left. The late 1950s saw a rebirth of student activism in the United States and the emergence of some of those organizations and political concerns which contributed to the student movement of the 1960s. A number of crucial developments were taking place outside the campus which had a major impact on the student movement. The end of the Korean War and a period of somewhat greater tolerance in the United States made political activism a bit easier. The "beatniks" indicated the first stirrings of a major counter-culture. The 1954 Supreme Court decision on segregation and the beginning of an active and militant civil rights movement focused the attention of students on a key issue in American society for perhaps the first time. The growing consciousness of the dangers of nuclear war stimulated the resurgence of a peace movement. It is significant that the student movements of the postwar period placed little emphasis on university-related issues. This lack of concern with the environment of the student continued until the early 1960s, when questions of educational reform and of the university generally became important issues.

The student movement of the late 1950s had strong intellectual concerns. It was interested in moving beyond the stale ideologies of the "old Left" sects and in breaking new ground. Substantial disil-

lusionment with the Communist party was evident after Khrush-
chev's speech denouncing Stalin, and especially after the Soviet invasion of Hungary in 1956. Several new journals were founded which
reflected a searching for fresh ideological currents. *Studies on the
Left*, founded by graduate students at the University of Wisconsin in
1959, *New University Thought*, from the University of Chicago, and
several other journals began to establish the ideological and tactical
basis for a new radical movement.

The New Concerns

Several new student organizations and campaigns emerged at the
end of the 1950s which reflected new concerns of politically conscious
American students. The Students for a Democratic Society (SDS),
perhaps the most publicized organization of the New Left, emerged
from the Social-Democratic Student League for Industrial Democracy. While SLID changed its name to SDS in 1959, ties were maintained with the adult League for Industrial Democracy until 1963,
and SDS received a financial subsidy during this period. The ideological and tactical development of the SDS, while beyond the scope of
this essay, reflects some of the changing emphases of the student
movement. As the SDS became more radical it broke its ties with the
LID, indicating a trend away from student involvement in the adult
"old Left" political organizations.

The three main threads of student activism in the late 1950s were
civil liberties, peace, and civil rights, in chronological order. Ad hoc
civil liberties groups such as the Committee to Abolish the House
Committee on Un-American Activities aroused interest in issues of
academic freedom and civil liberties. These efforts culminated in
violent demonstrations in San Francisco in 1960. The peace movement emerged from two major trends—the traditional pacifist organizations such as the Fellowship of Reconciliation, and newer,
liberal groups such as the National Committee for a Sane Nuclear
Policy (SANE). The student affiliate of SANE was founded in 1958
and, although it included many left-wing students, it generally followed SANE's liberal policies. Its major focus was on ending nuclear
testing. The other major student peace organization, the Student
Peace Union (SPU), was founded in 1959 by a combination of pacifists and moderate radicals. The SPU was for a period the largest
radical student group in the United States, with a membership of
about 5,000 in some 100 campus groups. The civil rights movement is

perhaps the most important stimulus for the recent upsurge in student activism. While the major successes of the campus civil rights movement took place in the early 1960s, many of the roots were established in the fifties. Many students supported groups like CORE and the NAACP, and small civil rights demonstrations occasionally took place. In the days before black power, it was easier for white middle-class students to involve themselves in campaigns for equality and integration, and the plight of the Negro caught the attention and sympathy of the campus.

While the 1950s saw a re-establishment of radical and social action organizations on campus, the major mood of the campus remained, in the words of *The Nation*, silent and apathetic. Only a tiny proportion of the student population was involved in any of the new organizations, and most campuses remained placid. Yet, groups like SDS, SPU, and the newly formed Student Nonviolent Coordinating Committee (SNCC) caught the attention of some students and indicated a trend away from reliance on adult guidance. New student journals helped to lay the ideological foundations for the new movement. The period can, in the words of one radical journal, be characterized as one of hope in the midst of apathy.

CONCLUSION

Easy generalizations concerning student activism in America are impossible. While there is a clear historical tradition of student activism, each period is marked by distinctive factors. The American student movement in the period under consideration was never a direct threat to the established order nor did it play a leading role in any of the social movements of the period. Nevertheless, American students in the 1920s were among the most socially conscious elements of the population. Students were influential in at least one political struggle, the antiwar movement of the thirties. Throughout the period under consideration, the majority of the American student community was never involved in a major way in politics. Even during the 1930s, most of the campuses were untouched by activism, and in the less active 1920s and 1950s only a tiny minority of the student population was involved in politics.

Perhaps more important than the number involved, however, was the fact that the student political movement—mostly of a radical nature—helped to shape the political and intellectual climate of the campus and particularly of the prestigious universities. The impact of the university on student activism has hardly been mentioned in this essay, although it is of importance. During this period, the numbers of students on American campuses increased from 355,000 in 1910 to 3,580,000 in 1960. The university was transformed from an important yet somewhat "ivory tower" institution into the "multiversity" at the center of economic and political life. Higher education was transformed from a preserve of the upper middle classes to a much broader phenomenon.

Despite substantial differences between periods and among organizations, there are a number of generalizations that can be made with regard to the period between 1900 and 1960.

(1) There is little evidence of generational conflict in the organized student movement. There was discontent with adult cultural forms in the twenties and some conflicts between youth and adults in groups ranging from the YMCA to the YPSL, but few direct attacks on adult institutions. Throughout this period, student activists worked closely with and generally took direction from the adult political movement.

(2) The student movement generally limited its tactics to educational campaigns and non-violent and legal direct action. This generalization seems to hold regardless of political ideology throughout the period.

(3) The thrust of the student movement was in general directed at broad social issues and not basically concerned with the university itself. Although there was some concern with academic issues in the twenties, most activists were more interested in political questions.

(4) The organized student movement was not part of any kind of a "counter-culture" or other similar effort. The radical political groups felt that the basic necessity was a change in power relationships in society and social reform.

(5) Student activism involved not only radical (or conservative) organizations, but religious and other groups. For several periods, groups like the YM-YWCA were in the forefront of student social action programs.

(6) With the exception of the late 1950s, the student movement followed political trends in society and in the adult radical movement.

A comparative analysis of the student movement of the pre- and post-1960 period is beyond our present scope. It is clear that while there are some similarities, there are also important differences. Quick comparisons will probably result in errors, as student activism has been shaped by the different circumstances of varying historical periods. If there is any lesson from this consideration, it is perhaps that student activism is very much tied to events in society and on the campus. Although the movement on a number of occasions acted as a conscience for its generation, or at least kept radical traditions alive, it never exhibited the potential for revolution.

.2. *The Development of the New Left*

JAMES P. O'BRIEN

IN THE spring of 1969, less than ten years after the first tentative stirrings of student protest activity on northern college campuses, President Nixon traveled to General Beadle State College in South Dakota to deliver a commencement speech on the subject of campus unrest. He went there because it was one of the very few colleges out of the more than one thousand four-year schools in the country at which the President of the United States could speak in 1969 without having to face hostile demonstrations. Thus far had the student movement spread in less than a decade. There have been many answers to the question of where it will go next, but the Cambodian crisis of May 1970 should provide a clear warning against those who argue that we are merely on the upswing of a cycle, or that, in the words of a United Press International news analysis two months before the Cambodian crisis, "the student revolution, like a bad fever, appears to have run its course."[1] A look at the history of the student movement in the 1960s, and the stages through which it has passed, will not provide ready-made answers to its future, but it is a necessary precondition for such speculation.

THE FIRST THREE YEARS

Although there had been scattered campus rallies in support of the Hungarian revolution in 1956, and although the provision for a student loyalty oath in the National Defense Education Act of 1958 had

[1] *Wisconsin State Journal*, March 1, 1970.

drawn campus protests—almost entirely from administrators and faculty groups rather than students—it makes no sense to date the modern student movement from any time other than February, 1960. It was then that the sit-in movement, initiated and carried on by black college students in the South, touched off sympathy picketing by northern students at local branches of national variety store chains (especially Woolworth's) whose southern branches refused to serve blacks at their lunch counters. This northern support activity was on a far smaller scale than were the sit-ins themselves; it was also far less risky—no northern students were arrested and convicted for this activity, while close to two thousand sit-in arrests were made in the South over a four-month period. Still, it broke the ice. Perhaps six to eight thousand northern students took part in picketing, an almost entirely unheard-of student activity within the memory of students who had been on campus in the late 1950s. Perhaps ten times as many students were involved in such lesser ways as signing petitions or contributing money in support of the Woolworth sit-ins.

The Issues Involved

The Woolworth pickets in the spring of 1960 marked the start of a distinctive three-year period in the history of the student movement. During this period the three great issues that stirred the activist minority were southern racial discrimination, atmospheric nuclear testing, and the House Un-American Activities Committee (HUAC). The amount of visible activity over these issues was not great: the only period after the spring of 1960 in which a large number of students took part in demonstrations was the fall and winter of 1961–62, when the principal issue was nuclear testing. The House Committee on Un-American Activities was an issue principally because it made a slanted and highly emotional film, "Operation Abolition," depicting as Communist dupes the students demonstrating against its May 1960 hearings in San Francisco. "Anti-HUAC" activity consisted primarily of speeches and pamphlets seeking to discredit the film, rather than further demonstrations against the committee itself.

At this time, the number of people involved in the student movement was only a small minority of the American student population. There were about fifty schools where there was some kind of recurrent political activity concerning civil rights and peace issues, but if we look for schools where this activity was well established and where it involved as much as four or five percent of the student body, we have a very small list of schools. On such a list we might include Berkeley, Reed, Minnesota, Carleton, Wisconsin, Chicago, Shimer, Michigan, Earlham, Oberlin, Antioch, Cornell, Harpur, Swarthmore, College of the City of New York, Columbia, and Harvard-Radcliffe.[2] Eight of these schools are liberal arts colleges, and even at the universities on the list, perhaps 90 percent of the students involved in political protest activity were liberal arts majors. Moreover, at these and other schools, the student movement was almost entirely based on a campus subculture characterized by folk music and by relative tolerance for unorthodoxy in dress and appearance.[3]

Even the largest active political rallies and demonstrations never drew more than five or six hundred people. During this period of 1960–63, the largest protest demonstration by white students was almost certainly at Ohio State in 1961, when five thousand students marched downtown to protest the faculty's rejection of a Rose Bowl bid.[4] The second largest may have been at the University of Mississippi a year later, when rioting occurred in an attempt to bar the admission of the school's first Negro student, James Meredith.

Another salient feature of the student movement during this period was that it was focused on somewhat remote issues and was not directed against the university itself. Even though the people involved in the student movement often felt stifled by academic and social regulations, this never led either to civil disobedience against the university—even at Berkeley, where the liberal political party SLATE was a persistent critic of the administration—or to an analysis of the university in terms of what interests controlled it. The basic rationale for participation in the student movement was not a personal sense of oppression but a feeling that, as an Oberlin student put it, the student "can and must be the one to criticize, to examine. He is the only one who, because of his inherent status, is in the logical position to do these things, so essential to a progressive and democratic society."[5]

[2] This list is, of course, not entirely precise. It is based on estimates derived from my use of the student newspapers of most of these schools and from a large number of interviews with activist leaders from these and other schools during the 1960–63 period.

[3] These generalizations are based on approximately eighty interviews with students active in campus politics during this period.

[4] *Wisconsin Daily Cardinal*, November 29, 1961.

[5] *Oberlin Review*, November 11, 1960.

The university was seen not as a field of confrontation, but as an institution that was important for its intellectual resources and its at least nominal tradition of critical thought. It was no accident that the schools where the student movement was strongest were, in general, far above the average American colleges and universities in their academic standing.

The Political Groups

Of the quasi-national student political organizations which helped to provide a vehicle for the student movement during this period, five are worthy of notice. The National Student Association, composed of the student governments of several hundred campuses and secretly funded in some of its overseas activities by the United States government, held a liberal stance that led it to seek the support of northern students for civil rights activity. Although NSA's annual congresses provided a meeting place and forum for liberal activists, the organization itself had no grass-roots support on its "member" campuses and actually played only a little role in its own right. The Student Peace Union, formed in the Midwest in 1959 and reaching an impressive membership of more than three thousand by 1961–62, was led by pacifists and—more important—members of the Young People's Socialist League, whose "Third Camp" perspective condemned the foreign policies of both the United States and the Communist bloc. The SPU went into a period of decline after the spring of 1962, when President Kennedy resumed atmospheric testing after a long period of indecision; the signing of a U.S.-Russian test ban treaty effectively killed both SPU and the student peace movement. The Young People's Socialist League, whose eight hundred members in 1962 made it by far the largest avowedly radical student organization during this period, fell into internal dissolution. Its decline was marked by the brandishing of old Socialist texts rather than by any sense of what was happening in the 1960s, and by the time of its temporary disbanding in 1964 it was an empty shell.

A much smaller Socialist group, the Trotskyist Young Socialist Alliance (YSA), was more successful in developing a solid cadre, but at this time the YSA was too small and too far Left to be able to play a significant role in the student movement. Finally, Students for a Democratic Society (formerly the Student League for Industrial Democracy) was able to attract a number of very bright leaders from the humanitarian-liberal edge of NSA and also able to produce the student movement's most important social critique, The Port Huron Statement. The SDS document, while not explicitly Socialist, nevertheless added up to a searching indictment of modern American society, with particular stress on the remoteness of ordinary citizens from control over the decision-making process.

THE IMPORTANT WATERSHED

The most important watershed of the student movement was the period starting with the Birmingham demonstrations in the late spring of 1963 and ending about two years later—one can choose to end it with the passing of President Johnson's voting rights bill in early August 1965 or with the Watts uprising shortly afterwards—when civil rights was the major public issue in the United States. This was an issue which a strong and relatively united civil rights movement kept forcing, and one which was almost impossible to ignore. For white college students, this period saw a deepening of involvement on the part of an activist minority. Hundreds of students went into the Deep South to risk their lives in working for the Student Nonviolent Coordinating Committee (SNCC)—an offspring of the 1960 sit-ins—and other civil rights groups, most notably in the Mississippi Summer Project of 1964.

In the North itself, large numbers of students were arrested for civil disobedience in Baltimore, New York, San Francisco, Ann Arbor, Chester, and elsewhere; in addition, several hundred students got experience as community organizers in urban poverty areas as part of the Economic Research and Action Project of Students for a Democratic Society (SDS), which was now entering its first period of self-sustaining membership growth. Even for students who were not involved directly in the civil rights movement, there was a possibility of vicarious identification with it. Students from a great variety of schools took part in the Mississippi Summer Project, in particular, and the project got extensive press and television coverage during the summer. "Friends of SNCC" fund-raising groups existed on nearly a hundred campuses, and these groups helped to bring the reality of the civil rights movement home to college students.

The moral and political issues posed by the civil rights movement were seemingly clear and uncomplicated. Blacks were demanding rights and freedoms that white people took for granted, and more generally they were protesting the sub-human status to which they were assigned, especially in the South. It was not a complex situation in which both sides could make equally persuasive cases, or in which direct exposure to reality made simple judgments seem invalid. Indeed, the experience of the students who went South only deepened their sense of outrage at racial discrimination.[6] This clear-cut sense of the rights and wrongs of the discrimination issue was important, because it carried over even beyond this period and beyond the discrimination issue itself.

The clarity of the issues that were involved in the civil rights movement led to the first important radicalizing experience for the student movement. This was the experience in seeking aid from the federal government and the Democratic party. Even before 1963, SNCC had had countless frustrating experiences in trying to get the Justice Department to act on pleas for protection—under laws passed during the Reconstruction period but still valid—against harassment by local southern officials.[7] Despite a greatly strengthened federal presence in Mississippi during the Summer Project of 1964, the government was still seen as holding back from using its full statutory powers. A frequently heard slogan was, "There is a town in Mississippi named Liberty. There is a department in Washington named Justice." The failure of the Mississippi Freedom Democratic party delegation to win seats at the 1964 Democratic convention in Atlantic City, as a result of a last-minute "compromise" worked out with Administration support, was an especially disillusioning experience. During 1965, SNCC took an increasingly anti-Administration stance, focusing much of its energies on an attempt—successfully blocked by the House Democratic leadership—to unseat the Mississippi representatives because of the widespread denial of voting rights to Negroes in the state.

The Free Speech Movement

The historic Free Speech Movement at Berkeley occurred in the fall of 1964, and there was nothing coincidental about the fact that it took place during the civil rights upsurge. Berkeley students had

[6]See Elizabeth Sutherland, ed., *Letters from Mississippi* (New York: McGraw-Hill, 1965), for a sensitive rendering of the volunteers' reaction to southern conditions.

[7]Several writings by Howard Zinn convey the SNCC workers' indignation and the legal basis for it: *A Study in National Responsibility* (Atlanta: Southern Regional Council, 1962); "Kennedy: The Reluctant Emancipator," *The Nation* 195 (December 1, 1962): 373–76; and *SNCC: The New Abolitionists* (Boston: Beacon Press, 1965), pp. 190–215.

taken an active part in civil rights demonstrations the previous year, both in San Francisco and in Berkeley, and several students—including Mario Savio, who became the Free Speech Movement's major spokesman—had taken part in the Mississippi Summer Project. The administrative ruling that touched off the FSM, a ban on campus solicitation for off-campus political action, seemed to be aimed specifically at civil rights groups, especially when it was amended to allow campaigning for the November elections. Regardless of the administration's motives, the two campus political groups that provided the major tactical leadership for the FSM were Campus CORE and the Friends of SNCC groups. Prominent civil rights leaders such as James Farmer of CORE and John Lewis of SNCC helped lend national support for the FSM objective.

The major significance of the Free Speech Movement is that it brought home to the university campus itself, for the first time during the decade, the tactics of the civil rights movement, including civil disobedience. The struggle was also invested by its supporters—and, in an entirely different way, by its opponents—with the aura of righteousness that surrounded the civil rights movement. The political freedoms demanded by the FSM were freedoms that had been well established at nearly all the other schools that had seen political activity in the 1960s, and it was hard to see a good reason why they should not exist at Berkeley as well. The revolt also fed on a cultural alienation from the university that expressed itself in the frequent references in FSM oratory to IBM cards and to the university as a factory. The FSM also spawned the first serious attempt by students to come to grips with the question of university control by the corporations—Marvin Garson's pamphlet on the University Regents—though this was not a major theme in the FSM itself.[8]

THE VIETNAM WAR

It was in February, 1965 that the Vietnam War became a major issue on the campuses. At that time the Johnson Administration began systematic bombing of North Vietnam and made a clear commitment to send as many American troops as were necessary to "win." Since mid-1965, Vietnam has been the overriding political issue

[8]For materials on the Berkeley Free Speech Movement, see Max Heirich, *The Beginning: Berkeley, 1964*. (New York: Columbia University Press, 1971); Hal Draper, *Berkeley: The New Student Revolt* (New York: Grove Press, 1965), and Seymour M. Lipset and Sheldon S. Wolin, eds., *The Berkeley Student Revolt* (Garden City, N.Y.: Anchor Books, 1965).

that has powered the growing student movement. Still, it is possible to distinguish two fairly distinct periods in the Vietnam protest movement: one lasting from 1965 until 1967 and the other lasting at least until mid–1970. If we compare these two periods, we can see the way in which the student movement has expanded, both in its size and in the breadth of its critique of society.

During its first two years, the Vietnam protest movement followed fairly conventional lines—public demonstrations were the central element. The high points were the SDS–sponsored March on Washington in April, 1965, which drew over 15,000 participants, most of them students, and the International Days of Protest in mid–October, 1965, in which an estimated 100,000 persons took part in local demonstrations across the country. The teach-in movement, which began in the spring of 1965 and continued to spread during the following school year, represented the major innovative tactic in the protests. For many students, the teach-ins represented a refreshing contrast to the normal routine of the university, and embodied a social relevance that they felt was lacking in the regular curriculum. At the same time, the fact that the teach-ins depended heavily on faculty members' expertise and status was a sign that the Vietnam protest was not directed at the universities themselves.[9] Only at about a half-dozen schools—notably Chicago, Wisconsin, Roosevelt, and a few others where sit-ins took place in the spring of 1966 to protest against universities' furnishing class-rank information to draft boards—did protesters link the universities to the war in any way.

Draft Resistance

The spring of 1967 marked a watershed in the antiwar movement in at least three ways. First, after a disappointing series of mass demonstrations with dwindling turnouts in 1966, the April, 1967 mobilization in New York and San Francisco drew a total of perhaps three or four hundred thousand people.[10] The antiwar movement was larger than most people had believed. A second important development in the spring of 1967 was the growth of a serious draft resistance movement, sparked in large part by SDS. Draft resistance was a failure as

[9]On the teach-ins, see especially Louis Menashe and Ronald Radosh, eds., *Teach-ins U.S.A.* (New York: Praeger, 1967).

[10]The police estimate for the New York march was 125,000, although march organizers claimed at least 400,000; for the San Francisco march, the respective estimates were 50,000 and 75,000. *The New York Times,* April 16, 1967; *The Militant,* April 24, 1967.

a mass organizing tactic—some of its adherents had expected to actually break the Selective Service system—but with such slogans as "Not with my life, you don't" and with the risk of long jail sentences, it put the war on an individual level and connected the somewhat remote issue of Vietnam to the students' own lives. A third development was the spontaneous outbreak of campus protests, often obstructive, against symbols of the military and the war. Early examples were the blockading of Defense Secretary McNamara's car at Harvard and protest against recruiters for Dow Chemical (napalm manfacturers) at Brown, Wisconsin, and several other schools. In the fall of 1967, such protests multiplied and in many instances became more violent. Although SDS chapters often took an active part in these protests, SDS as a national organization was essentially taken by surprise, and played no role in coordinating them. This was true of other national groups as well, including the Young Socialist Alliance, the Trotskyist youth group which played a key role in the national antiwar demonstrations.

Radicalism Emerges

Together with the heightened campus antiwar movement, 1967 was also marked by the emergence of a cultural radicalism. Although drugs, especially marijuana, had become steadily more common on campuses since the year 1964–65, it was in 1967 that the phenomenon of the "hippies"—youthful dropouts from middle-class environments, who used drugs as a central part of their informal community life— became widespread. While the "hippies" themselves generally eschewed politics, they were responding to many of the same stimuli as the war protesters, and there was a strong aura of cultural rebellion in the antiwar movement. Underground newspapers, which began to spread rapidly in 1967, represented an attempt, often strikingly successful, to fuse the political and cultural concerns. At the end of 1967, the Youth International Party (YIP, or Yippies) was announced by Jerry Rubin and Abbie Hoffman, both of whom had been involved in "straight" protest politics for a number of years but who now sought a new political critique that would capture the imagination of alienated young people.[11]

[11]See Abbie Hoffman, *Revolution for the Hell of It* (New York: Dial Press, 1968) and *Woodstock Nation: A Talk-Rock Album* (New York: Random House, 1969); and Jerry Rubin, *Do It: Scenarios of the Revolution* (New York: Simon and Schuster, 1970).

The year 1968 was important not so much for what the student anti-war movement did as for the image that it established. The major ingredients of this image were the McCarthy campaign, the Columbia University uprising, and the street demonstrations in Chicago at the Democratic national convention. The student revolts in Germany, Czechoslovakia, and especially in France, in the spring and summer were also very important. The major lesson that all these episodes seemed to bring home was that young people, as such, could exert a great deal of power. President Johnson's forced withdrawal from the presidential campaign was certainly due, in large part, to the role that student volunteers played in the New Hampshire and Wisconsin primaries. As a result of the building seizures at Columbia, a major university was effectively shut down for the last month of the spring semester—a far greater paralysis than had occurred at Berkeley during the Free Speech Movement. Student uprisings in France in May led to a nationwide general strike and nearly brought down the De Gaulle government; similarly, Czech students played a major part in forcing the liberalization from the country's Communist regime that eventually led to armed intervention by Russia. The Chicago convention demonstrations, even though the turnout was much smaller than anticipated, provoked the police and Democratic party machinery into showing their most brutal face and, in a sense, dominated the proceedings of the convention. The number of American students who actually took part in the McCarthy campaign, who occupied buildings at Columbia, or who took to the streets in Chicago was very small—much smaller than, say, the number of students who took part in the April, 1967 mobilizations—but that is not a true measure of their importance. In a situation in which millions of young people were becoming personally uncomfortable with their lives—because of the draft, boring classes, drug laws, or any number of other reasons—the example of resistance was very important. By this time, especially after the Tet Offensive in February, 1968, opposition to the Vietnam War was no longer a minority phenomenon on the campuses, and Vietnam was becoming a symbol for American society as a whole.

Support of Black Students

During the 1968–69 school year, the most important theme in campus protests—which were more widespread than ever before—was support for the black students' demands, which usually included the establishment of Black Studies departments. These protests reflected several factors. One was the fact that since about 1965 the number of black students on predominantly white northern campuses had grown dramatically, although it was still far less than proportionate to the black population in the United States. Another was the fact that "white backlash" had never gained headway on the campuses. During the late 1960s, as the country moved toward what one presidential adviser has called a policy of "benign neglect" toward blacks, the campuses were moving in exactly the opposite direction, thus increasing the gap between student opinion and "adult" public opinion. A third factor was the continued ability of black students to exert a strong influence over the course of the white student movement, as had happened earlier in the decade with the sit-ins and then with SNCC. Still, even when these special factors relating to black students are considered, it is hard to escape the conclusion that in many cases the black demands were supported, not simply because they seemed to be right, but also because many white students were ready for an opportunity to act out of a generalized frustration with the university and with the society. Like other campus protests in the latter part of the 1960s, the movements in support of black demands fed, among white students, on a combination of political moralism—indignation that demands which seemed just and straightforward were not being granted—and an underlying cultural alienation based on the white students' own needs and frustrations. The combination was an explosive one, and had the potential of becoming even more so.

During 1969 and 1970, even before the Cambodia crisis, three important developments had already taken place. One was the reemergence of the antiwar movement in October and November, with the October moratorium showing an overwhelming antiwar consensus on the campuses and with the November mobilization drawing a much larger crowd (mostly young people) than any previous demonstrations.[12] A second development, to which Cambodia gave great impetus, was the steady advance of a movement to force Reserve Officer Training Corps programs off university campuses. Since ROTC is an important source of officers for the armed services, this campaign had at least the potential of inflicting real damage to the

[12]Washington police said that a "moderate" estimate for the march down Pennsylvania Avenue, which encompassed only part of the protesters, was 250,000 people. *The New York Times*, November 16, 1969.

military, unlike the more symbolic earlier protests against military-related targets. A third development was a marked increase in physical sabotage of university facilities. This might have been expected, since building seizures had led to thousands of arrests in the spring of 1969 and administrators at most schools had made it clear that a get-tough policy would be followed with known violators of campus rules. This left sabotage as a much less risky action. Additionally, such sabotage, together with the "trashing" of windows in off-campus areas in some cities, reflected a growing impatience with the kind of purely symbolic actions that had been the mainstay of the student movement during most of the decade.

Demise of SDS

The intensification of the student movements in 1969 and 1970 took place despite the demise of the largest and most important radical organization, Students for a Democratic Society. By the end of the spring of 1969, SDS probably had as many as fifty to seventy-five thousand students at least loosely affiliated with its hundreds of campus chapters. SDS split asunder at its June, 1969 convention, with a "national office" in Boston following the line of the Progressive Labor (PL) party, an old-line Left group that had split away from the Communist party in 1961–1962, and another "national office" in Chicago under the control of a small group known as the Weatherman faction. Half a year later, with the Weathermen having gone underground, only the PL-oriented group remained, and it was unable to play a major role in the student movement except in the Boston area. Its program for the year was to fight for improved conditions for campus workers, which was not a major theme of the year's student protests. The Weathermen, with their near-glorification of violence and of "trashing," probably exerted a greater influence on the student movement even though their numbers were quite small and they were universally condemned by other political groups. The fact that the student movement burgeoned despite the absence of an umbrella-type organization such as SDS illustrated the movement's basically spontaneous nature. At no time during the decade had any organization been able to maintain hegemony over the movement. Even SDS, during its period of rapid growth between 1965 and 1969, had found itself constantly giving belated "leadership" to a movement whose direction it was never able to predict.

The Cambodia Crisis

Undoubtedly, the most salient feature of the 1969–70 student protests, especially during the Cambodia crisis in May, was the dramatic evidence that the movement had spread far beyond its original base of top-ranking state universities and liberal arts schools. The major centers of campus protest in 1969–70 included, besides the universities of Michigan and Wisconsin, such schools as Kent State in Ohio, the University of California in Santa Barbara, Ohio State, Maryland, and the State University of New York at Buffalo. Students' strikes took place during the first weeks after American troops went into Cambodia at several hundred campuses, most of which had been almost completely quiescent during the early 1960s.[13] Although there were special circumstances—such as President Nixon's bitter remarks about student protesters and the shooting of four Kent State students by National Guardsmen—the response that ensued was clearly the result of a long period of radicalization and estrangement that had taken place among college students over the decade of the 1960s.

FUTURE POSSIBILITIES

It is commonplace that Marxists have always expected the working class, especially the blue-collar workers in basic production industries, to be the source of a possible Socialist revolution in an advanced capitalist society. Today in the United States there is an apparent paradox; a large and growing student movement is more and more adopting the rhetoric of revolution while seemingly in complete isolation from the working class. The adoption of classical Marxist-Leninist terminology by many people in the movement has, of course, done nothing to reduce this isolation. Yet it can be argued that, despite surface appearances, the growth of the student Left does portend a possible socialist revolution in the United States.

There are two ways in which this may be said to be true. The first is that the movement, especially in the last several years, has meant a weakening among young people of the social and cultural incentives that keep people going about their rounds in society. This is most evident in the rejection of the "consumer ethic" that appears in the haphazard life styles of so many students and college dropouts. If it

[13]At the end of the first and most important week of the strike, the National Student Association listed 437 schools as having been closed or affected by the strike. This list was almost certainly far from complete. *The New York Times*, April 10, 1970.

is true that the acquisition of consumer goods is the most important incentive for holding a regular job, and for following orders diligently while on the job, then the student movement is likely to have a profound effect on the attitudes of workers over the next several decades. The spread of the movement to many colleges attended primarily by children of lower-middle-class and working-class families, as well as the spread of rebelliousness in the armed forces over the past few years, is an indication that all American young people, regardless of class backgrounds in some degree are subject to the same radicalizing forces that have produced the student Left. A recent *Fortune* article indicates that young automobile workers are creating problems for management with their militancy and high absenteeism, because high wages do not have the same incentive value for them as for the older workers.[14]

Granted that the movement has brought a weakening of the cohesive forces of present-day capitalist society, has it also brought signs of hope that society could someday be reconstituted on a new basis? It is not out of the question, after all, that the present trend could lead only to social dissolution, open militarization, or both. There are, however, discernible signs that new values are perhaps being evolved by the youth movement. The rapid growth of interest in women's liberation, which has come largely out of the student movement without having been "instigated" by any political groups, is one such sign. Another is the groping attempt of people in the student movement and other young people to develop forms of voluntary and cooperative social arrangements. The rejection by many young people of narrow occupational roles, as well as the refusal to enter into a cycle of buying and then paying for expensive material possession, may also be similar signs.

To be sure, there is a vast amount of negativism in the movement; it is this very negativism—arising out of frustration and anger at existing institutions—that has given the movement most of its impetus. But to see only this side of the movement, and to ignore the ways in which it has led to tentative insights about the type of society that ought to be possible in the United States, is to distort the movement's meaning. A revolution of the classical Marxist-Leninist model has never occurred in an advanced capitalist society, and it may well be that a socialist revolution in this country will be simply an extension of the student movement that began in 1960.

[14]Judson Gooding, "Blue-Collar Blues on the Assembly Line," *Fortune* 82 (July 1970): 69–71.

.3. *The Changing Social Base of the American Student Movement*

MILTON MANKOFF and RICHARD FLACKS

EVER SINCE the rebirth of student protest in the early 1960s, social scientists have been almost exclusively interested in studying the social and psychological characteristics of movement participants. Over the past few years, as a result of intensive investigations of the activists in the Berkeley Free Speech Movement, Vietnam Summer, and other protests, a rather clear-cut consensus has emerged concerning the social and characterological base of student activism.

PORTRAIT OF THE YOUNG ACTIVIST

The collective portrait of the student protesters provided by the extant literature includes the following elements: First, activists tend to come disproportionately from upper-middle-class families living in large urban areas, and particularly those portions of the upper middle class that depend upon high levels of educational achievement. Both parents tend to be involved with "careers;" the fathers are very likely to be successful professionals as opposed to businessmen. Second, parents of movement-oriented youth are likely to be politically liberal. Relatively few activists come from conservative or apolitical backgrounds. Third, children raised in the Jewish tradition or without any formal religious training are significantly more likely to become activists than are Christian youth. Fourth, some studies have shown that activists have experienced relatively permissive early socialization practices, compared to non-activists. Their parents were willing to give them a considerable amount of freedom to develop their own life styles and values.

46

In addition to social background, research has shown that activists are more likely to be intellectually and academically oriented than non-activists; activists tend to be recruited from among those students who demonstrate relatively high academic achievement. Very few are drawn from the ranks of academic underachievers or persons of low intellectual ability. Moreover, activist students tend to specialize in the social sciences and humanities as compared to non-activists. Thus, their intellectual orientations and academic prowess are directed toward those areas of study which help to understand society and culture. Finally, activist students are particularly likely to eschew conventional instrumental attitudes toward education in favor of a conception which places education in the service of self-development rather than of material success.[1]

Thus, the consensus derived from the pioneering empirical research views the white student movement in the United States as the outcome of an interaction between students drawn from a particular family milieu and embodying particular values and aspirations with regard to the university system and the larger society. The student activist is, according to this body of research, explicitly socialized to be concerned about social problems, to be skeptical of authority, and to take university ideals seriously. Early socialization tended to de-emphasize personal, material success in favor of social consciousness, political participation, and intellectual fulfillment as central life goals.

A major implication of the early research on the socio-psychological underpinnings of student activism was that campus protest was likely to be substantially limited to those students who were raised in the "humanistic," liberal, intellectually oriented, middle-class social environments characteristic of the first waves of campus protesters. Indeed, given the notoriously apolitical upbringing of most Amer-

[1]The profile of the radical student activist of the 1960s is drawn from several empirical studies. The most widely cited include the following: Richard Flacks, "The Liberated Generation: An Exploration of the Roots of Student Protest," *Journal of Social Issues 23* (July 1967): 52–75; William Watts and David Whittaker, "Free Speech Advocates at Berkeley," *Journal of Applied Behavioral Science 2* (January–March 1966): 41–62; Kenneth Keniston, *Young Radicals: Notes on Committed Youth* (New York: Harcourt Brace and World, 1968); Paul Heist, "Intellect and Commitment: The Faces of Discontent," in O. W. Knorr and W. J. Minter, eds., *Order and Freedom on the Campus: The Rights and Responsibilities of Faculties and Students* (Boulder, Colo.: Western Interstate Commission for Higher Education, 1965), pp. 61–69; David Westby and Richard G. Braungart, "Class and Politics in the Family Backgrounds of Student Political Activists," *American Sociological Review* 31 (October 1966): 690–692.

icans and the apparent stability of the political system, it seemed plausible, even as recently as three years ago, to expect that radicalism and protest were destined to remain the property of an important but relatively small minority of American students.

THE MOVEMENT SPREADS

Events, however, have largely undermined such interpretations and expectations. By the late 1960s, several national studies provided statistical documentation for the generally expressed view that the student movement had rapidly grown during the second half of the decade. Peterson's well-known studies for the Educational Testing Service showed that campuses with New Left organizations had doubled between 1965 and 1968. Foster and Long demonstrated that by the 1967–68 academic year, more than 75 percent of American universities had experienced major incidents of protest and that protest activity had occurred in a substantial proportion of liberal arts and junior colleges. Moreover, by 1968, protests had spread from major coastal schools to every region of the country; more than a third of southern schools had experienced "incidents."[2]

Surveys of campus opinion show a similar trend, with substantial proportions of student bodies expressing agreement with New Left positions on the war, racism, and other major issues, supporting "student power," and favoring activism and mass protest. Although the great majority of students opposes student-initiated violence and is not made up of committed radicals or revolutionaries, there is unquestionably a widespread feeling among students across the country concerning the basic issues which have been foci of protest, representing a dramatic shift of student opinion to the Left over the past five years.[3] It seems likely, therefore, that the spread of student activism and "leftism" has resulted in a considerable change in the social composition of the activist core. In short, the classic portrait of the student activist needs fundamental reconsideration.

Indeed, recent cross-sectional studies comparing student activists

[2]Richard Peterson, *The Scope of Organized Student Protest in 1967–68* (Princeton, N.J.: Educational Testing Service, 1968); Julian Foster and Durward Long, "Levels of Protest," in J. Foster and D. Long, eds., *Protest! Student Activism in America* (New York: Morrow, 1970), pp. 81–88.

[3]The Scranton report cites May, 1970 Harris Poll data indicating that minorities of only around one-third of the American student body favored the complete removal of ROTC, the banning of Defense corporate recruiting on the campus, and the banning of the use of police to quell campus violence. About 11 percent of the Harris sample identified themselves with the "far or radical Left," a proportion three times larger than that found by Harris in 1968. On the other hand, three-

with inactivists have failed to show the same clearly patterned differences which were found in earlier work.[4]

Unfortunately, these provocative studies are deficient in regard to their relevance to the question of whether the social base of the student movement has changed in recent years—because they do not provide longitudinal data.

A SURVEY AT WISCONSIN

Data gathered by one of the authors at the University of Wisconsin, an elite institution and one noted for a tradition of student radicalism, address directly the question of the transformation of the activist population in at least one major university. These findings, reported below, will provide a starting point for some further discussion of the emergent sources of political socialization in the American student movement.[5]

"Generational" Trends Emerge

During October of 1967, several hundred student protesters prevented representatives of the Dow Chemical Company from recruiting personnel at the University of Wisconsin, Madison, because of Dow's role in producing napalm for the Vietnam War. Police were called in to quell the obstructive action, and scores of students and a few policemen required medical attention as a consequence of the violent confrontation that ensued. The campus community was extremely upset by the events, and when the chancellor of the uni-

---

fourths of the sample favored basic changes in the system, and nearly half believed that such changes were more likely to come about through "radical pressure from outside the system" than from actions of established institutions themselves. According to the Harris survey, 80 percent of the sampled schools had experienced protest during the Cambodian crisis, and these were supported by 75 percent of the students at these schools—indeed, nearly 60 percent had taken part in such protests. The Scranton Commission cites another study indicating that 80 percent of graduating seniors favored confrontation as a necessary means of social change. "The Scranton Report: Text of the President's Commission on Campus Unrest," *Chronicle of Higher Education* 5 (October 5, 1970): 7.

[4] Roger Kahn, "The Rank-and-File Student Activist: A Contextual Test of Three Hypotheses," unpublished paper, State University of New York at Stony Brook, 1969; Riley Dunlap, "Family Backgrounds of Radical and Conservative Political Activists at a Non-Elite University," unpublished paper, University of Oregon, 1969.

[5] A more detailed report of the following study may be found in Milton Mankoff, "The Political Socialization of Student Radicals and Militants in the Wisconsin Student Movement during the 1960s," unpublished doctoral dissertation, University of Wisconsin, 1970.

versity sought to invoke disciplinary action against leaders of the protest, approximately 2,250 students signed a *Declaration of Responsibility*, claiming that they too were "leaders" of the Dow protest. In May of the following year, after several students were expelled for their alleged role in the October 1967 events and relative peace prevailed on the campus, fixed-choice questionnaires pertaining largely to students' political life and social background were mailed to approximately 750 identifiable persons originally selected from a 50 percent random sample of *Declaration* signatories. The return rate on the questionnaire was 68.4 percent. It was felt, correctly, that this sample would include a large number of the movement cadre at Wisconsin. In order to obtain a cross section of Wisconsin students with which to compare activist youth, identical questionnaires were sent to 240 students selected at random from the *Wisconsin Student Directory*, excluding in advance the few students who were *Declaration* signers. The return rate for this sample was 63.4 percent.

In order to address the problem of "generational" trends within the student movement at the University of Wisconsin, it was necessary to determine which of the students within the sample of *Declaration* signatories would be considered as belonging to the movement cadre, and to distinguish between two distinct "generations" of such cadre. Simply to consider all *Declaration* signers as members of the movement cadre would be to include fairly sizable numbers of conservative, moderate, and liberal students who were upset over various aspects of the Dow affair but were neither radical ideologically nor very militant. Thus, it was decided that the movement cadre would be limited to radicals—that is, those students who described themselves as Socialists, Communists, anarchists, revolutionaries, or New Leftists on an item pertaining to political ideology. This group represented 46.6 percent of the *Declaration* signers and 2 percent of the cross section. It should be noted that 56.1 percent of the radical students claimed to have engaged in some form of civil disobedience, our criterion for militancy, so that we are selecting students who really constituted hard-core activists at the time of the study. If changes in the social base of this group could be demonstrated, they would probably indicate that even more significant changes are occurring at the periphery of the student movement.

The Veteran Cadre

In considering the question of generations within the movement, it was felt that students who claimed to have been active politically for three or more years prior to May 1968 (when the questionnaires were distributed) would be viewed as veteran cadre—regardless of the time spent or the nature of their work. It was believed that this cutting point between veteran and non-veteran cadre would distinguish fairly accurately between those who were politically involved when the movement was small and isolated during the pre-1965 period and those who probably became involved after the bombing of North Vietnam in February 1965.

RESULTS OF THE SURVEY

The table compares veteran and non-veteran radicals and a cross section of Wisconsin students in terms of demographic character- istics, family political-social relations, and aspects of student politi- cal-intellectual culture emphasized in the work of Watts and Whit- taker, Flacks, and Keniston. Several preliminary observations can be made after examining the table. To begin with, even though veteran cadre can be characterized as coming from well-educated, liberal, permissive families residing in large cities, in comparison to the cross section of Wisconsin students, it is worthwhile noting that, even among movement veterans, a large proportion comes from other backgrounds. A second general observation is that, although non- veteran radicals differ in several respects from veterans, the non- veterans are still distinct from the cross section in several ways. Thus, the changes in the social base of student radicalism at Wisconsin in- dicate tendencies rather than a complete alteration in the social base of the student movement, at least as of May 1968.

In examining the similarities and dissimilarities between verteran and non-veteran cadre on several selected variables, we can draw the following conclusions.

Demographic Characteristics

If we consider the size of the cities in which members of the movement cadre spent most of their lives, their fathers' educational

Comparison of Veteran and Non-Veteran Cadre and Student Cross Section on Selected Variables Relevant to Student Activism

	Demographic Characteristics (in Percentages)		
	City Size Students who lived in city of 100,000 or more for most of their lives	Educational Achievement Fathers with college degree	Religion Students raised in Jewish tradition or without any religious affiliation
Veteran Cadre (N = 137)	51.8	65.1	65.4
Non-Veteran Cadre (N = 94)	36.2	54.2	39.4
Cross Section (N = 153)	33.3	42.5	18.3
Chi-square Values for Veteran/Non-veteran Differences	$\chi^2 = 5.510$ $df = 1$ $p < 0.02$	$\chi^2 = 3.649$ $df = 2$ $p > 0.10$	$\chi^2 = 15.261$ $df = 1$ $p < 0.001$

	Family Political-Social Relations (in Percentages)		
	Fathers' Political Ideology Students who perceive their fathers as being "very liberal" or "radical"	Parental Discipline Students who claim highly permissive child-rearing during adolescence	Parental Approval Students who claim their parents approve of their present life style[b]
Veteran Cadre (N = 137)	32.8	47.4	49.6
Non-Veteran Cadre (N = 94)	15.9	35.1	31.9
Cross Section (N = 153)	5.3	32.4	75.6
Chi-square Values for Veteran/Non-veteran Differences	$\chi^2 = 10.002$ $df = 1$ $p < 0.01$	$\chi^2 = 3.850$ $df = 2$ $p > 0.10$	$\chi^2 = 8.734$ $df = 2$ $p < 0.02$

	Student Political-Intellectual Culture (in Percentages)			
	Academic Performance Students with B or better average as undergraduates[b]	Major Field Students specializing in social sciences or humanities	Success Ideology Students who consider it important to succeed in career	Informal Political Education Students who read many[a] political periodicals[b]
Veteran Cadre (N = 137)	58.4	81.0	58.5	32.1
Non-Veteran Cadre (N = 94)	52.1	79.8	51.1	14.9
Cross Section (N = 153)	43.1	36.2	92.1	2.6
Chi-square Values for Veteran/Non-veteran Differences	$\chi^2 = 0.888$ $df = 1$ $p > 0.30$	$\chi^2 = 0.054$ $df = 1$ $p > 0.80$	$\chi^2 = 1.234$ $df = 1$ $p > 0.20$	$\chi^2 = 10.877$ $df = 2$ $p < 0.001$

[a] Nine or more.

[b] Veteran and non-veteran cadre did not differ significantly in age distribution, a variable which might have affected parental approval of student life styles, grade point averages, and the volume of reading students engaged in.

achievement, and their religious heritage, it is clear that there is a genuine trend toward inclusion of more students from smaller cities and towns and with Christian upbringings. While somewhat more non-veteran cadre members' fathers are likely not to be college graduates than veterans' fathers, differences are not statistically significant. All these changes in the social base of student movement cadre members make the group more representative of the Wisconsin student body as a whole.

Family Political -Social Relations

When we consider the political and social relationships between parents and their activist offspring, it is clear that veteran students are considerably more likely to have fathers who were either very liberal or radical politically themselves than are the non-veterans. Moreover, while the differences in permissiveness are modest and not statistically significant, non-veteran students are significantly more likely to experience parental disapproval of their current life styles than are veteran cadre. These changes in parental-student relations show a definite convergence between non-veteran and veteran cadre.

Student Political-Intellectual Culture

Finally, if we consider what can best be called students' political-intellectual culture, it appears that academic performance and major field of specialization remain largely the same between the different generations of cadre. An interesting finding is that the newer recruits are actually slightly less likely—though, again, statistical significance is lacking—to consider it important to succeed in a career. If the extant literature has always described the "young radicals" as eschewing conventional materialism, one would certainly have expected that the movement, as it grew, would come to encompass those who sought more conventional career patterns but nevertheless could embrace a desire for radical social change. Apparently this has not been the case. Several interpretations of this finding are possible, perhaps the most likely being that to be a radical implies a serious commitment to devote oneself primarily to political activity, activity that is increasingly felt to preclude a normal career development.

The one area in which the political-intellectual culture of the newer movement cadre differs significantly from that of the veterans, and converges with that of the general student body, is in the realm of informal political education. Students were asked to list the political periodicals that they read at least occasionally, and the data show that veteran cadre are much more likely to read many political periodicals (nine or more) than the non-veterans. This finding, we believe, is of great potential import, and its implications for the development of a radical movement in the future will be considered below.

IMPLICATIONS FOR A RADICAL MOVEMENT

The finding that the radical activist core at the University of Wisconsin involves an increasing proportion of students from conventional backgrounds—that, in fact, it is increasingly difficult to differentiate the activists from the student body as a whole on the basis of family origin—is, we believe, likely to be replicated at other institutions. For instance, a study by Weissberg at the University of Chicago, conducted in 1966, showed that, even at an earlier time, there were similar distinctions between movement "veterans" and those who were participating in their first demonstration—the latter being substantially similar in social background to the student body as a whole, the former fitting closely the classic portrait.[6]

It seems clear, then, that the growth of the student movement in these years is not attributable simply to its appeal to the offspring of the liberal, educated middle class, although of course these young people continue to play a major role within it. Instead, the movement has spread well beyond its initial ranks to include increasing proportions of Roman Catholics and Protestants as well as Jews and "secular" youth, increasing proportions of the offspring of businessmen, white-collar and blue-collar workers as well as the children of professionals and intellectuals, increasing numbers of youth raised as Republicans in "middle America" as well as Democrats in big eastern cities.[7] Moreover, together with these changes in the social base of

[6]Charlotte Weissberg, "Students Against the Rank," unpublished master's essay, Department of Sociology, University of Chicago, 1968.

[7]In the Wisconsin study, an analysis of differences between veteran and non-veteran *Declaration* signers, encompassing marginal supporters of the movement as well as radicals and militants, indicates that changes in the social base of the movement are even more pronounced among peripheral participants than among the core activists. By 1971, with the 1968 Democratic convention, the Chicago conspiracy trial, and the Cambodian invasion increasing the radicalization of campuses, it is reasonable to assume that the trends outlined in the Wisconsin data collected in the spring of 1968 have become even more pronounced. Since the mid-sixties, and particularly in the past few years, the growth of black and so-called Third World student activism has also contributed to a need for a recasting of theoretical and empirical research on the student movement. This paper is limiting its concerns to the largely white student movement.

the movement have occurred changes in the definition of activist commitment. It is no longer possible to restrict that definition to those who belong to this or that organization or who have demonstrated some form of systematic commitment to political action. For the movement has developed a rich variety of ways in which allegiance to it can be symbolically and behaviorally expressed, among which the role of the "politico" is decreasingly central.

It is plausible to argue that students and young people generally have the capacity to develop a collective consciousness functionally akin to the "class consciousness" postulated by Marxism. Marx, for instance, argued that proletarian class consciousness would arise in part because workers had been brought together in situations of intense interaction and segregation, as a result of the emergence of the factory system. This circumstance is perhaps even more true for young people in industrialized and developed societies, who are herded together for prolonged periods under conditions of sharp segregation from other strata. In fact, in the United States, the sixties marked the first time in history that the great majority of young people, including those from 16 to 21, were thus agglomerated and segregated—in high schools, colleges and universities, in military camps, and in urban ghettoes. Thus, a critical and necessary condition for the emergence of collective consciousness has been created for young people, irrespective of their social origins.[8]

But, of course, collective consciousness with an oppositional thrust requires a bit more than simply the opportunity for intense interaction. The theory of revolutionary class consciousness roots such opposition in the fact that those who are gathered together have the common experience of exploitation, material deprivation, and permanent political powerlessness. Youth consciousness, however, has not been principally rooted in such material sources of discontent; indeed, youth movements everywhere have generally been started by students who came from economically and socially advantaged and privileged families.

Generational movements may be distinguished from class-based oppositional movements in that the roots of the former are found primarily in cultural crises while the latter are determined by crises in the political economy. To be very brief about it, students and young people are likely to move toward self-conscious rebellion when prevailing official values and symbols appear irrelevant or retrogressive

[8]For a fuller analysis of the segregation and concentration of American youth in the postwar period, compare Richard Flacks, *Youth and Social Change in American Society* (Chicago; Markham, 1971).

in the face of the need for radical social change. The classic condition for such a cultural crisis has been the situation of rapid modernization of feudal, agrarian societies. Under these conditions, young people experience profound dislocation as they leave their tradition-oriented communities and families; they experience the universities as centers of badly needed new values and ideological perspectives; they experience the regime as unwilling or unable to accept and implement these new perspectives. The cultural crisis of developing countries is thus experienced as both a national crisis of authority and a personal crisis of identity. Student movements have always represented a primary attempt to solve both the social and the personal problems at once.[9]

The depth and extent of student unrest in the United States and other advanced industrial societies in recent years lends credence to the view that these societies have now entered a period of cultural crisis—one which has no doubt been developing for several decades. This crisis has to do with the impact of general affluence and large-scale bureaucratic organization on allegiance to the "Protestant ethic," on modes of child rearing, on sexual identity, on attitudes toward work, property, competition, and self-expression. As the vitality of traditional values declines, young people, especially, experience cultural incoherence and chaos. Established institutions appear to operate at cross purposes and to lack internal consistency. For example, the media promulgate hedonism and indulgence while the schools continue to uphold self-discipline. Parents promote self-gratification and consumership while at the same time expecting self-control and achievement. Furthermore, in the quest for cultural coherence and stable meanings, young people find few established, authoritative voices or models. Under the circumstances, young people are increasingly disposed to question the official culture and established institutions, and they are increasingly likely to turn to each other in the quest for coherence and identity.[10]

[9]Compare S. N. Eisenstadt, *From Generation to Generation* (Glencoe, Ill.: Free Press, 1956); Philip Altbach, "Students and Politics," in S. M. Lipset, ed., *Student Politics* (New York: Basic Books, 1967), pp. 74–96; S. M. Lipset, "Students and Politics in Comparative Perspective," *Daedalus* 97 (Winter; 1968): 97–123.

[10]A provocative interpretation of America's cultural crisis which traces its roots to the "disaccumulation" period of capitalism in the twentieth century can be found in Martin Sklar, "On the Proletarian Revolution and the End of Political-Economic Society," *Radical America* 3 (May-June 1969): 1–41. Sklar's discussion of the alienated young intelligentsia in the 1920s shows parallels with contemporary dissident cultural themes. The collapse of the counter-culture of the 1920s in the face of economic depression suggests that one must eschew any linear theory of societal change. The cultural revolt of the present period presupposes economic stability

It is our argument, then, that the combination of deepening cultural crisis (rooted in the impact of advanced technology on traditional capitalist values) with a rapidly expanded incorporation of young people into segregated enclaves created the ground for the emergence of widespread generational consciousness—a consciousness in considerable tension with established authority. But the primary expression of that consciousness throughout the sixties was the so-called "youth culture"—a complex of music, drugs, fashion, language, and sentiment, exhibiting considerable alienated content, but also rather explicitly hostile to organized political involvement and action.

In the sixties, students and other young people who sought to express and resolve the cultural crisis through organized political action were very much a special minority. In retrospect, it is not at all surprising that these young people should have been primarily those who were reared with a special interest in politics and a particular emphasis on social concern. The average white child in this country is not raised to seek solutions through political means, or to possess any urgent sense of societal responsibility, or to feel any concrete skepticism about the claims of political authority.[11] Accordingly, conventionally reared students and youth who experienced cultural malaise turned predominantly to drugs, youth culture, religious experiment, and other apolitical models of expression.

Throughout much of the past decade, it was commonplace to believe that there was a more or less fundamental schism between the New Left and the "hippies"—that, in fact, political opposition and cultural alienation were mutually exclusive responses to social crisis. Many observers argued further that the narcotic, disaffiliative attractions of the youth culture would undoubtedly undermine impulses toward political activism; for example, a number of early civil rights activists found solace with "acid" after "burning themselves out" in Mississippi.

But the channeling of youthful malaise into "counter-cultural" experiment and away from politicized challenges to authority depends first of all on the continued legitimacy of established authority in the eyes of youth and, second, on the existence of an atmosphere in which unconventional and, indeed, extra-legal cultural experiment and innovation are permitted and, in certain respects, sponsored by

---

and affluence, conditions which, given the cyclical behavior of capitalist economies, should not be taken for granted.

[11]David Easton and Jack Dennis, "The Child's Image of Government," *The Annals* 361 (September 1965): 40–57.

the authorities. Since many young people were already predisposed to question the claims of authority, and since many persons of all ages in the society were, by the early sixties, already deeply troubled about the racial crisis, the Cold War, and the effects of advanced technology, student activism in favor of basic reform was received with considerable interest and sympathy on the campus from the beginning of the decade. On the other hand, even the early New Left activists tended to accept the basic legitimacy of the political system, and focused their protest on particularly racist and militarist elites rather than on the regime or the system as a whole.

A crucial factor in the delegitimation of the political system, for student activists in particular and for students in general, was the failure of established agencies of reform—such as the labor movement, liberal Democrats, liberal intellectual and religious elements—to mobilize an effective national coalition for fundamental reform.

Had the established liberal/labor/civil rights leadership coalition been able to break early from commitment to the Cold War, and to mount an aggressive grass-roots movement of reform (as SDS advocated in its early days), had the emergent southern movement and the early student activists been recognized and fully supported by the established liberal leadership, had charismatic figures not been eliminated and others not demoralized, then the widespread radicalization of the students—and particularly the "deauthorization" of the political system for them—would very likely not have occurred.

Of course, as has been widely observed, the growing mistrust of the political system, arising out of the racial crisis, was profoundly accelerated, deepened, and diffused by the Vietnam War, by the domestic consequences of the war, by the so-called "credibility gap," and by the failure in 1968 of the political parties to recognize popular antiwar feeling in any effective fashion.

In addition to sensing the unresponsiveness of the political system, apolitical young people in this period have come to experience the major institutions of the society as biased against their "cultural" needs, interests, and aspirations. In particular, as increasing numbers of young people have wished for the time, space, resources, and freedom to experiment with new values, life styles, and identities, they have found such opportunities limited or contradicted by the actual operation of the society. Many, especially those most attracted to political activism, hoped, for instance, that the universities would provide the resources and opportunities for the cultural quest. In this, they have been sharply frustrated—hence, the demand for "relevance,"—or they have experienced considerable repression—as, for instance, in the effort by the Berkeley administration to close the campus to recruitment for off-campus activism (thus precipitating the Free Speech Movement of 1964). Many young men experienced the draft and the associated system of "channeling" as a very concrete barrier to self-fulfillment. As drug use spread in the youth culture, increasing numbers of young people experienced regular harassment at the hands of the police, and the institutionalization of the youth culture was repeatedly undermined by the combined efforts of the police and by commercial exploiters, both legal and illegal. In short, virtually all efforts to sustain a counter-culture, to find time, space, resources, and freedom for experiment, have come up against the necessity of resisting efforts by the authority structure to undermine or frustrate these aspirations.

Data from the Wisconsin study demonstrate rather clearly the radicalizing effects of repression: Of the 125 students who claimed to have experienced some form of "political repression" as a consequence of their political belief or activity, 49 percent reported that they became more radical, and 41 percent reported that they became more politically active as a result. It seems plausible that many of these were among the more moderate, conventional students rather than among those who fit the classical portrait of the activist.

Our argument, then, has been this: Radical student activism has spread to include a much more diverse group of students than those depicted in the well-known research on the social-psychological characteristics of student protesters. Thus, such research, and its underlying premise that the effects of political socialization in the family are permanent and overriding, no longer serves as an adequate guide to understanding the processes of politicalization and radicalization among American youth. Instead, attention must now be focused on the hypothesis that a quasi-class consciousness has emerged among students, facilitated by the enormous concentration of young people in universities and fostered by the general cultural crisis in American society. This generational consciousness has been politicized and radicalized in part as a result of the catalytic efforts of the New Left, but primarily because political authority has been substantially delegitimated and institutional authority has been unable to accommodate the cultural aspirations of many students and young people.

These students and young people do not, however, form a class; their status is by definition transitory; their segregation, although enormously functional in the development of collective consciousness, ultimately walls them off from connection to the majority of the population and from access to decisive resources for power. There are, however, elements of the student situation which suggest the possible emergence of a more truly class-conscious movement in the Marxian sense.

One of the central findings of the classic research on the social base of the student movement was that student activists were the children of men and women who were themselves highly educated and who were involved in occupations for which advanced education was a requisite. These parents were concentrated in the social service professions—in education, medicine, law, social work—and in intellectual work. It is clear that this stratum—the "intelligentsia"—has been, on the one hand, in some degree of tension with the prevailing culture for several generations, and, on the other hand, constitutes the most rapidly growing sector of the labor force.[12]

Other data, provided by Samuel Lubell, suggest that students most likely to move Left and to be attracted to protest, even though socialized in conservative or conventional families, are those oriented to "intelligentsia"-related occupations.[13] Indeed, the Wisconsin data discussed here show that one continuing difference between new and veteran activists versus the student body as a whole is the concentration of the activists in the social sciences.

It is possible, then, that a major source of student radicalism, in addition to the situation of students and the cultural problems experienced by young people, is the emergence of a new type of alienated worker—the "educated" or "new" working class. The general point would be that advanced industrial capitalism requires the rapid growth of a mass intelligentsia, specially trained for technical and cultural innovation, for organizational problem-solving, and for modernization. These new workers experience alienation in their work partly because their training leads them to be critical of the status quo and because they find established authority recalcitrant in making needed reforms, partly because their conditions of work are "over-bureaucratized" and insufficiently autonomous, and partly because, in what they believed to be an imperialist and racist social order, they play roles of domination which are repugnant to their liberally educated sensibilities.[14]

On this analysis, university-style confrontations and related activity should begin to spread to other institutions in which the young intelli-

[12]See Richard Flacks, "The Revolt of the Young Intelligentsia," *Trans-action* 7 (June 1970): 47–55.

[13]Samuel Lubell, "That Generation Gap," *The Public Interest* (Fall 1968): 52–60.

[14]Herbert Gintis, "The New Working Class and Revolutionary Youth," *Socialist Revolution* 1 (June 1970): 13–43.

gentsia are concentrated: hospitals, newspaper offices, publishing houses, government bureaus, and the like. The 1968 Wisconsin data do not indicate that non-veteran radicals were any less likely to be specializing in the social sciences and humanities than were veteran radicals. The failure, thus far, of radical political ideology to make substantial inroads among students in the physical, natural, and engineering sciences would lead one to predict that future confrontations would be limited largely to public and private service bureaucracies and "culture" industries. This would leave the productive sector of private industry relatively immune to the radical activity by scientific-technical workers that played such a crucial role in the massive rebellion in France in May, 1968. Nevertheless, the recent development of "proletarianization" in scientific-technical fields, complete with job insecurity and coupled with a growing awareness of the relationship between capitalist production and ecological catastrophe, may serve to radicalize students in these fields, who were previously indifferent or hostile toward radical ideology. Further, if "educated labor" comes to conceive of itself in working-class rather than in "professional" terms, the grounds for linkage between student radicalism and the more traditional sectors of the working class might come into existence.

In addition to becoming rooted in the class consciousness of new occupational groups, generational consciousness can be institutionalized in another way—that is, through what might be called the "territorialization" of the youth revolt. As increasing numbers of diverse young people become attracted to radical politics and countercultural life styles, they tend to congregate in neighborhoods near large universities and in major cities. Recently, such locations have begun to be perceived as the places in which the time, space, resources, and freedom for cultural innovation and political mobilization can be at least partially sustained. Increasingly, as such territorial consciousness has taken hold, these locales have been the arenas of severe police-youth confrontations, providing incidents which generally heighten the sense of solidarity and community within these locales. As the youth revolt moves off campus in this way, it is clear that the social base of the movement will become increasingly heterogeneous, spreading beyond the ranks of those who can attend school and attracting increasing numbers of working-class and "drop-out" young people and young adults.

The rising receptivity to violent street fighting and sabotage in the youth movement is perceived as primarily a consequence of the failure of the political system to be an effective instrument of change.

But it is also a function of the increasing heterogeneity of the youth movement. The original student activist, raised in a "humanistic" family, was overwhelmingly pacifist in temperament. Indeed, those few "old" New Leftists who have joined such groups as Weathermen have gone through veritable agonies of self-transformation in order to become capable of street combat. Our observations during the recent period of severe physical confrontation in Isla Vista suggest that it is not the organized veteran radicals who are most active but the less politicized, newly radicalized youth, socialized in "mainstream" American homes, who view pacifism as unmasculine and violence as more normal.[15]

Disciplined violence and spontaneous insurrection apparently have been a necessary part of social revolutionary change as well as of reform movements elsewhere.[16] Yet genuine revolution, unlike reform or elite or minority revolutions (for instance, Japan, Turkey, the Soviet Union), requires the widespread mobilization of masses of people from many walks of life. Such a process can only be realized by the widespread delegitimation of the existing elites and official culture. Moreover, it involves the development of an appealing vision of the new society which can begin to be implemented during the revolutionary struggle itself. Violence, in such an effort, although not absent, plays a distinctly subordinate role to political mobilization.

If the student movement merely becomes fixed at the stage of sporadic insurrection and sabotage, it can at best lead to co-optive reform from above, as has a total devotion to parliamentary strategy, and at worst to a fully authoritarian political regime.

That new recruits to the movement are generally less involved in political discourse is perhaps reflected in the finding (see Table) that veterans are much more likely to read political periodicals and journals than are new recruits. It would seem clear that the long-term viability of the movement depends, in part, on the capacity of those within it to synthesize the spontaneous, anti-political "gut" radicalism of the new recruits with the more systematically politicized and intellectual radicalism of the veterans.

[15]Richard Flacks and Milton Mankoff, "Revolt in Santa Barbara: Why They Burned the Bank," *The Nation* 210 (March 23, 1970): 337–40.

[16]Barrington Moore, Jr., *The Social Origins of Dictatorship and Democracy: Lord and Peasant in the Making of the Modern World* (Boston: Beacon, 1966); Richard Rubenstein, *Rebels in Eden: Mass Political Violence in the United States* (Boston: Little, Brown, 1970).

.4. The Political Future of Activist Generations*

SEYMOUR MARTIN LIPSET and EVERETT CARLL LADD, JR.

THE RISE of student activism and the apparent radicalization of large segments of the undergraduate population since 1965, have led to considerable speculation as to what the future politics of today's students will be. It is certainly clear that the students and graduates of the latter half of the 1960s and early 1970s are much more liberal and radical than those of the 1950s. A host of opinion surveys have confirmed that the large majority of the more recent graduates adhere to the camp of Kennedy-McCarthy liberalism, thoroughly oppose the Vietnam War, are committed to egalitarianism and special help for black and other underprivileged minorities, and are concerned with the elimination of poverty, etc.[1] The proportion of self-described "radicals" rose gradually from 1965 on to a high point of 11 percent in a Harris Poll in May 1970. It declined again to between 4 and 7 percent in Gallup and Harris surveys taken during the year of the "ebbing wave," 1970–71. Yet a Gallup Poll of college students in late 1970 found 44 percent maintaining that violence is justified to bring about social change in the United States (compared to just 14 percent of the public at large), 49 percent maintaining that personal freedom and the right of dissent are being curbed in this country, and 37 percent describing themselves "far left" or "left" politically as against

---

*An earlier version of this chapter appeared as "College Generations from the 1930s to the 1960s," *The Public Interest*, 25 (Fall 1971): 99–113.

[1]For a detailed summary of the opinion polls of college students gathered from 1965 to 1971, see Seymour Martin Lipset, "Polls and Protests," Chapter 2 of Seymour Martin Lipset and Gerald Schaflander, *Passion and Politics: Student Activism in America* (Boston: Little, Brown, 1971), pp. 38–79.

just 17 percent "right" and "far right." The students overwhelmingly favored liberal candidates for the presidency. (Their non-college age-mates, however, show a sharply different political orientation. Over 25 percent of the newly enfranchised 18–21 age group not attending college preferred George Wallace to Muskie or Nixon, over twice the proportion of older voters, according to an April, 1971 Gallup Poll. Non-college young people have consistently shown greater support for the Vietnam War than those in any other age stratum, college or non-college, while the college-educated young have become the most opposed to the war.)

As the students of this college "generation" have graduated and entered the junior ranks of the professions, the media, business, government, of academe itself, it would appear that they have brought to these occupational environments a deep concern for applying egalitarian, populist, often strongly radical principles. Young journalists press for advocacy rather than "objective" reporting; new physicians support socialized medicine; architects demand plans which "serve the people;" young academics back "relevance," i.e., an orientation to radical social change, in their teaching and research. And from a variety of young college graduates has come support for the "New Politics."

What does the emergence of a liberalized, partially-radicalized college stratum portend for the future? Will they remain a force for major social change as they climb the occupational hierarchies? Will they become much more moderate and "socially responsible" as they marry, have children, gain income, status, power and personal responsibilities? Some fear or hope the first is true; others that the saying "radical at twenty, conservative at forty," will prove valid.

GENERATIONS OR AGING: PERSISTENCE OR CHANGE?

This question, in a general sense, is not a new one for social scientists, yet unfortunately the existing literature does not provide a clear and unambiguous guide. The basic confusion, as John Crittenden has so well pointed out, lies in the contrasting emphases on the experiences of *political generations* on the one hand, and upon the effects of *aging* on the other.[2]

[2]John Crittenden, "Aging and Party Affiliation," *Public Opinion Quarterly* 26 (Winter 1962): 648.

Such scholars as Karl Mannheim, Sigmund Neumann, and Rudolf Heberle contended that people form a frame of reference, which then informs their subsequent values and actions, from the major events of the period when they first come to political consciousness, usually in their late teens or early twenties.[3] The prevailing climate in which a cohort "comes of age politically," in this view, is of decisive importance to its future political orientations.

The idea of the political generation has been frequently used in analyses of Weimar Germany. The weakness of the Weimar Republic has been interpreted, in part, as stemming from the fact that a dominant generation of the years 1929–33 was formed politically during the period of war, defeat, revolution, and inflation, i.e., from 1914–24.[4] More recently, political analysts have stressed the impact of the Great Depression of the 1930s in creating a generation disposed to fear economic insecurity and to favor welfare state measures, while those who came of age in the prosperous 1940s and 1950s have been said to be more cautious in their acceptance of the welfare state and less committed to New Deal liberalism.[5] Similarly, the support for an activist-interventionist foreign policy in the early 1960s has been credited in part to the reactions of a "generation" which had learned the "lessons of Munich" and of World War II, that democratic powers must support small, weak states against totalitarian aggression.

Of course, those who speak of generations do not suggest that all or most people in the same age category react identically to key

[3]See this volume, Chapter 6. See also Karl Mannheim, *Ideology and Utopia* (New York: Harcourt, Brace, 1936), p. 270; Sigmund Neumann, "The Conflict of Generations in Contemporary Europe." *Vital Speeches* 5 (1939): 623–28; Sigmund Neumann, *Permanent Revolution* (New York: Harper and Brothers, 1942), pp. 234–44; Rudolf Heberle, *Social Movements* (New York: Appleton-Century-Crofts, 1951), pp. 118–27; Francois Mentre, *Les generations sociales* (Paris: Editions Bossard, 1920); R. Behrendt, "Die offentliche Meinung und das Generationsproblem," *Kölner Vierteljahrshefts für soziologie* 11 (1932): 290–309; José Ortega y Gasset, *Man and Crisis* (New York: W. W. Norton, 1958), pp. 50–84; Bruno Bettelheim, "The Problem of Generations," in Erik Erikson, ed., *Youth: Change and Challenge* (New York: Basic Books, 1963), pp. 64–92; S. N. Eisenstadt, *From Generation to Generation* (Glencoe: The Free Press, 1956).

[4]Arthur Dix, *Die Deutschen Reichstagsvahlen, 1871–1930, and die Wandlungen der Volkgliederung* (Tubingen: J. B. C. Mohr, Paul Siebeck, 1930), pp. 34–35; Hans Gerth, "The Nazi Party: Its Leadership and Composition," *American Journal of Sociology* 55 (1940): 530–41.

[5]Seymour Martin Lipset, *Political Man* (Garden City: Doubleday-Anchor Books, 1963), pp. 281–86.

political events. Mannheim wrote of "generation-units," which are different groups within the same age stratum who adhere to alternative, often conflicting values. And more recently Bennett Berger noted that "it is essential, when using the concept of the generation, in a cultural sense, to specify generations of what, because it is only in a demographic sense that people in the same age-group constitute a homogeneous unit. . . ."[6] Obviously, the rich and the poor youth, factory workers and college students, blacks and whites do not experience events in the same way. During the Great Depression, some were reared in families whose real income actually increased, while others had unemployed fathers. Any effort to evaluate the impact of political events on generations has to take into account the diverse units within an age stratum, and their varying personal experiences. Within the framework of our present inquiry, college students would seem to meet the standard of a reasonably coherent "generation-unit."

Emphasis upon the effects of aging have led to quite different conclusions or expectations. For both social and psychological reasons, it has been argued, people tend to move from the political extremes as they grow older, toward a more "moderate" or centrist position. Actions defined by society as "deviant"—e.g., delinquent, bohemian, and radical—tend to be largely phenomena of youth.[7] As they grow older, the overwhelming majority of "deviants" become "respectable" and "settle down." In politics, this has meant that young people, as they grow older, tend to move toward the political center, as then defined. Parties of the extreme left and right almost invariably draw disproportionate support from young voters.

The moderating influence of aging has been stressed in a very diverse array of studies, but no one, perhaps, has made the argument as cogently as Aristotle in his *Rhetoric:*

Young men have strong passions, and tend to gratify them indiscriminately. . . . They are hot-tempered and quick tempered, . . . owing to their love of honor they cannot bear being slighted, and are indignant if they imagine themselves unfairly treated. . . . They love . . . money . . . very little, not having yet learnt what it means to be without it. . . . They have exalted notions, because they have not yet been humbled by life or learnt its necessary

[6]Bennett M. Berger, "How Long is a Generation?" from his book, *Looking for America* (Englewood Cliffs, N. J.: Prentice-Hall, 1971), p. 29.

[7]David Matza, "Subterranean Traditions of Youth," *The Annals* 338 (November 1961): 106.

limitations. . . . They would rather do noble deeds than useful ones: their lives are regulated more by moral feeling than by reasoning. . . . They think they know everything and are always quite sure about it; this, in fact, is why they overdo everything.

The elderly, however, are characterized by quite opposite qualities:

They have lived many years; they have often been taken in, and often made mistakes; and life on the whole is a bad business. The result is that they are sure about nothing and *under-do* everything. They "think" but they never "know;" and perhaps because of their hesitation they always add a "possibly" or a "perhaps. . . ." Further, their experience makes them distrustful and therefore suspicious of evil. . . . They guide their lives too much by considerations of what is useful and too little by what is noble—for the useful is what is good for oneself and the noble what is good absolutely. . . . They lack confidence in the future; partly through experience—for most things go wrong, or anyway worse than one expects. . . .

As a middle-aged man, Aristotle saw virtue resting in the middle, "between that of the young and that of the old, free from the extremes of either." And these moderate views are held by "men in their prime," a period which occurs intellectually at age 49.[8]

Max Weber reiterated an aspect of Aristotle's analysis when he suggested that the young are more disposed to adhere to the "ethic of ultimate ends," the older to the "ethic of responsibility." That is, the latter seek to accomplish what limited good is practically possible even though to do so may mean to compromise with evil, while new generations seek to protect their sense of virtue by refusing to compromise.[9]

Beyond the changes in views and behavior which accompany aging as such are the adjustments which may be a consequence of relating to politically relevant events. People not only may retain views reflecting events and climates of opinion when young, but may as well adjust these opinions because subsequent experiences challenge them. And since societies at times move from stable to crisis-ridden situations, from periods in which conservatism is dominant to those in which the legitimacy of basic social and political institutions are being challenged, men sometimes may become more radical as they grow older. The social psychologist, Herbert Hyman, has

[8]The "Rhetorica" of Aristotle, in Richard McKeon ed., *The Basic Works of Aristotle* (New York: Random House, 1941), pp. 1403–06.

[9]From *Max Weber: Essays in Sociology*, edited by H. H. Gerth and C. Wright Mills, (New York: Oxford University Press, 1946), pp. 120–8.

pointed up the analytic complexities in considering the ways in which opinion varies with age:

Thus, if we compare young vs. old *in the same calendar year*, we do not know which aspect of the "generational complex" is at work. The contrasted groups grew up in different eras and different worlds, but they are also of different chronological ages. Even the meaning of the chronological age component of the "generational complex" is itself complex. We have the status implications of age plus the inevitable elements of aging such as infirmity, pessimism, etc., plus the fact that aging may simply mean the cumulative influence of *more* exposure to the *same* kind of environment (or a sharply different one).[10]

The issue of generations is hardly an "academic" one. Conservatives recognizing the link between youth and radicalism have long taken comfort in the aphorism: "He who is not a radical (Socialist, Communist) at 20 does not have a heart; he who is still one at 40 does not have a head."[11] Yet even if a variety of impressionistic evidence attests to the validity of Aristotle's and Weber's assertion that men become more moderate, less passionate, in their views as they grow older, this does not necessarily refute the thesis that "generations" remain as a distinct factor, predisposed to the left or right by the frame of reference formed in their youth.

Returning to our immediate problem—the likely future politics of the students who passed through the radicalized political climate of academe in the late 1960s—we would not expect either the "generations" or the "aging" thesis to provide a complete or fully satisfactory guide. Nor are the two mutually exclusive; there could be both the persistence of a distinctive generational orientation and still a "moderation" in views with age. But the question remains of *relatively* how important the very distinctive experiences of the college cohort of the late 1960s are likely to be to their future political commitments and behavior.

THE COLLEGE "GENERATION"
OF THE 1930s

It is possible to cast some limited light on these issues by examining what happened to the political orientations of an earlier generation

[10]Herbert H. Hyman, *Political Socialization* (Glencoe: The Free Press, 1959), p. 130 (emphases in original).

[11]We have seen varients of this statement attributed to many different people in a number of countries.

of college students who were, in their time, also liberalized and radicalized—the students of the 1930s. A variety of literary impressions as well as statistical evidence indicates that the events of the Great Depression moved the students of that day considerably to the left of students of the prosperous 1920s. Thus, "straw polls" taken on college campuses each presidential election year point to a marked shift from the 1920s to the 1930s. They show that the GOP had a substantial majority among students in the 1920s, but lost this position in 1932 and 1936. Though these straw polls cannot claim reliability by the strictest academic standards, the absence of contrary findings makes them generally credible. Indeed, a more systematic though still inherently unrepresentative poll of student opinion on foreign policy issues was conducted by the *Literary Digest* in 1934–35. Ballots were returned by 112,607 students among the 318,-414 who received them. The large majority of those who replied took a strong peace oriented position. Thus, 82 percent said they would not bear arms if the United States were involved "in the invasion of the borders of another country;" 63 percent disagreed that "a national policy of *an American navy and air force second to none* is a sound method of insuring us against being drawn into another great war;" 91 percent favored "government control of armaments and the munitions industry;" and 82 percent supported "the principle of universal conscription of all resources of capital and labor in order to control all profits in time of war."[12] A recent report on the results of various academic surveys of student political attitudes on assorted campuses at different times in the 1930s, concluded that "students expressed more liberal views toward economic planning and change than their counterparts before the Depression and this liberalism increased during the four years of college attendance. Polls repeatedly showed that President Roosevelt was held in high regard among the younger generation."[13]

The first significant effort to take a systematic sample of the national population of students made in the spring of 1936 by Elmo Roper for *Fortune*, furnished impressive evidence that the scattered

[12]See "*Digest* Helps Poll Articulate College Generation," *The Literary Digest* 119 (January 12, 1935): 38; "League Loses By Slim Margin in College Vote," *The Literary Digest* 119 (February 16, 1935): 7.

[13]C. Michael Stanton, "Student Protest: Youth Response to Depression and Affluence," Newton, Mass., Boston College, unpublished manuscript, chapter 2, p. 7. A detailed report on activism and student opinion in the 1930s may be found in Seymour Martin Lipset, "Historical Background: The Twenties Through the Fifties," in Lipset and Schaflander *Passion and Politics*, pp. 159–96.

local campus surveys and the presidential "straw votes" were describing accurately the direction, if not the actual magnititudes, of the changing attitudes of students in the 1930s. *Fortune*, reporting the survey in non-quantitative terms, pointed out that "liberals and Democrats form the thick equatorial bulge of the (campus political) turnip. . . ."[14] The more quantitative unpublished report by Roper supplied detailed documentation of the predominant liberal to left sentiments of the students. Close to one-quarter (24 percent) of those interviewed, when asked about various terms which "suggest ideas toward which you feel sympathetic," picked "socialism" as a positive one, and 6 percent identified with "communism," as contrasted to but 15 percent for "conservatism," and 45 percent for "liberalism." Over two-thirds indicated that they favored changes in the Constitution to enable people "to live comfortably . . . even if this means a revision in our attitude about property rights."[15]

The history of student activism during the 1930s is covered elsewhere in this book (see Chapter 1) and we will not repeat it here. It is worth noting, however, that the radicals of the 1930s were not less numerous in proportionate terms than those of the 1960s. The demonstrations and strikes held on Peace Day in April, 1935 are reported to have included 185,000 students out of a total population of not much more than a million.[16] The most important organization, the American Student Union (ASU), is reputed to have had 20,000 dues paying members at its height in 1937–38.[17] To put this figure in some historical perspective, it may be noted that SDS (Students for a Democratic Society) never claimed more than 7,000 national dues paying members with another 30,000 to 35,000 participants in local chapter activities in 1969, out of a student population six times as large. Further indication of the radicalization of the campus in the "Red Decade," was the commitment of many national Protestant and Jewish campus groups to socialism, and their direct affiliation to the Communist-controlled American Youth Congress.

[14]"Youth in College," *Fortune* 13 (June 1936): 99–102, 155–62.

[15]Unpublished report of the 1936 national college student study prepared by Cherington, Roper and Wood for *Fortune*. We are indebted to Burns Roper for making this report available to us.

[16]William R. McIntyre, "Student Movements," *Editorial Research Reports* 2 (December 1957): 925; Murray Kempton, *Part of Our Time* (New York: Simon and Schuster, 1955), pp. 302–03.

[17]Daniel Bell, *Marxian Socialism in the United States* (Princeton: Princeton University Press, 1967), pp. 148–49.

These data clearly point to the creation of a unique politicized generation or generations of American students, who may be presumed to have played an important role through succeeding decades. Daniel Bell reports: "Members of the ASU went into the professions, government, and trade-union bodies."[18] It is possible to point to visible, often spectacular, examples of student activists of the 1930s who went on to prominence: the Reuther brothers in the labor movement; Robert Lane, national president of the American Student Union in 1940 and of the American Political Science Association in 1969; Adam Yarmolinsky, active in the ASU in the late 1930s and in the Defense Department in the 1960s; Theodore Draper, editor of the National Student League's magazine in the early 1930s and anti-Communist chronicler of the Communist party and of Castroism in recent years; Joseph Lash and James Wechsler, the most durable staff executives of the ASU for some years, as national secretary and editor of the organization's paper who have been major editorial figures on the *New York Post* during the fifties and sixties; George Edwards, first national chairman of the ASU, became a police commissioner and later a judge in Detroit; Pete Seeger, involved in the ASU at Harvard, and subsequently a major contributor to American folk song culture; Lewis Feuer, active on the left as a graduate student at Harvard in the thirties and sharp scholarly critic of student activism at Berkeley and elsewhere during the sixties; Hal Draper, student Trotskyist leader in the Depression decade, and major adult counselor to the Berkeley Free Speech Movement as a staff member in the university library in 1964–65; Alvin Gouldner, ASU activist in the late thirties and leading radical critic of dominant trends in sociology in 1970 as the Max Weber Professor of Sociology at Washington University; Irving Howe, Trotskyist leader at City College of New York in the same period, major literary critic, professor at various schools, and editor of the Democratic Socialist journal *Dissent* from the early fifties to the present. Yet how representative are these? Most of them, though less radical than in their college days, remain identified with liberal or moderately left politics.

These men, and hundreds of others who have achieved eminence and influence, are but a tiny fraction of the total who passed through various wings of the radical movement. Estimates of the numbers who belonged to the Communist party alone during the

[18]*Ibid.*, p. 148.

late 1930s and early 1940s number 750,000.[19] Reports indicate that it experienced 90 percent turnover per annum. What makes the figures concerning rapid turnover within the Communist party particularly relevant for an analysis of student politics is that the overwhelming majority of those who joined were of college age. "The peak age appears to be 18–23. In fact a majority of the rank and file have not only joined but have left the party by the time they are 23. The late teens seem to be an especially susceptible time." It is clear that "the proportion of party members who have been to college is very high. Even more striking is the number of graduate degrees among them."[20] In addition to the Communists, there were, of course, many more close "fellow-travelers," plus a much smaller number of Socialists, and members of radical "splinter groups."

There is obviously no absolutely reliable way to determine the enduring impact of the 1930s on the students of that period. But a variety of opinion data gathered for other purposes do permit some specifications of the ways in which the attitudes and political behavior of the graduates of the 1930s have differed from those of preceding and succeeding generations. Thus, data from a 1947 study of a national sample of 9,000 college alumni, conducted by the Columbia Bureau of Applied Social Research on behalf of *Time* magazine, make possible some detailed comparisons of variations in the attitudes of those who had attended school in the Depression decade with earlier and later academic generations.[21] Another source of data, which covers a much greater time span, is contained in the hundreds of thousands of interviews collected by the American Institute of Public Opinion (Gallup) since its origin. Gallup has been in continuous operation since 1935 and conducts surveys at close and frequent intervals throughout the year. By combining surveys made during fixed periods of time, and separating out those who went to college, it is possible to locate a sufficiently large sample of former students, and to see how they vary in opinions according to the time in which they attended college. Gallup's questions, of course, differ from month to month, but the poll has regularly asked respondents about their choices in presidential elections. It is therefore possible to compare

[19]Irving Howe and Lewis Coser, *The American Communist Party* (Boston: Beacon Press, 1957), p. 529; Morris L. Ernst and David Loth, *Report on the American Communist* (New York: Henry Holt and Company, 1952), p. 14.

[20]*Ibid.*, pp. 2–4.

[21]Ernest Havemann and Patricia Salter West report on this survey in *They Went to College* (New York: Harcourt, Brace, 1952).

the presidential voting behavior over three decades of different college generations. In addition, two surveys of faculty opinions, one of nearly 2,300 social scientists in 1933, the other of 60,000 academics in all disciplines in 1969, permit an examination of the way in which college students who have gone on to an academic career have reacted politically.[22] Because college professors are among the most liberal professional groups in the nation, an analysis of the way in which they vary by college generation seems particularly appropriate.

The 1947 Time Survey

The most striking feature of the *Time* survey data (Table 1) on the political orientation of graduating classes, is the steady increase in

Table 1. Political Positions of the College-educated, by Years of College Attendance (*Time* College Graduate Survey; as percentages of *n*)

Year Span When Graduated from College	Party I.D.[1] Rep.	Party I.D.[1] Dem.	1944 Preference for FDR[2]	Expect to Vote Rep. in 1948[3]	Favorable to Wallace[4]	Favorable to Taft[4]	Favorable to Byrd[4]
1944–48 (n = 1062)	27	31	61	27	25	26	26
1939–43 (n = 2074)	31	31	55	31	17	30	29
1934–38 (n = 1583)	37	28	47	37	15	32	37
1929–33 (n = 1257)	40	26	44	41	16	37	43
1919–28 (n = 1588)	43	23	40	48	15	42	54
1918 and earlier (n = 1156)	55	17	32	60	12	51	63
All (n = 8720)	38	26	47	40	16	36	41

[1] Do you consider yourself: (Republican? Democrat? Other party? Independent?)

[2] In the 1944 Presidential Election did you favor: (Roosevelt? Dewey? Or other candidate?)

[3] Of course no one knows who the presidential candidates or just exactly what the issues will be, but as you feel now, how will you most likely vote in the 1948 presidential election? (Democratic; Republican; Other party; Depends)

[4] Of the following men, which do you like, which do you dislike, and on which do you feel neutral? (Henry A. Wallace; Robert H. Taft; Harry F. Byrd)

[22] The 1955 survey is reported in Paul F. Lazarsfeld and Wagner Thielens, Jr., *The Academic Mind* (Glencoe, Illinois: The Free Press, 1958). The 1969 study was conducted under the sponsorship of the Carnegie Commission on Higher Education, with the financial support of the United States Office of Education, Department of Health, Education and Welfare. We are presently engaged in the analysis of the Carnegie data, and wish to acknowledge our debt to Clark Kerr, Chairman of the Carnegie Commission, Martin Trow of the University of California, Berkeley, who directed the administration of the survey, and to their colleagues. For a complete

conservatism with movement from the youngest to the oldest cohort. Democrats outnumbered Republicans (in terms of party identification) only among the 1944–48 college graduates.[23] The parties drew even in the 1939–43 group, and the Republican margin over the Democrats increased with each preceding generation. Franklin Roosevelt, certainly the more liberal candidate in 1944, was favored by 61 percent of the most recent college graduates but by only 32 percent of those in college prior to 1919. Just 27 percent of the former, in contrast to 60 pcercent of the latter, said they expected to vote Republican in the upcoming 1948 presidential election. The college alumni were asked to react positively or negatively to a number of prominent political figures. Conservative Senators Harry Byrd of Virginia and Robert Taft of Ohio received favorable ratings from only one quarter of the 1944–48 graduates, but the proportion of favorable ratings climbed steadily with each earlier cohort to a figure roughly twice as great among those who graduated before the 1920s. As might be expected, the opposite pattern occurred with respect to opinions on men with leftist images such as Henry Wallace.

Furthermore, the progression which Table 1 describes among the cohorts persists *within* them. For example, the 27 percent Republican identification of the 1944–48 graduates is made up of 29 percent support among the classes of 1944 and 1945, and 25 percent adherence in the 1946–48 classes. Sixty-four percent of the latter favored Roosevelt in 1944 compared to 58 percent of the former.

The *Time* study data show no indication, then, that the left-wing campus politics of the Depression decade left a mark on the students, taken collectively, who then passed through academe. Those graduating between 1934 and 1938 were, in 1947, considerably more conservative than the postwar graduates, just as they were somewhat more liberal than the cohorts which came before them. The percentage favoring FDR in 1944 was 17 points lower among the classes of 1934–38 than among those of 1946–48. Henry Wallace, who a year later was to run for the presidency on a third party Progressive ticket with strong Communist support, received a "favorable" rating by

---

description of the sampling and weighting procedures followed in this survey, and for a copy of the questionnaire with marginals, see Alan E. Bayer, *College and University Faculty: A Statistical Description* (Washington, D. C.: American Council on Education, 1970).

[23]Although the survey was conducted in 1947, it included some still completing their bachelor's degree, with a projected graduation date of 1948.

26 percent of 1946–48 graduates compared to just 15 percent of the 1934–38 cohort. Overall, the steady age progression revealed by Table 1 contradicts the notion of "college generations" whose politics are influenced in a long-term way by the political climate prevailing in academe when they were undergraduates.

It is important to keep in mind that the *Time* data show earlier college graduates relatively more conservative than later grads— not that aging is necessarily associated with an increasing conservatism in any absolute sense. The politics of any group must be affected by its political experience and by larger currents in national politics. Many of the policy innovations of the New Deal, so vigorously contested in the 1930s, came in the 1940s and 1950s to be widely accepted; and if the New Deal is thought of as a set of "liberal" political commitments, then Americans generally were more "liberally" inclined in 1947 than in 1927.

Table 2.   Presidential Choice in 1948, 1956, 1964 and 1968;
The College-educated, by Years of College Attendance[a]

Years of College Attendance	Dewey	Truman	1948 Wallace	Thurmond	Other
1946–48 (*n* = 115)	47	41	9	2	*
1944–48 (*n* = 247)	53	37	8	1	*
1939–43 (*n* = 302)	57	34	5	3	*
1934–38 (*n* = 491)	56	34	7	1	*
1929–33 (*n* = 518)	64	29	3	3	*
1919–28 (*n* = 752)	70	25	2	3	*
1918 and earlier (*n* = 574)	69	27	1	2	*
All college-age cohorts (*n* = 2,999)	62	30	4	3	*
Actual Presidential vote, total population (48,790,414)	45.1	49.6	2.4	2.4	*

Years of College Attendance	Eisenhower	1956 Stevenson	Other
1954–56 (*n* = 40)[b]	70	30	*
1949–53 (*n* = 164)	55	44	*
1944–48 (*n* = 215)	59	41	*
1939–43 (*n* = 292)	66	34	*
1934–38 (*n* = 272)	64	35	*
1929–33 (*n* = 175)	55	45	*
1919–28 (*n* = 274)	75	25	*
1918 and earlier (*n* = 241)	75	24	*
All college-age cohorts (*n* = 1,673)	62	38	*
Actual Presidential vote, total population (61,825,206)	57.4	42.1	*

Table 2—Continued

Years of College Attendance	1964		
	Goldwater	Johnson	Other
1962–64 (n = 159)	27	73	*
1956–61 (n = 310)	30	70	*
1950–55 (n = 330)	35	65	*
1944–49 (n = 321)	42	58	*
1939–43 (n = 367)	34	66	*
1934–38 (n = 307)	42	57	*
1929–33 (n = 191)	30	70	*
1919–28 (n = 271)	46	53	*
1918 and earlier (n = 109)	57	43	*
All college-age cohorts (n = 2,365)	37	62	*
Actual Presidential vote, total population (70,420,910)	38.5	61.1	*

Years of College Attendance	1968			
	Nixon	Humphrey	Wallace	Other
1966–68 (n = 59)[b]	41	48	12	*
1962–65 (n = 221)	45	42	12	*
1956–61 (n = 289)	51	36	13	*
1950–55 (n = 115)	57	31	11	*
1944–49 (n = 111)	60	32	8	*
1939–43 (n = 184)	56	30	13	*
1934–38 (n = 134)	56	35	9	*
1929–33 (n = 109)	47	44	8	*
1928 and earlier (n = 235)	67	22	11	*
All college-age cohorts (n = 1,457)	54	33	12	*
Actual Presidential vote, total population (73,188,253)	43.4	42.7	13.5	*

*Less than one percent.

[a] The following Gallup surveys were included in the above analysis. Those for each presidential election year were added together and treated as a single sample. The Gallup organization has commented on this procedure (*Gallup Opinion Index*, report no. 36, June 1968):

The findings for political affiliation ... are based on over 10,000 cases, with several surveys being combined. Results based on 1,500 cases (the minimum number of cases in a typical Gallup survey) are highly reliable, but this large sample of 10,000 cases enables us to give detailed breakdowns. For example, we can have reliable information not only by age groups, but age groups by region of the country.

In each election year, we selected a cluster of surveys immediately preceding and following the election. The pre-election surveys, of course, asked the respondents how they expected to vote; the post-election studies asked them how they actually voted. *1948:* #428, September; #429, September; #430, October; #431, October; #432, November 1; #433, November 24. *1956:* #570, September; #571, September; #572, October; #573, October; #574, November 7; #576, December. *1964:* #696, August; #697, August; #698, September; #699, October; #701, November 4; #702, November 18. *1968:* #768, September; #769, September; #770, October; #771, November 7; #773, December.

[b] The number of respondents is too small for reliability.

The Gallup Surveys

Turning to the Gallup data, we have less on which to assess political orientations and smaller samples of the college educated—but pick up the "plus" of a time span, being able to look at a college-age cohort over two decades. Table 2 presents Gallup data on the presidential election choices of the college-educated portion of the population, by the years in which they were undergraduates, for the elections of 1948, 1956, 1964, and 1968.

These Gallup survey findings support the picture developed from the *Time* study. Table 2 shows a persistent age association in the voting preferences of the college "generations." As a basic generalization (and the sample sizes are such that we cannot attribute significance to minor differences and fluctuations), the younger the voter, the greater the preference for the more liberal nominee. Thus, those who were in college in the Republican twenties and earlier were in all of the elections the most Republican, but the undergraduates of the 1930s were generally more Republican than those whose education occurred in the postwar years.

A substantial majority of the alumni of the thirties voted for the Republican presidential nominee in all the elections considered here, with the single exception of 1964, when Barry Goldwater was the G.O.P. candidate, and received the lowest Republican percentage in any two party contest since the Civil War. And even in that election, a larger percentage of the college students of the 1930s voted Republican than was true for the electorate as a whole. And the one major postwar effort for a leftist third party candidate, Henry Wallace in 1948, also found that his support among the college educated was associated with age, rather than generation experience.

The one seemingly important exception to the overall pattern of an association between younger age and liberal candidate support, involves those who were in college immediately after the Great Collapse, during Herbert Hoover's term in office. In 1956, 1964 and 1968, those who were undergraduates between 1929 and 1933 show up as markedly less Republican than the immediately preceding *and the immediately following* (i.e., younger), college cohorts. In other words, those in school in the darkest hours of the Depression, not the undergraduates of the latter half of the thirties when organized campus radicalism was at its height, stand out as the one aberrant college group. Seemingly, it was not exposure to the more conspicuous and self-conscious radicalism of the later 1930s that left a mark in terms of a continuing propensity to support the more liberal candidates; rather that experiencing the directionless gloom of the Hoover years bequeathed on the college population of that time a disproportionate antipathy toward the Republican party. Even here, however, there is an exception, for the 1948 data do not show such aberrant behavior by the 1929–33 cohort. And more importantly, none of the data from the other surveys show comparable behavior for this college-age stratum.

The Lazarsfeld-Thielens and Carnegie Faculty Surveys

In Tables 3 and 4, we shift attention from the college-educated population at large to a special subgroup thereof—those who went on to careers in higher education. Professors are, we know, among the most liberal professional groups, and are well to the left politically of the general body of college graduates.[24] But it is still fruitful to inquire whether the pattern of political orientations by college-age cohorts, which we have presented for the whole college population, persists in this special substratum.

Tables 3 and 4 make clear that it does. Among the social scientists interviewed in the Lazarsfeld-Thielens study, those who did their undergraduate work in the 1930s displayed a higher proportion having belonged at some time to a "controversial political group" than those in school before the thirties or in the forties. This is as expected, given the strength of Socialist, Trotskyist, and Communist groups on college campuses in the Depression decade. But examining present politics, the Lazarsfeld-Thielens data indicate a strongly age-related progression. Thus, the percentage voting for Henry Wallace or for one of the other left-wing candidates in 1948 (mainly Norman Thomas) was considerably higher for those who did their undergraduate work between 1944 and 1949 than among the "generation of the 1930s," and there is a steady decline as one moves back through earlier college generations (Table 3).[25] Similarly,

[24]For a review of the extant literature on the politics of American faculty, see Seymour Martin Lipset, "The Politics of Academia," in David C. Nicols ed., *Perspectives on Campus Tensions* (Washington, D. C., American Council on Education, 1970), pp. 85–118.

For preliminary reports on the Carnegie study, see Lipset and Ladd, ". . . And What Professors Think," in *Psychology Today* 4 (November 1970): 49–51, 61; and "The Divided Professoriate," *Change* 3 (May-June 1971): 54–60.

[25]The coding used in the Lazarsfeld-Thielens study prevent us, in our secondary analysis, from getting finer college-age breaks than those shown in Table 3.

Table 3. Political Commitments of American Social Science Professors by Years in Which They Were Undergraduates (Lazarafeld-Thielens *Academic Mind* Study, 1955)

Years in College as Undergraduates	1948 Vote			
	Dewey	Truman	Wallace and Other Left Candidates	Thurmond
1944–49 (*n* = 202)	25	59	17	*
1933–43 (*n* = 936)	22	66	12	*
1923–32 (*n* = 632)	25	69	6	*
1913–22 (*n* = 465)	38	56	4	2
1912 and earlier (*n* = 202)	41	54	3	1
All college-age cohorts (*n* = 2,437)	28	63	8	

	Rights of Communists on Campus[a]		
	Low	Medium	High
1944–49 (*n* = 202)	36	31	33
1933–43 (*n* = 936)	44	25	31
1923–32 (*n* = 632)	54	25	22
1913–22 (*n* = 465)	61	23	16
1912 and earlier (*n* = 202)	69	18	13
All college-age cohorts (*n* = 2,437)	51	24	24

	Ever Member of a Controversial Political Group?[b]	
	Yes	No
1944–49 (*n* = 202)	30	70
1933–43 (*n* = 936)	35	64
1923–32 (*n* = 632)	29	71
1913–22 (*n* = 465)	25	74
1912 and earlier (*n* = 202)	26	74
All college-age cohorts (*n* = 2,437)	30	69

*Less than one percent.

[a]A two-item index based upon the following variables: "Now, I should like to ask you some questions about a man *who admits he is a Communist.* (1) Suppose he is teaching in a college. Should he be fired, or not? (2) If there are students who want to join it, do you think that a Young Communist League ought to be allowed on this campus or not?

The question asked was: Have you ever been a member of a political group which advocated a program or a cause which has been unpopular or controversial, or haven't you been a member of any such group?

support for the rights of Communists in university communities during the (Joe) McCarthy era was greatest among the youngest, the postwar cohort, who supposedly went to college in a relatively apolitical period, and grew progressively weaker among each preceding cohort.

A decade and a half later, the Carnegie survey of the entire professoriate reveals the same age progression, for the faculty as a whole

Table 4.   Political Commitments of American College Professors, by Years in Which They Were Undergraduates; Entire Professoriate, and Social Scientists only (in parentheses) (as percentages of *n*, 1969 Carnegie Survey)

Years in College as Undergraduates	Percentage "Left" Today[1]	Percentage for Immediate Vietnam Withdrawal[2]	Percentage Very Supportive and Supportive of Campus Political Activism[3]	Percentage Favoring Humphrey Over McCarthy, 1968 Democratic Convention[4]
During or before the early 1920s				
(*n* = 1,351)	1	9	16	64
(*n* = 126)	(3)	(11)	(31)	(53)
1922–26				
(*n* = 2,932)	1	14	21	57
(*n* = 250)	(5)	(18)	(43)	(56)
1927–31				
(*n* = 3,839)	2	15	25	57
(*n* = 413)	(6)	(22)	(49)	(55)
1932–36				
(*n* = 5,431)	2	17	30	55
(*n* = 573)	(6)	(25)	(48)	(51)
1937–41				
(*n* = 7,492)	3	17	34	53
(*n* = 845)	(9)	(28)	(57)	(48)
1942–48				
(*n* = 8,503)	4	18	39	50
(*n* = 1,017)	(10)	(27)	(62)	(45)
1947–51				
(*n* = 10,019)	5	18	43	47
(*n* = 1,178)	(11)	(25)	(62)	(45)
1952–56				
(*n* = 10,503)	7	19	48	39
(*n* = 1,396)	(13)	(25)	(68)	(35)
1957–63				
(*n* = 8,590)	9	24	51	32
(*n* = 1,270)	(16)	(33)	(70)	(27)
All college-age cohorts				
(*n* = 58,660)	5	18	39	47
(*n* = 7,068)	(11)	(27)	(61)	(42)

[1] How would you characterize yourself politically at this time?
[2] Which of these positions on Vietnam is closest to your own?
[3] The variable is a four-item scale created to measure faculty support for and opposition to campus political activism.
[4] Whom would you have favored at the Democratic Convention?

and for the social scientists within it. Their present politics show a straight line age progression. The percentage of those who were in college in the "conservative" campus atmosphere of the "silent"

1950s describing their current political orientation as "left" is roughly three times as high (7 to 9) as for those who completed their undergraduate studies in the "radical" climate of the 1930s (Table 4). The college "generation" of the 1930s was similarly much less supportive of the recent campus political activism that that of the 1950s, and showed a markedly greater preference for Hubert Humphrey over Eugene McCarthy in their contest for the Democratic nomination for the presidency in 1968.

The Spaeth-Greeley N. O. R. C. Study of the 1961 Alumni

All of the surveys presented thus far essentially involve comparisons of the political views or electoral choices of populations of college graduates of varying ages. Although consistent in their results, they do not demonstrate that processes associated with aging per se have influenced attitudes, since we do not actually know the actual views of the respondents when young. To conclusively prove change, it would be necessary to have longitudinal evidence, that is, to collect the information from the same group of people over a prolonged period of time. There is one such survey, a study of the college alumni of the class of 1961. The National Opinion Research Center surveyed a sample of this class with respect to some political issues three years after graduation, in 1964, and again in 1968. They graduated as the Kennedy years began, and have been subjected to all the experiences of the frustrations of liberal administrations, the rise of the militant civil rights movement, the antiwar agitation, and student activism.

In the four year period from 1964 to 1968, the proportion of alumni who described themselves as "conservatives" grew from 42 to 46 percent; liberals dropped from 56 to 52 percent. Put in partisan terms, the Republican support increased from 38 to 43 percent, while the Democrats declined from 36 to 30 percent. These changes are, of course, small, but they do go in the conservative direction. More interesting, perhaps, is the report that when these alumni of 1961 are themselves differentiated by age, the younger are much more liberal with respect to position on student activism than the older members of the class. Thus, those under twenty-eight are twice as likely to score high (32 percent) on the support for student militancy index as those over 31 years of age (15 percent), with the twenty-nine to thirty-one year age group falling in the middle (23 percent). These large differences which are associated with such narrow variations in age among members of the same college class point up in dramatic fashion the power of factors associated with aging on political opinions.[26]

CONCLUSIONS.

By all of the measures we have been able to locate, then, the variations in political orientation among college generations over the last half century follow an essentially linear and age-related progression. They do not reveal irregularly dispersed peaks and valleys associated with the academic climate prevailing at the time their undergraduate studies were pursued. There is simply no indication, for example, that exposure to the radical-liberal politics which prevailed on university campuses in the late 1930s left its mark on the rank and file of students, in the sense of inclining them to an orientation which was to manifest itself in a relatively greater commitment to liberal-left politics after they left school. The events of the Depression and post-Depression years certainly produced massive changes in the political thinking of Americans generally, but no college cohort emerged from the 1930s with a *distinctive* politics which was to persist.

These generalizations are meant to apply largely to the mass of a given cohort, not to the small core group of committed activists who may emerge in periods of intense politicization such as occurred during the 1930s and again in the second half of the 1960s. Studies of extremist political movements in many countries indicate that their inner core of leaders and activists were first recruited as undergraduates. Relatively few highly educated radical leaders joined as mature adults. Often a given college generation has gone down in revolutionary history for having contributed the leaders of specific movements. Hence, though the mass of students revert to political passivity or moderation in response to post-graduation experiences, generation-units of leaders may continue to reflect the lessons which they learned as student activists.

Since past American experience shows clearly that periods of campus activism have not created generation-units, it must be considered likely that the cohort which passed through the radical and activist campus politics of the late 1960s will not behave as one in the future either. Colleges are encapsulated communities. Their students have been abruptly removed from the various constraints of their parental family experience, and placed in an environment in which peer group

[26]Joe L. Spaeth and Andrew M. Greeley, *Recent Alumni and Higher Education* (New York: McGraw-Hill, 1970), pp. 102, 109.

pressures are especially intense and pervasive. For four years they inhabit this world apart, a remarkably homogeneous and unstratified society. After graduation, however, most—even today when the number rejecting affluence, a "careerist" outlook, and the regular occupational system, is far greater than ever before—re-enter the highly differentiated larger society and take part in middle-class life in job, family and community. The intellectual legacies of college are by no means all lost, but the intense pressures of the encapsulated community which make for the distinctive and wildly fluctuating bodies of student political opinion are, for most, removed as abruptly as they have been introduced.

There is a new factor to be noted here: the factor of size. The college population of the late 1960s was approximately seven times as great as that of the 1930s (seven million compared to one million), which would mean that the same percentage of committed radicals (say five) would add up to 350,000 today instead of 50,000. The left-inclined students now are a large enough group to sustain a wide variety of institutions, including "free schools" for their children, communes, the "underground" press, and the like. Those who have graduated in recent years, and who are "alienated" from the larger society, may find a home in encapsulated communities composed of others like themselves.[27] Hence, the radical or counter-culture community

[27]Some indication that a strongly supportive social environment will help maintain views formed in college is suggested in a study of Bennington College students of the classes of 1938–40, who had been intensively interviewed as undergraduates, and then restudied in 1960–64. The original analysis had documented the fact that at Bennington, then a new, very small experimental college with a young and very liberal faculty, the large majority of the students had become increasingly liberal in their political opinions. Two decades later, they seemed to have retained their liberal political orientations; two-thirds "reported participating in at least one "liberal cause" or "liberal" organization." The radicals among them may have changed more than the liberals. Thus, out of 91 respondents who listed party references in 1960, nine had been Socialists or Communists in 1938. All had shifted to a major party, eight Democrats and one Republican. More interestingly, four out of these nine student radicals were above the median in an Index of Conservatism administered in 1960. Seemingly, the pulls of career, family, and high social status, had not conservatized the group of liberal women, though the vast majority were married to men with a high income and/or were in professional positions. There is some indication that as a highly politicized group, many of them chose a post-collegiate environment which supported liberal views, particularly with respect to choice of husband and friends. "Those who were able to maintain attitudes similar to the ones with which they left college were, by and large, women who lived in social environments which supported these attitudes, and those who changed their attitudes since college were primarily individuals who associated with others who had different opinions." See Theodore M. Newcomb, Kathryn E. Koenig, Richard Flacks, and Donald P. Warwick, *Persistence and Change* (New York: John Wiley, 1967), pp. 24–25, 35, 53, and *passim*.

of the 1970s may turn out to be more supportive of radical views than the environment experienced by graduates of the 1930s. But the overwhelming majority of recent graduates who had moved to the left during their college years will surely not live in communes, or choose to drop out of society and be downwardly mobile.

The future politics of today's students will, of course, reflect larger movements in American political culture, and aging will not necessarily be accompanied by "conservatizing" in any *fixed ideological sense* of the term. Thus, as noted earlier, public opinion has generally moved to the left from the 1930s to the 1970s. Richard Nixon advocates politics with respect to welfare, Keynesian economics and state payment for medical care, which Republicans denounced as outright socialism or communism during the 1930s. Support for minority rights has grown steadily among the population, particularly among college graduates. Hence, even though the older alumni may be much more conservative, *relative* to younger ones at any given present or future time, they also may be more liberal in an *absolute* sense than when they left college. But whatever the political climate in the United States in 1980, the college cohort of the late 1960s will be *relatively* less receptive to the dominant change-directed thrusts of the day, and in that sense more moderate or conservative, than its succeeding cohorts in academe. In essence, in so far as we can generalize from the available data, they suggest that Aristotle's emphasis on the moderating effects of experience and aging turns out to be more predictive than Mannheim's stress on the long-term consequences of the formation of generation-units among the young.

.5. On the New Working Class and Strategies for Social Change

RICHARD FLACKS

THE MAJOR stumbling block to the articulation of a workable critical theory has been the problem of specifying the "agency" of social change—that class in society, capable of embodying both the consciousness and the political energy to lead the struggle for a new society, in the interests of the people as a whole. This problem has, of course, been created by the empirical failure of the classic Marxist expectation that the industrial proletariat was such an agency. That failure led superficial social scientists to celebrate the end of Marxism. It led more serious intellectuals to believe either that social initiative would rest indefinitely with managerial and/or technocratic elites or that it would come primarily from the colonialized periphery, rather than the center, of the capitalist system.

But the student movement, the youth culture, and related happenings of the past decade have forced a re-examination of such conclusions. The effort to comprehend these new happenings within a neo-Marxian perspective has led a number of writers, quite independently of one another, and starting from rather different points of departure, to arrive at strikingly similar conclusions. The basic point of convergence is that advanced capitalism has, over several decades, undergone a fundamental series of interrelated changes, and that in the process of transformation, a "new working class" has come into being—a class which fits many of the criteria of the long-sought revolutionary agency. This class in formation has many names—none of which are entirely satisfactory—but it is perhaps best understood as the "intelligentsia" (a label which stresses its distinctness from other sectors) or "educated labor" (a label which emphasizes that it is a component of the working class).

I want to call attention here to some of the recent work to which I am referring. Space permits only a superficial listing of some recent work done in the U.S. The reader would be well advised to consult the works cited, rather than accept what follows as an adequate review. There is, on the one hand, the substantial contribution made by "bourgeois" social analysts in recent years—for instance John Kenneth Galbraith, and Daniel Bell—in calling attention to the "post-industrial" character of contemporary society. In this view, the decisive problems of the society cease to be those relating to industrial production, but rather, have to do with consumption, planning, management, and coordination. Such theorists argue, further, that the key institutions of post-industrial society are those involved with the production and distribution of knowledge, rather than material goods.

It has remained for young radical intellectuals, however, to perceive that this situation might have revolutionary implications—that the emergence of a post-industrial system represents the final realization of capitalism and hence its demise. One glimpse of this possibility was provided by Martin Nicolaus in his brilliant essay, "The Unknown Marx," which appeared in the *New Left Review* in 1968. This essay suggests that Marx, in his untranslated *Grundrisse*, anticipated that capitalism could develop to the point of providing the technological *capacity* to eliminate the proletariat, while continuing, by definition, to maintain a political and economic organization which would *prevent* the fulfillment of that potentiality. Under these conditions, the proletariat, by now well-fed and intellectually sophisticated, would make the revolution in order to achieve the abolition of alienated labor and the human promise embodied in the technological capacities of society.

An impressive development of this line of thought appears in a piece by Martin Sklar in *Radical America* (May-June 1969). Sklar argues that in the twentieth century, American capitalism moved from a phase of accumulation to one of "disaccumulation." In the disaccumulation phase, human labor is increasingly extricated from immediate processes of production, and people are freed to engage in other lines of endeavor. At the same time, the rising economic surplus must be consumed, technological unemployment has to be managed, and economic growth sustained. Thus, in the disaccumulation phase, capitalism creates major new contradictions for itself: it creates visions of a society freed from preoccupation with the production of material goods, but it cannot create that freedom; it generates a continuously rising number of people who seek mental and creative work, but continuously extends the imperatives of the profit system to all spheres of life, etc.

In addition to these general arguments and insights, Sklar provides, in his essay, some specific data on the rise of an anti-capitalist intelligentsia after World War I, and suggests how the perspectives of the young intellectuals of that decade resonate with the new radicalism of the sixties and beyond. It should be mentioned, in this regard, that similar suggestions about the emergence of an anti-capitalist consciousness among American intellectuals were presented by Christopher Lasch, in his book, *The New Radicalism in America* (1965), and by other historians as well.

Another important recent piece, by Herbert Gintis, appears in *Socialist Revolution* for June, 1970. Gintis' starting point is somewhat different from Sklar's—rather than emphasizing the *extrication* of workers from the production process, he emphasizes the increasing *centrality* of "educated labor" in the political economy. Gintis goes on to suggest that the rising power of educated labor as a class will be accompanied by the emergence of socialist consciousness: first, because the satisfaction of material needs under capitalism undercuts the demands of the system for economic growth, second, because the conditions of schooling and work for the intelligentsia are at least as alienating as those of industrial workers.

My own work has had still another starting point—more cultural and socio-psychological. Beginning with the observation that the New Left began among a definitely circumscribed cultural type—the sons and daughters of educated, intellectual "middle-class" mothers and fathers—I tried to understand how political consciousness might arise in such families, and how such families came to be carriers of a definite subcultural tradition—one which had become quite decidedly anti-capitalist in character. I arrived at conclusions similar to those of Sklar and Gintis. Like Sklar, I noted that this tradition seemed to have its origins among young intellectuals earlier in the century, and that it had greatest appeal to those educated persons whose sources of income lay outside the primary production process. Like Gintis, I called attention to the strategic importance of this sector. But in accounting for the social impact of new radical consciousness, emphasized mainly the cultural dislocations of post-industrial society and their impact on many types of youth, and neglected the kinds of politico-economic analysis sketched by Sklar and Gintis.

These lines of argument are complementary and interpenetrating. No one has yet brought them all together into a full-fledged theory. But the bare bones of such a theory are there to be articulated and fleshed.

There is a deep, far-reaching crisis in advanced capitalism. The root of this crisis lies in the contradiction between the technological capacities and the social organization of the society. The technology frees increasing numbers from direct dependence on material production for making a living, and frees increasing numbers from material insecurity. But it cannot provide either the social institutions or cultural meanings for such a post-industrial situation. Moreover, it cannot provide such conditions of life to the whole people. On the one hand, aspirations to fulfill the liberating promises of the system are profoundly threatening and destabilizing to it; on the other hand, the continuing imperatives of profit, economic growth, and individual consumption perpetuate an endlessly ramifying network of irrationalities and barbarities.

But this situation has also created its own oppositions. On one hand, there are millions who are systematically colonized or cast-off—and who either have not or cannot be integrated on the system's own terms—as workers, consumers and citizens. On the other hand, there are *those whose social position is already post-industrial*—who have been able or aspire to be able to make a life outside of the goods producing sector—i.e., in the production and distribution of knowledge, culture and human services, or as free persons—and those whose needs in a material sense have been satiated by the existing system.

There are many interrelated reasons for the oppositional character of this stratum of the working class:

Its separation from the goods-producing sector tends to free members from much of the discipline of, and commitment to the profit system. Its dependence on public subsidy makes it side with the public sector and its expansion against the private sector. Exposure to social criticism in school, and the rational, problem-solving perspectives on the job, predisposes members to take a critical stance. Family socialization prepares many for a less submissive attitude toward authority, and provides many with a social rather than a competitive ethic. The felt competence of many members leads them to seek more control over their lives and the institutions within which they find themselves; their relative material security weakens the hold of material incentives over them (and leads many to seek for life styles based on terms other than material consumption). In short, this stratum contains many whose childhood and adolescent experience leads them to feel constrained and repelled by many aspects of the prevailing culture and social order, to be extremely restless with the career opportunities for which they are programmed, and to have a considerable sense of alternative, more liberated, personal, and social futures.

As the experience of the past decade shows, such traits, aspirations, and sentiments are powerfully reinforced if not instilled by the contemporary university experience. For students who do not enter the university with these sentiments, the prolonged, intimate, and exclusive contact with their peers, with the movement and the youth culture which occurs on the campus, awakens previously latent feelings of unrest. Moreover the university embodies its own contradictions—contradictions which are continuous with those in the larger society. On the one hand, the university offers considerable time, freedom, opportunity, and resources for self-expression, personal development, and the free play of imagination, intellect, and feeling. But on the other hand, its formal educational program, its structured competitive discipline, its impersonality, its authoritarianism, serve to continuously corrode the liberating possibilities one glimpses within it, serve as constant reminders that the spontaneous, autonomous life of upper-middle-class youth is a momentary privilege which one loses with adulthood, and which the rest of the world never has a chance to taste.

In these terms, the youth culture and the student movement may be seen as an intensifying effort by participants to bring into being the cultural and social basis for a post-industrial society. Increasingly, these currents are expressing a vision of such a society in definite terms. It is a vision of a society in which the *primary vocational activities* would be focused around the production and distribution of knowledge and art, around the provision of a vast array of human services, and around collective efforts to create maximally beneficial communal and natural environments. It is a vision of a society in which *technological development and economic investment* are guided, not by imperatives of profit, economic growth, and empire but rather by drives to eliminate "alienated" labor, and to promote public happiness and personal self-actualization. It is a *culture* which values cooperation and love over competition and dominance, self-expression over self-denial, equality over materially-based status differentiation. It is a quest for a *political order* in which the nation-state is replaced by self-governing communities.

The sixties may well have been the decade in which this post-industrial consciousness began to be rooted in a definite class. At least it was the moment at which large segments of the youth in advanced industrial societies developed solidarity in terms of that consciousness, began to define a collective identity, began to oppose some of the features of existing society which most threatened the possibility of an alternative future, and began to try to *test that future by implementing it within the universities.*

By the end of the decade, it had become clear that the university struggle was, in large measure, self-isolating and ultimately self-defeating in certain respects. Moreover, it became obvious that the freedom to use the university as a base for constructing a post-industrial culture, life style, and social organization was extremely limited. At the same time, however, the youth of the sixties were of necessity moving en masse into the larger society. For all of these reasons and more, the student movement is now undergoing a process of self-transcendence.

Several years ago, Rudi Dutschke, in discussing the strategy of the German student movement, talked about the necessity for "a long march through all the institutions of society." The phrase implies that fundamental social change in advanced industrial society is not initiated or mediated through the political system, nor is it likely to result from mass insurrections and rebellions. Instead, fundamental political change occurs only after a prolonged period of ferment and conflict within the principal cultural, social, and economic institutions of the society. In this view, the campus revolt is but the first step in the long march.

It is already evident that the spirit of the student movement has come to be a significant presence in a variety of institutions other than the university. This has happened, in part, because the student movement has served as an example to people in other milieus; in part, because graduates of the student movement have entered a variety of professions and other institutional roles; in part, because young people off the campus have been influenced by the symbols and sentiments of the new youth culture. But most fundamentally it is because contradictions we have been discussing are at least as evident in these other institutions as they are within the universities.

Among the many examples of institutional revolt are the following:

Efforts by young health professionals to develop a social medicine, to challenge the policies of the AMA, to confront the class-based structure of medical care, the authoritarian and elitist practices of hospital complexes.

Efforts by young lawyers to serve the legal needs of insurgent movements, to provide legal services to the poor, to engage in exposure and legal contest in behalf of consumers, to find ways to use the legal system to promote social change.

Efforts by young academics to form radical caucuses within academic disciplines in order to foster the development of critical and humanistic perspectives within the disciplines, and pressure for social responsibility among intellectuals.

Parallel efforts by radical school teachers, social workers, city planners, architects, scientists—indeed there is hardly a professional organization or convention which does not now have some kind of radical caucus. And perhaps of most fundamental importance in the intellectual disciplines has been the emergence of increasingly coherent, substantial intellectual work deriving from socially critical perspectives.

But institutional revolt and protest is not restricted to the professions and academic disciplines. The organization of priests and nuns within the Catholic Church has been a significant fact for several years. A significant protest movement with respect to the war, civil rights and other policy issues is evident among high-level civil service employees of certain federal departments, while Peace Corps and Vista volunteers and returnees have undertaken similar activity. Antiwar and related political organization has begun to occur within the staffs of major newspapers and other mass media institutions. Each day brings new evidence that a kind of class struggle—rooted in post-industrial issues—is breaking out in many institutional locales.

Like the campus revolts, these forms of institutional protest have two fundamental aims. On the one hand, they challenge the structure of power, prestige and decision-making within the institutions and professions—so as to promote cooperative work relations; end the corruption of the professions resulting from careerist competition; increase the individual worker's autonomy and voice in the "product." On the other hand, they challenge the domination of the institutions and professions by corporate, militarist, or conservative interests and ideological perspectives, and instead, compel the institutions to serve the interests of the people as a whole. The strategy of institutional opposition thus far, has involved a mix of exposure and criticism; theatrical and symbolic confrontation; efforts to develop alternative work roles and counter-institutional experiments; and forms of trade unionism.

These forms of institutional struggle are, of course, heartwarming to the new working-class theorist—for they certainly supply some concrete empirical evidence for the view that a new type of class struggle is flowing out of the university revolt. But viewed close up, these protests are considerably more ambiguous. First, they are not, as yet, "revolutionary;" indeed they call for, at best, institutional structural reform. Second, it is only a minority of employees who are typically involved; indeed, some of the most reactionary energy in the society seems, at present, to be flowing from the ranks of such mental workers as: university faculty, public school teachers, doctors, etc. Third, the comfortable status of most of the institutionally employed intelligentsia is more plausibly a check on revolutionary boldness than a spur to liberation. Still, these struggles *are* deepening *and* spreading, and the institutions have yet to feel the full impact of the late sixties' college graduates. During the Cambodian crisis, it did not seem at all fanciful to imagine a spreading general strike a la France developing in medical complexes, government offices, the media, publishing outfits, law firms, etc. Meanwhile, it is inescapable that a full-fledged political and cultural revolutionary movement *requires* the institutional struggle of the intelligentsia, for it is the *work* of educated labor which will provide a good part of the content of a post-industrial cultural and social order.

If the new working-class theory, however, claims to have *the* key to the problem of revolutionary agency, it must confront some additional conceptual problems—specifically, the fact that the most significant institutional struggles are not being waged by the intelligentsia *qua* intelligentsia, but in other arenas entirely.

There is, for example, the intensifying and impressive struggle within the prisons, sparked quite obviously by the spread of revolutionary consciousness among black youth—a spread which is easy enough to understand on its own terms, but not easily integrated into the class analysis which I have been arguing for thus far.

The same might be said for the resistance movement and less organized expressions of disaffection which are widely obvious in the military—a movement which derives a lot of its energy from the black revolution, as well as the white youth culture, and the war itself.

Clearly, the burgeoning struggles within the prison and military systems have a more immediately revolutionary significance than the institutional struggles of the new intelligentsia. They are clear signs of the fact that the legitimacy of the American state is undergoing a surprisingly rapid process of erosion. They also appear to represent a surprising convergence of the, hitherto, separate alienations of black and white youth. At a theoretical level, one can intuit a variety of direct and indirect connections between these revolts and the general crisis of advanced capitalism to which I have been alluding. But they also show up the (fortunate) fact that revolutionary "practice" still far outruns developments in critical theory. For instance, we are still unable to systematically comprehend the links among imperialism, racism and the "disaccumulation" crisis, and, therefore, we are still unable to provide a coherent theoretical argument for the (intuited) interdependence of the Third World, black, and new working-class struggles.

There are more problems than these, however, for a neo-Marxian theory of revolutionary social change.[1] In a real sense, the most profound confrontation in the long march through American institutions is now emerging in the family.

The Women's Liberation Movement is very recent, yet it has raised or dramatized a number of issues which are, it is already apparent, very central ones for understanding the potentialities for socio-cultural change in this society. For instance: is the link between sex and power, both within the family and in the larger society, at the core of motives to dominate, compete with, and subjugate fellow humans? Is it plausible that authentically egalitarian sexual relations and child-raising would greatly enhance the capacity of individuals to love, cooperate, and share? For another instance: is the

---

[1]Let me be clear: by calling attention to "problems" I am not trying to argue against such a theoretical development; rather I am suggesting the exhilarating fact that the practical struggles of people are well beyond any existing efforts to comprehend the social process as a whole—a very healthy state of affairs all around.

masculine monopoly on occupational status, and the feminine monopoly on consumership—i.e., role differentiation in the American family—the primary mechanism for sustaining the rat-race? Is it plausible that the privatized, competitive, anxiety-ridden individualism, which constitutes the fundamental motivational energy for middle-class economic behavior, could be substantially alleviated if the nuclear family ceased to be the principal unit of personal consumption, and if women had full equality in the labor market? As far as I am concerned, the deepest significance of the Women's Liberation Movement is not the drive for equality of women within the existing social structure, but rather that it calls into question the fundamental sources of motivational support for the central values of capitalist culture. Further, to the extent that women experiment with communal modes of family life and child-raising, and press for genuine occupational equality, they offer very concrete ways of making a serious cultural revolution.

It is therefore intuitively apparent that the women's struggle and the transformation of the family is directly related to the general crisis of capitalism. But again, no one has, to my knowledge, worked this out fully (although feminist theory has already supplied some, hitherto, unavailable and central insights into the nature of that crisis). More than that, how does this struggle fit, conceptually and practically, into a theory rooted in class analysis?

At any rate, my argument so far has been this: we are beginning to see the emergence of a new critical theory capable of providing real, practical comprehension of the contemporary American crisis. One element of such a theory has been the effort to interpret the student movement and the youth culture as the first expression of a new class-conscious and potentially revolutionary working class, the decisive component of which we have been calling the "intelligentsia." If this stratum has been defined by the university struggle, during the sixties, it has now begun to transcend that struggle, and there are clear signs that a multi-faceted institutional "long march" is now underway. But the institutional struggles are not primarily, or even mainly, expressions of the intelligentsia as such. In any case, whatever they are the expression of theoretically, it ought to be clear that they are of critical importance for defining a strategy for fundamental social change in the next period.

But the long march is not the only strategic direction which can be discerned for those who have formed their political consciousness through the youth movement of the sixties. It is clear, for example, that a significant proportion of students and other youth do not intend to enter the occupational roles assigned to educated labor; moreover, such withdrawal is likely to be intensified by the contraction of opportunity for certain types of educated youth.

Until recently, young people who sought to postpone or refuse entry into the labor force or conventional adult roles, have had great difficulty defining viable, collective alternatives. Increasingly, they have tended to aggregate in neighborhoods adjacent to large universities, or in traditional or new bohemian quarters of major cities. For several years, such locales have been inchoate, anomic, deeply troubled places.

It is now evident, however, that a new consciousness of territory and community is emerging in many of these youth ghettoes. This consciousness has developed, in part, because the population of these ghettoes is increasingly representative of American youth, rather than being primarily composed of an ultra freaked-out fringe. More importantly, territorial and communal sentiments have resulted from the increasingly systematic efforts to control, police, and repress these communities. Finally, the new consciousness is an outcome of the youth culture, which has clearly generated a sense of solidarity around a set of symbols and sentiments of opposition to the official culture.

Once community consciousness begins to take root in the youth ghetto, the sensed possibilities become exhilaratingly attractive for many members. For it becomes clear that the youth ghetto can be the locale in which genuine institutional alternatives can be created and tested, newly acquired values and aspirations and identities supported and implemented.

Consider, for example, what has happened in Isla Vista since the burning of the Bank of America and the police occupations which resulted from it: a city council, elected by all Isla Vistans, 16 years or older, and representing a great diversity of tendencies and styles, now functions as a kind of shadow government. It represents the community to outside agencies; draws up plans for community development; is the effective, legitimate political expression of the community, although it has no legal status or formal power. A variety of institutions has emerged alongside this. A cooperative food service seeks to compete with local supermarkets. A People's Patrol conducts surveillance of local police activity. A local clinic, legal defense center, switchboard counseling center, free elementary school, humanistic dating service, organic vegetable garden, credit union—all initiated by the community—have opened, or are planned. Hundreds in the community are engaged in studying and planning ways to increase the political leverage and power of the community. Hundreds of others are studying and planning ways to redesign the economic and land use arrangements in the community.

Meanwhile, at a more personal level, the community becomes the place for seriously working out alternative life styles. It fosters the development of communal living and child care and family arrangements. It fosters the possibility for collective aesthetic activity. Political radicalism and religious experiment flourish. Increasingly, the aspiration grows to build a self-determining free territory, a piece of the future right in the midst of the repressive present.

Isla Vista has its counterparts in many parts of the country. It is hard to know what the longer run implications of the "free territory" consciousness emerging in these communities might be. Conceivably, a liberal, managerially sophisticated, authority structure could discover ways to achieve a stable *modus vivendi* within such communities. But at present there seems to be little likelihood that such communities are destined to be protected enclaves of cultural innovation. On the contrary, some youth ghettoes are threatened by urban renewal (e.g., Telegraph Avenue in Berkeley). Most are victimized by a great variety of commercial interests—realtors, store-owners, hip capitalists, hard drug dealers. Above all, youth ghettoes increasingly confront a violently antagonistic law enforcement system. Isla Vista accounts for a huge proportion of the felony arrests in Santa Barbara County. Nearly 10 percent of its population has been arrested during demonstrations and disorders over the past six months. During those disorders, a veritable police state was imposed; scores of persons were beaten and terrorized, dozens of private dwellings were raided, with occupants brutalized and property wrecked.

Clearly, the long-term viability of "liberated" youth communities is open to questions of many kinds. Still, it appears likely that these communities are going to be the primary centers of cultural and political opposition in the coming period. They are likely to be powerfully attractive to increasing numbers of non-school youths and young adults; moreover, what happens in and to them is likely to be powerfully catalytic for large numbers of people who live in "straight" society. They will constitute the principal locales for the construction of the post-industrial life—provided, of course, their inhabitants continue to have the energy to both build and defend it.

The "long march" and the "liberated zone"—as we have defined them here—are the emergent strategies of radical opposition. They have, in my opinion, authentically revolutionary significance because they express the recognition that a genuine revolution begins and ends with transformations of consciousness, social relations and identity at every level of society. But they seem to have the quality of romantic naivete to many observers for two important reasons. First, the majority of Americans are not situated in the locales within which these struggles are emerging, and at least so far, experience them as remote, threatening, or unintelligible. Anyone can see that this is dangerous; moreover, it seems clear, intuitively, that since the crisis of capitalism is as damaging to the traditional working class and other strata as it is to the intelligentsia, there is no *necessary* reason for the former to be antagonistic to the latter. Second, the emergent strategies do not deal directly with the "problem of state power"—in fact, in the last couple of years, almost all *political* initiative on the national level has been left in the hands of those who have direct access to state power.

It is obvious that if the movement would enter into a new national coalition based on a neo-Social Democratic or left-liberal program, it could "solve" the problem of isolation fairly easily, and at least put off the questions of "fascism" and "armed struggle" which now haunt and fascinate so many radicals and liberals.

But it is not so simple. There are at least three persuasive arguments for the extra-parliamentary movements.

1. The principle source of energy for all that has been most creative and promising in the past decade has been supplied by the *failure* of the political system to even give the appearance of being an effective instrument of change. *The socio-cultural transformation of the society must continue*—no one has shown how action within the political system can substitute for it. It seems very clear that the same people cannot simultaneously be both political reformers and socio-cultural revolutionaries. But it is plausible that each type of activity can support the other. If that is true, then it is functional for them not to coalesce—and even to be in considerable tension with each other.

2. The only acceptable coalition would be one which was substantially anti-imperialist, anti-corporate, and supportive of commu-

nity self-determination. Perhaps, such a program could be put together among forces that now have substantial leverage within
the parliamentary system. If by some chance, such a coalition
could come to power nationally, it would not have the power to
implement very much of its program by conventional means.
There would still be the need for mass movement in the streets.

3. There are other ways to unify the disparate forces of opposition
and begin to "reach" the white working class. For instance, a
locally based grass-roots socialist politics could begin to emerge
out of the neighborhoods and communities which have high con-
centrations of intelligentsia and youth. For another instance,
students and intellectuals could do infinitely more than they have
to approach factory workers directly and with concrete proposals
for cooperative action. Indeed, it may well be very premature to
argue that the main drift of white workers is toward the right, and
that this drift can only be neutralized by a conventional politics
of economic reform.

Sooner or later, the forces of insurgency will, of course, have to
deal directly with national politics and the problem of state power.
But it is really too early to decide the political forms which will be
necessary. For one thing, the nature of the adult majority in this
country will be utterly transformed during the next five years. For
another, no one knows whether a major political blunder by the authorities will precipitate some new national crisis like France's May
or our Cambodian May—a crisis which could have major transforming effect on the political system. Further, no one knows whether
continuing economic pressure on white workers, combined with
other factors, will set off processes of radicalization in people who
now appear supportive of the status quo.

In any case, the coming of the eighteen-year old vote, combined
with the burgeoning of the young adult population, has already begun to revive interest in electoral action among radicals. The
achievement of post-industrial society requires majority consensus
on behalf of such change—and such a consensus must be expressed
through the political system. If it is hard, right now, to discern the
means to achieve such a consensus and such expression, it nevertheless seems plausible that one of the crucial arenas within which
those means will be found will be the locales within which the youth
vote is concentrated. Perhaps, it is in the closeup experience of
striving for local power that the new forces of opposition will come
to understand what must be done.

Part II

Generational Conflict

.6. *The Problem of Generations*

KARL MANNHEIM

THE SOCIOLOGICAL PROBLEM OF GENERATIONS

THE PROBLEM of generations is important enough to merit serious consideration. It is one of the indispensable guides to an understanding of the structure of social and intellectual movements. Its practical importance becomes clear as soon as one tries to obtain a more exact understanding of the accelerated pace of social change characteristic of our time. It would be regrettable if extra-scientific methods were permanently to conceal elements of the problem capable of immediate investigation.

It is clear from a brief survey of the problem as it stands today that a commonly accepted approach to it does not exist. The social sciences in various countries only sporadically take account of the achievements of their neighbors. In particular, German research into the problem of generations has ignored results obtained abroad. Moreover, the problem has been tackled by specialists in many different sciences in succession; thus, we possess a number of interesting sidelights on the problem as well as contributions to an overall solution, but no consciously directed research on the basis of a clear formulation of the problem as a whole.

The multiplicity of points of view, resulting both from the peculiarities of the intellectual traditions of various nations and from those of the individual sciences, is both attractive and fruitful; and there can be no doubt that such a wide problem can only be solved as a result of cooperation between the most diverse disciplines and nationalities. However, the cooperation must somehow be planned and directed from an organic center. The present status of the problem of generations thus affords a striking illustration of the anarchy in the social and cultural sciences, where everyone starts out afresh from his own point of view (to a certain extent, of course, this is both necessary and fruitful), never pausing to consider the various aspects as part of a single general problem, so that the contributions of the various disciplines to the collective solution could be planned.

Any attempt at over-organization of the social and cultural sciences is naturally undesirable: but it is at least worth considering whether there is not perhaps one discipline—according to the nature of the problem in question—which could act as the organizing center for work on it by all the others. As far as generations are concerned, the task of sketching the layout of the problem undoubtedly falls to sociology. It seems to be the task of *formal sociology* to work out the simplest, but at the same time the most fundamental facts relating to the phenomenon of generations. Within the sphere of formal sociology, however, the problem lies on the border line between the static and the dynamic types of investigation. Whereas formal sociology up to now has tended for the most part to study the social existence of man exclusively *statically*, this particular problem seems to be one of those which have to do with the ascertainment of the origin of social dynamism and of the laws governing the action of the dynamic components of the social process. Accordingly, this is the point where we have to make the transition from the formal static to the formal dynamic and from thence to applied historical sociology —all three together comprising the complete field of sociological research.

In the succeeding pages we shall attempt to work out in formal sociological terms all the most elementary facts regarding the phenomenon of generations, without the elucidation of which historical research into the problem cannot even begin. We shall try to incorporate any results of past investigations, which have proved themselves relevant, ignoring those which do not seem to be sufficiently well founded.

A. Concrete Group—Social Location (Lagerung)

To obtain a clear idea of the basic structure of the phenomenon of generations, we must clarify the specific interrelations of the individuals comprising a single generation-unit.

The unity of a generation does not consist primarily in a social bond of the kind that leads to the formation of a concrete group, although it may sometimes happen that a feeling for the unity of a generation is consciously developed into a basis for the formation of concrete groups, as in the case of the modern German Youth Movement.[1] But in this case, the groups are most often mere cliques, with the one distinguishing characteristic that group-formation is based upon the consciousness of belonging to one generation, rather than upon definite objectives.

Apart from such a particular case, however, it is possible in general to draw a distinction between generations as mere collective facts on the one hand, and *concrete social groups* on the other.

Organizations for specific purposes, the family, tribe, sect, are all examples of such *concrete groups*. Their common characteristic is that the individuals of which they are composed do actually *in concrete* form a group, whether the entity is based on vital, existential ties of 'proximity' or on the conscious application of the rational will. All 'community' groups (*Gemeinschaftsgebilde*), such as the family and the tribe, come under the former heading, while the latter comprises 'association' groups (*Gesellschaftsgebilde*).

The generation is not a concrete group in the sense of a community, i.e., a group which cannot exist without its members having concrete knowledge of each other, and which ceases to exist as a mental and spiritual unit as soon as physical proximity is destroyed. On the other hand, it is in no way comparable to associations such as organizations formed for a specific purpose, for the latter are characterized by a deliberate act of foundation, written statutes, and a machinery for dissolving the organization—features serving to hold the group together, even though it lacks the ties of spatial proximity and of community of life.

By a concrete group, then, we mean the union of a number of individuals through naturally developed or consciously willed ties. Although the members of a generation are undoubtedly bound together in certain ways, the ties between them have not resulted in a concrete group. How, then, can we define and understand the nature of the generation as a social phenomenon?

An answer may perhaps be found if we reflect upon the character

---

[1] In this connection it would be desirable to work out the exact differences between modern youth movements and the age-groups of men's societies formed amongst primitive peoples, carefully described by H. Schurtz (31).

of a different sort of social category, materially quite unlike the generation but bearing a certain structural resemblance to it—namely, the class position (*Klassenlage*) of an individual in society.

In its wider sense class-position can be defined as the common 'location' (*Lagerung*) certain individuals hold in the economic and power structure of a given society as their 'lot'. One is proletarian, entrepreneur, or *rentier*, and he is what he is because he is constantly aware of the nature of his specific 'location' in the social structure, i.e., of the pressures or possibilities of gain resulting from that position. This place in society does not resemble membership of an organization terminable by a conscious act of will. Nor is it at all binding in the same way as membership of a community (*Gemeinschaft*) which means that a concrete group affects every aspect of an individual's existence.

It is possible to abandon one's class position through an individual or collective rise or fall in the social scale, irrespective for the moment whether this is due to personal merit, personal effort, social upheaval, or mere chance.

Membership of an organization lapses as soon as we give notice of our intention to leave it; the cohesion of the community group *ceases to exist* if the mental and spiritual dispositions on which its existence has been based cease to operate in us or in our partners; and our previous class position loses its relevance for us as soon as we acquire a new position as a result of a change in our economic and power status.

Class position is an objective fact, whether the individual in question knows his class position or not, and whether he acknowledges it or not.

Class-consciousness does not necessarily accompany a class position, although in certain social conditions the latter can give rise to the former, lending it certain features, and resulting in the formation of a 'conscious class'.[2] At the moment, however, we are only interested in the general phenomenon of social *location* as such. Besides the concrete social group, there is also the phenomenon of similar location of a number of individuals in a social structure—under which heading both classes and generations fall.

---

[2] It is a matter for historical and sociological research to discover at what stage in its development, and under what conditions, a class becomes class-conscious, and similarly, when individual members of a generation become conscious of their common situation and make this consciousness the basis of their group solidarity. Why have generations become so conscious of their unity to-day? This is the first question we have to answer in this context.

We have now taken the first step towards an analysis of the 'location' phenomenon as distinct from the phenomenon '*concrete group*', and this much at any rate is clear—*viz.*, the unity of generations is constituted essentially by a similarity of location of a number of individuals within a social whole.

B. The Biological and Sociological Formulation of the Problem of Generations

Similarity of location can be defined only by specifying the structure within which and through which location groups emerge in historical-social reality. Class-position was based upon the existence of a changing economic and power structure in society. Generation location is based on the existence of biological rhythm in human existence—the factors of life and death, a limited span of life, and aging. Individuals who belong to the same generation, who share the same year of birth, are endowed, to that extent, with a common location in the historical dimension of the social process.

Now, one might assume that the sociological phenomenon of location can be explained by, and deduced from, these basic biological factors. But this would be to make the mistake of all naturalistic theories which try to deduce sociological phenomena directly from natural facts, or lose sight of the social phenomenon altogether in a mass of primarily anthropological data. Anthropology and biology only help us explain the phenomena of life and death, the limited span of life, and the mental, spiritual, and physical changes accompanying aging as such; they offer no explanation of the relevance these primary factors have for the shaping of social interrelationships in their historic flux.

The sociological phenomenon of generations is ultimately based on the biological rhythm of birth and death. But to be *based* on a factor does not necessarily mean to be *deducible* from it, or to be implied in it. If a phenomenon is *based* on another, it could not exist without the latter; however, it possesses certain characteristics peculiar to itself, characteristics in no way borrowed from the basic phenomenon. Were it not for the existence of social interaction between human beings—were there no definable social structure, no history based on a particular sort of continuity, the generation would not exist as a social location phenomenon; there would merely be birth, aging, and death. The *sociological* problem of generations therefore begins at that point where the sociological relevance of these biological factors is discovered. Starting with the elementary phenomenon itself, then, we must first of all try to understand the generation as a particular type of social location.

C. The Tendency 'Inherent In' a Social Location

The fact of belonging to the same class, and that of belonging to the same generation or age group, have this in common, that both endow the individuals sharing in them with a common location in the social and historical process, and thereby limit them to a specific range of potential experience, predisposing them for a certain characteristic mode of thought and experience, and a characteristic type of historically relevant action. Any given location, then, excludes a large number of possible modes of thought, experience, feeling, and action, and restricts the range of self-expression open to the individual to certain circumscribed possibilities. This *negative* delimitation, however, does not exhaust the matter. Inherent in a *positive* sense in every location is a tendency pointing toward certain definite modes of behavior, feeling, and thought.

We shall therefore speak in this sense of a tendency 'inherent in' every social location; a tendency which can be determined from the particular nature of the location as such.

For any group of individuals sharing the same class position, society always appears under the same aspect, familiarized by constantly repeated experience. It may be said in general that the experiential, intellectual, and emotional data which are available to the members of a certain society are not uniformly 'given' to all of them; the fact is rather that each class has access to only one set of those data, restricted to one particular 'aspect'. Thus, the proletarian most probably appropriates only a fraction of the cultural heritage of his society, and that in the manner of his group. Even a mental climate as rigorously uniform as that of the Catholic Middle Ages presented itself differently according to whether one were a theologizing cleric, a knight, or a monk. But even where the intellectual material is more or less uniform or at least uniformly accessible to all, the *approach* to the material, the way in which it is assimilated and applied, is determined in its direction by social factors. We usually say in such cases that the approach is determined by the special traditions of the social stratum concerned. But these traditions themselves are explicable and understandable not only in terms of the history of the stratum but above all in terms of the location relationships of its members within the society. Traditions bearing in a particular direction only persist so long as the location relationships of the group acknowledging them remain more or less unchanged. The concrete form of an existing behavior pattern or of a cultural product does not derive from the history of a particular tradition but ultimately from the history of the location relationships in which it originally arose and hardened itself into a tradition.

D. Fundamental Facts in Relation to Generations

According to what we have said so far, the social phenomenon 'generation' represents nothing more than a particular kind of identity of location, embracing related 'age groups' embedded in a historical-social process. While the nature of class location can be explained in terms of economic and social conditions, generation location is determined by the way in which certain patterns of experience and thought tend to be brought into existence by the *natural data* of the transition from one generation to another.

The best way to appreciate which features of social life result from the existence of generations is to make the experiment of imagining what the social life of man would be like if one generation lived on for ever and none followed to replace it. In contrast to such a utopian, imaginary society, our own has the following characteristics:[3]

(*a*) new participants in the cultural process are emerging, whilst
(*b*) former participants in that process are continually disappearing;
(*c*) members of any one generation can participate only in a temporally limited section of the historical process, and
(*d*) it is therefore necessary continually to transmit the accumulated cultural heritage;
(*e*) the transition from generation to generation is a continuous process.

These are the basic phenomena implied by the mere fact of the existence of generations, apart from one specific phenomenon we choose to ignore for the moment, that of physical and mental aging.[4]

[3]Since actual experiments are precluded by the nature of the social sciences, such a 'mental experiment' can often help to isolate the important factors.

[4]Cf. Spranger (32) on 'being young' and 'becoming old', and the intellectual and spiritual significance of these phenomena. (He also gives references to other literature on the psychology of the adolescent—whereon see also Honigsheim (15)). Further, see A. E. Brinckmann (5) (who proceeds by way of interpretive analysis of works of art), Jacob Grimm (16), F. Boll (6), Giese (17). Literature relating to the youth movement, which constitutes a problem in itself, is not included in the bibliography at the end of this essay.

With this as a beginning, let us then investigate the bearing of these elementary facts upon formal sociology.

(a) The continuous emergence of new participants in the cultural process

In contrast to the imaginary society with no generations, our own —in which generation follows generation—is principally characterized by the fact that cultural creation and cultural accumulation are not accomplished by the same individuals—instead, we have the continuous emergence of new age groups.

This means, in the first place, that our culture is developed by individuals who come into contact anew with the accumulated heritage. In the nature of our psychical make-up, a fresh contact (meeting something anew) always means a changed relationship of distance from the object and a novel approach in assimilating, using, and developing the proffered material. The phenomenon of 'fresh contact' is, incidentally, of great significance in many social contexts; the problem of generations is only one among those upon which it has a bearing. Fresh contacts play an important part in the life of the individual when he is forced by events to leave his own social group and enter a new one—when, for example, an adolescent leaves home, or a peasant the countryside for the town, or when an emigrant changes his home, or a social climber his social status or class. It is well known that in all these cases a quite visible and striking transformation of the consciousness of the individual in question takes place: a change, not merely in the content of experience, but in the individual's mental and spiritual adjustment to it. In all these cases, however, the fresh contact is an event in one individual biography, whereas in the case of generations, we may speak of 'fresh contacts' in the sense of the addition of new psycho-physical units who are in the literal sense beginning a 'new life'. Whereas the adolescent, peasant, emigrant, and social climber can only in a more or less restricted sense be said to begin a 'new life', in the case of generations, the 'fresh contact' with the social and cultural heritage is determined not by mere social change, but by fundamental biological factors. We can accordingly differentiate between two types of 'fresh contact': one based on a shift in social relations, and the other on vital factors (the change from one generation to another). The latter type is *potentially* much more radical, since with the advent of the new participant in the process of culture, the change of attitude takes place in a different individual whose attitude towards the heritage handed down by his predecessors is a novel one.

Were there no change of generation, there would be no 'fresh contact' of this biological type. If the cultural process were always carried on and developed by the same individuals, then, to be sure, 'fresh contacts' might still result from shifts in social relationships, but the more radical form of 'fresh contact' would be missing. Once established, any fundamental social pattern (attitude or intellectual trend) would probably be perpetuated—in itself an advantage, but not if we consider the dangers resulting from one-sidedness. There might be a certain compensation for the loss of fresh generations in such a utopian society only if the people living in it were possessed, as befits the denizens of a Utopia, of perfectly universal minds— minds capable of experiencing all that there was to experience and of knowing all there was to know, and enjoying an elasticity such as to make it possible at any time to start afresh. 'Fresh contacts' resulting from shifts in the historical and social situation could suffice to bring about the changes in thought and practice necessitated by changed conditions only if the individuals experiencing these fresh contacts had such a perfect 'elasticity of mind'. Thus the continuous emergence of new human beings in our own society acts as compensation for the restricted and partial nature of the individual consciousness. The continuous emergence of new human beings certainly results in some loss of accumulated cultural possessions; but, on the other hand, it alone makes a fresh selection possible when it becomes necessary; it facilitates re-evaluation of our inventory and teaches us both to forget that which is no longer useful and to covet that which has yet to be won.

(*b*) *The continuous withdrawal of previous participants in the process of culture*

The function of this second factor is implied in what has already been said. It serves the necessary social purpose of enabling us to forget. If society is to continue, social remembering is just as important as forgetting and action starting from scratch.

At this point we must make clear in what social form remembering manifests itself and how the cultural heritage is actually accumulated. All psychic and cultural data only really exist in so far as they are produced and reproduced in the present: hence past experience is only relevant when it exists concretely incorporated in the present.

In our present context, we have to consider two ways in which past experience can be incorporated in the present:

(i) as consciously recognized models[5] on which men pattern their behavior (for example, the majority of subsequent revolutions tended to model themselves more or less consciously on the French Revolution); or

(ii) as unconsciously 'condensed', merely 'implicit' or 'virtual' patterns; consider, for instance, how past experiences are 'virtually' contained in such specific manifestations as that of sentimentality. Every present performance operates a certain selection among handed-down data, for the most part unconsciously. That is, the traditional material is transformed to fit a prevailing new situation, or hitherto unnoticed or neglected potentialities inherent in that material are discovered in the course of developing new patterns of action.[6]

At the more primitive levels of social life, we mostly encounter unconscious selection. There the past tends to be present in a 'condensed', 'implicit', and 'virtual' form only. Even at the present level of social reality, we see this unconscious selection at work in the deeper regions of our intellectual and spiritual lives, where the tempo of transformation is of less significance. A conscious and reflective selection becomes necessary only when a semi-conscious transformation, such as can be effected by the traditionalist mind, is no longer sufficient. In general, rational elucidation and reflectiveness invade only those realms of experience which become problematic as a result of a change in the historical and social situation; where that is the case, the necessary transformation can no longer be effected without conscious reflection and its technique of destabilization.

We are directly aware primarily of those aspects of our culture which have become subject to reflection; and these contain only those elements which in the course of development have somehow, at some

[5]This is not the place to enumerate all the many forms of social memory. We will therefore deliberately simplify the matter by limiting ourselves to two extreme alternatives. 'Consciously recognized models' include, in the wider sense, also the body of global knowledge, stored in libraries. But this sort of knowledge is only effective insofar as it is continually actualized. This can happen in two ways—either intellectually, when it is used as a pattern or guide for action, or spontaneously, when it is 'virtually present' as condensed experience.

Instinct, as well as repressed and unconscious knowledge, as dealt with in particular by Freud, would need separate treatment.

[6]This process of discovery of hidden possibilities inherent in transmitted material alone makes it clear why it is that so many revolutionary and reformist movements are able to graft their new truths on to old ones.

point, become problematical. This is not to say, however, that once having become conscious and reflective, they cannot again sink back into the aproblematical, untouched region of vegetative life. In any case, that form of memory which contains the past in the form of reflection is much less significant—e.g., it extends over a much more restricted range of experience—than that in which the past is only 'implicitly', 'virtually' present; and reflective elements are more often dependent on unreflective elements than vice versa.

Here we must make a fundamental distinction between *appropriated* memories and *personally acquired* memories (a distinction applicable both to reflective and unreflective elements). It makes a great difference whether I acquire memories for myself in the process of personal development, or whether I simply take them over from someone else. I only really possess those 'memories' which I have created directly for myself, only that 'knowledge' I have personally gained in real situations. This is the only sort of knowledge which really 'sticks' and it alone has real binding power. Hence, although it would appear desirable that man's spiritual and intellectual possessions should consist of nothing but individually acquired memories, this would also involve the danger that the earlier ways of possession and acquisition will inhibit the new acquisition of knowledge. That experience goes with age is in many ways an advantage. That, on the other hand, youth lacks experience means a lightening of the ballast for the young; it facilitates their living on in a changing world. One is old primarily insofar as[7] he comes to live within a specific, individually acquired, framework of usable past experience, so that every new experience has its form and its place largely marked out for it in advance. In youth, on the other hand, where life is new, formative forces are just coming into being, and basic attitudes in the process of development can take advantage of the molding power of new situations. Thus a human race living on for ever would have to learn to forget to compensate for the lack of new generations.

(c) *Members of any one generation can only participate in a temporally limited section of the historical process*

The implications of this basic fact can also be worked out in the light of what has been said so far. The first two factors, (*a*) and (*b*), were only concerned with the aspects of constant 'rejuvenation' of

[7]That is, if we ignore—as we said we would—the biological factors of physical and psychological aging.

society. To be able to start afresh with a new life, to build a new destiny, a new framework of anticipations, upon a new set of experiences, are things which can come into the world only through the fact of new birth. All this is implied by the factor of social rejuvenation. The factor we are dealing with now, however, can be adequately analyzed only in terms of the category of 'similarity of location' which we have mentioned but not discussed in detail above.[8]

Members of a generation are 'similarly located', first of all, insofar as they all are exposed to the same phase of the collective process. This, however, is a merely mechanical and external criterion of the phenomenon of 'similar location'. For a deeper understanding, we must turn to the phenomenon of the 'stratification' of experience (*Erlebnisschichtung*), just as before we turned to 'memory'. The fact that people are born at the same time, or that their youth, adulthood, and old age coincide, does not in itself involve similarity of location; what does create a similar location is that they are in a position to experience the same events and data, etc., and especially that these experiences impinge upon a similarly 'stratified' consciousness. It

[8]It must be emphasized that this 'ability to start afresh' of which we are speaking has nothing to do with 'conservative' and 'progressive' in the usual sense of these terms. Nothing is more false than the usual assumption uncritically shared by most students of generations, that the younger generation is 'progressive' and the older generation *eo ipso* conservative. Recent experiences have shown well enough that the old liberal generation tends to be more politically progressive than certain sections of the youth (e.g., the German Students' Associations—*Burschenschaften*— etc.). 'Conservative' and 'progressive' are categories of historical sociology, designed to deal with the descriptive contents of the dynamism of a historical period of history, whereas 'old' and 'young' and the concept of the 'fresh contact' of a generation are categories belonging to formal sociology. Whether youth will be conservative, reactionary, or progressive, depends (if not entirely, at least primarily) on whether or not the existing social structure and the position they occupy in it provide opportunities for the promotion of their own social and intellectual ends. Their 'being young', the 'freshness' of their contact with the world, manifest themselves in the fact that they are able to re-orient any movement they embrace, to adopt it to the total situation. (Thus, for instance, they must seek within Conservatism the particular form of this political and intellectual current best suited to the requirements of the modern situation: or within Socialism, in the same way, an up-to-date formulation.) This lends considerable support to the fundamental thesis of this essay, which will have to be further substantiated later—that biological factors (such as youth and age) do not of themselves involve a definite intellectual or practical orientation (youth cannot be automatically correlated with a progressive attitude and so on); they merely *initiate* certain formal tendencies, the actual manifestations of which will ultimately depend on the prevailing social and cultural context. Any attempt to establish a direct identity or correlation between biological and cultural data leads to a *quid pro quo* which can only confuse the issue.

is not difficult to see why mere chronological contemporaneity cannot of itself produce a common generation location. No one, for example, would assert that there was community of location between the young people of China and Germany about 1800. Only where contemporaries definitely are in a position to participate as an integrated group in certain common experiences can we rightly speak of community of location of a generation. Mere contemporaneity becomes sociologically significant only when it also involves participation in the same historical and social circumstances. Further, we have to take into consideration at this point the phenomenon of 'stratification', mentioned above. Some older generation groups experience certain historical processes together with the young generation and yet we cannot say that they have the same generation location. The fact that their location is a different one, however, can be explained primarily by the different 'stratification' of their lives. The human consciousness, structurally speaking, is characterized by a particular inner 'dialectic'. It is of considerable importance for the formation of the consciousness which experiences happen to make those all-important 'first impressions', 'childhood experiences'—and which follow to form the second, third, and other 'strata'. Conversely, in estimating the biographical significance of a particular experience, it is important to know whether it is undergone by an individual as a decisive childhood experience, or later in life, superimposed upon other basic and early impressions. Early impressions tend to coalesce into a *natural view* of the world. All later experiences then tend to receive their meaning from this original set, whether they appear as that set's verification and fulfilment or as its negation and antithesis. Experiences are not accumulated in the course of a lifetime through a process of summation or agglomeration, but are 'dialectically' articulated in the way described. We cannot here analyze the specific forms of this dialectical articulation, which is potentially present whenever we act, think, or feel, in more detail (the relationship of 'antithesis' is only one way in which new experiences may graft themselves upon old ones). This much, however, is certain, that even if the rest of one's life consisted in one long process of negation and destruction of the natural world view acquired in youth, the determining influence of these early impressions would still be predominant. For even in negation our orientation is fundamentally centered upon that which is being negated, and we are thus still unwittingly determined by it. If we bear in mind that every concrete experience acquires its particular face and form from its relation to this primary stratum of experiences from which all others receive their meaning, we can appreciate its importance for the further development of the human consciousness. Another fact, closely related to the phenomenon just described, is that any two generations following one another always fight different opponents, both within and without. While the older people may still be combating something in themselves or in the external world in such fashion that all their feelings and efforts and even their concepts and categories of thought are determined by that adversary, for the younger people this adversary may be simply non-existent: their primary orientation is an entirely different one. That historical development does not proceed in a straight line—a feature frequently observed particularly in the cultural sphere—is largely attributed to this shifting of the 'polar' components of life, that is, to the fact that internal or external adversaries constantly disappear and are replaced by others. Now this particular dialectic, of changing generations, would be absent from our imaginary society. The only dialectical features of such a society would be those which would arise from social polarities—provided such polarities were present. The primary experiential stratum of the members of this imaginary society would simply consist of the earliest experiences of mankind; all later experience would receive its meaning from that stratum.

(d) The necessity for constant transmission of the cultural heritage

Some structural facts which follow from this must at least be indicated here. To mention one problem only: a utopian, immortal society would not have to face this necessity of cultural transmission, the most important aspect of which is the automatic passing on to the new generations of the traditional ways of life, feelings, and attitudes. The data transmitted by conscious teaching are of more limited importance, both quantitatively and qualitatively. All those attitudes and ideas which go on functioning satisfactorily in the new situation and serve as the basic inventory of group life are unconsciously and unwittingly handed on and transmitted: they seep in without either the teacher or pupil knowing anything about it. What is consciously learned or inculcated belongs to those things which in the course of time have somehow, somewhere, become problematic and therefore invited conscious reflection. This is why that inventory of experience which is absorbed by infiltration from the environment in early youth often becomes the historically oldest stratum of consciousness, which tends to stabilize itself as the natural view of the world.[9]

But in early childhood even many reflective elements are assimilated in the same 'aproblematical' fashion as those elements of the basic inventory had been. The new germ of an original intellectual and spiritual life which is latent in the new human being has by no means as yet come into its own. The possibility of really questioning and reflecting on things only emerges at the point where personal experimentation with life begins—round about the age of 17, sometimes a little earlier and sometimes a little later.[10] It is only then that life's problems begin to be located in a 'present' and are experienced as such. That level of data and attitudes which social change has rendered problematical, and which therefore requires reflection, has now been reached; for the first time, one lives 'in the present'. Combative juvenile groups struggle to clarify these issues, but never realize that, however radical they are, they are merely out to transform the uppermost stratum of consciousness which is open to conscious reflection. For it seems that the deeper strata are not easily destabilized[11] and that when this becomes necessary, the process must

[9]It is difficult to decide just at what point this process is complete in an individual—at what point this unconscious vital inventory (which also contains the national and provincial peculiarities out of which national and provincial entelechies can develop) is stabilized. The process seems to stop once the inventory of aproblematical experience has virtually acquired its final form. The child or adolescent is always open to new influences if placed in a new milieu. They readily assimilate new unconscious mental attitudes and habits, and change their language or dialect. The adult, transferred into a new environment, consciously transforms certain aspects of his modes of thought and behavior, but never acclimatizes himself in so radical and thoroughgoing a fashion. His fundamental attitudes, his vital inventory, and, among external manifestations, his language and dialect, remain for the most part on an earlier level. It appears that language and accent offer an indirect indication as to how far the foundations of a person's consciousness are laid, his basic view of the word stabilized. If the point can be determined at which a man's language and dialect cease to change, there is at least an external criterion for the determination also of the point at which his unconscious inventory of experience ceases to accumulate. According to A. Meillet, the spoken language and dialect does not change in an individual after the age of 25 years. (A. Meillet: *Méthode dans les sciences*, Paris, Alcan, 1911; also his *'Introduction à l'etude comparative des langues indo-européennes'* 1903, as quoted in Mentré (23), p. 306 ff.)

[10]Spranger (32) also assumes an important turning point about the age of 17 or so (p. 145).

[11]This throws some light on the way in which 'ideas' appear to precede real social transformation. 'Ideas' are understood here in the French rather than in the Platonic sense. This 'modern idea' has a tendency to destabilize and set in motion the social structure. It does not exist in static social units—for example, in self-contained peasant communities—which tend to draw on an unconscious, traditional way of life. In such societies, we do not find the younger generation, associated with ideas

start out from the level of reflection and work down to the stratum of habits.[12] The 'up-to-dateness' of youth therefore consists in their being closer to the 'present' problems (as a result of their 'potentially fresh contact' discussed above), and in the fact that they are dramatically aware of a process of destabilization and take sides in it. All this while, the older generation cling to the reorientation that had been the drama of *their* youth.

From this angle, we can see that an adequate education or instruction of the young (in the sense of the complete transmission of all experiential stimuli which underlie pragmatic knowledge) would encounter a formidable difficulty in the fact that the experiential problems of the young are defined by a different set of adversaries from those of their teachers. Thus (apart from the exact sciences), the teacher-pupil relationship is not as between one representative of 'consciousness in general' and another, but as between one possible subjective center of vital orientation and another subsequent one. This tension[13] appears incapable of solution except for one compensating factor: not only does the teacher educate his pupil, but the pupil educates his teacher too. Generations are in a state of constant interaction.

This leads us to our next point:

(e) The uninterrupted generation series

The fact that the transition from one generation to another takes place continuously tends to render this interaction smoother; in the process of this interaction, it is not the oldest who meet the youngest

---

of this kind, rising against their elders. 'Being young' here is a question of biological differentiation. More on this matter later.

[12]The following seems to be the sequence in which this process unfolds: first the 'conditions' change. Then concrete behavior begins unconsciously to transform itself in the new situation. The individual seeks to react to the new situation, by instinctive, unconscious adjustment. (Even the most fanatical adherent of an orthodoxy constantly indulges in an adaptive change of his behaviour in respects which are not open to conscious observation.) If the dynamic of the situation results in too quick cultural change and the upheaval is too great, if unconscious adjustment proves inadequate and behavior adaptations fail to 'function' in the sudden new situation, so that an aspect of reality becomes problematic, then that aspect of reality will be made conscious—on the level of either mythology, philosophy, or science, according to the stage of cultural evolution reached. From this point on, the unravelling of the deeper layers proceeds, as required by the situation.

[13]L. von Wiese (35), gives a vivid description of this father-son antagonism. Of considerable importance is the suggestion that the father is more or less forced into the role of representing 'Society' to his son (p. 196).

at once; the first contacts are made by other 'intermediary' generations, less removed from each other.

Fortunately, it is not as most students of the generation problem suggest—the thirty-year interval is not solely decisive. Actually, all intermediary groups play their part; although they cannot wipe out the biological difference between generations, they can at least mitigate its consequences. The extent to which the problems of younger generations are reflected back upon the older one becomes greater in the measure that the dynamism of society increases. Static conditions make for attitudes of piety—the younger generation tends to adapt itself to the older, even to the point of making itself appear older. With the strengthening of the social dynamic, however, the older generation becomes increasingly receptive to influences from the younger.[14] This process can be so intensified that, with an elasticity of mind won in the course of experience, the older generation may even achieve greater adaptability in certain spheres than the intermediary generations, who may not yet be in a position to relinquish their original approach.[15]

Thus, the continuous shift in objective conditions has its counterpart in a continuous shift in the oncoming new generations which are first to incorporate the changes in their behavior system. As the tempo of change becomes faster, smaller and smaller modifications are experienced by young people as significant ones, and more and more intermediary shades of novel impulses become interpolated between the oldest and newest reorientation systems. The underlying inventory of vital responses, which remains unaffected by the change, acts in itself as a unifying factor; constant interaction, on the other hand, mitigates the differences in the top layer where the change takes place, while the continuous nature of the transition in normal times lessens the frictions involved. To sum up: if the social process involved no change of generations, the new impulses that can originate only in new organisms could not be reflected back upon the representatives of the tradition; and if the transition between generations were not continuous, this reciprocal action could not take place without friction.

[14]It should be noted, on the other hand, as L. von Wiese (36), p. 197 points out, that with the modern trend towards individualism, every individual claims more than before the right to 'live his own life'.

[15]This is a further proof that natural biological factors characteristic of old age can be invalidated by social forces, and that biological data can almost be turned into their opposites by social forces.

E. Generation Status, Generation as Actuality, Generation-Unit

This, then, broadly constitutes those aspects of generation phenomena which can be deduced by formal analysis. They would completely determine the effects resulting from the existence of generations if they could unfold themselves in a purely biological context,
or if the generation phenomenon could be understood as a mere
location phenomenon. However, a generation in the sense of a location phenomenon falls short of encompassing the generation phenomenon in its full actuality.[16] The latter is something more than the
former, in the same way as the mere fact of class position does not
yet involve the existence of a consciously constituted class. The location as such only contains potentialities which may materialize,
or be suppressed, or become embedded in other social forces and
manifest themselves in modified form. When we pointed out that
mere coexistence in time did not even suffice to bring about community of generation location, we came very near to making the distinction which is now claiming our attention. In order to share the
same generation location, i.e., in order to be able passively to undergo or actively to use the handicaps and privileges inherent in a
generation location, one must be born within the same historical
and cultural region. Generation as an actuality, however, involves
even more than mere co-presence in such a historical and social region. A further concrete nexus is needed to constitute generation
as an actuality. This additional nexus may be described as *participation in the common destiny* of this historical and social unit.[17] This
is the phenomenon we have to examine next.

We said above that, for example, young people in Prussia about
1800 did not share a common generation location with young people
in China at the same period. Membership in the same historical
community, then, is the widest criterion of community of generation
location. But what is its narrowest criterion? Do we put the peasants,
scattered as they are in remote districts and almost untouched by
current upheavals, in a common actual generation group with the
urban youth of the same period? Certainly not!—And precisely be-

[16]Up till now we have not differentiated between generation location, generation as
actuality, etc. These distinctions will now be made.

[17]Cf. the quotation from Heidegger, in Mannheim, "The Problem of Generations," *Essays on the Sociology of Knowledge* (London: Routledge and Kegan Paul,
1952), p. 282.

cause they remain unaffected by the events which move the youth of the towns. We shall therefore speak of a *generation as an actuality* only where a concrete bond is created between members of a generation by their being exposed to the social and intellectual symptoms of a process of dynamic destabilization. Thus, the young peasants we mentioned above only share the same generation location, without, however, being members of the same generation as an actuality, with the youth of the town. They are similarly located, insofar as they are *potentially* capable of being sucked into the vortex of social change, and, in fact, this is what happened in the wars against Napoleon, which stirred up all German classes. For these peasants' sons, a mere generation location was transformed into membership of a generation as an actuality. Individuals of the same age, they were and are, however, only united as an actual generation insofar as they participate in the characteristic social and intellectual currents of their society and period, and insofar as they have an active or passive experience of the interactions of forces which made up the new situation. At the time of the wars against Napoleon, nearly all social strata were engaged in such a process of give and take, first in a wave of war enthusiasm, and later in a movement of religious revivalism. Here, however, a new question arises. Suppose we disregard all groups which do *not* actively participate in the process of social transformation—does this mean that all those groups which *do* so participate, constitute one generation? From 1800 on, for instance, we see two contrasting groups—one which became more and more conservative as time went on, as against a youth group tending to become rationalistic and liberal. It cannot be said that these two groups were unified by the *same* modern mentality. Can we then speak, in this case, of the same actual generation? We can, it seems, if we make a further terminological distinction. Both the romantic-conservative and the liberal-rationalist youth belonged to the same actual generation but form separate 'generation-units' within it. The *generation-unit* represents a much more concrete bond response to an historical stimulus experienced by all in common. Romantic-conservative youth, and liberal-rationalist group, belong to the same actual generation but form separate 'generation-units' within it. The *generation-unit* represents a much more concrete bond than the actual generation as such. *Youth experiencing the same concrete historical problems may be said to be part of the same actual generation; while those groups within the same actual generation which work up the material of their common experiences in different specific ways, constitute separate generation-units.*

F. The Origin of Generation-Units

The question now arises, what produces a generation-unit? In what does the greater intensity of the bond consist in this case? The first thing that strikes one on considering any particular generation unit is the great similarity in the data making up the consciousness of its members. Mental data are of sociological importance not only because ot their actual content, but also because they cause the individuals sharing them to form one group—they have a socializing effect. The concept of Freedom, for example, was important for the Liberal generation-unit, not merely because of the material demands implied by it, but also because in and through it it was possible to unite individuals scattered spatially and otherwise.[18] The data as such, however, are not the primary factor producing a group—this function belongs to a far greater extent to those formative forces which shape the data and give them character and direction. From the casual slogan to a reasoned system of thought, from the apparently isolated gesture to the finished work of art, the same formative tendency is often at work—the social importance of which lies in its power to bind individuals socially together. The profound emotional significance of a slogan, of an expressive gesture, or of a work of art lies in the fact that we not merely absorb them as objective data, but also as vehicles of formative tendencies and fundamental integrative attitudes, thus identifying ourselves with a set of collective strivings.

Fundamental integrative attitudes and formative principles are all-important also in the handing down of every tradition, firstly because they alone can bind groups together, secondly, and, what is perhaps even more important, they alone are really capable of becoming the basis of continuing practice. A mere statement of fact has a minimum capacity of initiating a continuing practice. Potentialities of a continued thought process, on the other hand, are contained in

[18]Mental data can both bind and differentiate socially. The same concept of Freedom, for example, had totally different meanings for the liberal and the conservative generation-unit. Thus, it is possible to obtain an indication of the extent to which a generation is divided into generation-units by analysing the different meanings given to a current idea.

every thesis that has real group-forming potency; intuitions, feelings, and works of art which create a spiritual community among men also contain in themselves the potentially new manner in which the intuition, feeling, or work of art in question can be re-created, rejuvenated and reinterpreted in novel situations. That is why unambiguousness, too great clarity, is not an unqualified social value; productive misunderstanding is often a condition of continuing life. Fundamental integrative attitudes and formative principles are the primary socializing forces in the history of society, and it is necessary to live them fully in order really to participate in collective life.

Modern psychology provides more and more conclusive evidence in favor of the *Gestalt* theory of human perception: even in our most elementary perceptions of objects, we do not behave as the old atomistic psychology would have us believe; that is, we do not proceed towards a global impression by the gradual summation of a number of elementary sense data, but on the contrary, we start off with a global impression of the object as a whole. Now if even sense perception is governed by the *Gestalt* principle, the same applies, to an even greater extent, to the process of intellectual interpretation. There may be a number of reasons why the functioning of human consciousness should be based on the *Gestalt* principle, but a likely factor is the relatively limited capacity of the human consciousness when confronted with the infinity of elementary data which can be dealt with only by means of the simplifying and summarizing *Gestalt* approach. Seeing things in terms of *Gestalt*, however, also has its social roots with which we must deal here. Perceptions and their linguistic expressions never exist exclusively for the isolated individual who happens to entertain them, but also for the social group which stands behind the individual. Thus, the way in which seeing in terms of *Gestalt* modifies the datum as such—partly simplifying and abbreviating it, partly elaborating and filling it out —always corresponds to the meaning which the object in question has for the social groups as a whole. We always see things already formed in a special way; we think concepts defined in terms of a specific context. Form and context depend, in any case, on the group to which we belong. To become really assimilated into a group involves more than the mere acceptance of its characteristic values—it involves the ability to see things from its particular 'aspect', to endow concepts with its particular shade of meaning, and to experience psychological and intellectual impulses in the configuration characteristic of the group. It means, further, to absorb those interpretive formative principles which enable the individual to deal with new impressions and events in a fashion broadly predetermined by the group.

The social importance of these formative and interpretive principles is that they form a link between spatially separated individuals who may never come into personal contact at all. Whereas mere common 'location' in a generation is of only potential significance, a generation as an actuality is constituted when similarly 'located' contemporaries participate in a common destiny and in the ideas and concepts which are in some way bound up with its unfolding. Within this community of people with a common destiny there can then arise particular *generation-units*. These are characterized by the fact that they do not merely involve a loose participation by a number of individuals in a pattern of events shared by all alike though interpreted by the different individuals differently, but an identity of responses, a certain affinity in the way in which all move with and are formed by their common experiences.

Thus within any generation there can exist a number of differentiated, antagonistic generation-units. Together they constitute an 'actual' generation precisely because they are oriented toward each other, even though only in the sense of fighting one another. Those who were young about 1810 in Germany constituted one actual generation whether they adhered to the then current version of liberal or conservative ideas. But insofar as they were conservative or liberal, they belonged to different units of that actual generation.

The generation-unit tends to impose a much more concrete and binding tie on its members because of the parallelism of responses it involves. As a matter of fact, such new, overtly created, partisan integrative attitudes characterizing generation-units do not come into being spontaneously, without a personal contact among individuals, but within *concrete groups* where mutual stimulation in a close-knit vital unit inflames the participants and enables them to develop integrative attitudes which do justice to the requirements inherent in their common 'location'. Once developed in this way, however, these attitudes and formative tendencies are capable of being detached from the concrete groups of their origin and of exercising an appeal and binding force over a much wider area.

The generation-unit as we have described it is not, as such, a con-

crete group, although it does have as its nucleus a concrete group
which has developed the most essential new conceptions which are
subsequently developed by the unit. Thus, for example, the set of
basic ideas which became prevalent in the development of modern
German Conservatism had its origin in the concrete association
'*Christlich-deutsche Tischgesellschaft*'. This association was first
to take up and reformulate all the irrational tendencies corresponding to the overall situation prevailing at that time, and to the particular 'location', in terms of generation, shared by the young Conservatives. Ideas which later were to have recruiting power in far
wider circles originated in this particular concrete group.

The reason for the influence exercised beyond the limits of the
original concrete group by such integrative attitudes originally
evolved within the group is primarily that they provide a more or
less adequate expression of the particular 'location' of a generation
as a whole. Hence, individuals outside the narrow group but nevertheless similarly located find in them the satisfying expression of their
location in the prevailing *historical configuration*. Class ideology, for
example, originates in more closely knit concrete groups and can
gain ground only to the extent that other individuals see in it a
more or less adequate expression and interpretation of the experiences peculiar to their particular *social* location. Similarly, the
basic integrative attitudes and formative principles represented by a
generation-unit, which are originally evolved within such a concrete
group, are only really effective and capable of expansion into wider
spheres when they formulate the typical experiences of the individuals sharing a generation location. Concrete groups can become
influential in this sense if they succeed in evolving a 'fresh contact'
in terms of a 'stratification of experience', such as we have described
above. There is, in this respect, a further analogy between the
phenomenon of class and that of generation. Just as a class ideology
may, in epochs favorable to it, exercise an appeal beyond the 'location' which is its proper habitat,[19] certain impulses particular to a
generation may, if the trend of the times is favorable to them, also
attract individual members of earlier or later age-groups.

But this is not all; it occurs very frequently that the nucleus of attitudes particular to a new generation is first evolved and practised by

[19]In the forties in Germany, for example, when oppositional ideas were in vogue,
young men of the nobility also shared them. Cf. Karl Marx: 'Revolution and Counter-revolution in Germany'. (German edition, Stuttgart, 1913, pp. 20 f. and 25).

older people who are isolated in their own generation (forerunners),[20] just as it is often the case that the forerunners in the development of a particular class ideology belong to a quite alien class.

All this, however, does not invalidate our thesis that there are new basic impulses attributable to a particular generation location which, then, may call forth generation units. The main thing in this respect is that the proper vehicle of these new impulses is always a collectivity. The real seat of the class ideology remains the class itself, with its own typical opportunities and handicaps—even when the author of the ideology, as it may happen, belongs to a different class, or when the ideology expands and becomes influential beyond the limits of the class location. Similary, the real seat of new impulses remains the generation location (which will selectively encourage one form of experience and eliminate others), even when they may have been fostered by other age-groups.

The most important point we have to notice is the following: not every generation location—not even every age-group—creates new collective impulses and formative principles original to itself and adequate to its particular situation. Where this does happen, we shall speak of a *realization of potentialities inherent* in location, and it appears probable that the frequency of such realizations is closely connected with the tempo of social change.[21] When as a result of an acceleration in the tempo of social and cultural transformation basic attitudes must change so quickly that the latent, continuous adaptation and modification of traditional patterns of experience, thought, and expression are no longer possible, then the various new phases of experience are consolidated somewhere, forming a clearly distinguishable new impulse, and a new center of configuration. We speak

[20]For instance, Nietzsche may be considered the forerunner of the present neo-romanticism. An eminent example of the same thing in France is Taine, who under the influence of the events of 1870–71 turned towards patriotism, and so became the forerunner of a nationalistic generation. (Cf. Platz (29), pp. 43 ff.) In such cases involving forerunners, it would be advisable to make individual case-analyses and establish in what respect the basic structure of experience in the forerunner differs from that of the new generation which actually starts at the point where the forerunner leaves off. In this connection, the history of German Conservatism contains an interesting example, i.e., that of the jurist Hugo, whom we may consider as the founder of the 'historical school'. Nevertheless, he never thought in *irrationalistic* terms as did the members of the school (e.g., Savigny) in the next generation which lived through the Napoleonic wars.

[21]The speed of social change, for its part, is never influenced by the speed of the succession of generations, since this remains constant.

in such cases of the formation of a new generation style, or of a new *generation entelechy*.

Here too, we may distinguish two possibilities. On the one hand, the generation-unit may produce its work and deeds unconsciously out of the new impulse evolved by itself, having an intuitive awareness of its existence as a group but failing to realize the group's character as a generation-unit. On the other hand, groups may consciously experience and emphasize their character as generation-units—as is the case with the contemporary German youth movement, or even to a certain extent with its forerunner, the Student's Association (*Burschenschaft*) Movement in the first half of the nineteenth century, which already manifested many of the characteristics of the modern youth movement.

The importance of the acceleration of social change for the realization of the potentialities inherent in a generation location is clearly demonstrated by the fact that largely static or very slowly changing communities like the peasantry display no such phenomenon as new generation-units sharply set off from their predecessors by virtue of an individual entelechy proper to them; in such communities, the tempo of change is so gradual that new generations evolve away from their predecessors without any visible break, and all we can see is the purely biological differentiation and affinity based upon difference or identity of age. Such biological factors are effective, of course, in modern society too, youth being attracted to youth and age to age. The generation-unit as we have described it, however, could not arise solely on the basis of this simple factor of attraction between members of the same age-group.

The quicker the tempo of social and cultural change is, then, the greater are the chances that particular generation location groups will react to changed situations by producing their own entelechy. On the other hand, it is conceivable that too greatly accelerated a tempo might lead to mutual destruction of the embryo entelechies. As contemporaries, we can observe, if we look closely, various finely graded patterns of response of age-groups closely following upon each other and living side by side; these age-groups, however, are so closely packed together that they do not succeed in achieving a fruitful new formulation of distinct generation entelechies and formative principles. Such generations, frustrated in the production of an individual entelechy, tend to attach themselves, where possible, to an earlier generation which may have achieved a satisfactory form, or to a younger generation which is capable of evolving a newer form. Crucial group experiences can act in this way as 'crystallizing agents', and it is characteristic of cultural life that unattached elements are always attracted to perfected configurations, even when the unformed, groping impulse differs in many respects from the configuration to which it is attracted. In this way the impulses and trends peculiar to a generation may remain concealed because of the existence of the clear-cut form of another generation to which they have become attached.

From all this emerges the fact that each generation need not evolve its own, distinctive pattern of interpreting and influencing the world; the rhythm of successive generation locations, which is largely based upon biological factors, need not necessarily involve a parallel rhythm of successive motivation patterns and formative principles. Most generation theories, however, have this in common, that they try to establish a direct correlation between waves of decisive year classes of birth—set at intervals of thirty years, and conceived in a purely naturalistic, quantifying spirit—on the one hand, and waves of cultural changes on the other. Thus they ignore the important fact that the realization of hidden potentialities inherent in the generation location is governed by extra-biological factors, principally, as we have seen, by the prevailing tempo and impact of social change.

Whether a new *generation style* emerges every year, every thirty, every hundred years, or whether it emerges rhythmically at all, depends entirely on the trigger action of the social and cultural process. One may ask, in this connection, whether the social dynamic operates predominantly through the agency of the economic or of one or the other 'ideological' spheres: but this is a problem which has to be examined separately. It is immaterial in our context how this question is answered; all we have to bear in mind is that it depends on this group of social and cultural factors whether the impulses of a generation shall achieve a distinctive unity of style, or whether they shall remain latent. The biological fact of the existence of generations merely provides the *possibility* that generation entelechies may emerge at all—if there were no different generations succeeding each other, we should never encounter the phenomenon of generation styles. But the question which generation locations will realize the potentialities inherent in them, finds its answer at the level of the social and cultural structure—a level regularly skipped by the usual kind of theory which starts from naturalism and then abruptly lands in the most extreme kind of spiritualism.

A formal sociological clarification of the distinction between the categories 'generation location', 'generation as actuality', and 'generation unit', is important and indeed indispensable for any deeper analysis, since we can never grasp the dominant factors in this field without making that distinction. If we speak simply of 'generations' without any further differentiation, we risk jumbling together purely biological phenomena and others which are the product of social and cultural forces: thus we arrive at a sort of sociology of chronological tables (*Geschichtstabellensoziologie*), which uses its bird's-eye perspective to 'discover' fictitious generation movements to correspond to the crucial turning-points in historical chronology.

It must be admitted that biological data constitute the most basic stratum of factors determining generation phenomena; but for this very reason, we cannot observe the effect of biological factors directly; we must, instead, see how they are reflected through the medium of social and cultural forces.

As a matter of fact, the most striking feature of the historical process seems to be that the most basic biological factors operate in the most latent form, and can only be grasped in the medium of the social and historical phenomena which constitute a secondary sphere above them. In practice this means that the student of the generation problem cannot try to specify the effects attributable to the factor of generations before he has separated all the effects due to the specific dynamism of the historical and social sphere. If this intermediary sphere is skipped, one will be tempted to resort immediately to naturalistic principles, such as generation, race, or geographical situation, in explaining phenomena due to environmental or temporal influences.

The fault of this naturalistic approach lies not so much in the fact that it emphasizes the role of natural factors in human life, as in its attempt to explain *dynamic* phenomena directly by something *constant*, thus ignoring and distorting precisely that intermediate sphere in which dynamism really originates. Dynamic factors operate on the basis of constant factors—on the basis of anthropological, geographical, etc., data—but on each occasion the dynamic factors seize upon different potentialities inherent in the constant factors. If we want to understand the primary, constant factors, we must observe them in the framework of the historical and social system of forces from which they receive their shape. Natural factors, including the succession of generations, provide the basic range of potentialities for the historical and social process. *But precisely because they*

*are constant and therefore always present in any situation, the parti-
cular features of a given process of modification cannot be explained
by reference to them.*

Their varying relevance (the particular way in which they can
manifest themselves in this or that situation) can be clearly seen only
if we pay proper attention to the formative layer of social and cultural
forces.

G. The Generation in Relation to Other Formative Factors in History

It has been the merit of past theorizing about generations that it
has kept alive scientific interest in this undoubtedly important factor
in the history of mankind. Its one-sidedness, however—this may
now be said in the light of the foregoing analysis—lay in the attempt
to explain the whole dynamic of history from this one factor—an ex-
cusable one-sidedness easily explained by the fact that discoverers
often tend to be over-enthusiastic about phenomena they are the first
to see. The innumerable theories of history which have sprung up so
luxuriantly recently all manifest this one-sidedness: they all single out
just one factor as the sole determinant in historical development.
Theories of race, generation, 'national spirit', economic determinism,
etc., suffer from this one-sidedness, but it may be said to their credit
that they bring at least one partial factor into sharp focus and also
direct attention to the general problem of the structural factors shaping history. In this they are definitely superior to that brand of histor-
iography which limits itself to the ascertainment of causal connections between individual events and to the description of individual
characters, and repudiates all interest in structural factors in history,
an attitude which eventually had to result in the conclusion that nothing after all can be learned from history, since all of its manifestations are unique and incomparable. That this cannot be so, must be
realized by anyone who takes the liberty to think about history rather
than merely to collect data, and also observe in everyday life how
every new departure or outstanding personality has to operate in a
given field which, although in constant process of change, is capable
of description in structural terms.

If in our attempts to visualize the structure of the historical dynamic we refuse to deduce everything from a single factor, the next
question is whether it is not perhaps possible to fix some sort of
definite order to importance in the structural factors involved, either
for a particular period or in general—for of course it cannot be as-

sumed *a priori* that the relative importance of the various social or other factors (economy, power, race, etc.), must always be the same. We cannot here attempt to solve the whole problem: all that can be done is to examine more closely our own problem of generation in relation to the other formative factors in history.

Petersen (26) had the merit of breaking away from that historical monism which characterized most earlier theories of generations. In dealing with the concrete case of romanticism, he tried to treat the problem of generations in conjunction with other historical determinants such as the ethnic unit, the region, the national character, the spirit of the epoch, the social structure, etc.

But however welcome this break with monistic theory is, we cannot agree with a mere juxtaposition of these factors (apparently this is only a provisional feature of the theory); the sociologist, moreover, cannot yet feel satisfied with the treatment of the social factor, at least in its present form.

If we are speaking of the 'spirit of an epoch', for example, we must realize, as in the case of other factors, too, that this *Zeitgeist*, the mentality of a period, does not pervade the whole society at a given time. The mentality which is commonly attributed to an epoch has its proper seat in one (homogeneous or heterogeneous) social group which acquires special significance at a particular time, and is thus able to put its own intellectual stamp on all the other groups without either destroying or absorbing them.

We must try to break up the category of *Zeitgeist* in another fashion than Pinder did. With Pinder, the *Zeitgeist* as a fictitious unit was dissolved, so as to make the real units, i.e., for Pinder, the generation entelechies, visible. According to them, the *Zeitgeist* is not one organic individuality, since there is no real, organic entelechy corresponding to it. It would seem to us, too, that there is no such *Zeitgeist* entelechy which would confer organic unity on the spirit of an epoch; but in our view the real units which have to be substituted for the fictitious unit of *Zeitgeist* are entelechies of social currents giving polar tension to each temporal segment of history.

Thus the nineteenth century has no unitary *Zeitgeist*, but a composite mentality made up (if we consider its political manifestations)[22] of the mutually antagonistic conservative-traditional and

[22]We draw on examples deliberately from the history of political ideas, partly to counterbalance the tendency (especially evident in Germany) to study the problem of generations exclusively in the context of the history of literature or art; and partly to show that we believe that *the structural situation of decisive social impulses and*

liberal impulses, to which was later added the proletarian-socialistic one.

We would, however, not go quite as far as Pinder does in his denial of any temporal unity, and in his determination to attribute any homo-geneity found in the manifestations of an epoch to a quite accidental crossing of various otherwise separate entelechies (accidental chords). The *Zeitgeist* is a unitary entity (otherwise, it would be meaningless to speak of it), insofar as we are able to view it in a dynamic-antinomical light.

The dynamic-antinomical unity of an epoch consists in the fact that polar opposites in an epoch always interpret their world in terms of one another, and that the various and opposing political orientations only become really comprehensible if viewed as so many different attempts to master the same destiny and solve the same social and intellectual problems that go with it.[23] Thus from this point of view the spirit of an age is no accidental coincidence of contemporary entelechies (as with Pinder); nor does it constitute itself an entelechy (a unified centre of volition—or formative principle, as with Petersen) on a par with other entelechies. We conceive it, rather, as a dynamic relationship of tension which we may well scrutinize in terms of its specific character but which should never be taken as a substantial 'thing'.

Genuine entelechies are primarily displayed by the social and in-tellectual trends or currents of which we spoke above. Each of these trends or currents (which may well be explained in terms of the social structure) evolves certain basic attitudes which exist over and above the change of generations as enduring (though nevertheless constantly changing) formative principles underlying social and historical de-velopment. Successively emerging new generations, then, superim-pose their own generation entelechies upon the more comprehensive,

---

also the differentiation between generations is clearest at this point. The other en-telechies and changes of style must of course be studied for their own sake inde-pendently, and cannot be derived in any way from political factors, but their recip-rocal relations and affinities can best be understood and made clear from this angle. The artist certainly lives in the first instance in his artistic world with its par-ticular traditions, but as a human being he is always linked with the driving forces of his generation even when politically indifferent, and this influence must always transform even purely artistic relations and entelechies. As a point of orientation for a survey of the whole structure, the history of political ideas seems to us to be most important. This matter will be further dealt with below.

[23]From our point of view, the 'spirit of an age' is thus the outcome of the dynamic interaction of actual generations succeeding one another in a continuous series.

stable entelechies of the various polar trends; this is how entelechies of the liberal, conservative, or socialist trends come to be transformed from generation to generation. We may conclude from this: generation-units are no mere constructs, since they have their own entelechies; but these entelechies cannot be grasped in and for themselves: they must be viewed within the wider framework of the trend entelechies. It follows, furthermore, that it is quite impossible either to delimit or to count intellectual generations (generation-units) except as articulations of certain overall trends. The trend entelechy is prior to the generation entelechy, and the latter can only become effective and distinguishable within the former—but this does not mean to say that every one of the conflicting trends at a given point of time will necessarily cause new generation-entelechies to arise.

It is quite wrong to assume, for example, that in the first decades of the nineteenth century there existed in Germany only one romantic-conservative generation,[24] which was succeeded later by a liberal-rationalistic one. We should say, more precisely, that in the first decades of the nineteenth century the situation was such that only that section of the younger generation which had its roots in the romantic-conservative tradition was able to develop new generation-entelechies. This section alone was able to leave its own mark on the prevailing tone of the age. What happened in the thirties, then, was not that a 'new generation' emerged which somehow happened to be liberal and rationalistic—but the situation changed, and it now became possible for the first time for the other section of the younger generation to reconstitute the tradition from which it derived in such a way as to produce its own generation-entelechy. The fundamental differentiation and polarization were undoubtedly always there, and each current had its own younger generation: but the opportunity for creative development of its basic impulse was granted first to the romantic-conservatives, and only later to the liberal-rationalists.

We may say in this sense, that Petersen's[25] distinction between a *leading*, a *diverted*, and a *suppressed* type of generation is both correct and important, but it is not yet expressed in a sufficiently precise form, because Petersen failed to analyze the corresponding sociological differentiation.

Petersen assumes a direct interaction between supra-temporal character types on the one hand, and the *Zeitgeist* (which he con-

---

[24]Romanticism and Conservatism did not always go together. Romanticism was originally a revolutionary movement in Germany, the same as in France.

[25]Petersen (26), pp. 146 ff.

siders as an unambiguously ascertainable datum) on the other, as if the historic process consisted in these two factors struggling with each other, and the fate of the single individuals were actually determined by their reciprocal interpenetration. Let us take, as an illustration of Petersen's method, an individual of an emotional type; he would be what Petersen would call a 'romantically inclined' character. If we further suppose that this man lives in an age the spirit of which is essentially romantic, this coincidence may well result in a heightening of his romantic inclinations, so that he will belong to the 'leading type' of his generation. Another individual, however, in whom emotional and rational inclinations tended more or less to balance one another, could in similar circumstances be drawn over into the romantic camp. Thus he would represent Petersen's *diverted* type. If we take finally, a third individual who by nature was rationalistically inclined but living in a romantic epoch, he would represent the *suppressed* type. Only two alternatives would be open to him: either he could swim with the tide and, against his own inclinations, follow the romantic tendencies of his time—a course which would lead to stultification—or, alternatively, if he insisted on maintaining his ground, he could remain isolated in his time, an epigone of a past, or the forerunner of a future generation.

Apart from the somewhat cursory way in which 'emotional' and 'romantically inclined' are taken as synonymous, there is something essentially correct in this classification of generation types into *leading*, *diverted*, and *suppressed*. But what occurs is no clash between supra-temporal individual dispositions existing in a supra-social realm on the one hand, and an undifferentiated unitary *Zeitgeist* (because no such thing really exists) on the other. The individual is primarily molded by those contemporary intellectual influences and currents which are indigenous to the particular social group to which he belongs. That is to say, he is in the first instance in no way affected or attracted by the *Zeitgeist* as a whole, but only by those currents and trends of the time which are a living tradition in his particular social environment. But that just these particular trends and not others should have taken root and maintained themselves in his world is ultimately due to the fact that they afford the typical 'chances' of his life situation their most adequate expression. There is therefore no question of an undifferentiated 'spirit of the age' promoting or inhibiting the potentialities inherent in individual characters: *in concreto* the individual is always exposed to differentiated, polarized trends or currents within the 'global spirit of the age', and in particular to that trend which had found its home in his immediate environment. The individual's personality structure will be confronted, in the first place, with their particular trend.

The reason why literary historians tend to overlook the fact that most people are confined to an existence within the limits of one of the trends of their time, and that the 'spirit of the age' is always split up into a number of tendencies rather than being now exclusively romantic, now exclusively rationalistic, is that their material consists primarily of biographies of *hommes de lettres*, a social group of a very particular character.

In our society only the *hommes de lettres* exist as a relatively unattached (*freischwebend*) group (this being, of course, a sociological determinant of their situation); hence, they alone can vacillate, joining now one trend, now another. In the first half of the nineteenth century, they tended to embrace trends supported by a young generation which, favored by circumstances of the time, had just achieved an intellectually dominant position—i.e., trends which permitted the formation of entelechies. The period of the Restoration and the social and political weakness of the German bourgeoisie at the beginning of the nineteenth century favored the development of entelechies at the romantic-conservative pole of the younger generation, which also attracted a large part of the socially unattached *literati*. From the thirties on, the July revolution and the growing industrialization of the country favored the development of new liberal rationalist entelechies among the younger generation; and many of the *literati* promptly joined this camp.

The behavior of these *hommes de lettres*, then, gives the impression that at one moment the 'spirit of the age' is entirely romantic, and at the next entirely liberal-rationalist, and further that whether the spirit of the age is to be romantic or rationalist is exclusively determined by these *literati*—poets and thinkers. In actual fact, however, the decisive impulses which determine the direction of social evolution do not originate with them at all, but with the much more compact, mutually antagonistic social groups which stand behind them, polarized into antagonistic trends. This wave-like rhythm in the change of the *Zeitgeist* is merely due to the fact that—according to the prevailing conditions—now one, and then the other pole succeeds in rallying an active youth which, then, carries the "intermediary' generations and in particular the socially unattached individuals along. We do not wish to underrate the enormous importance of these literary strata (a social group to which many of the greatest thinkers and poets belong), for indeed they alone endow the entelechies radiating from the social sphere with real depth and form. But if we pay exclusive attention to them, we shall not be able really to account for this vector structure of intellectual currents. Taking the whole historical and social process into consideration, we can say that there has never been an epoch *entirely* romantic, or *entirely* rationalist in character; at least since the nineteenth century, we clearly have to deal with a culture polarized in this respect. It may very well be asserted, however, that it is now the one, now the other of these two trends that takes the upper hand and becomes *dominant*. In sociological terms, to sum up once more, this means simply that the circumstances of the time favour the formation of a new generation-entelechy at one or the other pole, and that this new entelechy always attracts the vacillating middle strata, primarily the literary people of the time. Thus the socially attached individual (to whatever psychological 'type' he may belong) allies himself with that current which happens to prevail in his particular social circle; the socially unattached *homme de lettres* of whatever psychological type, on the other hand, generally must clarify his position with regard to the *dominant* trend of his time. The outcome for the individual of this battle between his own natural disposition, the mental attitude most appropriate to his social situation, and the dominant trend of his time, undoubtedly differs from case to case; but only a very strong personality will be in a position to maintain his individual disposition in face of the antagonistic mental attitude of the social circle of his origin, especially if his group happens to be in process of rising in the social scale. An irrationally inclined 'bourgeois' would find it as difficult to come into his own in the forties of the nineteenth century as a young aristocrat with rational inclinations to preserve his rationalism in face of the rise of romanticism and religious revivalism in his social circle. We find for the most part that the opponents of a new generation-entelechy consist mainly of people who, because of their 'location' in an older generation, are unable or unwilling to assimilate themselves into the new entelechy growing up in their midst.

The generation location always exists as a potentiality seeking realization—the medium of such realization, however, is not a unitary *Zeitgeist* but rather one or the other of the concrete trends prevailing at a given time.[26] Whether new generation-entelechies will be formed at one pole in the social vector space or another depends, as we have seen, on historical group destinies.

There remains one further factor which we have not yet considered and which must be added to the others, complicated enough as they are.

We have not yet considered the fact that a newly rising generation-entelechy has not equal possibilities of asserting itself in every field of intellectual pursuit. Some of these fields tend to promote the emergence of new entelechies; others, to hinder it. And we can grade the different fields according to the degree to which they evidence the existence of generation entelechies.

Thus, for example, the natural sciences in which factors of total orientation (*Weltanschauung*) play a less important part than in other fields, definitely tend to conceal generation-entelechies.

The sphere of 'civilization'[27] in general, by virtue of the unilinear nature of developments falling within it, tends to conceal experiential and volitional transformations to a far greater extent than does the sphere of 'culture'. And within the sphere of 'culture' itself, Pinder is certainly right in ascribing to linguistic manifestations (religion, philosophy, poetry, and letters) a role different from that played by the plastic arts and music.[28]

In this field, however, we need a finer differentiation. It will have to be shown how far the various social and generation impulses and formative principles have peculiar affinities to this or that art form, and also whether they do not in certain cases bring new art forms into existence.

We must also consider the degree to which *forms of social intercourse* show stratification according to generations. Here, too, we find that certain forms of intercourse are more adequate to one particular set of social and generation trends than others. Mentré (23) has already shown that an association deliberately organized on

[26]This can also be observed in the modern youth movement, which is constantly in process of social and political polarization. Purely as a social phenomenon, it represents a coherent actual generation entity, but it can only be understood concretely in terms of the 'generation-units' into which it is socially and intellectually differentiated.

[27]Cf. A. Weber: 'Prinzipielles zur Kultursoziologie' (*Archiv für Soz. Wiss. u. Soz. Politik*, 1920).

[28]Pinder (27), p. 156.

the basis of written statutes is much less capable of being molded by new generation impulses than are less formal groupings (such as literary *salons* for example). Thus, it appears that in the same way as factors in the social and historical realm exercise either a restrictive or encouraging influence on the emergence of generation-entelechies, the degree to which various cultural 'fields' lend themselves to serving as sounding-boards for a new generation cannot be exactly determined in advance. All this indicates from yet another point of view that the generation factor—which at the biological level operates with the uniformity of a natural law—becomes the most elusive one at the social and cultural level, where its effects can be ascertained only with great difficulty and by indirect methods.

The phenomenon of generations is one of the basic factors contributing to the genesis of the dynamic of historical development. The analysis of the interaction of forces in this connection is a large task in itself, without which the nature of historical development cannot be properly understood. The problem can only be solved on the basis of a strict and careful analysis of all its component elements.

The *formal sociological* analysis of the generation phenomenon can be of help insofar as we may possibly learn from it what can and what cannot be attributed to the generation factor as one of the factors impinging upon the social process.

BIBLIOGRAPHY

1. Agathon, *Les jeunes gens d'aujourd'hui.* Paris (Plon Nourrit), 1912.
2. Ageorges, *La marche montante d'une génération (1890–1910),* 1912.
3. Bainville, *Histoire de trois générations.*
4. Boas, F., *Changes in Bodily Form of Descendants of Immigrants.* Washington, 1911.
5. Brinckmann, A. E., *Spätwerke grosser Meister.* Frankfurt, 1925.
6. Boll, F., *Die Lebensalter, Ein Beitrag zur antiken Ethnologie und zur Geschichte der Zahlen.* Berlin, 1913.
7. Cournot, *Considérations.* 1872.
8. Curtius, E. R., *Die literarischen Wegbereiter des neuen Frankreichs.* Potsdam.
9. Dilthey, *Über das Studium der Geschichte der Wissenschaften vom Menschen, der Gesellschaft und dem Staat.* 1875. Abgedr. Ges. Schr. Bd. V., pp. 36–41. (Abbreviated: Dilthey.)

10. ———, *Leben Schleiermachers.* Bd. 1, 2. Aufl. Berlin, Leipzig, 1922.

11. Dromel, Justin, *La loi des revolutions, les générations, les nationalités, les dynasties, les réligions.* Didier & Co., 1862.

12. Ferrari, G., *Teoria dei periodi politici.* Milano (Hoepli), 1874.

13. Heidegger, 'Sein und Zeit'. *Fahrb. f. Philosophie u. phänomenologische Forschg.*, Bd. VIII, Halle a.d.S., 1927, pp. 384 f.

14. Herbst, F., *Ideale und Irrlümer des akademischen Lebens in unserer Zeit.* Stuttgart, 1823.

15. Honigsheim, P., 'Die Pubertät'. *Kölner Vierteljahrshefte für Soziologie.* Jahrg. III (1924), Heft 4.

16. Grimm, Jakob, *Über das Alter.* Reclams Universal-Bibl. No. 5311.

17. Giese, 'Erlebnisform des Alterns', *Deutsche Psychologie*, 5 (2). Halle, 1928.

18. Joel, K., 'Der sekuiäre Rhythmus der Geschichte'. *Fahrb. f. Soziologie*, Bd. I, Karlsruhe, 1925.

19. Korschelt, E., *Lebensdauer, Altern und Tod.* 3. Aufl. 1924. (Bibliogr.)

20. Kummer, F., *Deutsche Literalurgeschichte des 19. Fahrhunderts. Dargestellt nach Generationen.* Dresden, 1900.

21. Landsberger, Franz, 'Das Generationsproblem in der Kunstgeschichte'. *Kritische Berichte*, Jahrg. 1927, Heft 2.

22. Lorenz, O., *Die Geschichtswissenschaft in Hauptrichtungen und Aufgaben kritisch erörtert*, Teil I, Berlin, 1886; Teil II, 1891.

23. Mentré, F., *Les générations sociales.* Ed. Bossard, Paris, 1920.

24. Nohl, H., 'Das Verhältnis der Generationen in der Pädagogik'. *Die Tat* (Monatsschrift), Mai 1914.

25. Ortega y Gasset, *Die Aufgabe unserer Zeit.* Introd. by E. R. Curtius. Zürich, 1928. (Kap. I, 'Der Begriff der Generation'.) Verl. d. Neuen Schweizer Rundschau.

26. Petersen, *Die Wessensbestimmung der Romantik.* (Kap. 6, 'Generation'.) Leipzig, 1925.

27. Pinder, *Kunstgeschichte nach Generationen. Zwischen Philosophie und Kunst.* Johann Volkelt zum 100. Lehrsemester dargebracht. Leipzig, 1926.

28. ———, *Das Problem der Generation in der Kunstgeschichte Europas.* Berlin, 1926. (Abbreviated: Pinder.)

29. Platz, R., *Geistige Kämpfe in modernen Frankreich.* Kempten, 1922.

30. Rümelin. 'Über den Begriff und die Dauer einer Generation', *Reden und Aufsätze* I. Tübingen, 1875.
31. Schurtz, H., *Altersklassen und Männerbunde. Eine Darstellung der Grundformen der Gesellschaft.* Berlin, 1902.
32. Spranger, *Psychologie des Fugendalters.* Leipzig, 1925.
33. Scherer, W., *Geschichte der deutschen Literatur*, 3. Aufl. Berlin, 1885.
34. Valois, G., *D'un siècle à l'autre. Chronique d'une génération (1885-1920).* Nouvelle librairie nationale. Paris, 1921.
35. von Wiese, L., *Allgemeine Soziologie als Lehre von den Beziehungsgebilden*, Teil I. Beziehungslehre. Munchen and Leipzïg, 1924.
36. ———, 'Väter und Söhne', *Der Neue Strom*, Jahrg. I, Heft 3.
37. Zeuthen, H. G., 'Quelques traits de la propagation de la science de génération en génération'. *Rivista di Scienza*, 1909.

.7. Generational Conflict and Intellectual Antinomianism

SHMUEL N. EISENSTADT

STUDENT REBELLION and adolescent violence are not new in the history of human society. Student violence was reported in the Middle Ages, and student rebellion and student movements—especially as parts of wider social and national movements—have been an integral part of the history of modern societies.

Similarly, various types of adolescent rebellion or deviance, rooted to no small degree in generational discontinuity or conflict, can be found throughout the history of human society.[1]

In some cases these two phenomena—youth deviance or violence and student rebellion—have tended to converge, and some element of intergenerational conflict has probably been present in many student movements.[2]

Most of such features which could have been discerned in the types of youth rebellion or student movements throughout history, and modern history in particular, can also be found in many of the contemporary expressions of youth rebellion and student radicalism.

But beyond these, contemporary student movements evince also some new features as well. Of these, two are perhaps outstanding. First, as Edward Shils has noted,[3] probably for the first time in his-

---

[1]See S. N. Eisenstadt, *From Generation to Generation* (New York: Free Press, 1956 and 1962).

[2]See L. Feuer, *The Conflict of Generations* (New York: Basic Books, 1969).

[3]See Edward Shils, "Dreams of Plenitude, Nightmares of Scarcity," in Seymour Martin Lipset and Philip G. Altbach, *Students in Revolt* (Boston: Houghton Mifflin, 1969), pp. 1–35.

tory at least some parts of these movements tend to become entirely dissociated from broader social or national movements and from the adult world, and tend not to accept any adult models or associations— thus stressing intergenerational discontinuity and conflict to an unprecedented extent.

Second, many of these movements tend also to combine their political activities with violence and a destructive orientation which go much beyond the anarchist or bohemian traditions of youth or the artistic, intellectual subcultures, combining these with a very far-reaching, general, and widespread alienation from the existing social order. Although these specifically new characteristics are certainly not the only ones to be found in the contemporary youth scene, and certainly do not obliterate many older types of youth culture, youth rebellion, and student protest, yet they are indeed among the most salient new features on this scene.

Many explanations of these new features have been offered elsewhere and it would not be possible to repeat or summarize them all here. Rather, I would like to propose that at least part of the explanation of these new features of youth rebellion and student protest lies in the convergence and mutual reinforcement of the two major sets of conditions or processes—namely, of widespread intellectual antinomianism on the one hand, and of generational discontinuity and conflict on the other, and of their simultaneous extension to the central zones of society as well as to very broad groups and strata.

THE BASES OF ANTINOMIANISM

Intellectual antinomianism is not new in the history of mankind. It constitutes an extreme manifestation of the tensions and ambivalence between intellectuals and authority which exist to a large extent in all human societies. These tensions and ambivalence are rooted in two distinct yet strongly interconnected bases. One is the close relation between the activities and orientation of intellectuals and the authorities in the formation and crystallization of the specific cultural and social contours. This includes charismatic orientation, tradition, centers, and symbols of the society or civilization. The second is the close relation between some, at least, of the skills and technical knowledge of certain groups of intellectuals and the organizational exigencies of the exercise of power and authority in any society.[4]

[4]See, for instance, Edward Shils, "Intellectuals," *International Encyclopedia of the Social Sciences*; Karl Mannheim, *Ideology and Utopia* (New York: Har-

This tension is due not only to the antithesis, often stressed in Western thought, between the organization and exercise of power and the participation in the maintenance of broad socio-cultural order, although this antithesis may indeed constitute an important basis of this tension. Beyond this, tension is also inherent in the fact that the charismatic qualities of social order, and the quest to participate in them, are not focused or centered in only one institutional sphere, and that they become dispersed in different ways in each institutional sphere. This in itself tends to explain, to some extent, the existence of a plurality of authorities in any society, as well as the "natural" predilection of the holders of political power to attempt to monopolize and regulate the central institutions of the society and its charismatic orientation, and their ultimate inability to do so.

The problematics and variety of such tensions can perhaps most clearly be seen in the symbolism of political power and authority that can be found in most civilizations. In all cultural traditions, one of the major foci of political symbols and thought is the concern with the relations between the political order and the other types of "symbolic/institutional"—cosmic, moral, and social—orders, and especially with those orders which are conceived in the tradition of a given society or culture as the most central and important delineators of its basic and collective identity and as the most important parameters of human existence.

The problematics of this relation are usually conceived in terms of the mutual symbolic and organizational relevance of these orders, of their legitimation, autonomy, and responsibility: Are the nonpolitical orders highly relevant to the political one? And, whatever the degree of their relevance, how are they conceived, and how are these relations perceived and organized?[5]

This tension is also rooted in the structural interdependence and relations between the intellectuals and the political powers. Political authorities need the basic legitimation and support which can be provided mostly by intellectuals—that is, by religious or secular intellectual elites. The intellectuals and intellectual organizations tend to need the protection and help of the political institutions for the establishment and maintenance of their own organizations and posi-

court, Brace, 1936), and *Man and Society in an Age of Reconstruction* (New York: Harcourt, Brace, 1940); and the selections in G. B. de Huszar, ed., *The Intellectuals: A Controversial Portrait* (New York: Free Press, 1960).

[5]See S. N. Eisenstadt, "The Scope and Problem of Political Sociology," in idem, ed., *Political Sociology* (New York: Basic books, 1970).

tions. Hence, the continuous tension and ambivalence, on the symbolic and structural levels alike, between the intellectuals and the holders of power or authority, focus around the respective nature, scope, and relative autonomy of participation of the intellectuals and the political powers in the socio-political and cultural orders, and are rooted in their continuous mutual interdependence.

Political authorities may naturally attempt to control entirely the activities of the intellectuals, and to claim for themselves the sole right to represent the major religious and cultural symbols of the society; and they may also expect the intellectual organizations to assure a certain level of political activity and involvement in central political activities which their respective regimes may need.

Against this, the intellectual elites often attempt to become the sole or major representatives of the purely social and cultural orders, to usurp central political offices, and to remove their organizations from the political control and influence of the rulers.[6]

THE TENSIONS BEHIND PROTEST

The potentially antinomian tendencies of intellectuals become especially articulated insofar as the tensions between them and political authorities tend to converge with some of the major themes of protest, rebellion, and heterodoxy. Such themes have continually reoccurred in the history of human societies and civilizations, and are largely rooted in the tensions inherent in any process of institutionalization of social life in general, and of authority in particular.

Among these themes is the tension between the very complexity and fragmentation of human relations inherent in any insitutional division of labor, as against the possibilities of full freedom of participation in the basic social and cultural order.

Parallel to this are also the tensions inherent in the temporal dimension of the human and social condition, the tensions between the deferment of gratification in the present and the possibility of its attainment in the future.

Hence, many movements of protest tend to emphasize the suspension or negation of the structural and organizational division of labor in general, and to emphasize the ideal of "communitas," of direct, unmediated participation in the social and cultural orders.

[6]For analysis of one such historical case, see Eisenstadt, *The Political Systems of Empires* (New York: Free Press, 1963, 1969), especially ch. 8; and Eisenstadt, "Religious Organization and Political Process in Centralized Empires," *The Journal of Asian Studies* 21 (May 1962): 74–94.

They tend also to emphasize, together with such participation, the suspension of the tensions between "productivity" and "distribution," and tend to merge these two together through a basic commitment to unconditional participation in the community.

Similarly, many such movements contain a strong emphasis on the suspension of the differences between various time dimensions—between past, present, and future—and on the suspension of the relation between such dimensions to patterns of gratification and allocation of rewards.

The two institutional/symbolic foci around which the ambivalence to traditions and orders tends to converge are, first, that of authority, especially as vested in the various political and cultural centers, and second, the system of stratification in which the symbolic dimensions of hierarchy are combined with the structural aspects of the division of labor. It is thus that symbols of authority and of hierarchy constitute the most common objects of ambivalence and foci for demands for change in any society.

These various tendencies to heterodoxy, antinomy, and rebellion are most clearly articulated by intellectuals, but it would be wrong to assume that they are oriented only against the political authority. They may also be oriented against intellectual authority, and it is perhaps in this fact that the antinomian tendencies of intellectuals may tend to become most clearly articulated.

Needless to say, such antinomianism is an extreme phenomenon often found only within small groups of intellectuals; it tends to develop under very specific conditions. Yet it may also be an important ingredient in the orientation of wider groups of intellectuals—an ingredient which under certain conditions may indeed become more widespread.

Such conditions, conducive to a more pervasive spread of such antinomian attitudes and dispositions, have been most prevalent in modern societies in general and in contemporary ones in particular; and they are closely related to the actual spread of modernity, its structural characteristics and its ideological premises and symbols.[7]

The revolutionary orientation which was at the root of most breakthroughs to modernity has been, whatever its concrete contents, pointed toward a complete transformation of the nature and contents of the centers of the social and cultural orders, of the rules of parti-

[7]For a fuller analysis of these varied aspects of modernity, see S. N. Eisenstadt, *Modernization, Protest and Change* (Englewood Cliffs, N.J.: Prentice-Hall, 1966); and *Political Sociology* (New York: Basic Books, 1970).

cipation in them and of access to them, and of the relations between these centers and the periphery.

From the point of view of the contents of these centers, the major transformation concomitant with modernity has been in the growing secularization of the centers and in the "opening up" of their contents. There has been a growing non-acceptance of the inherent rightness of these contents; a spreading of the assumption that these contents can indeed be formulated anew.

This has been closely connected with changes in the structure of the political, cultural, societal centers and the relations among them—that is, with the growing autonomy of such centers and, above all, with changes in the relations between the centers and the periphery.

Modern social orders have been characterized by the growing impingement of the periphery on the center, by the improved access to the center from the periphery, by the permeation of the periphery by the center, and by the concomitant tendency toward the obliteration of the differences between center and periphery, thus making membership in any part of the periphery tantamount to participation in the center.

This impingement on the center can best be seen in the political field. The broader groups and strata of society tend more and more to impinge on the central institutions, not only in making various concrete demands on them, but also by developing the aspiration to participate in the actual crystallization of the center, its symbols, and its institutional contours. The major social movements that have developed with the onset of modernization—be they national, social, or cultural—all manifest this tendency in varying degrees and scope.

These processes are, of course, closely connected with the second major trend concomitant with modernization, namely, that of growing structural differentiation in general, and of the spheres of intellectual, scientific, and professional endeavor in particular. The development of specialized scientific and technological roles and institutions and the growing impact of these on the occupational structure are too well known to need any lengthy specification.

THE EDUCATIONAL SYSTEM CHANGES

But perhaps the most important change related to these developments from the present point of view takes place in the social organization of the educational sphere. In most pre-modern societies, the process of education was usually divided into several rather compartmentalized aspects. The central educational institutions were oriented mainly to the education of an elite and of the upper strata, and to the upholding and development of the central cultural tradition in its varied manifestations.

The local educational institutions, which were usually only loosely connected with the central ones, were oriented chiefly to the maintenance of a certain general, diffuse, and rather passive identification of the various strata with the overall symbols of society—without, however, being permitted any closer participation in the central political and cultural activities. These local institutions were also expected to provide some technical know-how which would be appropriate to their position in society. Between the central and the local institutions were several educational institutions which served either as channels of restricted, "sponsored" mobility into the central spheres of society or as centers of some specific vocational preparation.

On the whole, the educational system in these societies was geared to the maintenance and perpetuation of a given, relatively unchanging, cultural tradition, and did not serve either as a channel of widespread occupational and social mobility or of overall, active participation by the broader strata in the cultural and political order with the center. The type of education given to different classes was greatly, although not entirely, determined by their socio-economic position, and not vice versa.

This situation began to change with the onset of modernity. Education started to deal with the problems of forging new national communities and their common symbols, access to which tended to become more widely spread among different strata. At the same time, education began to serve increasingly as a channel of more general occupational, and allegedly achievement-based, selection. Moreover, the system of education tended to become more centralized and unified, thus assuring its permeation into wider strata of the society.

THE RESULTING CONTRADICTIONS

This societal unification of the education system, when combined with the continuous developments of the structural and symbolic aspects of modernity, gave rise to a series of social and cultural contradictions and discontinuities which has become extremely widespread throughout the society and at the same time has tended to become more and more focused on the society's central symbols.

Most of these contradictions and discontinuities have tended to focus on the tension between the premises of plenitude, full participation inherent in the symbolism of modernity, and the various structural limitations on the realization of these premises.

These problems and tendencies have developed in all the social spheres, but in the literature special emphasis has been given to the occupational and economic spheres. Thus, it is often emphasized that the most important such developments in these fields were the bureaucratization of most types of economic markets and the growth of bureaucratization, specialization, and professionalization in the occupational structure, increasing the close interrelationship between educational attainment and occupational placement.

These developments have given rise to problems and discontinuity in areas like social mobility, educational selection, development of patterns of consumption, and above all, in the special service occupations.

But beyond these developments in the occupational and economic fields, parallel processes have developed also in the cultural field, and it is on these that we would like to focus our analysis here. Perhaps the most important single, overall development in this field —which, in a great variety of ways, has arisen in many different countries—has been the transfer of emphasis from the creation of and participation in future-oriented collective values to the growing institutionalization of such values. This has been closely related to a very important shift in the whole pattern of protest in modern societies. Here, as in so many other cases, when much of the initial charismatic orientation and many of the goals have indeed become— through attainment of political independence, broadening of the scope of political participation, revolutionary changes of regime, development of welfare state policies, and the like—at least partially institutionalized, they give rise to new processes of change, to new series of problems and tensions, and to new foci of protest.

It is important to emphasize that the same shift in the pattern of protest is true of youth movements and activities, when the goals and values toward whose realization these movements aim become institutionalized through their acceptance as part of the structure of society. This has happened in most modern societies. Thus, in Russia, youth movements became fully institutionalized through the organization of the Komsomol. In many European countries the institutionalizing of youth groups, agencies, and ideologies came through association with political parties, or through acceptance as part of the educational system. In the United States, many (such as the Boy Scouts) have become an accepted part of community life and, to some extent, a symbol of differences in social status. In many Asian and African countries, organized youth movements have become part of the official educational organizations.

All these changes have also been associated with a marked decline of ideology in the traditional nineteenth- and early-twentieth-century sense, and a general flattening of traditional politico-ideological interest. This decline, in turn, has been connected with the growth of the feeling of spiritual or cultural shallowness in the new social and economic benefits accruing from the welfare state or from the "consumer society."

This tendency has been intensified by the fact that in many such countries, be they the new states of Asia and Africa or Russian postrevolutionary or European welfare states, the new generation of young people and students faces not only reactionary parents but also successful revolutionaries who have become part of a new "establishment," creating a new collective reality which young people have to face, a reality that evinces all the characteristics of a bureaucratized establishment but at the same time presents itself as the embodiment of revolutionary collective and spiritual values.

Later this tendency was also reinforced by the weakening of the ideological dimension of the Cold War and by the consequent loss of the negative images and symbols.

THE BREAKDOWN OF CONTINUITY

Within this general framework of development of the cultural sphere, several special developments or processes stand out. One such development is what may be called the breakdown of continuity in the historical consciousness or awareness. It is not only that the new generations have not experienced such events as the Depression or the two World Wars, which were crucial in the formation of their parents. What is more significant is that, probably partly due to the very process of institutionalization of the collective goals of their parents on the one hand, and their growing affluence on the other, the parent generation failed to transmit to the new generation the significance of the meaning of these historical events. The very emphasis on the new goals has increased a tendency to stress the novelty of the world created by the parents—a tendency taken up and reinforced by the younger generations.

Another cultural process, closely related to the proceding one and especially prominent in Western societies in general and in America in particular, has been the reversal of the former relation between the different age-spans and social and cultural creativity. In contrast to the not-so-distant past, youth has come to be seen more and more not only as the age for preparation for the possibilities of independent and creative participation in social and cultural life, but as the very embodiment of permissive, often unstructured, creativity—only to be faced later on with the constants of a relatively highly organized, constrictive, meritocratic, and bureaucratic environment.

It has probably not been these constraints as such—in themselves they were probably not greater than those in most past societies—but rather the discrepancy between the permissive premises of family and educational life and the realities of adult life, which have tended to create their feelings of frustration and disappointment. Moreover, their feelings have often been shared by many members of the parent generation and reinforced by its guilt feeling about the incomplete realization of the goals of their own youth and of the movements in which they participated—because of this very process of institutionalization.

THE FOCI OF DISCONTINUITY

As a result of all these trends, there has tended to develop in many contemporary societies, and particularly in the highly developed and industrialized societies, a whole series of structural and symbolical discontinuities—all related to the spread and development of the institutional and symbolic dimensions of modernity. All of them have gradually converged on both intergenerational conflicts and widespread intellectual antinomian tendencies. These discontinuities are much more variegated than those between a relatively closed, traditional familial structure and more specialized and universalistic occupational and political systems. The latter have given rise in the first stages of modernity to various types of intergenerational conflicts.[8]

They have tended to become transposed beyond the direct opposition between family on the one hand, and educational and occupational sectors on the other, to the different sectors of the society through which young people pass; and therefore the foci of such discontinuity tend to become, in modern societies in general and in contemporary societies in particular, much more diversified. They may include discontinuity between the family and the educational and occupational spheres; between the family and educational institutions on the one hand, and the occupational sector on the other; between the productive and the consumer roles in the economic sector; between the values and orientations inculcated in the family and the educational institutions and the central collective symbols of the society; between the premises of these symbols and the actual political roles of the parents and younger people alike, thus cutting across family roles themselves.

These new types of discontinuity have tended also to impinge most intensively on the social and cultural situation of young people and on the concrete mainfestations of youth problems and protest. Here several such repercussions can be singled out. One is that the span of areas of social life that the specific youth or student culture encompasses has tended to expand continuously. First, it has extended over longer periods of life, reaching, through the impact of the extension of higher education, to what before was seen as early adulthood. Second, it tends more and more to include areas of work, of leisure time activity, and of many interpersonal relations. Third, the potential and actual autonomy of these groups, and the possibility their members have of direct access to work, to marriage and family life, to political rights, and to consumption, have greatly increased, while their dependence on adults has greatly decreased.

Because of this, paradoxically enough, the growing direct access of young people to various areas of life has given rise to a growing insecurity of status and self-identity and to an increasing ambiguity in adult roles.

This insecurity and ambiguity tend to be enhanced, first, by the prolongation of the span between biological and social maturity and by the extension of the number of years spent in basically "preparatory" (educational) institutions. Second, they are enhanced by the

[8]Eisenstadt, *From Generation to Generation* (Glencoe, Ill.: Free Press, 1956).

growing dissociation between the values of these institutions and the future—especially the occupational and parental roles—of those participating in them. Third, they are enhanced by the fact that for a long period of time many "young" people may as yet have no clear occupational roles or responsibilities, may be dependent on their parents or on public institutions for their economic needs, while at the same time they constitute an important economic force as consumers and certainly exercise political rights.

In turn, this situation may become intensified or aggravated by the fact of the growing demographic preponderance of the "young" in the whole population and by the increasing possibilities of ecological mobility.

These discontinuities have very often tended to culminate in a crisis of weakening of authority—evident in the lack of development of adequate role-models, on the one hand, and the erosion of many of the bases of legitimation of existing authority, on the other.

As a result of all these processes, the possibility of linking personal transition to social groups and to cultural values alike, to societal and cosmic time—so strongly emphasized in the youth movements and observable to some extent even in the earlier, looser youth culture—has become greatly weakened. In general, these developments have depressed the image of the societal and cultural future and have deprived it of its allure. Either the ideological separation between present and future has become smaller or the two have tended to become entirely dissociated. Out of the first of these conditions has grown what Riesman has called the cult of immediacy; out of the second, a total negation of the present in the name of an entirely different future—both, in principle, totally unrelated to any consciousness of the past.

A SHIFT IN ORIENTATION

The various processes just analyzed have given rise to a shift in the orientations and foci of protest in modern societies, and it is in this shift that the antinomian tendencies of intellectual protests can be most clearly discerned.

Unlike the older, classical movements of protest of early modernity —the major social and national movements, which tended to assume that the framework and centers of the nation-state constituted the major cultural and social reference points of personal identity and that the major task before modern societies was to facilitate the access of broader strata of the society to these centers—the new movements of protest are characterized by their skepticism toward the new modern centers, by their lack of commitment to them, and by their tendency toward a lack of responsibility to the institutional and organizational frameworks of these centers.

The foci of protest tend to shift from demands for greater participation in national/political centers, or from attempts to influence their socio-economic policies, to new directions. The most important of these directions seem to be: first, attempts to "disrobe" those centers of their charismatic legitimacy, and perhaps of any legitimacy at all; second, continuous searches for new loci of meaningful participation beyond these existing socio-political centers, and the concomitant attempts to create new centers which would be independent of them; third, attempts to couch the patterns of participation in their centers not so much in socio-political or economic terms as in symbols of primordial or direct social participation.

Thus, it seems that these developments touch not only on some of the most important structural developments in post-modern societies, but also on the relations of these developments to some of the basic symbolic constituents of these societies—to basic components of their socio-cultural orders as well as of their cultural, collective, and personal identities.

Significantly enough much of the new orientation of protest was also directed not only against the bureaucratization and functional rationalization connected with a growing technology, but also against the supposed central place of science and scientific investigation in the socio-cultural order.

They all denote an important aspect of what has been called by Weber the "demystification" of the world—demystification which here becomes focused on the possibility that the attainment of participation in these centers may indeed be meaningless, that these centers may lose their mystery, that the king may be naked indeed.

This demystification may well be related to the relative success of the demand for accesss to these centers and to participation in them, and to the obliteration of the symbolic difference between centers and periphery. This, in its turn, may give rise to a new type of social alienation, focused not only on the feeling of being lost in a maze of large-scale, anonymous organizations and frameworks, but also on the possibility of the loss of the meaning of participation in these political and national centers.

In other words, these centers may be losing their special place as loci of the participation in a meaningful socio-cultural order, and as the major social and cultural referrents of personal identity. There tends to develop here a growing feeling of dissociation and lack of congruence between the quest for participation in the charismatic dimension of human and social existence and these specific types of social and political centers.

THE UNIVERSITY AS A FOCUS

But it is not just the contents of these antinomian tendencies that are important and new, but the convergence of these contents. It is highly significant, from the point of view of our analysis, that this type of protest is not borne only by small, closed intellectual groups but by widespread circles of novices and aspirants to intellectual status. These protesters constitute, on the one hand—given the spread of the modern educational system and the parallel efforts of the spread of the media of mass communication—a very large part of the educated public, while on the other hand, for the same structural reasons, they impinge on the centers of intellectual creativity and cultural transmission and become integral, even if transient, parts thereof. It is, indeed, owing to these processes that these institutions in general, and universities in particular, have become the loci in which the convergence of intergenerational conflict with potential intellectual protest and antinomianism has taken place. It is this also which explains why the university is chosen as one of the focal symbols and objects of such total attack against the existing order.

It is not that the various bureaucratic or meritocratic features are necessarily much more developed in the university than in other organizations and institutions, but rather that here the social and cultural orders tend to become more salient and articulated. The university is being here perceived as the major locus of the possibility of such participation, and as the very place in which the quest for such creativity could be institutionalized. In this way the university has tended to become the major focus of the legitimation of a modern social order, and the attack on it indicates not only dissatisfaction with its own internal arrangements or even with the fact that it serves also as one mechanism of occupational and meritocratic selection. The choice of the university as the object of such attack rather emphasizes the denial that the existing order can realize these basic premises of modernity: to establish and maintain an order which could do justice to the claims to creativity and participation in the broader social order, and to overcome the various contradictions which have developed within it from the point of view of these claims.

It is, of course, very significant that this denial is also often shared and emphasized by many of the faculty itself, which evinces here some of the guilt feelings alluded to before, of the parent generation in general and of the intellectuals among them in particular.

It is perhaps in the attack on the university that the new dimension of protest—the negation of the premises of modernity, the emphasis on the meaninglessness of the existing centers, and the symbols of collective identity—becomes articulated in the most extreme, although certainly not necessarily representative, way.

It is also here that the basic themes of youth rebellion become very strongly connected with those of intellectual antinomianism. It is here that the rebellion against authority, hierarchy, and organizational framework, directed by the dreams of plenitude and of permissive, unstructured creativity, tends to become prominent—especially as the university serves also as the institutional meeting point between the educational and the central cultural spheres of the society.

Perhaps the most significant fact about these movements against the university is that they develop throughout the world in macrosocietal situations which are structurally basically different—in the centers of highly developed modern nations, as well as in those of developing and underdeveloped ones—but which are at the same time perceived by those participating in them as symbolically similar. Those participating in them tend to develop somewhat similar attitudes to the symbolic aspects, to the premises and promises of modernity and the similar perceptions of being placed in situations of relative deprivation with regard to these premises and promises.

The fact that the bases of such deprivation or discontinuity differ greatly—that, for instance, in the underdeveloped countries they are mostly those between traditional and modern sectors, in the Communist regimes between an authoritarian regime and those who want to extend the realism of liberty, and in the highly industrialized societies mostly between the sons of affluence and the structural-organization aspects of their affluent society—does not necessarily abate their symbolic affinity, which cuts across different historical and social situations. In a sense, this symbolic affinity is reinforced by broad structural variety—connected with the similarity in the place of the university in the spread of the vision of modernity.

It is in the attack on the university and from within the university that these new extreme postures of rebellion and protest tend to become especially prominent, due to the convergence of generational conflict and intellectual antinomianism. Needless to say, these are indeed only extreme postures and they certainly do not constitute the whole picture of contemporary youth or the intellectual scene. Their relative importance, both for social organization and for the lives of individuals, may vary greatly and it is one of the tasks of social research—a task which is being more and more discharged[9]—to attempt to identify some of the specific conditions which tend to give rise in the modern setting to these as against other manifestations of youth rebellion.

But, whatever these specific conditions may prove to be, the very novelty of this phenomenon can, at least partially, be explained in terms of the conditions leading to the convergence of intergenerational conflict and intellectual antinomianism.

[9]See, for instance, among many others: P. Abrams, "*Rites de Passage:* The Conflict of Generations in Industrial Society," *Journal of Contemporary History*, vol 5, no. 1 (1970): 175–90; M. Brewster Smith, Norma Haan, and Joanne Black, "Social-Psychological Aspects of Student Activism," *Youth and Society*, vol. 1, no. 3 (March 1970): 261–89.

.8. Women and Children First

PHILIP E. SLATER

*Women may not be serious, but at least they're not a
damned fool!*
    SNOW WHITE[1]

*Your mother's ghost stands at your shoulder,
Face like ice—a little bit colder—*
    CROSBY

*Black, white, green, red,
Can I take my friend to bed?*
    LENNON AND MC CARTNEY

A CURIOUS event of the late sixties was the popularity of the film, *The Graduate*, the viewing of which became almost a ritual for a wide spectrum of middle-class youth, who went to see it over and over. It was a brilliant film, constructed almost entirely of movie cliches, but many middle-aged reviewers were disturbed by its fusion of satire and naive romanticism. With the intolerance for ambiguity that characterizes both the generation and the genre, some critics attempted either to maintain that it was really *all* satire, or to dismiss it as basically callow.

The satire is largely associated with the more modern aspects of the film; reflecting intergenerational hostility, its sources and consequences. But the heart of the film is its celebration of the old American Dream of love triumphant over culture. One might even say that it is a revival of a reformation of that Dream. Like Christianity, the Dream has always borne an almost antithetical relation to the everyday life of the society in which it is embedded, yet has still managed to dominate attitudes and even behavior within certain limited spheres. And like Christianity, the Dream became tarnished by this peculiar position in which it found itself.

Mike Nichols, the director of the film, was thus the Martin Luther of the Dream, reviving it and purifying it; clarifying, through satire, its ambiguous relation to the total culture, and restoring its original

[1]Donald Barthelme, *Snow White* (New York: Bantam, 1968), p. 131.

155

naive form. It is of no consequence that the hero and his bride will become corrupted as time goes by. What is important is that the confrontation has taken place and Love has won, however briefly. *The Graduate*, like its paler predecessors, is a ritual of purification and cleansing, a celebration of the *capacity* of feeling to triumph over pattern. The interruption of a wedding ceremony—always a popular theme in American films—is not merely a suspense gimmick. It is what the film is all about: the battle between social forms and human feeling. And it is important that human feelings should occasionally win—as important as occasional epiphanies and miracles are for religion. In our society this issue is a matter of life and death (of the society, if not the individual).

In earlier films the basic conflict was usually attenuated, revolving almost exclusively around the question of choosing the more romantic and less conventional of two prospective marital partners. The stop-the-wedding element tended to be approached either comically or in a very muted way (i.e., no disruption of the ceremony). *The Graduate* moves up to its climax with cinematic cliches so densely packed that we feel we have seen the film before. Once in the church, however, we find that the years' accumulations of compromises and dilutions have been ruthlessly cut away. The hero makes no attempt whatever to cover or mask his feelings, the ceremony is totally and irretrievably shattered, and the hero must physically battle the representatives of society's forms. In this scene the old theme is presented with a baldness so complete that it becomes new and revolutionary.

When an old theme is revived in its true form, stripped of its routinizations and redefinitions, it always seems shocking. Raw and literal Christianity has this kind of impact. That *The Graduate* achieved popular success therefore implies some change in values (middle-aged people tended to object to the church scene, while most young people did not). The major change seems to me to be a strengthening of the feeling side of the human-need-versus-social-form conflict. For the older generation rituals, ceremonies, and social institutions have an intrinsic validity which makes them intimidating— a validity which takes priority over human events. One would hesitate to disrupt a serious social occasion for even the most acute and fateful need unless it could be justified in social rather than personal terms. Doris Lessing and Shelley Berman have both observed, in the case of people confronted with aircraft whose integrity has been cast in doubt, that most people would quietly die rather than "make a scene."

The younger generation experiences a greater degree of freedom from this allegiance. They do not see social occasions as automatically having intrinsic and sovereign validity. Their attitude is more secular—social formality is deferred to only when human concerns are not pressing. A well-brought-up young man like the hero of *The Graduate* would have tended, thirty years ago, to stand passively watching while his personal disaster took place—thus the church scene at that time would have seemed much less realistic (or else the hero defined as severely disturbed). Indeed, much of the older cinematic comedy made use of this meek deference—we recall the cops-and-robbers chases in which both participants would briefly interrupt their frantic efforts in order to stand at attention while the flag or a funeral procession passed by.

This change is responsible both for the character of radical protest in the sixties and for the angry responses of older people to it. Sitting-in at a segregated restaurant, occupying a campus building, lying down in front of vehicles, pouring blood in office files, and all of the imaginative devices emerging from modern protest movements depend heavily on a willingness to make a scene—not to be intimidated by a social milieu. And this is precisely what so enrages their elders, who are shocked not so much by the students' radicalism as by their bad form. That students should be rude to a public figure is more important to their elders than that the public figure is sending their children to their deaths in an evil cause. Students faced with situations in which existing practices are having disastrous consequences (killing people, destroying neighborhoods, cheating the poor, stultifying the minds of children, starving or brutalizing people, or whatever) are skeptical when told they should at all costs go through proper channels, knowing that such channels are typically ineffectual or prohibitively slow.[2] To be told it is better to kill or be killed than to be rude or make a public scene arouses much youthful bitterness and disillusionment, deftly captured in the protest song, "It Isn't Nice."

A part of this mistrust is unfounded. The young assume that their elders are attempting to deceive them with this talk of proper chan-

[2]At my own university recently a proposal for curriculum reform was passed after seven years of moving through "normal faculty procedures," and of course long after those students who had sought the change were graduated.

nels—that it is deliberate obstruction, since the elders know that "proper channels" are designed to negate rather than to facilitate change. But while this motive is undoubtedly present (much less consciously than the young assume), the reaction is based primarily on a horror of social uproar that the young simply do not experience and cannot comprehend. The elders' notion that radical leaders are "just trying to get their names in the papers" expresses their own bafflement at the contrast.

Yet the change is one that the elders themselves created, for it is based on child-oriented family patterns. Europeans have always felt that American parents paid far too much regard to their children's needs and far too little to the demands of adult social occasions; but Spock's emphasis on allowing the child to develop according to his own potential and needs (starting with the abandonment of the fixed schedule fad that enjoyed brief popularity in the twenties and thirties) focused the parents' attention on the child as a future adult, who could be more or less intelligent, creative, healthy, and personable according to how the parents behaved toward him. This was unlike the older view that the child had a fixed personality to which the parents tried to give a socially acceptable expression as best they could. The old method was based on the military drill model: you take people who are all basically different and get them to behave outwardly in a uniform manner, regardless of whether they are inwardly committed to this behavior or not. Thus there is a sharp distinction between the outer and inner spheres. The child or recruit is expected to harbor inner feelings of rebellion or contempt, so long as these are not expressed outwardly.

The new method gives much more responsibility to the parents, for they must concern themselves with inner states. They are not merely trying to make the child well-behaved—for them personality is not a given, but something the parent can mold. The parents under the old method felt they had done their job well if the child was obedient, even if he turned out dull, unimaginative, surly, sadistic, and sexually incapacitated. Spockian parents feel that it is their responsibility to make their child into the most all-around perfect adult possible, which means paying a great deal of attention to his inner states and latent characteristics. The consequence of this is what is superficially defined as greater "permissiveness," but from an internal perspective is actually more totalitarian—the child no longer has a private sphere, but has his entire being involved with parental aspirations. What the child is *not* permitted to do is to take his own personality for granted.

Under the old system, for example, the parents would feel called upon to chastise a child defined as bright but lazy, and if they forced him to spend a fixed amount of time staring at a book—whether he learned anything or lost all interest in learning—they would feel justified and relieved of all moral responsibility for him ("I don't know why he's so bad, I beat him every day"). Today parents feel required not just to make him put in time but to make him motivated to learn.

The tradeoff for having his whole personality up for grabs is that the child's needs are paid much more attention. The old method demanded the subordination of these needs to social reality: for the most casual social encounter the parents would be willing to sacrifice the child's sense of truth and fair play ("kiss the nice lady"), bodily needs ("you'll just have to wait"), and even parental loyalty ("he's always stupid and shy with strangers"). For the parent who loved him to throw him to the dogs for something so trivial as etiquette makes a deep impression on the child. He sees the parent nurturant and protective in situations that seem much more important and dangerous, why not here? Since he cannot *see* anything so important as to justify this betrayal, all social situations tend to assume a sacred, awe-inspiring, inviolate quality. Since the parents put this mysterious situation above all else, it comes to assume the same sovereignty for the child.

But Spock-oriented parents, absorbed with the goal of molding the child's total character, were much less inclined to sacrifice the child to the etiquette concerns of strangers. The artist working on his masterpiece does not let guests use it to wipe their feet on. As a result, their children have grown up to feel that human needs have some validity of their own, and that social occasions are less sacred than they appeared to earlier generations. As an SDS leader observed: ". . . educational institutions exist to fit [the student] to the system and not vice versa, and that is a recognition that all of his careful socialization to upper-middle-class values has ill-prepared him to accept. We grew up feeling reasonably potent in influencing our personal milieu; and without our parents' deeper needs for economic and status security, we are in a much better position to challenge a society that promises to make us impotent."[3] When parents today enjoin their children to "face reality" (by which they mean *social* reality) there is a double irony: first, because their children have become so skillful at exposing how fictional "reality" is,

[3]Paul Potter, quoted by Warren G. Bennis in "Future of the Social Sciences," *Antioch Review*, 28 (Summer 1968): 239.

and second, because the parents themselves have never been able to "face" this reality but have always been stared down by it.

The hero of *The Graduate* is thus not intimidated by the wedding ceremony but wails out his pain, and the heroine, until then bewitched by social forms, is disenchanted, rescued, and redeemed. But what of the parents, who gave their children the power to confront what they are unable to resist themselves?[4] How do they react? In *The Graduate*, they show vindictive hatred, and this also is a new departure, for in the older films the representatives of social forms are merely left openmouthed, or slyly smiling (secretly glad), or futilely shaking their fists. But here they attack viciously and a true mêlée ensues. The hero fights off the mob by grabbing a large cross from the altar, beating them off with it, and then using it to bar the church door from the outside, permitting the couple to escape.

The cross incident is important for two reasons. First, the hero, by appropriating it, transforms it from a symbol of church convention and ritual to one of revolutionary Christianity, in which love takes precedence over ceremony. It is the final act of purification in the film, and it was shocking to adults who could not imagine religion being on the side of human feeling and against convention. But to young Christian activists it was not shocking at all, but a proper role for the cross to play. For was not Jesus himself impatient with traditional forms and rude to authority? Can it not be said of him that he acted in bad taste, and refused to seek reform through proper channels? Wasn't throwing the money changers out of the Temple a far more obstreperous act than occupying a building? But then Jesus was very much a Yippie, which is why he wound up in jail, Jerusalem being the Chicago of its day.

Second, the wielding of the cross exposed a peculiarity of contemporary parent-child relationships. As every movie-goer knows, one carries a cross to ward off vampires, and putting a cross on a door prevents the vampires from getting through. In *The Graduate*, as in upper-middle-class America generally, parents relate to their children in a somewhat vampiresque way. They feed on the child's accomplishments, sucking sustenance for their pale lives from vicarious

---

[4]This unique power that parents have—to give their children attributes they do not themselves possess—is perhaps the unconscious determinant of an otherwise incomprehensible theme that appears so often in fairy tales: that of the impoverished old parent or helper who gives the hero magic gifts that could have made the giver himself wealthy and powerful but apparently did not.

enjoyment of his or her development. In a sense this sucking is appropriate since the parents give so much—lavish so much care, love, thoughtfulness, and self-sacrifice on their blood bank. But this is little comfort for the child, who at some point must rise above his guilt and live his own life—the culture demands it of him. And after all, a vampire is a vampire.

We are shown this relationship at the very beginning of the film when a party is given to celebrate the hero's return from an honor-laden college career; family and friends clutch and paw him like a valuable artifact. Much of the satire throughout the film centers on this theme, perhaps best exemplified by the pool scene, in which the hero becomes a mannikin on which his father can display his affluence to his friends. The hero's struggle to shed his diving gear —to disentangle his own motivation from the vicarious aspirations of his parents—takes up the entire movie.

In this process Mrs. Robinson is a crucial transitional figure. Unlike the parents, she is not a crypto-vampire but an absolutely open one. She gives nothing whatever and thus induces no guilt. Nor does she want to derive any vicarious satisfaction from Ben's achievements. She wants only to feed on his youth and obtain sexual gratification from him. In this relationship—initially an expression of his Oedipal enthralment—Ben can extricate himself from these familial entanglements, for Mrs. Robinson's cold exploitativeness enables his own motivation to separate itself out and became coherent. In shifting his interest to her daughter he moves a step further—perhaps as far as he is able. It is significant that at the beginning of this new relationship he adopts a very uncharacteristic mode of behavior—one which resembles Mrs. Robinson's—as if he were using her cold and distant personality as a lever to establish his own separateness prior to forming a serious relationship.

The cross, then, is necessary to ward off the elders, whose vampiresque involvement with the hero has been insufficiently exorcized. The intense new relationship threatens to arouse all of his old symbiotic responses, and these must be magically neutralized—much in the way puberty rites in primitive societies neutralize the young boy's attachment to his mother.

Before leaving *The Graduate* we should take note of the hostile reaction of older adults in the society to the cross incident, which was widely criticized as being "unnecessary" and "in bad taste." That they should pick up this issue of "taste" and ignore the meaning of the incident exemplifies a characteristic tendency toward irrelevance that exasperates their children. In the midst of a dramatic confrontation between the generations they are distracted by the unorthodox use of a religious symbol. In the midst of a dramatic confrontation between blacks and whites they are distracted by a four-letter word. In the midst of a dramatic confrontation between those who espouse and those who oppose the Vietnam War, they are distracted by the long hair of some of the participants.

The young are baffled, amused, and enraged by these bizarre responses. They alternately view the middle-aged as hopelessly detached from reality and as willfully perverse. What they overlook is the terror. The young are challenging the fundamental premises on which their elders have based their lives, and they are attacking at all of the weakest points. No one likes to admit that they have spent their lives in a foolish, evil, or crazy manner. Furthermore, the elders were always taught to lie about their feelings. They are not likely to say: "You frighten and depress us. We are afraid we have spent our lives in narrow self-aggrandizement, neglecting and brutalizing our neighbors, pursuing useless and trivial artifacts, and creating a joyless environment. It always seemed the right thing to do, but now we are a little unsure, and anyway we wouldn't know how to behave differently." Instead, they suppress their doubts and fears about themselves by refusing to perceive the meaning of the stimulus. When their children cry for peace or social justice they say, "don't talk dirty" or "get a haircut." This is a way of saying, "There is nothing important or disturbing going on here—this is just my child who is mischievous or careless at times—it is just a family affair" ("But Mother, I'm going to jail—I'm a political prisoner." ... "Well, at least they'll give you a decent haircut"). It is a desperate attempt to view the world as unchanging—to convert the deep social unrest of the day into the blank torpor of suburban life—to translate Watts into *Julia*, Berkeley and Columbia into *Dobie Gillis*, Chicago into *Mayberry*, and Vietnam into *McHale's Navy*.

This is precisely the way the parents of schizophrenic children typically respond to emotional crises of a personal kind. Lidz and his colleagues illustrate this pattern by telling of a patient who, after much struggle and resistance, finally was able to pour out her anguish and bewilderment to her parents and plead for their understanding and help. At the height of her plaintive entreaty her mother "offhandedly turned to one of the psychiatrists, tugged at the waist of her dress and blandly remarked, 'My dress is getting tight. I suppose I should go on a diet.' "[5] The kind of communication pattern that characterizes the families of schizophrenics appears in a number of contemporary dramas, suggesting that it speaks to a much larger social phenomenon. How, for example, can matters so intrinsically trivial as hair length or apparel arouse reactions of such intensity in people who present themselves as the most sane, stable, and effective members of our society? The answer is that two compatible processes are taking place at once: the elders are expressing anger, while pretending to themselves that the causes of that anger do not exist.

THE SPOCKIAN CHALLENGE

More deeply revealing of the generational issue than *The Graduate* was the odd non-event that followed the arrest of Dr. Spock.[6] Many people expected that the arrest, on such a basis, of a man who had been doctor, teacher, and adviser to millions of American mothers would cause a torrent of protest. Instead it was met with a profound and malicious silence.

Why did the mothers turn against their benefactor? What was Spock's impact upon American society and why did it try to revenge itself upon him? Since a man does not write a child-rearing manual as successful as this one unless it strikes extremely responsive chords in its readers, it appears that we have found yet another example of Americans raging against the consequences of their own inclinations.

Spock's book reinforced three trends in American family and child-rearing patterns: permissiveness, individualism, and feminine domesticity. The first two are patterns that have been with us for two centuries, but the last is a relatively recent (post-World War II) reversal of an older trend in the opposite direction. Curiously enough, it is also the only one about which Spock does not caution against excess, even in his latest edition.

[5]Theodore Lidz, et al., *Schizophrenia and the Family* (New York: International Universities Press, 1965), p. 182.

[6]Spock was arrested through a device that has became increasingly prominent in modern America: the selective enforcement of laws so vague, broad, and universally violated that they enable any law enforcement officer to arrest almost anyone any time he wishes. This is a modern version of the Bill of Attainder, outlawed by our Constitution, but revived, to all intents and purposes, by the convenient chaos of our legal system.

Current popular discussion has centered around permissiveness, but this is due to two misunderstandings. First, it is usually assumed that permissiveness in child-rearing is a recent American development, which is quite clearly not the case. Every generation of Americans since the first landing has imagined itself to be more permissive than the previous one, while foreign visitors have resolutely refused to recognize any variation in an unremitting stream of American laxity.[7] Second, it would be absurd in any case to blame parental permissiveness on Spock, who places great emphasis on the child's need for parental control and the importance of not letting the child become a tyrant in the home. The areas in which Spock reinforced "permissiveness" had to do not with social behavior, but with such matters as feeding schedules, toilet training, and the like. Even here he did not advance totally new approaches, but merely revived practices current in America and England prior to the middle of the eighteenth century. While I do not wish to minimize the extent to which Spock has become a *symbol* of permissiveness in child-rearing, I think we will learn more about the nature of his impact and the reaction against him by examining the other two variables.

Spock's work epitomizes the old American tradition that every individual is somehow unique. Furthermore, he implicitly endorses a concept that pervades popular American thinking about education—the notion of an individual having a "potential." This potential is seen as innate, partially hidden, gradually unfolding, fluid, and malleable.[8] The parent cannot simply coerce the child into a set uniform pattern of behavior, because it is important, given our achievement ethic, that a child realize his maximum potential, and this means taking into account present, anticipated, or fantasied characteristics of his own. The concept of potential is thus rooted in individualism and achievement ideology. It also serves, however, as a kind of compromise between biological and environmental determinism. The parent is given not clay but some more differentiated substance with which to mold an adult.

In any case, the notion of individual differences, of special unfolding potentialities, is fundamental in Spock, although the latest

[7]See W. G. Bennis and P. E. Slater, *The Temporary Society*, (New York: Harper and Row, 1968), Chapter 2.

[8]John L. Fischer and Ann Fischer, "The New Englanders of Orchard Town, U.S.A.," in Beatrice Whiting, ed., *Six Cultures: Studies of Child Rearing* (New York: Wiley, 1963), pp. 921–28.

edition makes a modest effort to stress more universal social demands on the individual. Indeed, it is curious that he talks of the need to instill social consciousness as if this were something that his previous approach failed to do (presumably because he makes no explicit mention of it in earlier editions). Yet the product of child-centered, Spockian child-rearing is the most socially conscious youth America has ever known. This should warn all of us (including Spock) against the simple assumption that a deliberate push in a given direction will produce the expected outcome.

Spock is nonetheless concerned about what he feels to be our excessive child-centeredness, although he sees no escape from it: "I doubt that Americans will ever want their children's ambitions to be subordinated to the wishes of the family or the needs of our country."[9] He suggests that the children would be happier if they did, and advises parents to stick to whatever principled guns they have. But this hardly balances the general thrust of his work. From the very beginning Spock's book has tended both to encourage Pygmalionesque fantasies in mothers and to stress the complexity of the task of creating a person out of an infant. His good sense, tolerance, humanity, and uncanny ability to anticipate the anxieties that everyday child-rearing experiences arouse in young mothers helped seduce them into accepting the implicit (and probably unintended) challenge. Underneath all of the qualifications and demurrals, most middle-class, Spock-oriented mothers believe, deep in their hearts, that if they did their job well enough all of their children would be creative, intelligent, kind, generous, happy, brave, spontaneous, and good—each, of course, in his or her own special way.

It is this challenge and this responsibility that have led mothers to accept the third pattern that Spock has reinforced—feminine domesticity. For Spock makes quite explicit, even in his latest edition, his belief that a woman's place is in the home. He lays great emphasis on the importance and the difficulty of the task of child-rearing, and gives it priority over all other possible activities. He suggests government allowances for mothers otherwise compelled to work, on the grounds that it "would save money in the end"—thus implying that only a full-time mother can avoid bringing up a child who is a social problem. He allows reluctantly that "a few mothers, particularly those with professional training" might be so unhappy

---

[9]Benjamin Spock, *Baby and Child Care* (New York: Pocket Books, 1968), p. 12. See also pp. xvi, 10–23.

if they did not work that it would affect the children—the understanding here is that the professional training was a kind of unfortunate accident the effects of which can no longer be undone. The mother must feel "strongly" about it and have an "ideal arrangement" for child care. Otherwise Spock tries to induce guilt: "If a mother realizes clearly how vital this kind of care is to a small child, it may make it easier for her to decide that the extra money she might earn, or the satisfaction she might receive from an outside job, is not so important after all."[10]

Although in other respects Spock merely endorses existing cultural patterns—reinforcing them or making them explicit—one could conceivably make a case for his having contributed to the postwar ultradomestication of the American female, since his book was first published in 1946 when it all began. I personally feel that the flight into the home was only a part of a general postwar retreat from the world—a flight that would have occurred even without *Baby and Child Care.* Yet Spock gave it a certain focus, and supported a set of social arrangements which is now yielding both good and bad results. I raise this point because although Spock is as American as apple pie, he has been attacked as if he had introduced some foreign element into the American socialization process. For the most part, he has been a scapegoat for the ambivalence Americans feel about their own society. Only in his emphasis on domesticity did he introduce a broad departure from the past.

American women have always had a reputation for independence (De Tocqueville commented upon it in 1830). The culture as a whole tends to exert a certain pressure for sexual equality, and women in the nineteenth century were not as protected as in Europe (although they were expected to guard their own chastity as vigorously as if men were guarding it for them). In frontier settings they were too important to yield much power or deference to husbands, and among immigrant groups they were often more employable than their husbands. During the present century labor-saving devices reduced the demands of the home to a minimum, education for women increased, women obtained the vote, and contraception undermined the double standard. The direction of events seemed clear.

After World War II, however, a strange phenomenon occurred. Although more women were working than ever before, this was not true for the professions. Despite more women going to college, a

[10]*Ibid.*, pp. 563–64.

smaller percentage were using this education in any way. In short, while single middle-class women were becoming more and more liberated, married middle-class women were embracing a more totally domestic existence than ever before. But how was this achieved? How could educated women devote their entire lives to a task so shrunken? How could they make it fill the day, let alone fill their minds?[11] To some extent Parkinson's Law ("work expands to fill the time available to complete it") can be relied upon in such situations, especially with the aid of the advertising industry, which continually invents new make-work chores and new standards of domestic perfection. Television also fills many gaps.

But the main factor facilitating the ultradomestication of the middle-class American female was the magnification of the child-rearing role. Child-rearing is not a full-time job at any age in and of itself. In every other society throughout history women have been busy with other tasks, and reared their children as a kind of parallel activity. The idea of devoting the better part of one's day to child care seldom occurred to anyone because few women ever had time for it before, and when they did they usually turned the job over to a servant. Occasionally someone fiercely determined to produce a genius would devote many hours a day trying to teach an infant Greek, or whatever, but these were eccentricities. In our society it is as if every middle-class parent were determined to rear a John Stuart Mill; it turns one a bit queasy to see them walking about with signs on them so their three-year-olds will learn to read, or complaining that their children are not learning enough in nursery school.

This is not to say that child care *cannot* fill a day. There have been many social inventions that have successfully filled the time gaps created by home appliances. The modern suburban home is neither built nor equipped in a manner that allows for the comfortable or healthy management of an eighteen-month-old child. Living in the suburbs also involves the mother in constantly driving her children about from one activity to another. Anyone could add to the list of anomalies created by our being a child-oriented society in the face

[11]Soviet women achieve "equality" by working twice as hard and long as men do, since Russian men are reluctant to engage in domestic chores. The women work a full-time job and then a full-time domestic job, largely unassisted by either men or machines. Middle-class American women, on the other hand, have much more *opportunity* to make this equality real, since (a) their domestic task is much easier, with more labor-saving devices, (b) American middle-class males are not averse to helping out, and (c) they can obtain outside jobs with shorter hours.

of a technological environment that is essentially child-antagonistic or at least child-alien. One has only to see a village community in which women work and socialize in groups with children playing nearby, also in groups, supervised by the older ones, or by some of the mothers on a haphazardly shared basis, to realize what is awkward about the domestic role in America. Because the American mother is isolated, she can engage in only one of these three activities at a time—with effort, two. Even taken together they hardly constitute a satisfying occupation for a civilized woman.

But the most important factor here is that the American wife has accepted the Spockian challenge. She has been told: "You have the capacity to rear a genius, a masterpiece. Such an activity is the most important thing you can do and should therefore rightfully absorb all of your time and energy." Given such an attitude it is relatively easy to expand child-rearing into a full-time job. For although Spock has many sensible passages about not martyring oneself to one's children ("needless self-sacrifice sours everybody"), the temptation to do so is enormous given the fact that there is so little else. In all the tedium and meaninglessness of her domestic chores this is the only area that is important enough to be worthy of her attention. We are a product-oriented society, and she has been given the opportunity to turn out a really outstanding product.

Unfortunately, however, there really isn't that much she can do to bring about this end. At first the child sleeps most of the time, and later he spends more and more time amusing himself or playing with other children. It is not particularly helpful to waken a sleeping infant, and parents are not very good playmates for older children. The only way she can feel that she is putting a proper amount of effort into the task is by cultivating the child's natural entropic tendencies to make more housework for herself; or by upsetting and then comforting the child so she can flex her nurturant and therapeutic skills. Since she really doesn't know how to create an outstanding adult and perhaps recognizes, deep in some uncorrupted sanctuary of good sense, that the more actively she seeks it the less likely she is to attain it, the only time she will feel she is engaged in her primary task is when she is meeting minor crises. Naturally this produces a great temptation to induce such crises, indirectly and, of course, without conscious intent.

In a prior discussion of this issue, I suggested that the frequent jovial references to the multiplicity of roles played by housewives in our society serve to mask the fact that the housewife is a nobody.[12] Another custom with a similar function is the laughing narration of the events of a particularly chaotic day, in which one minor disaster follows hard upon another, or several occur simultaneously (". . . and there I was, the baby in one hand, the phone and doorbell both ringing . . ."). These sagas are enjoyed because they conceal the fundamental vacuity of the housewife's existence.[13] Saying, "everything happened at once" is an antidote to the knowledge that nothing ever happens, really.

The emotional and intellectual poverty of the housewife's role is nicely expressed in the almost universal complaint: "I get to talking baby talk with no one around all day but the children." There are societies in which the domestic role works, but in those societies the housewife is not isolated. She is either part of a large extended family household in which domestic activities are a communal effort, or participates in a tightly knit village community, or both. The idea of imprisoning each woman alone in a small, self-contained, architecturally isolating dwelling is a modern invention, dependent upon an advanced technology. In Moslem societies, for example, the wife may be a prisoner but she is at least not in solitary confinement. In our society the housewife may move about freely, but since she has nowhere to go and is not a part of anything anyway, her prison needs no walls.

This is in striking contrast to her premarital life, if she is a college graduate. In college she is typically embedded in an active group life with constant emotional and intellectual stimulation. College life is in this sense an urban life. Marriage typically eliminates much of this way of life for her, and children deliver the *coup de grâce*. Her only significant relationship tends to be her husband, who, however, is absent most of the day. Most of her social and emotional needs must be satisfied by her children, who are hardly adequate to the task. Furthermore, since she is supposed to be molding them into superior beings she cannot lean too heavily upon them for her own needs, although she is sorely tempted to do so.

This is, in fact, the most vulnerable point in the whole system. Even if the American housewife were not a rather deprived person, it would be the essence of vanity for anyone to assume that an un-

---

[12]P. E. Slater, *The Glory of Hera* (Boston: Beacon Press, 1968), pp. 450–451; see also Bennis and Slater, *The Temporary Society*, pp. 91–92.

[13]I am indebted to Dori Appel Slater for this observation.

formed child could tolerate such massive inputs of one person's personality. In most societies the impact of neuroses and defects in the mother's character is diluted by the presence of many other nurturing agents. In middle-class America the mother tends to be not only the exclusive daytime adult contact of the child, but also a contact with a mission to create a near-perfect being. This means that every maternal quirk, every maternal hang-up, and every maternal deprivation will be experienced by the child as heavily amplified noise from which there is no respite.

We know a little bit about the consequences of one aspect of this situation. Societies in which deprived mothers turn to their children for what they cannot obtain from adults tend to produce males who are vain, boastful, aggressive, and skittish toward women. Such males have great fear of losing self-control, of becoming dependent upon women, of weakness. Male gangs often assume great importance.[14]

Now middle-class American males do not, by and large, fit this description, although American foreign policy is deeply rooted in *machismo* philosophies. One of the reasons may be that in the societies that do produce this kind of male there is a strong sexual component in the maternal imvolvement with the son, resulting from a voluntary or involuntary sexual distance between husband and wife. But although individual American families often show such sexual displacement (the clinical literature is full of them), the American housewife taken as a general type is not a very sexy creature. Indeed, perhaps her major characteristic is that she has been so thoroughly desexualized.

This is no accident. A seductive mother in a family system involving many caretakers has nothing like the impact she has in a society like ours, where she is almost the whole world to the child. The fact that maternal seductiveness is so often associated with male schizophrenia is closely tied to the sexlessness of American housewives as a group. There seems to be some unconscious recognition of the fact that even ordinary feminine seductiveness, given the magnification that motherhood receives in our society, tends to be disorganizing to the child. Since the American mother is so omnipresent and intensely

[14]Slater, *The Glory of Hera*, Chapters 1, 14, 15. See also Beatrice Whiting, "Sex Identity Conflict and Physical Violence: A Comparative Study," *American Anthropologist*, 68 (December 1965) Supplement: 123–40; R.V. Burton and J.W.M. Whiting, "The Absent Father and Cross-Sex Identity," *Merrill-Palmer Quarterly*, 7 (1961): 85–95.

committed to her role, she must be defused, as it were. Her desexualization is necessary in order not to add unduly to the already somewhat overwhelming maternal input the child receives.

Let us consider this desexualization further, since it is both a remarkable phenomenon, given the sexual preoccupations of the society as a whole, and rather poorly understood. In many societies a woman is viewed as relatively neuter until she is married—it is at this point that she becomes a full-fledged female, a sexual being. This is especially the case in societies that are strict about permarital sexuality but indifferent toward extramarital affairs. Yet even in societies in which the exact reverse is true, single girls, however promiscuous, are sometimes viewed as merely children playing. In dress, manner, and interpersonal style it is often the married woman alone who is fully sexual.

In our society the exact opposite is true. Stylistically, it is only young unmarried girls who are allowed to be entirely female. Their appearance is given strong sexual emphasis even before there is anything to emphasize, but as soon as they are married they are expected to mute their sexuality somewhat, and when they become mothers this neutralization is carried even further. This means that whatever sexual appeal exists in a malnourished nymphet is made highly explicit, while the kind of mature and full-blown femininity that has excited Europeans for centuries is masked almost beyond recognition. Suburban housewives in particular often affect hard, severe, tight, and rectangular hair and clothing styles. The effect is rather masculine, especially when combined with a bluff, hearty, and sarcastic conversational style, as it so frequently is.

It is tempting to see in this pattern a compensatory process: women cheated of a career express their "masculinity" in the only form left to them. Certainly it seems appropriate to describe as "masculine" a behavioral style which is a transparent imitation of the way men in our society behave in all-male groups, and the hair and clothing style suggests mobilization—a readiness to participate in some vigorous activity outside the home (Chinese peasant women on their way to the factories seem more casually feminine by comparison).

But what is "masculine" and what is "feminine?" Contemporary psychoanalytic literature is full of absurd statements based on the assumption that sex roles in our own society embody biological universals. We know by now, however, that there is virtually nothing in the way of personal characteristics or behavior that is defined in every culture as masculine or feminine. In some societies women are assumed to be stronger, and carry all the heavy burdens. In some societies women are supposed to be impractical and intuitive, in others men are. In most societies women are seen as earthy, men as spiritual, but Victorian England reversed this order. Even within our own society there are odd contradictions: activity is seen as a masculine characteristic, passivity as feminine. Yet men are supposed to move and talk slowly, while women are expected to be birdlike in body movement—constantly moving their hands, using many more facial muscles, talking rapidly. Paradoxically, a man who is too active in the most physical sense of using many muscles from moment to moment is considered "effeminate."

It should be emphasized, then, that when we talk of "masculine" and "feminine" we are referring only to the ways in which these are customarily defined in our culture, and since sex role definitions change from time to time there is ample room for confusion. If women behave in ways that seem imitative of men, we call this masculine, but if customs change, and certain kinds of activities become redefined as appropriate for females are they "masculine" for doing them? One suddenly realizes that we have stumbled upon a powerful weapon for "keeping women in their place." It is really a very old and familiar weapon, used with great effect against minority groups. It begins with a stereotype—"women cannot think logically," for example. If a woman then demonstrates a capacity for logical thought she is stigmatized as "masculine." The same device is used to discourage women from engaging in professional careers.[15] The ancient Greeks were extremely adept at this device—so much so that they succeeded for over two millennia in distracting attention from the fact that Greek heroes almost never knew what to do without help or advice from some woman ("with a mind like a man," of course).

Today's black militants are the first minority group clever enough to have invented a solution to this ruse. Instead of trying to escape the black stereotype and become "white," they have in a sense accepted the stereotype and said "black, even in your stereotypical sense, is better than white." Since American society was in danger of being strangulated by its alienation from the body, this meant, as

---

[15]This has a particularly nasty side-effect upon the medical profession. To show that it is really "a man's job" the nurturing, helping aspects must be deemphasized. Thus the recruitment of physicians selectively favors cold, ungiving, exploitative, competitive, and mercenary personality types, with a result familiar to all.

Eldridge Cleaver has so brilliantly shown, that blacks could quite reasonably view themselves as saviors of the whites, helping them rediscover their own roots.[16] This is a lesson from which American women could learn a great deal. The missions are not even that dissimilar, since alienation from the body, from the emotional life, is largely a white male invention.

Consider, for example, the question with which we began this dicussion: have suburban matrons adopted a desexualized, "masculine" style because they have been deprived of careers? Many people would object that most women don't *want* careers. I suspect the women themselves would agree, but I also wonder if deep inside they don't feel the kind of puzzled uneasiness that we always experience when obliged to accept a formulation that makes us lose either way. The problem is that "career" is in itself a masculine concept (i.e., designed for males in our society). When we say "career" it connotes a demanding, rigorous, preordinated life pattern, to whose goals everything else is ruthlessly subordinated—everything pleasurable, human, emotional, bodily, frivolous. It is a stern, Calvinistic word, which is why it always has a humorous effect when it is applied to occupational patterns of a less puritanical sort. Thus when a man asks a woman if she wants a career, it is intimidating. He is saying, are you willing to suppress half of your being as I am, neglect your family as I do, exploit personal relationships as I do, renounce all personal spontaneity as I do? Naturally, she shudders a bit and shuffles back to the broom closet. She even feels a little sorry for him, and bewails the unkind fate that has forced him against his will to become such a despicable person. The perennial success of this hoax perhaps contributes to the low opinion that men so often have of feminine intelligence (an opinion which, as any teacher knows, is otherwise utterly unfounded).

A more effective (revolutionary, confronting) response would be to admit that a "career," thus defined, is indeed undesirable—that (now that you mention it) it seems like a pernicious activity for *any* human being to engage in, and should be eschewed by both men *and* women. Of course she doesn't want a "career," nor do most humans, with the exception of a few males crazed, by childhood deprivation or Oedipal titillation, with insatiable desires for fame, power, or wealth. What she wants is a meaningful and stimulating activity,

[16]Eldridge Cleaver, *Soul on Ice* (New York: McGraw-Hill, 1968), pp. 191–204.

excitement, challenge, social satisfactions—all the things that middle-class males get from their jobs, whether they are defined as "careers" or not. Rarely is she willing, however, to pay the price that masculine narcissism seduces men into paying in our society. She therefore accepts the definition of herself as the inferior sex, instead of adopting the revolutionary stance of the black militant ("black is beautiful"), and saying: "My unwillingness to sacrifice a host of human values to my personal narcissism and self-aggrandizement makes me the *superior* sex." Such a stance would in fact liberate both sexes: women would be freed from the suffocating stagnation of the artificial domestic role in which they have been imprisoned; men would be liberated from their enslavement to the empty promise (ever receding, always redefined as just out of reach, and unsatisfying even when grasped) of "success." Both could then live in a gratifying present, instead of an illusory future and an ill-remembered past.

This revolutionary response, however, is never made. Women have long been stereotyped as bastions of conservatism—a stereotype which receives considerable empirical support from attitude surveys. Even war, the most absurd and vicious of all the games that men play, has rarely produced a feminine revolt. Despite their antipathy toward it, despite the fact that they play no part in it and cannot control it, that it is most hurtful to them and destroys what they have created, women seldom resist war, and in some societies are more chauvinistic and bloodthirsty than the men. *Lysistrata* was, after all, a man's fantasy.

The reasons for this are complex and varied, but in our society, at least, feminine conservatism, like the domesticity pattern, is part of a role into which women are inducted by men. Having created a technological and social-structural juggernaut by which they are daily buffeted, men tend to use their wives as opiates to soften the impact of the forces they have set into motion against themselves. Consider, for example, the suburban living pattern: husbands go to the city and participate in the twentieth century, while their wives are assigned the hopeless task of trying to act out a rather pathetic bucolic fantasy oriented toward the nineteenth. Men in their jobs must accept change—even welcome it and foster it—however threatening and disruptive it may seem. They do not know how to abstain from colluding daily in their own obsolescence, and they are frightened. Such men tend to make of their wives an island of stability in a sea of change. The wife becomes a kind of memento, like the bit of earth the immigrant brings from the old country and puts under his bed. He subtly encourages her to espouse absurdly old-fashioned views which he then ridicules when he is with his male associates. There is a special tone of good-natured condescension with which married men gathered together discuss the conservatism of their wives, and one senses how elegantly their ambivalence has been apportioned between them ("it's a great opportunity for me but of course the wife doesn't like to move—she has a lot of ties in the community, and of course the children in school and all . . ."). It permits the husband to be far more adaptable and amenable to change than he really feels.

Ultimately, of course, this kind of emotional division of labor tends to backfire, and this case is no exception. Freed from the necessity of confronting his own resistance to change, and having insulated his wife from experiencing the more exciting and enjoyable aspects of such novelty, he tends to become bored with her and somewhat lonely. She is left behind, "outgrown," as William H. Whyte, Jr., puts it.[17]

The domestication and neutralization of the wife is part of the same process. That is, it is important not only that the wife have low stimulus value for her child, but also that she have low stimulus value for her husband. Our society is presently founded on overstimulation—on the generation of needs and desires which cannot directly be gratified, but which ensure a great deal of striving and buying in an effort to gratify them. Much if not most of this stimulation is sexual—erotic delights are implicitly attached to almost every product that can be bought in America today, at least by adults. The goal of commercial America, therefore, is to maximize sexual stimulation and minimize sexual availability—in this way an infinite number of products can be inserted in the resulting gap. It is the role of the wife to reverse the process for her beleaguered husband—to combine maximum availability with minimum stimulation. This also backfires, of course, since it is a prescription for boredom.

The only real solution for the housewife in this situation is a revolutionary one—to abandon the opiate role and combat the forces that make her opiate role necessary. This is extremely unlikely to

[17]William H. Whyte, Jr., "The Wife Problem," in R.F. Winch, et al. eds., *Selected Studies in Marriage and the Family* (New York: Holt, Rinehart, and Winston, 1962), pp. 472–77.

occur. On the other hand there is a powerful force for change in the increasingly bizarre contradiction between premarital and marital feminine roles. Women can be expected more and more to resist induction into such a hopelessly unrewarding life style, as cultural alternatives become increasingly available.

I would like to make one further point before moving on to consider the consequences of this constellation. Men, like all dominant groups, have generally been successful in getting women (like other "minority" groups) to accept whatever definition of their essential character has been convenient for men. One of the oldest gambits, for example, has been to maintain that dominance is sex-linked (as indeed it is, in some species). Thus if a woman assumes any other than a submissive pose she is accused of being "unfeminine." This is an ingenious device for maintaining superior status and has been quite successful. On the other hand, males lose considerably by thus hobbling the personalities of their womenfolk. Whenever men have succeeded in convincing their wives that some human response is "unfeminine," they have sought other women who possessed it.

One has only to think of Sophia Loren or Elizabeth Taylor (to name only the most conspicuous examples) to realize that dominance and aggressiveness in women need detract nothing from their sexual attractiveness. On the contrary, women who have been taught too well that aggressiveness is "unladylike" often seem a bit asexual. There is a depth in the human psyche at which all feelings are one, and the disparagement of any contaminates and constricts all. The universality of aggression-release in fertility rituals illustrates this communality.

There is a limit, in any case, to the amount of emotional crippling that can be borne, and as American women (who, after all, have had a long tradition of being defined as spirited) have been inducted more and more into a colorless, ultradomestic role, they have tended to reject submissiveness as a feminine adjunct. This has led to the rather unattractive combination of the strident drudge, an image strongly reinforced by television and other media.

When we realize that the justification for this horror is the welfare of the child, we begin to see why this same child will encounter some resentment when he or she grows up. The child is not really responsible for the bad bargain the parents have made with each other (and with themselves), but he lends moral credit to it. Indeed, "for the children" is a kind of priest's blessing or notary seal given to all bad marital bargains. And since the child is the sanction for the parents' neurotic division of labor, they cannot help but blame him when they begin to suffer from it. Furthermore, as the suffering increases, this sanction tends more and more to be the only force holding them to it. The husband's ambition and the wife's domesticity originally promised their own rewards and did not need to be buttressed by thoughts of the child's future—just as a voluntary and mutually profitable deal between two businessmen does not initially require a written contract. But such a contract binds them if there is a change of heart, at which point one of them might say, "if it weren't for the contract I wouldn't go on with this." Similarly, as ambition and domesticity fail to bring happiness to husband and wife, respectively, both begin to say, "if it weren't for the children I might chuck this and do something more interesting (enjoyable, fulfilling, exciting, relaxing)." One can admit wanting to tear up a contract, however, and one cannot admit wanting to tear up a child. Nor is it easy for the parents to admit their initial error (if indeed they can even comprehend it). This means that the child is not only a scapegoat but a scapegoat that cannot be attacked. The result is a free-floating resentment with a vague tropism toward youth—a resentment with roots in the parents' discontent with their own lives. This condition would seem ideally suited to produce anger toward young people who show tendencies to live (a) differently and (b) more pleasurably than did the parental generation. In the fantasies of adults, at least, there is a very large group of young people—especially those rather sloppily designated as "hippies"—who do both. It is perhaps for this reason that hippies rouse such extravagant rage in their elders.

This is not to say that the parents do not in fact make sacrifices for their children—in a child-oriented society like ours such sacrifices are very considerable. I am trying to explain why these sacrifices are resented. Parents in many societies make severe sacrifices for their children which never cause any hostile reaction later on, largely because the sacrifices "pay off" in some way, or lead to some predictable outcome. In our society parents never know exactly what their sacrifices will lead to, although they have many fantasies about it.

In the recent past, for example, and in working-class families today, parents sacrificed in order to prepare their children to be economically and socially better off than the parents were, and often hated them for fulfilling this goal and leaving the parents behind. Now middle-class parents sacrifice in order to prepare their children to be emotionally better off—more loving, expressive, creative, co-operative, honest[18]—and once again, resent being outdistanced. In both cases the parents feel left out of the triumphs they made possible; and the children feel ashamed of the parents who wanted them to be superior. The parents want their fantasies of vicarious success fulfilled, but never seem to recognize that both kinds of success involve a change to a new milieu from which the parents are automatically excluded. The earlier group of parents wanted their children to become rich and respectable and still remain somehow part of the working-class milieu. The latter group want their children to be more cultured, less money-grubbing, more spontaneous and creative, yet still somehow willing to remain on the same treadmill with the parents.

SEX AND THE GENERATION GAP

The most striking phenomenon in the current conflict between the generations is that each generation, in different ways, attempts to disallow the sexuality of the other. Many societies attempt to restrict sexual behavior in the young—our society is peculiar only in that it does so in the context of simultaneously maximizing their sexual significance. At the same time, the sexuality of those to whom sexuality is freely allowed is severely de-emphasized. As noted earlier, there is a severe dissociation between sexual availability and sexual interest in the norms of the society. The fact that the young no longer adhere to these sexual norms arouses an anger in their elders which probably owes something to the stylistic desexualization which the elders themselves must undergo in our society. Within the nuclear family itself, after all, the older generation holds an almost universal sexual monopoly (this is what the incest taboo means), but in American society this sexuality is masked. Portrayals of the middle-aged in films and television have traditionally catered to the preoccupations of latency-age school children, who cannot imagine their parents having sexual intercourse. This reached some sort of zenith in a recent film on intermarriage (*Guess Who's Coming for Dinner*) in which the tradeoff for accepting interracial sexuality

[18]See Melvin L. Kohn, "Social Class and Parental Values," *American Journal of Sociology*, 64 (1959): 337–51, for a study of the different child-rearing aspirations of middle-class and working-class families. The latter seek obedience, neatness, and cleanliness, while middle-class parents seem to take these for granted and seek internal qualities such as curiosity, self-control, and happiness.

(highly muted) was the fantasy that sexual interest disappears around the age of fifty or sixty anyway. When sexuality in the middle-aged or elderly does occur it is always in a comic context (e.g., *The Producers*).

Parents contribute to this process by denying their own sexuality to their children. In many societies and subcultures children are as aware that their parents copulate as that they eat, and children imitate the act of love long before they are competent to perform it. But in our society parental sexuality is hidden. The reason for this is that while in these more candid societies parental socialization is broad, shallow, and multifunctional, in our society, at least in the middle class, the family is first and foremost an institution for teaching emotional control. Researchers have found that corporation executives are more reluctant to reveal indecision and doubt to their subordinates than any other characteristic—their primary function is, after all, to make decisions. Similarly, parents are more reluctant to reveal sexual impulses to their children than any other characteristic, because their primary function is to control such impulses. It is certainly not simply a matter of the incest taboo, since primitive societies in which parents make little effort to hide their sexuality from their children often have an even more profound horror of incest than does our own.

The importance of the norm becomes clear when it is violated. Young people who are very comfortable with their own sexuality display great uneasiness when confronted with that of their parents or their parents' generation, and Thomas Cottle has shown dramatically the disruptive psychological impact that parental sexual confidences have upon the children.[19] Yet although I agree with Cottle's main point that destruction of the asymmetry of parent-child relationships is pathogenic, I suspect that these sexual revelations are particularly disorienting in our society, in which the parent-child relationship is emotionally overloaded even without them. There are many societies in which revelation of the parents' sexuality as such (that is, without the role reversal of which Cottle speaks) would no more constitute an abandonment of asymmetry than revelation of the parent eating or sleeping or defecating.

One would imagine that in a society like ours, in which parental sexuality is surrounded with so much anxiety and mystery, children

[19]Thomas Cottle, "Parent and Child—The Hazards of Equality," *Saturday Review* (February 1, 1969), pp. 16 ff.

would grow up beset with negative sexual attitudes. Yet today's youth appear strikingly liberated from the repressive sexual norms of their parents—not only have they ignored them behaviorally (as their parents often did, albeit clandestinely) but also attitudinally, and apparently without residual guilt. How did this arise? How could such a marked change occur in so short a time and leave so few traces? Changes in sexual mores have been very frequent in Western history, but it usually takes a few generations both to establish and to dissolve a given type of prudery. However hypocritical the parental generation may seem, they obviously feel strongly about the norms themselves and are infuriated by the open and casual manner in which their children disregard them. Given these strong feelings and the degree of internalization of parental values that typifies middle-class socialization, we would expect the children to be just a little defensive, at least in relation to their parents. Yet this does not seem to be the case. It is possible that sexual problems such as impotence and frigidity may be on the increase and that these are guilt-induced, but there are no sound data on which such a statement can be based. Nor does the existence of an ideology of sexual freedom account for the lack of irrational guilt: the two have coexisted for some time.

Yet I think ideology provides the answer to the question, in a rather oblique way. The younger generation has rid itself of its parents' sexual guilt by displacing it into other spheres. Although they violate their parents' sexual norms with relatively little discomfort, one of the striking characteristics of contemporary youth is a kind of diffuse moral absolutism. It is as if every act must have not merely a practical or pleasurable but also a moral foundation. The puritanism of youth displays itself in an inability to act without ideological justification. Every act becomes a moral act. It is this that both requires and enables them to confide in their parents about concerns the initial premises of which the parents reject.

What today's youth seem incapable of is amoral defiance. They cannot assume the responsibility of committing an act that they define as immoral but too pleasurable to forego. The only way this is possible is to make an ideological issue out of it ("it's good for people to get back into their bodies" or "you have to do what you want to do"). They spend a great deal of time trying not to "cop out" in a society whose corruption generates moral dilemmas that compel a hundred cop-outs a day even for the most obsessionally pure radical. And all of this, of course, makes them extremely vulnerable to moral contamination: when confronted with situations in which they took the easy way out, they are unusually demoralized. The radicalism of contemporary youth thus derives its emotional energy from guilt more than anger. One reason (there are many others, some quite practical) why compromising liberals are so despised and extreme conservatives sometimes respected is that the greater moral absolutism of the latter, no matter how antithetical in content, strikes a sympathetic chord.

I have suggested that these characteristics, along with parental desexualization and the intensified child-rearing process, all derive from the emphasis the American middle-class family places on the regulation of emotion—in particular, sexual impulses. Why is this function so important? Why is there so much preoccupation in America with sexual stimulation and with the control of sexual gratification?

.9. *The New History*

ROBERT J. LIFTON

THERE ARE psychological and historical stirrings of a revolutionary
nature throughout the world, especially (but by no means exclusively)
among the young. They are influenced by, but at the same time independent of, the Maoist visions. Indeed they can be understood as part
of a vast effort to bring about what we may term a New History.

What is a New History? And why do the young seek one? Let me
define a New History as a radical and widely shared re-creation of the
forms of human culture—biological, experiential, institutional, technological, aesthetic, and interpretative. The newness of these cultural
forms derives not from their spontaneous generation but from extension and transformations of existing psychic and physical components,
that is, from previously unknown or inadequately known combinations. A New History, then, is both an extension and a resetting of
boundaries.

The shapers of a New History can be political revolutionaries, revolutionary thinkers, extreme holocausts, or techological breakthroughs. These and the great events surrounding them, in different
ways, cause, reflect, and symbolize historical shifts. I have suggested
elsewhere that the combination of Nazi genocide and American
atomic bombings of Hiroshima and Nagasaki terminated man's sense
of limits concerning his self-destructive potential, and thereby inau-
gurated an era in which he is devoid of assurance of living on eternally
as a species. It has taken almost twenty-five years for beginning formulations of the significance of these events to emerge—formulations
which cannot be separated from the technological developments of

the same quarter century, or from the increasing sense of the universal world-society that has accompanied them.

Our own New History, then, is built upon the ultimate paradox of two competing and closely related images: that of technologically induced historical extinction, and that of man's increasingly profound awareness of himself as a single species. It may be more correct to say that this is just one image, extraordinarily divided.

I think we should take seriously the assertion by the young framers of the celebrated 1962 Port Huron Statement of the Students for a Democratic Society, still something of a manifesto for the American New Left, that: "Our work is guided by the sense that we may be the last generation in the experiment with living." What I wish to stress is the overriding significance for every post-Hiroshima generation of precisely this threat of historical extinction. The end of the next era becomes associated, psychologically speaking, with the end of everything. And even those who deny any special concern with this threat share in the general undercurrent of death anxiety.

This anxiety becomes closely associated with other symbolic impairments of our time, with the confusions of the knowledge revolution and the unprecedented dissemination of half-knowledge through media whose psychological impact has barely begun to be discerned.

There is a very real sense in which the world itself has become a 'total environment,' a closed psychic chamber with continuous reverberations bouncing about chaotically and dangerously. The symbolic death perceived, then, is this combination of formlessness and totality, of the inadequacy of existing forms and imprisonment within them. The boundaries of the environment are felt to be in one sense absolute, in another nonexistent. And the young are exquisitely sensitive to this kind of 'historical death,' whatever their capacity for resisting an awareness of the biological kind. They are struck by the fact that most of mankind simply goes about its business, as if these extreme dislocations did not exist—as if there were no such thing as ultimate technological violence or existence rendered absurd. The war in Vietnam did not create these murderous incongruities, but it does exemplify them, and it consumes American youth in them. No wonder, then, that, in their symbolic questions, or (to use Cassirer's phrase), in their "conversations with themselves," the young everywhere ask: "How can we bring the world—and ourselves—back to life?"

Students of revolution and rebellion have recognized the close relationship of both to death symbolism, and to visions of transcending death by achieving an eternal historical imprint. Hannah Arendt speaks of revolution as containing an "all-pervasive preoccupation with permanence, with a 'perpetual state . . . for . . . posterity.' " And Albert Camus describes insurrection, "in its exalted and tragic forms," as "a prolonged protest against death, a violent accusation against the universal death penalty," and as "the desire for immortality." But Camus also stresses the rebel's "appeal to the essence of being," his quest "not . . . for life, but for reasons for living." And this brings us to an all-important question concerning mental participation in revolution: what is the place of ideology, and of images and ideas, and of the self in relationship to all three?

Most of the revolutionary ideologies of the past have been notable in providing elaborate blueprints for individual and collective immortality, specifications of ultimate cause and ultimate effect, theological in tone and scientific in claim. For present-day revolutionaries to reject these Cartesian litanies is to take seriously some of the important psychological and historical insights of the last few decades. For they are rejecting an oppressive ideological totalism—with its demand for control of all communication in a milieu, its imposed guilt and cult of purity and confession, its loading of the language, its principles of doctrine over person and even of the dispensing of existence itself (in the sense that sharp lines are drawn between those whose right to exist can be recognized and those who possess no such right). This rejection, at its best, represents a quest by the young for a new kind of revolution—one perhaps no less enduring in historical impact, but devoid of the claim to omniscience, and of the catastrophic chain of human manipulations stemming from that claim. In other words, the young resist the suffocating personal boundaries imposed by earlier revolutions.

It is of course possible that their anti-ideological stance could turn out to be a transitory phenomenon, a version of the euphoric denial of dogma that so frequently appears during the early moments of revolution, only to be overwhelmed by absolutist doctrine and suffocating organization in the name of revolutionary discipline. Yet there is reason for believing that the present antipathy to total ideology is something more, that it is an expression of a powerful and highly appropriate contemporary style. The shift we are witnessing from fixed and total forms of ideology to more fluid *ideological fragments* represents, to a considerable degree, the emergence of contemporary or Protean man as rebel. It is an effort to remain open, while in rebellion, to the extraordinarily rich, confusing, liberating, and threatening array of contemporary historical possibilities—and to retain, in the process, a continuing capacity for shape-shifting.

The fluidity of the Protean style greatly enhances tactical leverage. For instance, Daniel Cohn-Bendit, the leader of the French student uprisings of May 1968, in an interesting dialogue with Jean-Paul Sartre, insisted that the classical Marxist-Leninist principle of the omniscient revolutionary vanguard (the working class as represented by the Communist party) be replaced with "a much simpler and more honourable one, the theory of an active minority, acting you might say as a permanent ferment, pushing forward without trying to control events." He went on to characterize this process as "uncontrollable spontaneity." In the same spirit are the warnings of Tom Hayden, a key figure in the American New Left, to his SDS colleagues and followers, against what he calls "fixed leaders," and his insistence upon "participatory democracy" as well as upon ideology of a kind that is secondary to, and largely achieved through, revolutionary action. So widespread has this approach been that the American New Left has been characterized as more a process than a program.

I would suggest that the general principle of "uncontrollable spontaneity" represents a meeting ground between tactic and deeper psychological inclination. The underlying inclination consists precisely of the Protean style of multiple identifications, shifting beliefs, and constant search for new combinations that extend both individual-psychological and political boundaries. Whatever its pitfalls, this style of revolutionary behavior is an attempt to mobilize twentieth-century fluidity as a weapon against two kinds of stagnation: the old, unresponsive institutions (universities, governments, families), and the newly-emerging but fixed technological visions (people 'programmed' by computers in a 'technotronic society'). The young thus feel hemmed in by boundaries formed both by legacies of the past and visions of the future.

Throughout the world, the young seek active involvement in the institutional decisions governing their lives, new paths of significance as alternatives to consuming and being consumed, and liberating rhythms of individual and (especially) community existence. Non-specific and ephemeral as these goals may seem, they are early expressions of a quest for historical rebirth, for re-attachment to the Great Chain of Being, for reassertion of a viable sense of immortality.

The French example is again revealing in its extraordinary flowering of graffiti. Here one must take note of the prominence of the genre—of the informal slogan-on-the wall virtually replacing formal revolutionary doctrine—no less than the content. But one is struck by the stress of many of the slogans, sometimes to the point of intentional absurdity, upon enlarging the individual life space, on saying yes to more and no to less. Characteristic were such slogans as "Think of your desires as realities," "Prohibiting is forbidden," "Imagination in power," and "Imagination is revolution." Sartre made an apt comment upon both the graffiti and the young revolutionaries themselves when he said, "I would like to describe what you have done as extending the field of possibilities."

Precisely such extending of the field of possibilities is at the heart of the world-wide youth rebellion, for hippies no less than political radicals—and at the heart of the Protean insistence upon continuous psychic re-creation of the self. Around this image of unlimited extension and perpetual recreation, as projected into a dimly imagined future, the young seek to create a new mode of *revolutionary* immorality.

Of enormous importance for these rebellions is another basic component of the Protean style, the spirit of mockery. While young rebels are by no means immune from the most pedantic and humorless discourse, they come alive to others and themselves only when giving way to—or seizing upon—their very strong inclination toward mockery. The mocking political rebel merges with the hippie and with a variety of exponents of pop culture to 'put on'—that is, mislead or deceive by means of some form of mockery or absurdity—his uncomprehending cohorts, his elders, or anyone in authority. (Despite important differences, there has always been a fundamental unity in the rebellions of hippies and young radicals, which is perhaps just now becoming fully manifest.) In dress, hair, and general social and sexual style, the mocking rebel is not only "extending the field of possibilities," but making telling commentary—teasing, ironic, contemptuous—on the absurd folkways of 'the others.' The mockery can be gentle and even loving, or it can be bitter and provocative in the extreme.

One thinks of the widely publicized slogan of the Columbia uprising: "Up against the wall, motherfucker!" with its complex relationships to blacks and whites, to police and their antagonists, and to the principle of authority in general. The bandying about of the phrase was a way of playing with, and mocking, an image of ultimate violation and of retribution for that violation.

The tone of mockery can be a source of great unifying power. At its more affirmative border are such slogans of the French students as: "We are all undesirables!" or the much more powerful "We are all German Jews!" The slogans refer directly to the origins of Cohn-Bendit, the student leader, but their significance extends much further. They mock not only anti-Semitism and national-racial chauvinism, but the overall process of victimization itself, and the 'old history' for harboring such victimization. At this affirmative border of mockery, then, and at the far reaches of Protean style, is a call for man to cease his folly in dividing himself into pseudo-species and to respond to the ethical and technological mandate to see himself as the single species he is.

Mockery thus breaks down the false boundaries imposed by victimization, and encourages every variety of odd combination. One can observe a related if much more confusing impulse toward inclusiveness in the diversity of ideological fragments young rebels embrace. Thus hippies, for their experiments with the self, draw upon Eastern and Western mysticism, chemically induced ecstasy, and various traditions, new and old, of polymorphous sexuality. Young radicals may incorporate any of these aspects of hippie culture, and combine them with ideas and images drawn from many different revolutionary experiences (pre-Marxist utopians, anarchists, Marx, Trotsky, Lenin, Rosa Luxemburg, Mao, Castro, Guevara, Debray, Ho, Gandhi, Fanon, Malcolm X, Martin Luther King, Stokely Carmichael, and H. Rap Brown); from recent psychological and social theorists (Sartre, Camus, C. Wright Mills, Herbert Marcuse, Norman Brown, Erik Erikson, Abraham Maslow, and Paul Goodman); and from just about any kind of evolving cultural style (derived from jazz or black power or 'soul,' from the small-group movement and the Esalen-type stress upon joy, or from camp-mockery of Victorian or other retrospectively amusing periods), including all of the revolutionary and intellectual traditions just mentioned.

The overall process can be seen as a revolutionary equivalent to the artist's inclination to borrow freely, selectively, impressionistically, and distortingly from contemporaries as a means of finding his own way. To dismiss all of this as a 'style revolution,' as some have, is to miss the point—unless one is aware of the sense in which style is everything. One does better to speak of a 'revolution of forms,' of a quest for images of rebirth which reassert connectedness, and as a 'process revolution' consistent with the principles of action painting and kinetic sculpture, in which active rebelling both expresses and creates the basic images of rebellion. The novelist Donald Barthelme's statement, "Fragments are the only form I trust," has ramifications far beyond the literary. However severe the problems posed by such a principle for social and especially political revolutions, we deceive ourselves unless we learn to focus upon these shifting forms—in styles of life as well as in relations to institutions and ideas. Indeed we require a little revolutionizing of our psychological assumptions, so that both the young and the old can be understood, not as bound by static behavioral categories, but as in continuous historical motion.

There has been much discussion about young rebels' selection of the university as a primary target for recent upheavals. Many distinguished commentators have cautioned students about the dangers of confusing the vulnerable centers of learning they attack, and for periods of time 'bring down,' with society at large. Stephen Spender put the matter eloquently when he said that "However much the university needs a revolution, and the society needs a revolution, it would be disastrous . . . not to keep the two revolutions apart." He went on to point out, as have others also, that the university is "an arsenal from which [student-rebels] can draw the arms from which they can change society;" and that "To say, 'I won't have a university until society has a revolution,' is as though Karl Marx were to say 'I won't go to the reading room of the British Museum until it has a revolution.' " Yet wise as these cautionary thoughts undoubtedly are, one also has to consider the ways in which the university's special symbolic significance makes it all too logical (if at times unfortunate) a target for would-be revolutionaries.

For the university is unique as a formative area. It is the place where the prevailing concepts of a society are simultaneously and with varying weightings presented, imposed, examined and criticized— where intellectual and ethical boundaries are examined and either narrowed or extended, but in any case redefined. The university is indeed a training ground for available occupational slots in society, as young rebels are quick to point out, and can, at its worst, approach a technical instrument in the hands of the military-industrial complex. But it can also be precisely the opposite, a training ground for undermining social institutions, as the young rebels themselves attest to by the extent to which they are campus products.

In most cases, the university is a great many things in between. It provides for students four years of crucial personal transition, a *rite de passage* from relatively unformed adolescence to a relatively formed adulthood. And the fact that many are likely to move through continuing Protean explorations during the post-university years renders especially important whatever initial adult formation the university makes possible. For these reasons, and because students and teachers are *there*, the university is the best place for the rebellious young to confront their ostensible mentors—their 'formative fathers'—and thereby both define themselves and make a statement about society at large. The statement they make has to do not only with social inequities and outmoded institutions but with the general historical dislocations of everyone. And in this sense the target of the young is not so much the university, or the older generation, as the continuing commitment of both to the discredited past.

Now, one can hardly speak of definitive conclusions about something just beginning. Nor would I claim a position of omniscient detachment from the events of the New History—I have in no way been immune from the complex combinations of feelings about them known to my generation of Left intellectuals. But having earlier in this talk affirmed the significance of the New History, I wish now to suggest some of its pitfalls, and then, finally, some of our present-day potentialities for avoiding these pitfalls.

From the standpoint of the young, these pitfalls are related to what is best called 'romantic totalism.' I refer here to a post-Cartesian absolutism, to a new quest for old feelings. Its controlling image, at whatever level of consciousness, is that of *replacing history with experience*.

This is, to a considerable extent, the romanticism of the 'youth movement.' I have heard a number of thoughtful European-born intellectuals tell, with some anxiety, how the tone and atmosphere now emanating from young American rebels is reminiscent of that of the German youth movement of the late Weimar Republic (and the Hitler Youth into which it was so readily converted). What they find common to both is a cult of feeling and a disdain for restraint and reason. While I would emphasize the differences between the two groups much more than any similarities, there is a current in contemporary youth movements that is more Nietzschean than Marxist-Leninist. It consists of a stress upon what I call experiential transcendence, upon the cultivation of states of feelings so intense and so absorbing that time and death cease to exist. (Drugs are of great importance here but as part of a general quest.) The pattern becomes totalistic when it begins to tamper with history to the extent of victimizing opponents in order to reinforce these feelings; and a danger signal is the absolute denial of the principle of historical continuity.

The replacement of history with experience—with totally liberated feeling—is by no means a new idea and has long found expression in · classical forms of mysticism and ecstasy. But it has reappeared with considerable force in the present-day drug revolution, and in the writings of a number of articulate spokesmen, such as Norman O. Brown. This increasing stress upon experiential forms of transcendence would seem to be related to the impairment of alternative modes of symbolic immortality. That is, the undermining of biological, cultural, and theological modes of immortality by both the speed of historical change, and by the threat posed by nuclear and other weapons, profoundly intensifies man's anxiety about both his death and his manner of life. One response to this anxiety, and to the quest for new forms, is the unique contemporary blending of experiential transcendence—in which boundaries of the self are felt to be eliminated—with social and political revolution.

At times entire historical traditions can be condemned or negated, largely by calling into play a single judgmental criterion: What feels revolutionary is good, what does not is counter-revolutionary. A related equally romantic pitfall is that of 'generational totalism.' The problem is not so much the slogan "Don't trust anybody over thirty," as the unconscious assumption that can be behind it: that youth power knows no limits because youth equals immortality. That is, an assumption that youth and only youth has access to boundarylessness. Conversely, members of older generations can, just as totalistically, view every innovative action of the young as destructive or 'deadly.' Indeed, the larger significance and greatest potential danger of what we call the 'generation gap' reside in differing solutions to these questions of broken historical connection and impaired sense of immortality.

The recent slogan of French students, "The young make love, the old make obscene gestures" is patronizing rather than totalistic, and its mocking blend of truth and absurdity permits a chuckle all around. But when the same students refer to older critics as "people who do not exist," or when young American radicals label everyone and everything either "relevant" ("revolutionary") or "irrelevant" ("counter-revolutionary") on the basis of whether or not the person, idea, or event is consistent or inconsistent with their own point of view—then we are dealing with something more potentially malignant. We approach the totalistic tendency I referred to before as the dispensing of existence, the drawing of a sharp line between people and non-people.

A related form of image-focused totalism is the all-encompassing concept of the 'Establishment.' Taken over from British rebels, it has come to mean everything from the American (or Russian, or just about any other) political or bureaucratic leadership, to businessmen large and small, university administrators and teachers of all colorings, and including even many of the student and youth leaders who are themselves very much at odds with people in the other categories. And just as Establishment becomes a devil-image, so do other terms—such as (in different ways) 'confrontation' and 'youth'—become god-images. At issue here is the degree to which a particular image is given a transcendent status, and is then uncritically applied to the most complex situations, in a way that makes it the start and finish of any ethical judgment or conceptual analysis.

This image-focused totalism can enter into the ultimate romanticization, that of death and immortality. While the *sense* of immortality, of unending historical continuity, is central to ordinary psychological experience, romantic totalism tends to *confuse death with immortality*, and even to equate them. And behind this confusion lurks the romantic temptation to court death in the service of immortality, to view dying and in some cases even killing as the only true avenues to immortality.

The great majority of today's radical young embrace no such imagery—they are in fact intent upon exploring the furthest outreach of the life process. But they can at times be prone to a glorification of life and death stances, so that all-or-none 'revolutionary tactics' can be applied to petty disputes, hardly worthy of these cosmic images. In such situations, their sense of mockery, especially self-mockery, deserts them, and at considerable cost.

Despite several paradoxes surrounding the romantic totalism of Mao Tse-tung and his conduct of the Chinese Cultural Revolution, Mao has nonetheless had great appeal for many young rebels throughout the world, especially because of his anti-institutional impulse.

But young rebels who embrace from afar Mao's stress on "permanent revolution" may too easily overlook the consequences of his recent programs: irreparable national dissension, convoluted and

meaningless forms of violence, and extreme confusion and disillusionment among Chinese youth (as well as their elders), perhaps especially among those who initially responded most enthusiastically to
the call for national transformation. Nor are young rebels in the West
aware of the extent to which the Maoist vision has had to be modified
and in some ways abandoned in response to the deep-seated opposition it encountered throughout China.

Intrinsic to Mao's romantic totalism is the pattern I regard as
psychism—the confusion between mind and its material products,
the attempt to control the external world and achieve strongly desired technological goals by means of intrapsychic exercises and
assertions of revolutionary will. Now, the radical young in more
affluent societies have a different relationship to technology; rather
than desperately seeking technology, they feel trapped and suffo-
cated by it (though they live in it, use much of it easily, and also feel
some of its attraction). But they too can succumb to a similar kind of
confusion, which in their case takes the form of mistaking a rewarding inner sense of group solidarity with mastery of the larger human
and technological world 'outside.' The recent Maoist experience
can find its counterpart in a sequence of experiences of young
rebels in the West: deep inner satisfaction accompanying bold
collective action, disillusionment at the limited effects achieved, and
more reckless and ineffective action with even greater group solidarity. This is not to say that all or most behavior of young rebels falls
into this category—to the contrary, their political confrontations
have achieved a number of striking successes largely because they
were *not* merely assertions of will but could also mobilize a wide
radius of opposition to outmoded and destructive academic and national policies. Yet the enormous impact of high technology in the
post-modern world, and the universal tendency to surround it with
vast impersonal organizations, present an ever increasing temptation to transcend the whole system (or 'bag') by means of romantic
worship of the will as such, and especially the revolutionary will.

For many young rebels, Mao and Maoism are perceived less as
demarcated historical person and program than as a constellation of
heroic, and above all anti-bureaucratic, revolutionary images. The
problem for these young rebels is to recover the historical Mao in
all of his complexity—which means understanding his tragic transition from great revolutionary leader to despot. To come to terms with
their own Maoism they must sort out the various elements of the
original—on the one hand its call for continuous militant action on

behalf of the deprived and its opposition to stagnant institutions, exhilarating principles which are consistent with evolving forms of the New History; on the other, its apocalyptic totalism, psychism, and desperate rear-guard assault upon the openness—upon the expanding psychological boundaries—of contemporary man.

Yet precisely their Protean capacities may help the young to avoid definite commitments to these self-defeating patterns. They need not be bound by the excesses of either Cartesian rationalism or the contemporary cult of experience which feeds romantic totalism. Today's young have available for their formulations of self and world the great twentieth-century insights which liberate men from the senseless exclusions of the experiential-versus-rational bind. These insights can expand the boundaries of man's thought and his feelings in their varied combinations. I refer to the principles of symbolic thought, as expressed in the work of such people as Cassirer and Langer, and of Freud and Erikson. Of course, one can never know the exact effect of great insights upon the historical process, but it is quite possible that, with the decline of the total ideologies of the old history, ideas as such will become more important than ever in the shaping of the new. Having available an unprecedented variety of ideas and images, the young are likely to attempt more than did previous generations and perhaps make more mistakes, but also to show greater capacity to extricate themselves from a particular course and revise tactics, beliefs, and styles—all in the service of contributing to embryonic social forms.

What about the 'older generation,' those middle-aged Left intellectuals I referred to before? For them (us), the problem is a little different. It entails a struggle to retain (or achieve) Protean openness to the possibilities latent in the New History and to respond to that noble slogan of the French students, "Imagination in power." But at the same time, this generation does well to be its age, to call upon the experience specific to the lives of those who comprise it. It must tread the tenuous path of neither feeding upon its formative sons nor rejecting their capacity for innovative historical imagination. This is much more difficult than it may seem, because it requires those now in their forties and fifties to come to terms with the extremely painful history they have known, neither to deny that history nor to be blindly bound by it. Yet, however they may feel shunted aside by the young, there is special need for their own more seasoned, if now historically vulnerable, imaginations.

For both the intellectual young and old—together with society at large—are threatened by a violent, counter-reaction to the New History, by a restorationist impulse often centered in the lower middle classes, but not confined to any class or country. This impulse includes an urge to eliminate troublesome young rebels, along with their liberal-radical 'fathers,' and to return to a mythical past in which all was harmonious and no such disturbance of the historical peace existed. What is too often forgotten by the educated of all ages, preoccupied as they are with their own dislocations, is the extent to which such dislocations in others produce the very opposite kind of ideological inclination—in this case, a compensatory, strongly anti-Protean embrace of the simple 'purities' and absolutized boundaries of 'law and oder,' rampant militarism, narrow nationalism, and personal rectitude.

If man is successful in creating the New History he must create if he is to have any history at all, then the formative fathers and sons I have spoken of must pool their resources and succeed together. Should this not happen, the failure too will be shared, whether in the form of stagnation and suffering or of shared annihilation. Like most other things in our world, the issue remains open. There is nothing absolute or inevitable about the New History and its challenge to life boundaries, except perhaps the need to bring it into being.

.10. THE GENERATION GAP: A Review and Typology of Social-Psychological Perspectives

VERN L. BENGTSON

OF THOSE phenomena on which social scientists gather data and write analyses, there are few of more popular relevance today than discussions of the "generation gap." It is of course true that the problem of generations is one of the older issues in modern sociology; despite this, very few thorough studies have yet been made to illuminate the nature and extent of continuity or differences between age groups today. Even more importantly, there have been no empirical attempts to analyse the effect on social structure of such differences between generations. Indeed, all too often the discussion of such issues has been impressionistic, speculative, and even apocalyptic—not only in the popular press, but also in the pages of scholarly books and journals.

The purpose of this paper is to review some classical and some contemporary approaches to the problem of generations, and to order these perspectives in a typology reflecting some underlying dimensions of the social-psychological investigation of generations.

The term generation gap should be read as in quotation marks throughout this paper; for the phenomenon to which it refers is undoubtedly neither strictly generational nor is it a gap, using any reasonable definition of those terms. Be that as it may, the term has worldwide usage and a sort of connotative reality. The man on the

SOURCE: "The Generation Gap: A Review and Typology of Social-Psychological Perspectives" by Vern L. Bengtson is reprinted from *Youth and Society*, Volume 2, number 1 (September 1970), pp. 7–32, by permission of the publisher, Sage Publications, Inc.

street knows, in his own way, what the generation gap refers to, and social scientists have, rightly or wrongly, followed his lead in using the term.

THE GENERATION GAP AND MASS CULTURE TODAY

A fruitful way to begin this analysis is through a brief survey of the evidence of generational differences as portrayed in such everyday chronicles as the mass media and political rhetoric. For in the characterization of social movements and the identification of social problems, mass culture often antecedes social scientists by several years.

The message from the media is that differences between age groups are becoming a serious social problem, not only in America but in most Western industrialized countries (see Neugarten, 1970). Concern over the youth problem turns very often into outright hostility; and discrimination against the aged, more subtle but no less pervasive (see Butler, 1969), has serious implications in nations where increasingly longevity swells the ranks of the aged. One might say that *age-ism* has become a common theme in mass culture today, just as racism finally became acknowledged a decade ago in American society. Defined as prejudice by members of one age group against another age group (s), age-ism implies stereotyping, interpersonal distance, and often, conflict of interest. It describes the subjective experience implied in the popular definition of the generation gap (Butler, 1969; Neugarten, 1970).

Evidence of age-ism is found in almost any newspaper or mass distribution magazine picked at random during the past few months or years. For example, in one three-day period in the spring of 1970, the *Los Angeles Times* printed a variety of news items, editorials, and cartoons—and several advertisements—that portrayed relations between generations as cause for serious concern. One article explored the international ties of student protest movements; another reported the "get tough" reactions of several public officials toward campus demonstrations. A feature reporting the rapidly expanding commune movement and hippie subculture was presented on the same page as a brief article reporting on increasing drug arrests in an affluent suburb of Los Angeles. On the editorial page, a syndicated columnist described the immorality of student demonstrations, while the editorial urged that taxpayers not take out their grievances against student demonstrators at the polls by voting down school bond elections. One cartoon showed the President making a clumsy attempt to "rap" with youthful constituents, while another portrayed student protestors riding roughshod over Law, Order, and Justice. On the front page was a report of working class men assaulting student protesters; it was continued on an inside page next to a large advertisment suggesting that the purchase of a Mustang would "bridge the generation gap." Thus, in many ways, some humorous but most pensive, the mass-distribution newspaper reports substantial differences between youth and the mature generation today. The implication of most of this portrayal is that these differences lead to social disorganization: the nation is "coming apart at the seams" and an elite group of youth is doing most of the tearing.

Or to take another example, the alleged disorganization of the family by intergenerational tension is reflected in the titles of articles in American mass-distribution magazines between 1968 and 1970. *Life* discusses "The Gulf Between Parents and their Kids (Wider than Ever Before);" *Look* analyzes "The Way Between Mother and Daughter;" *Saturday Review* wonders "What Are Our Young People Telling Us?" while the *Ladies Home Journal* suggests, somewhat tentatively, that "We Can Close the Generation Gap—IF."

A third example of generational relations as seen in popular culture is in the political arena. Not only has the gap become a political issue, it has been elevated to the level of a national problem. In one of his first addresses to the nation following his election in 1968, President Nixon characterized differences between youth and adults in our society as "a yawning gulf . . . between the two halves of our people, a great divide and misunderstanding that weakens our body politic" (Dougherty, 1968). He proposed and later implemented a National Youth Agency to "bring us together again in this area." Since then, the charge of discrimination against youth, or at least youthful protesters, has been leveled against the administration with growing fury. In the California gubernatorial election of 1970, an important campaign issue was the warning of Governor Reagan that "there will be a bloodbath on our campuses" if protesters do not subside (*Los Angeles Times*, 1970). In the spring of 1970 thousands of campuses across the nation responded, in one way or another, to the deployment of U.S. troops in Cambodia, protesting not only on moral grounds but on the basis of discrimination against youth. The violence that has ensued is literally without precedent in American history; and the traditional political ploy of "nothing but the best for our kids" has become unpopular. As the *Wall Street Journal* (1969) editorialized:

Many middle-aged Americans are likely to feel that youth rebels not because it feels deep grievances, but because it has never felt any. What troubles the older generation is the nagging thought that this ill-mannered rebellion is reward not for its failures but for its success.

From the evidence available in the mass media, then, differences between age groups today are seen as an extensive social problem in contemporary society. Relations between the generations are seen as tenuous and often outright hostile. And the result of the differences and tensions between the generations is seen as an alarming disruption of present social organization.

When one turns to an analysis of the earlier sociological formulations of the problem of generations, however, an entirely different perspective is seen. In a tradition of research that was for the most part ignored in the United States, European sociologists made analyses of the cycle of generations to account for the inevitable ebb and flow of historical events.

CLASSICAL SOCIOLOGY AND THE PROBLEM OF GENERATIONS

Concern with discontinuity between generations dates as far back as recorded history goes (see Feuer, 1969, for an excellent review). Egyptian and Hebrew sages defined wisdom in terms that implied dire consequences for youth who forsook the way of their elders. The Maxims of Ptahhotep—the first document on ethics of which there is record—was, as Feuer notes, already concerned with the problem of generations. Plato and Aristotle incorporated generational struggle in their theories of political change. Aristotle suggested the cause of political struggle could be found in the conflict of fathers and sons.

In the late nineteenth century, Continental social historians—for the most part, followers of Hegel—began to systematically explore generations as a dimension of social organization and political change. As summarized by Mannheim (1952), Heberle (1951), and Marias (1968), the thesis they attempted to document was that the rhythm of changes in ideas and political institutions is associated with the emergence of new biological generations.

As Mannheim describes it, the goal of these early sociologists was to deal with the problem of social time to account for change in the nature of the social fabric from period to period. He contrasted the "positivist" with the "romantic-metaphysical" definition of generations—a distinction which is still useful when applied to current perspectives of generations. The early positivist school tied the movement of history to the fact that persons growing up in an identifiable span of time, came of age under basically the same set of social events —wars, economic conditions, political movements. A new generation, arising with predictable regularity every twenty-five to thirty years, produces an identifiable historical era and serves as a link in the chain of progress. By contrast, the romanticists defined generations, not in terms of time span, but in terms of common sharing of experiences of a purely qualitative sort. A generation is defined by the shared *geist* of an era which colors all its products and is in a sense, independent of historical time. Thus the classical period in art lasted for three calendar generations, while the expressionism of the late nineteenth century only one; yet both can be seen as a generation of definite perspective in expressing artistic perception. From this viewpoint, then, a generation lasts as long as a single art form or mode of expression prevails.

The problem with both these positions is that they both fail to account for the "noncontemporaneity of the contemporaneous." This was Pinder's (1926) figure of speech referring to the contrasts in outlook that exist between two or three generational cohorts who live together at the same point in time. Mannheim proposes that the concept of generation be used as nothing more than a kind of identity of location in time, embracing related age groups who are embedded in a historical-social process. There is a "trigger action" of social and historical events which determine whether a new generation emerges every year, or every thirty or one hundred years, or whether it emerges at all. Thus during some periods, generations do not appear as social change agents because there has not been a catalyst to produce their consciousness as a generation: that is, a group differentiated from other generations and a unity despite the distinctions that usually occur within any age group (see the excellent discussions by Berger (1960) and Troll (1970) for contemporary perspectives of the Mannheim theme and the problems in generational analysis).

The classical sociological analysis of generations has been most often employed to explain political movements. Mentré (1920),

Heberle (1951), and most recently Feuer (1969) have applied the concept to the rise of national parties and to political revolutions. Heberle suggested the concept of "decisive politically relevant experiences" to explain why succeeding generations may be oriented to interpret the institutions of society in different ways. However, he emphasizes that the entire generation will not have identical objective experiences, and a generation will include many subdivisions (social classes, for example) that create differences within them. Intragenerational divisions are still less pronounced than differences between generations. Such contrasts between generations will be greater in periods of rapid social change, and the longer a generation stays in power politically, the sharper will be the clash with the youngest generation (as in Germany in 1918 when the elderly leaders of old political parties blocked the rise of younger men). Feuer (1969), a contemporary writer in the classical sociological tradition, suggests that the "moral de-authorization of the older generation" is a principal component of revolutionary change based on generational distinctions.

A final position in the classical tradition of sociology is that suggested by Davis (1940) in analyzing "the sociology of parent-youth conflict." Whereas Mannheim, Pinder, and Heberle focus principally on historical and structural conditions producing differences between generations, Davis focuses more on interpersonal and developmental issues. Whereas Mannheim considers conflict between age groups usual but not inevitable, Davis suggests that it is unavoidable, without commenting on the ultimate social gain or loss to be derived from such changes between generations.

For Davis, conflict between generations is the result of three universals in human development, modified by four variables having to do with the modern condition. The three universal factors leading to parent-child conflict are: (1) the basic birth cycle difference between parent and child; (2) the decreasing rate of socialization with the coming of maturity (that is, youth changes rapidly in personal orientations, while their parents change more slowly); and (3) the resulting intrinsic differences between parents and children in the physiological, sociological, and psychosocial planes of behavior.

These factors, according to Davis, may lead to conflict; but whether they do so, and to what degree, depends on the variables of: (1) the rate of social change; (2) the extent of the complexity of the social structure; (3) the degree of integration of the culture; and (4) the velocity of movement within the culture.

A review of the classical sociological analysis of generations, then, reveals many ideas that are relevant to the current social concern about the generation gap. How do these ideas compare with contemporary scholarly analyses of the nature of differences between age groups, and the effect of such differences on the stability and change of the social order? The next section presents a review of current perspectives in the scholarly literature to allow such a comparison.

CURRENT PERSPECTIVES ON GENERATIONAL DIFFERENCES AND SOCIAL CHANGE

In the past few years there has been a renaissance of scholarly interest in the problem of generations. The author has compiled a bibliography of over one hundred references to generational differences, though the number of empirical papers in this list is very small. To attempt to summarize these many orientations is difficult; however, one can posit some underlying issues which form dimensions useful in categorizing the current perspectives.

First, there is the issue of the *extent* of differences between age groups. Is there a very wide gap, a little gap, or none really at all? Is the gap serious and disruptive of the social order, or is it the natural mechanism of social change? In what dimensions of human behavior, values, or attitudes is the gap most manifest; in which areas is continuity the greatest?

Second is the question of the *novelty* of the current character of relations between generations. Has the gap always been there; has it always been as wide as it is today? What factors lead to the conflict being more pervasive at some periods in history than in others? Is such conflict the result, or the cause, of rapid social change?

Third, there is the issue of the *permanence* of difference between generations, in the life history of both the individual and the society. Will the differences so evident between today's youth and their elders dissolve as a natural correlate of achieving maturity; will youth grow out of it? Or will the currently observed difference in attitudes and behaviors become part of a mature personality, leading to decided change in the society when today's youth become the command generation? And, finally, is such change predictive and perhaps cyclical over long periods of time, or is it random? Is it true as in the old proverb, that what one generation builds the second rejects, leading the third generation to build the same sort of social mores as the first?

Such questions reflect the nature of the problem facing social scientists attempting to deal with generational differences, their correlates and consequences (see Aldous, 1965; Adelson, 1970; Troll, 1970). Using such issues as guides, one can organize the many current opinions regarding this problem in several ways. The simplest way is to proceed using one dimension to organize the literature, and then add another to form a more complete typology.

The dimension to be used first here is that of the extent of differences between age groups. Three rough categories of theorists and data appear: those that point to a "Great Gap" between age groups; those at the other end of the spectrum who suggest that the "Gap is an Illusion;" and those in between who infer "Selective Continuity and Difference" between age groups in today's society. All three positions are well represented in the current literature, and all three have some antecedents in classical treatment of the problem.

The "Great Gap"

Some sociologists, anthropologists, and educators have published data and impressionistic essays that indicate profound differences between youth and adults today regarding value system, orientations toward social institutions, interpersonal relations and communication, and locus of control and authority. In its extreme, the message is that a social revolution along generational lines is sweeping the world, toppling established adult social structures. Richman (1968) suggests that the "bona fide generation gap, qualitatively different from those that have occurred before," finds its focus on overthrowing outdated political systems. Seeley (1969) views the present youth movements as the beginning of a transformation of society analogous to the Renaissance or Reformation—if they are not crushed by the Establishment. One psychologist, educator Walter Angel (1968), summarizes his position with this quote: "the whole glacier of tradition is breaking up, and . . . a generation gap wider than we suspect has opened up under us." The gap appears, Angel adds, not at the extreme edges of society—the hippies and radicals—but throughout America where "a new madness, a new social but not necessarily ephemeral fad, a new psychological disease has gripped our nation." He labels the malignancy "gaposis" and suggests four strains: affluence, values, education, and communication as forces which are pulling apart age groups in our society.

Margaret Mead (1970) explains the pulling apart in terms of differential environmental experiences while young. It is no longer possible for the middle-aged parent to tell his son, "I was once a youth like you." The father never was just like him. Being twenty years old in 1970 is different from being the same age in the 1930s. Youth grow up in an environment of instant visual news, a threat of mass annihilation, and a growing concern with the credibility of Establishment leadership.

Perhaps the most eloquent exponent of this perspective of youth-adult relations is Edgar Friedenberg (1959, 1965, 1969, 1969a). He has argued prolifically that adult institutions have failed to listen to, let alone understand, a youth group which is progressively alienated. In his epigrammatic way he suggests that "young people aren't rebelling against their parents; they're abandoning them." Most recently, he has argued that the generation gap reflects "a real and serious conflict of interest" rather than mutual misunderstanding: youth is a discriminated minority, he says, and the "genuine class conflict between a dominant and exploitive older generation and youth who are slowly becoming more aware of what is happening to them will escalate into open conflict before long" (Friedenberg, 1969).

Certain analyses of popular culture by social scientists substantiate the notion of significant differences between youth and the over-thirty group. A number of current films (*The Graduate; Wild in the Streets; Goodbye, Columbus*) portray variously exploitation, conflict, or simply difference in interpretation across generational lines. Herbert Goldberg (1968), a clinical psychologist as well as songwriter, has documented the revolution in popular music since 1962 in terms of the style and media employed, the youthfulness of the performers, and the thematic portrayal through lyrics of revolt, parent-child differences, humanistic values, and sensory stimulation. Korngold (1968) has similarly analyzed the burgeoning underground press movement as a new social institution serving the particular interests and needs of a youth subculture. These developments have led some sociologists to suggest that the culture gap between young and old is progressively widening (see Simmons and Winograd, 1967, Seeley, 1969) or at least that youth are fashioning a new, humanistic ethic to replace the protestant ethic of their elders (Myerhoff, 1969). Such cultural innovations may someday fulfill the prophesies of some current writers of an entirely new social order. (It is interesting to note, however, as Goldberg points out, how rapidly some cultural innovations of youth have been adopted by Establishment fashion—witness mod clothing and sideburned junior executives—and how easily youthful performers like the Beatles become sophisticated capitalists and behave in some respects much like the Jet Set their songs decry.)

From a psychodynamic perspective comes additional confirmation for the "Great Gap" view of relations between age groups. Freudians have long accepted the proposition that rebellion (challenging the power of an autocratic, authoritarian father-figure) is an essential step in the achievement of the power and independence essential to the masculine identity role. Bettleheim (1965) has observed that factors that traditionally have mitigated generational conflict even in this country have become feeble or inoperative. The family plays a decreasing role in the socialization of the young; the elder generation is no longer the resource it was for coping with the world. The result is that one simply has to rebel if one is to become socially as well as psychologically an adult.

In short, regardless of the many roots of generational difference, the "Great Gap" position emphasizes that there are basic and, in some sense, irreconcilable differences in behavioral predispositions between age groups in American society, and the force of these differences is resulting in rapid cultural transformation. Many would add that such transformations are all for the best. Margaret Mead (1970) has suggested that, in societies where there is rapid social change, generational discontinuity is more adaptive than is substantial similarity between cohorts, since old responses become inappropriate to radically new situations, and parents must learn from their children. Or, as Friedenberg ("The Generation Gap," 1969b:42) has put it:

If the confrontation between the generations does pose, as many portentous civic leaders and upper-case Educators fear, a lethal threat to the integrity of the American social system, that threat may perhaps be accepted with graceful irony. Is there, after all, so much to lose? The American social system has never been noted for its integrity. In fact, it would be rather like depriving the Swiss of their surfing.

The Gap is an Illusion

At the opposite end of the spectrum, a second position emphasizes the continuities between generations, arguing that contemporary anxiety over the differences between age groups is greatly overplayed; it also draws on historical analysis to indicate the seemingly inevitable recurrence of periods of heightened conflict between age groups. In this sense, "the more things change, the more they stay the same" can be applied to relations between age groups as well as to political changes. Several contemporary analyses suggest that, though there are inevitably behavioral differences between age groups, the continuities in various aspects of behavior between one generation and the next, and the substantial solidarity between youth and their parents, take precedence over these differences (see Campbell, 1969, pp. 827–33, for an excellent review of the evidence for this position).

Four examples can be given. In the most comprehensive analysis to date of student protest movements, Feuer (1969) has presented voluminous historical documentation to the effect that the conflict of generations can be seen as both inevitable and recurrent. The intensity of the conflict varies, however, under such conditions as gerontocratic power structures and the obvious failure ("de-authorization") of the older generation to solve the problems facing the era. Current student movements are not to be considered simply as a manifestation of generational conflict: they have a more psychological base and end in failure unless attached to larger groups, defined not only on the basis of age. In short, youthful assault on the established structure is no more characteristic, nor revolutionary, in America in the 1960s than at other times and places within the modern era.

Similar findings are suggested in a second area, that of the so-called "sexual revolution," by Bell (1966) and Reiss (1968). The data of these studies may be interpreted to suggest that the greatest generational change in sexual behavior, at least with regard to premarital sex, occurred following World War I between the cohort born before, or after 1900, and not between today's youth and their parents. A survey by Walsh (1970) suggests that patterns of sexual behavior before marriage among current college students are remarkably similar to those characterizing their parents' generation.

Or, to give a third example, there are several studies which have touched on influence, sentiment, and interaction patterns between parents and youth. Some of these suggest that most adolescents and their parents perceive a decidedly satisfactory relationship in terms of communication, understanding, and closeness (Douvan and Adelson, 1966; Larson and Myerhoff, 1965; Adelson, 1968; Lubell, 1968; Bengtson, 1969). Others indicated that parents are more important referent persons than peers for some aspects of decision-making in adolescence (Kandel and Lesser, 1969). Musgrove (1965) has suggested an interesting variation on this theme: in his samples, adolescents have generally favorable orientations toward adults, while the adults in his sample displayed decidedly less favorable descriptions of young people in general.

The fourth perspective comes from the research or political attitudes of students and their parents. In the main, such intergenerational research has indicated substantial continuity among both activists and nonactivists. For example, Thomas (1970), in a study of sixty politically active parents (thirty liberal and thirty conservative) and their college-age children, found that "children of highly politicized parents tend to be like their parents both in their political attitudes and their political behavior." Westby and Braungart (1968) found considerable similarity between members of the Young Americans for Freedom and their parents' political identification, and slightly less for SDS members; their conclusion is that a stratification theory explains political activism better than a generational hypothesis (the young are rebelling against the parents, and that's why they demonstrate). Gamson, Goodman, and Gurin (1967) studied radicals, bystanders, and moderates during the 1966 University of Michigan uprising and concluded that "discontinuity between background and present beliefs is an inhibiting factor, making action *less* rather than more likely. . . . Freed from the cost of sharply breaking with their background, the activists are willing to go further in support of their beliefs." Such examples could be used to argue that "the gap is an illusion."

There are, of course, several factors at work that make generational conflict more visible today, and perhaps different in nature—factors such as rapid social change (Davis, 1940); technological advances which decrease the span between generations (Berger, 1960); the revolutionary effects of the mass media on socialization experiences (Hayakawa, 1968); the changing population distribution with the "pinching" in the middle-age range (Birren and Bengtson, 1969); and, finally, greater sensitization to differences between age groups brought about in part by the popular press. Despite factors such as the above, those who come down on the side of continuity in intergenerational behavior would hold that today's social conflict is not basically generational in nature at all. Perhaps, as Adelson (1968) has reported:

What we have tended to do is to translate ideological conflict into generational conflict; it may be easier to contemplate a rift between the generations than to confront the depth and extent of our current social discord . . . The feverish politics of the day do not align the young against the old, not in any significant way. Rather they reflect . . . the ideological differences in a deeply divided nation.

Selective Continuity and Difference

A possible position can be suggested as intermediate between these two extremes. Like the second position, it maintains that in most respects, conflict between the generations is peripheral; solidarity, and continuity of values are substantial across generational lines within the family and across cohort lines in the broader social order. However, like the first perspective, it emphasizes that the rapid pace of social change has created new modes of behavioral expressions that may be quite different from those of the preceding generation.

Selective continuity from one arena of behavior to another is seen in the three-generational studies of Aldous and Hill (1965) and Hill and Aldous (1969). This is probably the most extensive study to date of intergenerational continuity and difference. Among the eighty-four three-generational lineages in their research (all adults and all living in separate households), the greatest continuity of behavior appeared in the transmission of religious affiliation. Less transmission from generation to generation appeared in the pattern of dividing marital household tasks, educational achievement, and the making of decisions within the family.

An interesting side note of this research, in the context of social change, is the suggestion of greater similarity between middle-aged parents and their married children than between the parents and the grandparents. Hill and Aldous comment that the historical period of the 1930s may have represented a watershed between generations in family decision-making behavior—a comment consistent with other observations about the "sexual revolution" and changes in religious patterns between generations (see Birren and Bengtson, 1968).

Additionally, Aldous has made some analyses of the *consequences* of continuity between generations. For example, continuity in religious affiliation over three generations is associated with less marital tension for the youngest generation; continuity in occupation (for white-collar groups) appears to result in higher income for the younger generation than does lack of such a tradition.

Such evidence of generational continuity in some aspects of behavior, and of differences in others, points to a contrast that may be made between overt behavior and covert value systems. Behavior as outwardly manifest may vary substantially from generation to generation, while values or personal philosophy may in fact be similar. Taking this as a hypothesis, the literature suggests some confirming evidence.

For example, Keniston (1968) has suggested a distinction between "core" and "formal" values in his sample of young radicals. He emphasizes that the young radicals come from liberal or radical families, but denies that what has been called the "red diaper baby" hypothesis adequately explains the radical differences in means displayed by them. The accumulating literature of student activists supports this notion: rather than rebelling from parental values, many activists, both of right and left, are in fact carrying them to their logical conclusion (Flacks, 1967; Keniston, 1968; Thomas, 1970; Block et al., 1970). For example, Troll, Neugarten, and Kraines (1969: 333) present data that shows considerable similarity between young adults and their parents in the domain of values:

If one member of a family is dedicated to righting wrongs and changing the world (dedication to causes), it is likely that so will the others, even though the particular causes they espouse may not be the same; if one member values achievement (achievement need), probably so do the others; and so on. The salient values of this group of college students, whether they are activists or not, tend to be the salient values of their parents.

Troll's families exhibited greater similarity in the area of values than in other domains of personality—consistent with the "Selective Continuity" orientation.

Another way to look at the selective continuity is through the traditional value-norm differentiation proposed by Merton: specific values of the two cohorts—freedom, democracy, responsibility—may indeed be similar, but the norms, and therefore the behaviors, used by each age group to achieve the value ends may differ greatly (Bengtson, 1969). Or, to propose another perspective, differences in the structure and experiences of primary socialization agencies may account for the variability of the behavioral continuities present (see Larson and Myerhoff, 1967; Moriwaki and Bengtson, 1969). Block has recently presented data to substantiate the hypothesis that family patterns may account for this determined rebellion and selective continuity, at least as perceived by the child. Larson and Myerhoff suggested that continuity in socialization techniques lead to continuity in value patterns; these in turn were predictive of school adjustment patterns of adolescent boys (Larson, 1967).

The problem with the selective continuity is that it doesn't say much that is useful unless further specification is added, as in Troll's distinction between similarity in personality and similarity in values and the Hill-Aldous differentiation among family behaviors. That some things change, and some things stay the same, is simply irrefutable; and to say that there is neither a great gap nor a complete congruence between generations may be points worth emphasizing in order to allay anxieties of parents and taxpayers. But, unless researchers will specify more clearly what the points of difference are, how extensive they may be, and propose models to demonstrate what the consequences of intergenerational differences are, this field of investigation may continue to add a sea of interesting facts gathered from ad hoc studies of campus demonstrations to our already entrenched speculations.

In concluding this review, one is struck with the value-laden flavor of many of these positions. The three perspectives presented above, one or the other of which seem to crop up in the conclusion section of almost every paper in this field, come close to being value statements, reflecting either radical or conservative or mixed preferences on the part of the investigator. As such, much of this scholarly debate has added little to the development of predictive knowledge in the area of intergenerational relations.

PERSPECTIVES FOR FUTURE RESEARCH: A TYPOLOGY OF THE NATURE AND EXTENT OF GENERATIONAL DIFFERENCES

In the search for more scientifically useful analyses of social problems, the course of events usually goes from the review of past work on the issue to the creation of typologies that allow for the identification of ideal types, and thence to the gathering of data suggesting the analytic utility of these constructs. In the analysis thus far, reviews of contemporary and traditional approaches to the problem of generational differences have been made, and the contemporary approaches have been organized around a dimension derived from a mass culture approach to the problem: the extent of generational difference.

But to analyze the extent of differences between age groups is not a particularly productive enterprise when taken alone. More profitable, from a scientific perspective, is to add to this dimension some of the others discussed which have much broader sociological implications. When one considers the implication of social change in the light of the nature and the effect of generational difference, a number of interesting possibilities arise in terms of the effect of generational contrasts on the social structure.

Nature and Effect of Generational Difference

		Structural Factors; permanent change	Developmental Factors; temporary change
	1. "Great Gap"	A. Social revolution	B. Normal rebellion
Extent of Generational Difference	2. "Selective Gap"	C. Social evolution	D. Nothing really new
	3. "Illusory Gap"	E. Social change, but not by generations	F. Solidarity will prevail

Figure 1.   The Types of Consequences from Various Perspectives of Generational Differences

Figure I presents a typology that combines an identification of the extent, nature, and effect of differences between generational cohorts. The vertical dimension, used to order the preceeding section, has already been discussed. The horizontal dimension dichotomizes the predominant nature of differences into structural factors which lead therefore to permanent social change, and developmental or maturational factors whose effect is thus temporary in the life of the society. Individual cells represent various views on the effect of generational differences. The bivariate possibilities may be characterized thus:

Type A: Social revolution. There are substantial differences between age groups; the differences are induced by primarily structural factors, such as age-status inequities or adherence to an outmoded ethic. Major social change will be the result as youth move into adulthood, permanently imprinted by the inequities they have experienced (Friedenberg; Mead; Seeley; Mannheim).

Type B: Normal rebellion. There are substantial differences between age groups in norms, values, and behaviors; but these differences are primarily due to maturational factors. When children grow up and assume adult responsibilities, the great differences will disappear. Social change, therefore, will be minor, and the rebellion largely individual (Freud; Bettleheim; Reiss; Davis).

Type C: Social evolution. There are major differences between age groups in some areas, and major continuity in others. Behaviors and norms are different, while values are not. The normative differences and the acting out lead to new styles of life and thus social change. A selective gap between generations will result in major changes on issues, such as sexual mores, racism, and the like, but the changes will be gradual and selective, rather than sudden and revolutionary, because the value system is transmitted more or less continuously (Keniston; Block et al.).

Type D: Nothing really new. There are major differences in some areas because of normative contrasts, but continuity in others because the value system that youth will assume in adulthood is constant: responsibility, protection of home and family, necessary materialism. For example, youth become less permissive of premarital sex as they themselves become parents (Adelson; Bell).

Type E: Social change, but not by generations. There is great change evident in our society, but the change is not led primarily by generational conflict. All three generations are going through the social change, and to identify it with age group differences is to ignore the real ideological bases. Also, one must be aware of historical constancy in age group differences: there have always been certain differences, but today's are no greater and to call them a gap is a misnomer. The change is structure-wide (Feuer; Adelson).

Type F: Solidarity will prevail over tangential differences. There are some apparent differences between children and their parents over largely peripheral issues that have to do with maturational factors. Despite such inevitable disagreements there is overwhelming solidarity between generations in most families; there is a basic, permanent, and constant solidarity between generations that will continue to develop (Campbell; Douvan and Adelson; Walsh).

The Posing of More Refined Research Questions

As has been indicated, by now considerable work has been done in the study of generations; yet much of it is unsystematic and nonempirical. One can begin to build on what is accumulated and proceed to explore the uncharted areas. At the University of Southern California, a three-generational study is currently underway which will attempt to answer some of these questions.

It would seem that the first step toward collecting and ordering knowledge in this area would involve the systematic statement of important questions which remain to be answered. Perhaps the first question concerns the *nature and extent of differences between generational cohorts*, such investigations considered initially from outside the context of the family and its socialization implications. Despite imaginative cohort analyses using previously collected census and survey data such as Cain, 1967, 1968; Cutler, 1968, 1969; Glenn, 1968; Zody, 1969 and despite the growing body of social-psychological studies of student activists, it is simply not known how much the variation *within* a cohort on a given set of behavioral attributes compares with the variation *between* cohorts. Nor is it known which kinds of attitudes, values, or norms exhibit greatest variation between age groups; or what part aging plays in the causation of differences that are apparently generational.

Second, and perhaps even more important, is the dearth of knowledge concerning the *within-family differences* between generations. Building on the pioneering work of Hill and Aldous (1969), one might ask: To what degree do parents and children share a similar perspective of intergenerational interaction; is the definition of situation shared across generational lines? What are perceived as major sources of disagreement and discussion; why is solidarity higher in some families than in others?

Third, the *antecedents or correlates* of high or low generational similarity and high or low cross-generational solidarity await more systematic investigation. What are the family structure patterns of parent-child dyads evidencing high similarity in attitudes, values, and norms? Can model socialization patterns be found that characterize conformity or rebellion? What is the effect of social mobility between generations on cross cohort differences? What is the influence of nonfamily socialization agencies, such as strong peer group membership, on intergenerational continuity? What is the effect of immigration, as in those families where socialization of the grand-parental generation occurred in another society?

Finally, the *consequences* of high or low generational similarity or difference have only begun to be investigated (Aldous, 1965) either in terms of effects on individuals or in terms of the shape of broader social change. What does it mean to a parent, for example, to have a son who is extremely different from himself in opinions and basic life values? Is denial, or guilt, or a feeling of betrayal, or cheerful acceptance the more likely response? What does it mean to the son, who loses what Keniston and Erikson suggest may be of central importance to optimal personal development, a sense of continuity with the past? How do families cope with the inevitable instances of intergenerational conflict that occur within the family? Is it likely that continuity is deleterious in rapidly changing societies?

REFERENCES

ADELSON, J. 1970. What generation gap? *New York Times Magazine* (January 18): 10 ff.

———— 1968. The myth of adolescence: a polemic. Presented at the meeting of the American Psychological Association, San Francisco, September.

ALDOUS, J. 1965. The consequences of intergenerational continuity. *Journal of Marriage and the Family* 26: 462–68.

———— and HILL, R. 1965. Social cohesion, lineage type, and intergenerational transmission. *Social Forces* 43: 471–82.

ANGEL, W. 1968. Gaposis: the new social disease. *Vital Speeches* (August):671–72.

BELL, R. R. 1966. *Premarital Sex in a Changing Society.* Englewood Cliffs, N.J.: Prentice-Hall.

BENGTSON, V. L. 1969. The "generation gap:" differences by generation and by sex in the perception of parent-child relations. Presented at the annual meeting of the Pacific Sociological Association, Seattle, April 24.

BERGER, B. 1960. How long is a generation? *British Journal of Sociology* 2: 10–23.

BETTELHEIM, B. 1965. The problem of generations. In *The Challenge of Youth*, edited by E. Erikson, pp. 76–109. New York: Anchor.

BIRREN, J. E. and BENGTSON, V. L. 1961. The problem of generations:

emotions vs. reality. Presented at Senate Subcommittee on Aging, Santa Barbara, California. (Condensation in the *Center Magazine* 2:84–87.)

BLOCK, J. 1970. Rebellion re-examined: the role of identification and alienation. Unpublished, Institute of Human Development, University of California.

———, HAAN, N. and SMITH, M. B. 1970. Socialization correlates of student activism. *Journal of Social Issues* 26:25–38.

BUTLER, R. N. 1969. Age-ism: another form of bigotry. *Gerontologist* 9:243–46.

CAIN, L. D. 1968. Aging and the character of our times. *Gerontologist* 8:250–58.

——— 1967. Age status and generational phenomena: the new old people in contemporary America. *Gerontologist* 7:83–92.

CAMPBELL, E. Q. 1969. Adolescent socialization. In *Handbook of Socialization Theory and Research*, edited by D. A. Goslin, pp. 827–35. Chicago: Rand McNally.

CUTLER, N. E. 1969. Generation, maturation, and party affiliation: a cohort analysis. *Public Opinion Quarterly*.

——— 1968. The alternative effects of generations and aging upon political behavior: a cohort analysis of American attitudes toward foreign policy, 1946–66. Oak Ridge, Tenn.: Oak Ridge National Laboratory.

DAVIS, K. 1940. The sociology of parent-youth conflict. *American Sociological Review* 5:523–34.

DOUGHERTY, R. 1968. Nixon unveils plan for youth service agency. *Los Angeles Times*, Part 1 (Oct. 17):6.

DOUVAN, E. and ADELSON, J. 1966. *The Adolescent Experience*. New York: John Wiley.

ERIKSON, E. 1968. *Identity: Youth and Crisis*. New York: W. W. Norton.

——— 1965. Youth, fidelity and diversity. In the *Challenge of Youth*, pp. 1–28. New York: Anchor.

——— 1964. *Insight and Responsibility*. New York: W. W. Norton.

——— 1959. Identity and the life cycle. *Psychological Issues* 1.

——— 1950. *Childhood and Society*. New York: W. W. Norton.

FEUER, L. 1969. *The Conflict of Generations: The Character and Significance of Student Movements*. New York: Basic Books.

FLACKS, R. 1967. The liberated generation: an exploration of roots of student protest. *Journal of Social Issues* 23:52–72.

FRIEDENBERG, E. 1969a. Current patterns of generational conflict. *Journal of Social Issues* 25:21–38.

———— 1969b. The generation gap. *Annals of the American Academy of Political and Social Science* 382:32–42.

———— 1965. *Coming of Age in America*. New York: Vintage.

———— 1959. *The Vanishing Adolescent*. Boston: Beacon Press.

GAMSON, Z. F., GOODMAN, J., and GURIN, G. 1967. Radicals, moderates, and bystanders during a university protest. Presented at the meetings of the American Sociological Association, San Francisco, August 30.

GLENN, N., and GRIMES, M. 1968. Aging, voting, and political interest. *American Sociological Review* 33: 563–75.

GOLDBERG, H. 1968. Contemporary cultural innovations of youth: popular music. Presented at the meeting of the American Psychological Association, San Francisco, August 31.

HAYAKAWA, S. I. 1968. Mass media and family communications. Presented to the Seventy-Sixth Annual Convention of the American Psychological Association, San Francisco, September 2.

HEBERLE, R. 1951. *Social Movements*. New York: Appleton-Century-Crofts.

HILL, R. and ALDOUS, J. 1969. Socialization for marriage and parenthood. In *Handbook of Socialization Theory and Research*, edited by D. Goslin. Chicago: Rand McNally.

KANDEL, D. and LESSER, G. 1969. Parental and peer influences on educational plans of adolescents. *American Sociological Review* 34:212–23.

———— 1968. *Young Radicals*. New York: Harcourt, Brace & World.

KENISTON, K. 1965. *The Uncommitted: Alienated Youth in American Society*. New York: Harcourt, Brace & World.

KORNGOLD, B. 1968. Contemporary culture innovations of youth: needs or symptoms? Presented at the meeting of the American Psychological Association, San Francisco, August 31.

LARSON, W. R. 1967. Intrafamily relationships and adolescent school adjustment. A final report submitted to the United States Office of Education, on Cooperative Research Project no. 1353 and S-044. Youth Studies Center, University of Southern California.

———— and MYERHOFF, B. 1965. Primary and formal family organization and adolescent socialization. *Sociology and Social Research* 50:63–71.

LOS ANGELES TIMES. 1969. Reagan denounces Berkeley demands May 12.

LUBELL, S. 1968. That "generation gap." In *Confrontation*, edited by D. Bell and I. Kristol, pp. 58–66. New York: Basic Books.

MANNHEIM, K. 1952. *Essays on the Sociology of Knowledge*. London: Routledge & Kegan Paul.

MARIAS, J. 1968. Generations: the concept. *International Encyclopedia of the Social Sciences* 6:88–92. New York: Free Press.

MEAD, M. 1970. *Culture and Commitment: A Study of the Generation Gap*. New York: Basic Books.

MENTRÉ, F. 1920. *Les generations sociales*. Paris: Bossard.

MORIWAKI, S. and BENGTSON, V. L. 1969. Influence of sex lineage on intergenerational continuities. Presented at the Eighth International Congress of Gerontology, Washington, D.C.

MUSGROVE, F. 1965. *Youth and the Social Order*. Bloomington: Indiana University Press.

MYERHOFF, B. 1969. New styles of humanism: American youth. *Youth and Society* 1:151–77.

NEUGARTEN, B. 1970. The old and the young in modern societies. *American Behavioral Scientist* 14.

PINDER, A. 1926. *Das problem der generation in der kunstgeschichte Europas*. Berlin.

REISS, I. R. 1968. America's sex standards—how and why they're changing. *Trans-action* 5:26–32.

RICHMAN, F. 1968. The disenfranchised majority. *Greater Occasional Paper* 1:4–14.

SEELEY, J. 1969. Youth in revolt. *Britannica Book of the Year*. Chicago: University of Chicago Press.

SIMMONS, J. L. and WINOGRAD, B. 1966. *It's Happening*. Santa Barbara: Marc-Laird.

THOMAS, L. E., NEUGARTEN, B. and KRAINES, R. 1970. Family correlates of student political activism. *Journal of Developmental Psychology*. Forthcoming.

TROLL, L. 1970. The generation gap: conceptual models. *Aging and Human Development* 1.

—— et al. 1969. Similarities in values and other personality characteristics in college students and their parents. *Merrill-Palmer Quarterly* 15:323–36.

WALL STREET JOURNAL. 1968. What troubles the older generation? October 4.

WALSH, R. 1970. Intergenerational transmission of sexual standards. Presented at the meetings of the American Sociological Association. Washington, D.C. September 2.

WESTBY, D. and BRAUNGART, R. 1967. Utopian mentality and conservatism: the case of the Young Americans for Freedom. Presented at the annual meeting of the American Sociological Association, San Francisco, August 30.

.11. Sources of Generational Consciousness and Conflict

ROBERT S. LAUFER

SCHOLARLY WORK on the issue of generational conflict is presently a prime commodity in the cultural marketplace. Although there is a substantial literature on youth, the current interest in generational conflict is a product of mounting student protest against the political, economic, and cultural institutions of American society. One of the seminal works in the field, written in the midst of an earlier major crisis in the West, argues that generational conflict emerges in periods when rapid social change dramatically alters the position of youth in society.[1] In the transformation from an industrial to a post-industrial society, the structural position of a significant sector of youth is radically altered, and the problem of generational conflict can be seen as originating in these massive changes.

The last major crisis in the West occurred in the midst of a breakdown in industrial societies between the end of World War I and the beginning of World War II. This was the period of the "lost" generation and the Depression in America, and the dissolution of Imperial and Weimar Germany and the rise of Nazism. Varieties of fascism and communism attracted large numbers of Europeans and Americans. Although generational conflict became a matter of considerable interest, especially among German scholars, it did not become the dominant theme in either cultural thought or political conflict because the role of the industrial working class in the political and economic systems of Western capitalist societies remained unresolved. In the West in general, and America in particular, the

[1]Karl Mannheim, "The Sociological Problem of Generations," chapter 6.

Depression, World War II, and the Cold War finally stabilized the role of the working class in industrial society by incorporation into the major societal systems. In return, working-class organizations divested themselves of their more radical visions of social reconstruction. The Welfare State was the mechanism created to ensure minimal stability and allegiance from the working class.[2]

As the class structure of industrial societies stabilized, they began a process of transformation to what is today called the post-industrial society.[3] This transformation has profoundly altered Western societies. The most fundamental change is the new role of science in the development and growth process.[4] The scientist is the significant new actor in the post-industrial society.[5] The role of science and technology in a post-industrial society is one of the central sources of contemporary cultural and political instability because the technological revolution reconstitutes the conditions of middle-class existence.

The post-industrial society has radically transformed patterns of consumption, child-raising, occupational and career training, residential patterns, communication systems, warfare, and the decision-making process of the political and industrial system. These changes in post-industrial America have most dramatically affected the upper-middle and middle classes, and the lowest classes in the population. The latter were unable to take advantage of the new consumptive patterns and were made expendable by the lessening of demand for cheap, unskilled labor. The upper-middle and middle classes were the major beneficiaries of changes in patterns of consumption and communication, and the like. They, and especially

[2]Defined as, "a form of society characterized by a system of democratic, government-sponsored welfare placed on a new footing and offering a guarantee of collective social care to its citizens, concurrently with the maintenance of a capitalist system of production."—Piet Thoenes in *The Elite in the Welfare State*, J. A. Banks, ed. (London: Faber and Faber, 1966).

[3]Daniel Bell, "Notes on the Post-Industrial Society (I)," *The Public Interest*, Winter 1967; "Notes on the Post-Industrial Society (II)," *The Public Interest*, Spring 1968; and "The Measurement of Knowledge and Technology," *Indicators of Social Change*, E. B. Sheldon and W. E. Moore, eds. (New York: Russell Sage Foundation, 1968).

[4]Thoenes, *The Elite in the Welfare State*; Jean Meynaud, *Technocracy* (New York: Free Press, 1968); Robert Gilpin, *France in the Age of the Scientific State* (Princeton, N.J.: Princeton University Press, 1968); Bell, in *Indicators of Social Change*, and John K. Galbraith, *The New Industrial State* (New York: Signet, 1967).

[5]H. L. Nieburg, *In the Name of Science* (Chicago: Quadrangle Books, 1966).

their children, were also the most affected by the demands for academically trained manpower.

However, the transformations of the post-industrial society do not account for the specific content of generational consciousness. It is in the interplay between social structure and historical experience that we come to see the parameters of consciousness. By exploring the social base of generational conflict, the relation of this generation to the demands of its historical experience of post-industrial society becomes comprehensible.

Although this article focuses upon America, young people in advanced industrial societies throughout the world are involved in transforming mores and creating new social forms. As Barrington Moore, Jr. argues in his analysis of industrialization, there are different roads to the industrial world[6]; so, too, there are different roads to the post-industrial world. The process of post-industrial development is dependent upon certain structural changes in the social order which affect the political and cultural systems. The emergent patterns of development constitute the range of available responses of a given society to a general phenomenon. The differences in developmental process therefore represent variations on a theme rather than unique responses.

THE SOCIAL BASE OF GENERATIONAL CONFLICT

The first group to experience fully the effects of post-industrial existence is the children of the middle class. This sector of youth experiences the transformation of the occupational, decision-making, and communication patterns in the society directly through the primary agencies of socialization, the school, and the family. The class character of student protest has been the subject of considerable debate.[7] Studies have shown that student radicalism is expand-

[6]Barrington Moore, Jr., *Social Origins of Dictatorship and Democracy* (Boston: Beacon Press, 1966).

[7]Paul Heist, "Intellect and Commitment: The Faces of Discontent," *Order and Freedom on the Campus: The Rights and Responsibilities of Faculty and Students*, O. W. Knorr and W. J. Winters, eds. (Boulder: Western Interstate Commission on Higher Education, 1965); Richard E. Peterson, "The Student Left in American Higher Education," *Daedalus*, Winter, 1968; Richard Braungart, "SDS and YAF: A Comparison of Two Student Radical Groups in the Mid-1960s" (Paper delivered at the meeting of the American Sociological Association, Miami Beach, Florida, August-September, 1966); Richard Flacks, "The Liberated Generation: An Exploration of the Roots of Student Protest," *The Journal of Social Issues*

ing beyond its initially rather narrow base. All these studies have concentrated on university populations, and the vast majority of these studies has taken place at elite campuses. Nonetheless, local protests at such places as Wisconsin State University, Whitewater, and the State University of New York, Buffalo, as well as the widespread national protest against the invasion of Cambodia and the shooting of four students at Kent State and of two more students at Jackson State, lend observational support to this conclusion.

The question remains as to the significance of the broadened base of the protest movement. Precisely what new elements are expanding the movement, and how do they affect the problem of generational conflict? The expansion of the movement to which Flacks and Mankoff point is primarily an increase in the proportion of middle-class youth involved in protest. A number of studies underline the plausibility of this position by demonstrating that higher education is largely populated by children of the middle and upper-middle classes. A recent study on the system of higher education in California has shown this disparity.

Distributions by family income (among various types of institutions of higher education) clearly differ among (economic) groups. Median family incomes ... are highest for parents of University students, ... $12,000—followed by State College student families, ... $10,000—and Junior College student families, ... $8,000. Lowest of all is the median income for all families without children in the California system ... $7,900.[8]

Students attending either universities and colleges, or state colleges, have family incomes of between $10,000 and $12,000. Private institutions are not included in this estimate but it is fairly safe to assume that if we included them, the median income of the student families at universities and colleges would be even higher. Finally, class affects survival rates in higher education in favor of middle-class youth.[9] All these findings suggest that insofar as the issue of genera-

13, 3 (1967); Zelda Gamson, "The Academic Counterrevolution," mimeograph, 1968; Milton Mankoff, "The Political Socialization of Student Radicals and Militants in the Wisconsin Student Movement during the 1960s" doctoral dissertation, University of Wisconsin, 1970; and Richard Flacks and Milton Mankoff, chapter 5.

[8]W. Lee Hansen and Burton A. Weisbrod, *The Distribution of Costs and Direct Benefits of Public Higher Education: The Case of California* (Working Paper No. 7, Workshop on Human Resources, University of Wisconsin, September, 1968).

[9]William H. Sewell and Vimal P. Shah, "Socioeconomic Status, Intelligence, and the Attainment of Higher Education," *Sociology of Education* 40, 1 (1967).

tional conflict and contemporary protest is primarily a phenomenon involving university students, we are dealing with a problem of intra-class conflict within the upper-middle and middle classes.

THE SHAPING OF CONTEMPORARY CONSCIOUSNESS

The first generation to develop within post-industrial society is the present generation of middle-class youth. Such a society requires a larger proportion of its population to acquire academic training and technical skills than any other in history; this trained portion of the society is drawn overwhelmingly from the middle class and above. This means that the young spend a long, historically unique period in training. As the proportion of educated youth increases, the probability that an extended period of training will pay off in social and economic terms is reduced.[10] In other words, the relationship between academic training and class position begins to disappear as advanced-degree holders cease being a scarce commodity. Therefore, a portion of technically qualified youth faces the prospect of becoming déclassé—or, at least, under-employed—which, in turn, creates an unstable social situation. The demands for long periods of training also expand the age of "youth," the period of social, economic, and political impotence, while placing the young in an intellectual setting which provides the ideational equipment to develop new critiques and ideologies.[11]

As a consequence of the role of science in the development process, experts and expertise are a significant economic and political force. As a result, there has been a massive expansion of technical occupations; the university is the center for the production of scientific goods and trained personnel.[12] The tendency of post-industrial societies to rely upon experts in the decision-making process, plus the length of time it takes to acquire expert status, implicitly disenfranchises young people, as they have neither the credentials nor presumably the attendant skills to participate. Thus, the period of political impotency experienced by an incipient elite is greatly extended. Ambiguity, then, characterizes the position of middle-class youth: some are to move into elite positions, others are going to become déclassé,

[10]Raymond Boudon, chapter 16.

[11]Frank Musgrove, "The Problem of Youth and the Structure of Society in England," Youth and Society 1 (1969).

[12]Bell, in Indicators of Social Change.

but in ever-increasing numbers they are at universities and colleges. The position of middle-class youth in post-industrial society constitutes a necessary but not sufficient condition for student protest to become generational conflict.

THE FAMILY AND GENERATIONAL CONFLICT

Models that emphasize other than structural aspects are present in the literature. Both Lipset[13] and Feuer[14] propose models of generational conflict based upon Oedipal conflict. The treatment of cultural and political conflict as a problem of psychological growth implicitly denies significant substantive differences between generations, and suggests that the process of socialization and maturation is simply the reproduction of the younger generation in the image of the adult world. Youthful rebellion defined in terms of Oedipal conflict is the sowing of wild oats; depending upon the period, it may be fraternity hazing or student sit-ins. Youthful rebellion is based on the conflict between the personal needs of the young man and the normative demands of society. This formulation of the issues rejects the idea of historical location and consciousness, and seeks a universal theory to explain radically different situations in which youth plays a significant militant role.

The image which the Lipset-Feuer model brings to mind is the upwardly mobile immigrant child who successfully integrates into the dominant culture and whose parents discover too late that the world they encouraged him to enter takes him away from them. This we call assimilation and, whatever the difficulties, we see it as "healthy." As a society built upon the assimilation of immigrant generations, this is hardly surprising. However, the process of assimilation is by definition based upon a break with the real family and the acceptance of life styles and norms of the dominant culture. This type of relationship between personality and social structure demands the subordination of personality to the mores of the dominant culture. The parental generation, trapped by its own commitment to social mobility for its offspring, is left with the interpersonal arena to express its hostility. The process of assimilation, therefore, struc-

[13]Seymour M. Lipset, "University Student Politics," *The Berkeley Student Revolt*, Seymour Martin Lipset and Sheldon S. Wolin, eds. (New York: Anchor, 1965).

[14]Lewis S. Feuer, *The Conflict of Generations* (New York: Basic Books, 1969).

turally accentuates interpersonal conflict between the generations. As long as such conflict remains in the private domain, does not disturb public tranquility, it is viewed as "normal."

The present revolt of the young does not emerge out of issues related to assimilation. Rather, we are seeing a rebellion against the dominant culture of which the parental generation is a representative. Instead of private, interpersonal hostility we see public confrontations between representatives of different perspectives. The present parental generation has experienced socio-economic success. Instead of upwardly mobile young people who are experiencing a break with the parental sub-culture as they move into the dominant cultural system, we are confronted with middle and upper-middle class young people whose consciousness is being shaped by a historically unique environment.[15]The development of a historical consciousness by middle-class youth radically at odds with the parental generation's world view creates generational conflict on the cultural and political level. An analysis which insists upon the irrelevance of all but interpersonal conflict is woefully inadequate, because it does not explore the specific role of the family in post-industrial America in shaping this cultural and political confrontation.

A number of studies earlier in the decade revealed that student activists came from liberal professional families who approved their children's values.[16] Initially, this tended to focus attention away from the generational conflict issue. However, if the thesis that contemporary generational conflict occurs at the cultural and political level has merit, then value conflict and interpersonal compatibility are conceivable. In fact, several studies confirm this thesis; Bengtson's work revealed significant value differences between generations, although the interpersonal relations were satisfactory.[17]

The importance the present parental generation attached to the idea of the child's uniqueness provides several clues to the relationship between interpersonal compatibility and value conflict. As Philip Slater points out, the previous parental generations saw their responsibility in terms of getting the child to adjust to the demands of the society; insofar as personal needs were in opposition to social

[15]Margaret Mead, *Culture and Commitment* (Garden City: Doubleday, 1969).

[16]Flacks, in *The Journal of Social Issues*; and Braungart, "SDS and YAF."

[17]Vern L. Bengtson, "The 'Generation Gap': Differences by Generation and by Sex in the Perception of Parent-Child Relations" (Paper delivered at the meeting of the Pacific Sociological Association, Seattle Washington, April 24, 1969).

demands, that was just too bad.[18] The present parental generation
does not demand the child's submission to norms which are in direct
conflict with his inner needs and potential. The focus on self-actualization of personal potential calls for a much greater sensitivity
to the needs, feelings, and ideas of the child. This places a particularly heavy burden on interpersonal relations between parents and
children, and forces the parent to become a protective intermediary
between society and the child. However, the present middle-class
parental generation is able to sustain this burden because it does not
need to justify its role as parent through the financial, occupational,
or social success of its children. Instead, the present parental generation dwells on fantasies of intimacy with and autonomy for its
children.

Through the family, young people experience those issues which
were and are central to the older generation. They are the subjects
through which the older generation experiments with its fantasies
of "how it spozed to be," that is, how childhood should have been for
themselves. I would suggest that the rejection of intimacy described
by Caroline Bird as characteristic of the Depression, its destruction
of self-respect, independent action, and personality, made these become scarce but highly desirable attributes.[19] In the post–World
War II period, the organization man or the "Man in the Grey Flannel
Suit" became the prototype of an occupational world where security
was substituted for innovation and personality was submerged under
organizational identities. The fantasy of the older generation emerges
out of the deprivation it felt forced to tolerate in order to obtain the
rewards of security and status.

The uniqueness of the child, the importance of good interpersonal
relations between parents and children, and the importance of free
expression of inner needs are precisely what the parental generation
felt denied. The present generation of youth has in part been subject
to the parental generation's desire for the expression of self. As sociologists have pointed out, the family continues to be an arena where
personal needs of the members can be given priority.[20] For the older
generation, there was a clear understanding of the difference between private (family) and public worlds. Insofar as the young ex-

[18]Philip E. Slater, *The Pursuit of Loneliness* (Boston: Beacon Press, 1970).

[19]Caroline Bird, *The Invisible Scar* (New York: David McKay, 1966).

[20]Talcott Parsons, "The School Class as a Social System: Some of Its Functions
in American Society," *Harvard Educational Review* 29 (1959); and Robert Dreeben,
On What Is Learned in School (Reading: Addison-Wesley, 1968).

perience mediation between social demands and personal needs, there is a breakdown of private and public life styles.

The focus on human relations and the emphasis on individual integrity encourage the child to refuse the acceptance of social standards at the expense of internal needs. When primary value is placed on inner needs, the exacting scrutiny of societal norms becomes automatic. Hence, youth has found many of society's demands are counterproductive to its inner needs. Once this discovery is made in a context which allows and encourages exploration of its implications —as, for example, in the university's culture—then the possibilities for a radical transformation of middle-class youth exist.

Our model of contemporary generational conflict, like our model of generational conflict in the upwardly mobile immigrant family, must have room for the unanticipated consequences of parental behavior. Thus, the parents do not necessarily perceive correctly the outcome of their child-rearing patterns; in fact, the parental generation is often shocked. "This isn't what I wanted," is experienced dramatically. For an immigrant generation, interpersonal confrontation was the only potential outlet for hostility because successful occupational and social assimilation into the dominant culture was clearly the objective of the parental generation. Contrarily, a historic confrontation at the political and cultural level dominates contemporary generational conflict, because interpersonal relations and intrapersonal development are the focus of parental behavior.

In each case there is a basic ambivalence toward the child's behavior with which the parental generation cannot deal. In the upwardly mobile situation, the break with the concrete family and socio-economic success are intimately linked. In the present situation, the parental generation's focus upon autonomy and interpersonal compatibility creates conditions under which youth may legitimately question the validity of social forms which interfere with self-actualization, while the older generation attempts to contain this behavior in familial and non-institutional settings. The parents seek to liberate their children from institutional constraints they themselves find injurious, but which they respect because they provide security. The older generation tells the young that they are free to question institutional demands but not to challenge the institutions. Although the older generation has mechanisms which enable them to cope with these contradictions, the young do not. The young have not undergone the historical experience that would force them to accept contradictions between values and actions; instead, they reject the style of thought and the life style of their parents. Two movies, *M.A.S.H.* and *The Graduate*, clarify the thought and life styles of the contending generations.

The movie *M.A.S.H.* is a good example of a generation accustomed to diverting personal needs and resentment from political and/or cultural criticism. Although the war is horrifying, you do not oppose it; rather, you find ways of anaesthetizing your inner feelings. Hostility can then be safely expressed as a joke, through outrageous personal behavior or athletics. In fact, the entire movie is true to its Korean War setting. The validity of the war is never raised. War is hell, but there are ways of surviving. The war itself is never the subject of serious analysis. Humor is used to attack those caricatures of military life who seem overly committed to the more puritanical aspects of war. Sex seems to be the cure for whatever ails the military straight arrows. Sex, however, is not to be confused with love or tenderness, so that you get what you can between operations, so to speak. But around each corner lurks madness because the anaesthetic threatens to lose its effect and the self constantly threatens to break through. The difficulty of subjecting the inner self to institutional demands is never treated directly. The stars romp through guts and gore, but are forgiven their antics because they finish the job. They even give medical welfare to orphans, which shows they really do care, as we all must for those victims of our wars that we stumble upon. Once the orders for home come through, the immediate present and past are wiped out, our loved ones back home remembered, and responsibilities of civilian life reaffirmed.

If *M.A.S.H.* is representative of the world view of the older generation, *The Graduate*, as Philip Slater points out, demonstrates the triumph of personal needs over social forms and represents the thought of the younger generation.

The hero of *The Graduate* is . . . not intimidated by the wedding ceremony but wails out his pain, and the heroine until then bewitched by social forms, is disenchanted, rescued, and redeemed.[21]

The younger generation brings its inner needs to political and cultural consciousness and contemptuously rejects the sublimation practiced by the older generation. This is the primary source fueling

[21]Slater, *Pursuit of Loneliness.*

generational conflict. Although the older generation does theoretically believe in expanding intrapersonal autonomy, it has not experienced the translation of intrapersonal needs into public behavior in institutional settings; thus, the older generation does not extend its support for personal integrity when this development threatens the institutions to which it has sacrificed its own needs. The separation of private and public worlds by the older generation creates a system of thought which is hostile to attempts by youth to integrate private and public lives. It is much like the immigrant parent who says, "After all I've sacrificed for you, how can you reject all I stand for?" The young in each case are caught in the position of reluctant ingrate. They did not determine the pressures to which they were subjected, but they cannot go back to something they do not know. They did not understand that the older generation meant them to follow their inner needs only to the point where they impede, undermine, or conflict with the established institutional arrangements.

THE HISTORICAL EXPERIENCE OF YOUTH

The attempt to integrate private and public worlds, coupled with the position of youth in post-industrial society, is the basis for generational consciousness, but not generational conflict. It is the older generation's response to experiments with alternative life styles and political protest which transforms differences in consciousness into deep conflict. The hostility to both cultural experimentation and political protest ultimately drives cultural and political protesters together and forces the development of a counter-culture and a self-conscious world view among youth. If this development is foreshadowed by an ambivalence of the older generation to the issues of the relation of self to social forms, it was not necessarily ordained. It is in the historical experience of this generation with the older generation, in situations of collective conflict, that contemporary consciousness is developed. When youthful experimentation met heavy and deeply emotional resistance from adults of their own social class, the young also experienced shock, which was followed by a growing militancy on behalf of counter-cultural life styles and political protest. The expansion of the youth culture can in part be attributed to the opportunity which educational institutions, especially universities, and adolescent subcultures provide young people to discover their common understandings, operationalize their perspective, and collectively experience adult responses.

The university creates a climate which is conducive to exploration and experimentation. The intelligentsia is "engaged vocationally
in the production, distribution, interpretation, criticism, and incul-
cation of cultural values."[22] However, it should be emphasized that
neither university cultures nor other youth cultures are new phenomena. For example, during the 1950s, youth was oriented toward
clothes, music, athletics, and conformity.[23] This, however, was during the rather apolitical period of the "silent generation."

Activist youth successfully experimented in cultural and political
forms that are definitively different from those of the older generation.

Once politics, music, life styles, and drugs were integrated into
counter-cultural life styles, the adolescent peer culture was ripe for
penetration; and the increasing youthfulness of activists who were
engaged in cultural and/or political experimentation testifies to the
capacity of youth in post-industrial society to operate independently
of the older generation. This structural characteristic suggests that,
once student protest turns to generational conflict, the young may
well be able to effectively organize their collective world in spite of
or over adult opposition.

It is from institutions of higher education that the young have
gone into the society to seek change. It was to the university that
they later returned, demanding a cleansing of their own house.
They began their struggles with the assumption that they had the
support of their elders; and at the end of the decade they were convinced that the older generation preferred stability to change in
spite of the injustices that plagued society. The young have developed their view in the racial struggle, in the Vietnam War, and
through cultural experimentation. In each case, the support for
attempts to change patterns of social relations between whites and
nonwhites, of foreign policy, and of social mores has been experienced as a fraud. Instead of support, the young have experienced
hostility and punitiveness where they tried to bring about change.
The experience with the intractability of these institutions has profoundly shocked this generation; it has led the young to re-evaluate
the validity of existing mechanisms for social change. Thus, at the

[22]Richard Flacks, "The Revolt of the Young Intelligentsia: Revolutionary Class-
Consciousness in Post-Scarcity America," in *Revolution Reconsidered*, N. Miller
and R. Aya, eds. (New York: Free Press, 1970).

[23]James S. Coleman. *The Adolescent Society* (New York: Free Press, 1961).

heart of generational conflict is the ability of the present social system to meet human needs. How, where, and under what conditions did this affluent and protected generation experience the decline in their faith in the responsiveness of the American society?

REASONS FOR THE DECLINE OF FAITH IN AMERICA

Race

The decade began on a note of optimism with the election of John F. Kennedy, his offer of moral support for Martin Luther King, Jr., and student-initiated sit-ins in North Carolina. The Civil Rights Movement went sour as young blacks and whites demanded immediate freedom and older liberals offered token symbols of their good faith.[24] By the mid-sixties, riots, black power, and the Black Panthers replaced the emphasis on integration and the movement went North. The disillusionment of the young on the issue of black equality came with the recognition that officials and the public were more concerned with the style of protest than the issues involved, despite the fact that official documents clearly identified the sources of militancy and rioting in institutional racism.[25] Resources were disproportionately allocated to arming social control agencies against militants and potential rioters, and reputable white political leaders played on the racial fears of whites.

Vietnam

The Vietnam War and its ancillary issue of the military-university complex has been even more significant in the radicalization of the young. Lyndon Johnson ran for the presidency in 1964 on the promise to end the war in Vietnam. The slogan of Students for a Democratic Society, "Half the way with LBJ," reflected substantial support for the domestic program as well as their desire to end America's involvement in Vietnam. The aftermath of the election was the massive expansion of the war; the students reacted with endless protests, teach-ins, sit-ins, and massive marches. Every step of

[24]Jack Newfield, *The Prophetic Minority* (New York: Signet, 1965); and James P. O'Brien, chapter 2.

[25]Otto Kerner, chairman, *Report of the National Advisory Commission on Civil Disorders* (New York: Dutton, 1968).

escalation occurred among assurances that no escalation was planned, together with predictions by the antiwar movement of the next round of escalations. The protests drew the wrath of the Johnson Administration and accentuated the impotence of the antiwar movement.

The campaign to unseat Lyndon Johnson was started in New Hampshire by large contingents of young people, and ended with another Kennedy assassination in Los Angeles and a police riot at the Democratic National Convention. The anticlimax to the disaster was the election of Richard M. Nixon on the promise to end the war.

The years 1968–70 have seen massive protests by the young against the Vietnam War and its extension throughout Indochina. The Administration has responded by watching football on television, and vilification of the antiwar movement in general, and youth in particular.

In the process, four students were killed by the National Guard at Kent State University. Today, small groups of young people have become committed to revolutionary violence, others are prepared to participate in occasional violence such as "trashing," and many more are prepared to understand or tolerate violence against institutions directly involved in the war.

During the height of the crisis in May of 1970, President Nixon appointed a special adviser on university affairs and a special commission to study campus unrest. Since neither the adviser nor the commission presented answers acceptable to the White House, they have been ignored and repudiated in another demonstration of the resistance of the political and industrial institutions to pressures for change.

THE EXPERIMENTAL YOUTH CULTURE

The third area of major conflict between generations is experimentation by the young with counter-cultural life styles. The life style confrontation has occurred through presentation of a self radically at odds with the social and cultural expectations of the older generation. One aspect of this process consists of altering patterns of dress and appearance, especially body, hair, and style of communications (language, music, and art forms). The other side of the counter-culture plays on physical transformations and involves experiments with drugs, communal living, sexuality, especially the blurring of sexual differences, and explorations into intra- and inter-personal worlds in opposition to competitive and achievement behavior. As the young physically differentiated themselves from the older generation, they appeared strange and subversive. The older generation utilized social control agencies to combat what it perceived as deviance. The punitive use of schools, police, and courts failed to stop youthful experimentation. Counter-cultural presentations of self made it easy for the like-minded to identify each other. This allowed them to judge their strength among their peers.

One major accomplishment of punitive responses by the older generation was to legitimize "deviant" behavior for many young people who were cultural rather than political dissidents. Cultural experimentation, like political experimentation, focused the attention of the young on the restrictive character of the society and its limited capacity to tolerate alternatives to established social and cultural patterns. Furthermore, the punitive response by the older generation to cultural experimentation laid the groundwork for unifying cultural and political protest by identifying both types of experimenters as outsiders.

GENERATIONAL CONFLICT IN THE UNIVERSITY

The university has been at the center of generational conflict because of the middle-class character of the protest movement. The early 1960s were an era of mutual confidence between students and the rest of the academic community. By the end of the decade, mutual distrust and confrontation had become the dominant theme of campus life. Students saw the failure of faculty and administration to meet their demands for changes in the relationship between the university and minority communities, and the university and the political Center, as further proof of the inflexibility of American institutions. Faculty and administrators saw the university as a fragile institution being subjected to unreasonable confrontation tactics by students. Even in areas where faculty and administration were willing to make concessions, the process of confrontation left scars and lingering hostility. Students and faculty denounced each other for the militancy of the protest and harshness of the response.

Examples of this type of confrontation are the black studies and open-enrollment controversies. To a limited extent, protests aimed at expanding the quantity and quality of black participation in American universities have succeeded. Although black studies and the expansion of the black student body and faculty constitute one genuine area of success for the protest movement, they have been unable to prevent further estrangement between the generations in the academic community because the process of achieving gains has been so heavily dominated by the need to use militant extra-administrative and/or legislative channels. The process of negotiation has proceeded through confrontation politics which further de-authorize the older generation, because their contention that reason rather than power was the road to settlement of grievances proved inaccurate. Reason by itself only rarely proved sufficient to negotiate change. Second, black students have demanded curricular and admissions-policy changes. This clearly demands some reallocation of resources, but it does not demand the severing of critical and lucrative relationships with other institutions.

The attempt by the younger generation to effect a change in governmental policy on the Vietnam War issue has led to an expanded analysis of the character of the Cold War state. The role of academic institutions and personnel in providing knowledge for the American war machine has become a major source of contention between the generations. On this issue, the younger generation was indeed demanding an alteration of institutional relationships between the university and the political Center.

Department of Defense–sponsored research and research institutions, recruitment of defense-related industries and the military (ROTC), and foreign policy advisers located on university campuses, became significant targets of protest.

The university, because of the role of science and the manpower needs of the post-industrial society, became a microcosm of the larger society. University protests carried out by students on their own turf could also be directed at national issues and institutions, because of the relationship between universities and the national Center. Antagonism and conflict with the administration over the validity of this relationship led to an even further division between the generations, as the majority of the older generation saw the demands to terminate contracts, institute programs, and corporate recruitment as an invasion of its independence and academic freedom. Whatever the rhetoric, the young saw the university and its faculty as partisans of the military-industrial complex which directed the

Vietnam War. The faculty tended to support its right to make its own choices as to research and research funds.

Again, militant action brought down the agencies of social control on the protesters. The presence of police and National Guard on campus, a shocking development in 1964 at Berkeley, became commonplace. Here again youth directly experienced the use of social control agencies against those who could not or would not accept the positions of faculty administrators as to the correct institutional role vis-à-vis government, the military, and industry. Since neither side could verbally persuade the other of its position, each resorted to the power it could mobilize to force the issue. In the university, the young also confronted their inability to create the kind of institution they sought. In the final analysis, they simply lacked the power to force change.

PATTERNS OF INTRA-CLASS CONFLICT

Generational conflict emerged from the interplay between the location and experience of middle-class youth; and it has some peculiar characteristics because it sets members of the same social class against one another.

The pattern of confrontation between the generations suggests some of the problems of intra-class conflict. Initially, neither older nor younger generation found the stance of antagonist particularly confortable. Each generation has found it difficult to develop a stable definition of the other. The young are both part of the family and the ideological enemy. Do you label them as outsiders, unruly children, or reasonable critics? All these labels have been used at one time or another; what is most interesting is the inconsistency with which they have been used. The young likewise have tended to see the older generation as outsiders, irritable and irrational parents as well as men of good faith. At different times, the older generation has been treated in each way. As each generation has experienced what is felt to be a betrayal of commonly shared understandings about the style and content of protest, the ideological foundation of the confrontation has become increasingly clear, especially to the younger generation. The older generation developed labels of "outside agitator," "hard core" and "small minority of undesirables" to protect itself from the ideological character of conflict. These labels also justify the increasingly militant action of the young, as well as harsher reprisals by the older generation.

The intra-class character of the conflict initially obscures its ideological nature. However, over time the process of conflict clarifies the basic issues. These issues are: (1) the commitment of the younger and older generations to the existing institutional framework; and (2) the commitment of the younger and older generations to the creation of a "humane" society, that is, a society free of racism, poverty, and war, and open to multiple cultural styles. For the older generation, the movement toward a "humane" society is moderated by an overriding commitment to the established institutional framework. For the young, the validity of the institutional framework is determined by its responsiveness to meeting human needs.

This shift in emphasis constitutes a radical break in generational consciousness. The awareness of this discontinuity in thought is a necessary condition for the younger generation to see itself as an outsider vis-a-vis its own social class, as well as the society dominated by the older generation. Recognition by the young of these differences is slow, and dependent upon the development of a series of situations in which confrontation destroys the assumed similarity of interests and sentiments. The greater the degree to which each institution and issue appears interrelated, the greater the probability that ideological differentiation will develop. Social problems, as long as they remain independent problems, are insufficient to create ideological intra-class divisions. Only as social problems are experienced as a product of the internal logic of the system does ideological differentiation develop. In the early part of the decade, civil rights were seen as a social problem and produced a non-generational protest movement. The second half of the decade has seen the development of ideological conflict along generational lines; this is a consequence of the experience of the similarity of responses by the older generation to the attempt to create a more "humane" society through political and cultural experimentation.

Intra-class conflict allows for a moderation of conflict while at the same time it continually emphasizes generational differences. Interpersonal contact along generation lines within class boundaries has the effect of moderating the conflict. The pattern of interaction between the generations provides space for and sustains non-antagonistic relationships, and allows new ones to develop. Thus, parent/child, teacher/student, senior/junior colleague, friend/friend, constitute cross-cutting ties between generations. These contacts do not eliminate ideological differences, but they do humanize the antagonist. These role relationships create situations in which class sentiments are reinforced and generational differences muted. The humanization of the antagonist and multiple role relationships between the generations are significant factors in the erratic response of the older generation to the youth movement and the cyclical character of generational activism. Mutually rewarding interaction across generational lines reinforces non-ideological definitions of the antagonist; it creates the feeling of "we," and the expectation of some negotiability of differences. This reinforces ideas about hard-core outside agitators in situations where collective conflict blurs personal relationships. Both generations, in conflict situations, tend to fall back on personal knowledge of the antagonist rather than focus on the conflict of interest in the heart of the confrontation.

Role commitments (student, junior faculty, intern, and the like) take away time from political and cultural experimentation for the young and also limit the time the older generation must spend outside of its established roles, such as professor, doctor, or father. Again, the time limitations tend to reinforce beliefs on the part of the older generation that the younger generation is not, by and large, committed to political and cultural experimentation. In other words, the older generation wants to believe that only those young people who engage in full-time protest are involved in and sympathetic to the counter-culture. Actually, full-time youthful activists serve their constituency in the same way as the permanently organized "hard-core" political leaders and administrators who organize and lead the political and cultural institutions of the older generation.

The super-ordinate/subordinate character of the role relationships between the older and younger generations also provides a context in which hostility can develop, as a consequence of different generational interpretations of the proper content of the roles, providing a continual interplay between generational world views.

As crisis follows crisis, what emerges are clearly differentiated world views acted out between groups sharing social, economic, and occupational positions. Each group has its own cadre of permanently mobilized leadership representing the most advanced stages of its generational world view. Large sectors of each generation are available for a crisis or an event. Those of the younger generation who are not permanently mobilized divide their time between the roles they occupy and the experimental culture and political protest. Although not constantly active, this sector of each generation cannot be described as uninvolved, for it shares attitudes, feelings, and ideas with the more permanently mobilized. In fact, in a crisis, the attempt to punitively isolate the permanently mobilized sector of the younger generation usually activates this part of the population. Over the last few years, confrontations at Columbia, Wisconsin, Berkeley, and Harvard have demonstrated this at each institution.[26] And the events following Kent State have demonstrated the same thing on a national level.

CONCLUSION

The patterns of intra-class conflict between the older and younger generations in America are controlled by the structural transformation of the position of youth in post-industrial societies, patterns of childhood socialization which emphasize self-actualization over conformity to social forms, and the experience of this generation of youth with the hostile and punitive responses by the older generation to cultural and political experimentation. Most especially, the conflict between the generations has been exacerbated by the Vietnam War, the souring of the Civil Rights Movement, and the attempts by the older generation to stop experimentation with social forms and mores. The outcome has been an increasingly bitter series of confrontations in which the younger and older generations collectively express their hostility to each other. This pattern of conflict tends to be cyclical and sporadic because the pattern of interaction between the younger and older generations humanized enemies even as it creates multiple opportunities for friction in role-relationships which accentuate different views of appropriate behavior.

The pattern of generational conflict in America has been especially bitter and threatens to become increasingly violent, because specific political and cultural issues such as Vietnam and race relations and life styles remain unresolved. The attempt by the more rigid elements of leadership of the older generation to utilize generational hostility as a tool for political mobilization of a governing coalition creates the conditions for a particularly harsh confrontation over the shape of the future.

[26]Morgan and Judith Lyons, "Black Student Power: Protest and Reaction on Campus" (Unpublished paper, Florida State University, 1970).

.12. Stances and Substances

JOHN R. SEELEY

I HAVE not made a proper scientific count of column inches printed and man-seconds of speech and listening, but my impression is that, in the circles in which I move and in which those in those circles move, three topics have in the last six years been given the greatest total word-volume as well as word-passion: Hair, Drugs, and the War. And in that order.

Around these and related topics we are close to an undeclared psycho-social civil war, instituted, escalated, re-escalated and finally allowed to get utterly, or all but, out of hand. This war goes on over nearly the whole Western world, though here, as usual, America leads the way.

All three topics often proceed from and play back into discussions of "the Young." The Young are seemingly America's Number One love, Number One enemy, Number One public problem, and Number One private preoccupation. Locked in a love/hate relation to them, severally and collectively, those not young do more for them on a basis they take to be one of love and concern, while they also mount more weaponry and defeat-and-control gadgetry, material, social, and psychological against them, define them more into object-status as a problem, and "worry" more about them, than any other category of the population: women, blacks, browns, reds, or yellows, the old, the poor, the sick, the lonely, the criminal, even the unholy and deadly dangerous industrial-military-academic alliance.

THE YOUNG AND THEIR HAIR

First, as to hair: when young men reject the standard and hallmark and badge of conventionally defined virility, the clean-shaven (note

238

the odd connection of terms!) face and the close-cut (at its extreme, erectile) hair, and embrace a carefully cultivated, artistically elaborated sculpture of facial hirsute adornment, and a long, soft, flowing, sensual, and equally careful arrangement of head-hair, they are certainly saying something profound and threatening to those bearers of the traditional culture who say otherwise. They are saying, in an expressive gesture more powerful than any manifesto, all of the following things, among others: that artistic effect is more important to them than "efficient" appearance; that natural signs of sexuality and heightened sexual consciousness should not be restrained from the overt and public life and restricted to the covert and private one; that the overemphasis on categories like man/woman, public/private, active/passive, wooer/wooed, and the fixed labels and allotted roles connected therewith, are to be blurred and collapsed so that a finer sensibility for person and situation can replace labeling and label-reading; that sensuality, sexuality, play, and drama are not to be segregated from but infused into daily life; that personal style and taste must override the economies and conveniences of ready reading and identification; that hard, aggressive, determined, effortful pushiness, expressed in appearance, has not only nothing to do with what it is to be a man, but is a caricature, distortion, and miserable reduction of what that is.

At a deeper level, the transformation marks and expresses, in achievement and intent, the rejection of a whole phallic way of appearing and being in the world, in favor of a way that is at once more genital and more polymorph-perverse.

Such a shift presupposes a gradual shift in the center of gravity of a civilization, if not a new civilization—always provided we survive at all.

Let me, therefore, touch briefly on the war and then get down to drugs—or, perhaps, up!

THE YOUNG AND THE WAR

The resistance to the war moves at many levels, but in its symbolic meaning and in its intertwining with other issues it is unlike, greatly unlike, earlier forms of resistance to a draft or a particular war. For in some very large part this resistance carries and is carried by two deeper flows. They are closely related. The first flow is in a general movement against categorization, organization, role, obedience, and so on. The second flow is against the pre-existing notions of manhood and manliness, the values put upon assertive, aggressive, and proving and testing behavior for the person, and determining, ruling, controlling, expansive conquistadorial behavior for the nation or the state. It is not simply that the new people think this war foolish to the point of insanity and immoral to the point of bottomless depravity, but that they believe the whole conscience and consciousness out of which it flows is the source of a death-dealing disease for them, for us, for all mankind. When they say, at their mildest, that they "can't relate to it," they mean something far more significant than that they oppose it. They mean that, given their conscience and consciousness, they cannot comprehend it, and others cannot comprehend their incomprehension—that the very terms of the language that leads to this and all such enterprises are terms that have no meaning for them, or as little as "succubi" or "incubi" have (though one sometimes wonders) for the calculators and computers or for the games-theorists and power-balancers and games-players in the Pentagon. And by "all such enterprises," they mean not only all agressive wars but the whole mindless conquest of everything that there is to be conquered—at the cost of eviscerating well-nigh every other human capacity—which is the essence and arch-enterprise of the civilization itself. They do not even want all that much to conquer disease, if the price of conquest is just that much more calculation, control, regulation, bureaucracy, hassling, and extension of technarchy over all.

THE YOUNG AND DRUGS

It is time to turn to the drug problem, though the very use of the words "drug problem" prejudges and prejudices adequate apprehension of what is afoot. What is one man's "drug problem" is another man's "narc problem," and the right to name what a problem is is a pure expression of relative power. Moreover, the tendency to define almost everything as a problem is itself an expression of a particular form of consciousness, a certain way of being in the world, that is not given in nature but constructed in culture and, therefore, open to question, and now questioned. But since I cannot, I presume, hope to convince anyone on simple presentation that problem-constituting may be at or near the heart of a great part of our difficulties in every sphere, let me attempt to discuss the matter in the terms assigned.

Unfortunately, we must begin with some very elementary matters. What is a drug?

As soon as we define the term we may well be into the heart of the controversy and those much deeper matters it opens up. The word "drug" is old, but, interestingly, its etymological origin is lost in antiquity. A brief dictionary definition is "a medicinal substance." But what does "medicinal" mean? Medicinal means "pertaining to medicine." Medicine is the art of preserving or restoring health. Health means "wholeness." And wholeness is not only etymologically the twin of holiness, but, in a long tradition, either identical in meaning or so related that holiness includes wholeness. The holy is what is conformed to the divine. The divine is what is of surpassing excellence. Put it together: a drug is a substance requisite or helpful to an art that preserves, restores, or enhances surpassing excellence. I am not sure that, for a believer, the communion wafer, though simple bread in a secular apprehension, does not qualify as a drug in a sacred one.

I must assume that the reader is thinking that this is not what he means. And it is certainly not what any arm of government concerned with "dangerous drugs" thinks *it* means. It, too, might allow or insist that a drug is a medicinal substance. A medicinal substance, they would hold, however, is a substance that is or ought to be used exclusively in medicine. "Medicine" to them is an applied science. It is an applied science properly practiced only by physicians. Physicians are one class of state licensees. These licensees preserve or restore health. Health is adequate somatic or psychological (or, perhaps, psychosomatic) function. Adequate function is a notion definable in science, and its presence or absence is ascertainable by scientific enquiry. "Scientific" means essentially experimental. Table salt, if anyone were tempted to take it in fatal doses, would doubtless qualify as a drug, if physicians so declared, as glue perhaps does already.

The Polar Extremes

The drug problem in its modern form cannot be understood without recognition and deep appreciation of its two contending polar extremes as sketched, though much of what is problematic lies in what I would call the "muddled middle." The muddled middle is itself largely, however, the result of confusion engendered by the mutual failure of those at the purer poles to understand one another. Unless the two sides—the conventional side being clearly the aggressor—drive each other to insane excess, we are pushed neither to the madnesses of obsessive prohibition nor to the insanities of hysterical abandon.

It is no accident and no isolated phenomenon that the issues do appear framed on those terms: prohibition or abandonment; or, to put it more generally, conformity to peremptory demand based on the conventional wisdom, or exile—psycho-social or physical, or both.

The same alternatives, broadly, are commonly offered in the matter of male hair length, in other matters of costume, style, consumption, manners, or attire for both sexes, in male attitudes to and action about war and, often, female attitudes and actions in the realm of sex. At least, the alternatives offered are so perceived by the thousands of runaways or internal exiles of our society, becoming more numerous and younger each year. And if it is not the message consciously intended by thousands of parents, schools, and communities, it must be either the unconscious message communicated or a misunderstanding so massive that it taxes credulity to believe that the explanation lies in a "communications gap" in the usual sense. If there is a "communications gap" that is relevant, it lies more probably within the people than between them, most especially in the disjuncture between the conscious and unconscious wishes of parents and "parent-figures." It is such intrapersonal communications gaps that underlie interpersonal ones. A sense of fatherlessness, of having been unfathered or defathered, is the commonest report or complaint I have encountered in extended intimate conversation with those young most dangerously into and most in the muddled middle of the drug pattern. In those previously weak or badly damaged, this results in a sort of protracted or passive floating, chemically or otherwise induced or sustained. In the stronger, it results in more or less effective, more or less sad, attempts to father and mother themselves or each other anew, to be reborn, or, more commonly, to seek an unsatisfactory but next-best solution in substituting would-be responsponsible siblingship as a source of birth, nurture, sustenance, and support in place of effective parenting.

It would be wrong to let the impression lie that those setting such polar alternatives for their progeny or quasi-progeny do so simply wickedly, wantonly, or without agony and yearning for something other and better. What happens is more like—and probably an enlargement of—what happens in any time of religious transformation, such as the Reformation or, more markedly, the advent of Christianity or Islam. "Believers" and "unbelievers," especially perhaps the best of both, are simply unable to understand each other on almost any point or at almost any level; indeed, each can hardly believe either that the other believes what he says he believes, or that, if he does, he can be in any intelligible sense sane. Imagine Jesus trying to explain to the Roman High Command the doctrines of "love your enemies," "unto him that smiteth thee on one cheek, offer also the other," and "take no thought for the morrow"—not as strategic tricks or means to something else, but as samples of what is implied by the only proper way of being in the world!

I have, of course, up to this point drawn my prototypes too pure, though real people close to that degree of purity in their counterposed perceptions do exist. Most of the protagonists more muddily perceive the issue from points near one or the other pole. If we want to take in considerable numbers—still omitting a substantial middle—we should have to say that not a religion, but a religious movement or milling, or a movement or milling with marked religious overtones, confronts, over drugs, a debased physicianship backed by a debased secular power, the state. Something not yet fully formed confronts two somethings, long-formed and gone, past prime and seed-time, toward degeneration.

The Degenerate State

I will not argue in detail here, taking it to be obvious, that the state is degenerate. Its long-established monopoly of violence is now nearly matched by its monopoly of atrocity and major crime. No enterprise smaller than the state can effectively engage in genocide, biocide, and the noocide that we call national propaganda, as the core of communication at home and abroad. Nor can any other enterprise match the state *in hubris* as reflected in its galloping drift to totalism: the very volume of statute law and regulation, and the logarithmic rate at which it increases, even as it invades every manner and matter of being and behaving, sufficiently attest a cancerous character.

Hardly conscious any longer that men are more than citizens and subjects, that acts have many meanings and percussions and repercussions on many levels, the state (barely restrained in this country by the remnants and tatters of the Constitution) moves to rule and regulate more and more, in more and more detail, in more and more respects.

Medicine as an Art

The state is degenerate by bloating.

And medicine is degenerate both by its dependence on the state and by shrinkage due to the same cultural imperatives that make the state so bloated. The state can properly neither affirm nor deny professional proficiency, nor does such proficiency require the state's confirmation—always provided that there is a profession there to recognize the adept and withhold recognition from the apprentice or quack. But more serious than the profession's dependence on the state for "licensing," money and enforcement action, is its own shrinkage increasingly toward the ideal of "scientific medicine." Science, like love, is not enough! A profession whose responsibility is health or wholeness must practice a general art—the healing art, the art of aiding men become or remain whole—and science is of that art neither the basis nor the crown.

A "physician" means a "man who physics," who practices, it is assumed, in the physical order—so much so that a special word, "psychosomatic," had to be coined to patch the order, as though any medicine applied to man (or, probably, to anything living) could be other than psychosomatic or somatopsychic. Nothing can be done to or for a body that it not done to or for, or often against, a psyche— nor, for that matter, to the indivisible psychesoma or person, that is not done to or for or against the society, actual and virtual, in which he exists. A "doctor," the better term, means a "teacher," someone who causes someone to learn what that person needs to learn, that is, to grow or otherwise become more nearly whole.

In general, far from being such doctors, most physicians are ultra-competent engineer-managers, not even of whole bodies but of organs or organ-systems, or masters of mere procedures such as cutting or photography and photograph-reading. Were there real doctors, they would be, like good parents or teachers, those to whom persons would turn in warranted trust, to be told and shown by advice, practice, and example what was good for each, at a given moment in his expanding life, at a given instant in man's history and evolution. What would be good might be a drug, or a word, or a silence. Which would be good would be a matter for the art. The art would depend on a relation. And the relation could not have as one party a customer or an object of a technology or material for a craft.

Becoming Their Own Doctors

Failing such doctors, many have tried to become their own doctors or to engage with others in an amateur practice of the kind called for. It is probably about as silly for any man to be his own doctor as to be his own lawyer, teacher, or priest. It may even be a contradiction in terms. Yet a great part of the "drug problem" lies precisely in this: people, perhaps especially young people, take drugs —and do other things—acting validly on the aim of "expanding" their "consciousness" out of the consequent experience. They may well act imprudently as their own doctors, just as they may also unwisely attempt, in their desperate necessity, to be their own teachers and parents. That they will know what will best, or appropriately, or at all, expand their consciousness at any given moment is, I believe, almost by definition impossible. If they did know, it would argue that they had already achieved enough "expansion of consciousness" to know themselves and the moment and the context and the means so well that they knew beforehand what was most needed next.

That is unlikely. Most unlikely.

But, as the majority find themselves situated, as they look for alternative means to the valid end, they look one way to amateurs who have in a perhaps rather vague way the right ends in view, and the other way to certified practitioners who have not only the wrong ones, but a consciousness so constricted that they do not know (or, if they "know," only cognitively so) that they are wrong. Suppose both were to view with favor the ingestion of the same substance in the same dosage, say a "mood-elevator." The rankest amateur would know that a great part, perhaps the essence, of the effect would depend not on bare chemical properties, but upon who gave it to whom, with what message in words—and beyond or below words— and in whose company it was taken, in what surroundings, with what supported expectations, in what state of mind, open to what inner and outer clues and messages, at how many levels of consciousness. The scientific physician will generally, in the face of such knowledge, simply write an authoritative prescription, to be delivered to another commercial functionary, who will "make up" and dispense some pills, put them into a plastic bottle with a typed and printed instructional and restrictive label. The pills so dispensed will probably be taken privately, if not secretly or furtively perhaps gulped down, with no more special or appropriately directed awareness than is allowed for all other functions of life from which we thus normally also cut ourselves off.

This is the major underlying, very nearly ultimate, postural counterposition that makes nearly all talk about the drug problem merely fill the air with soundwaves, or conceal in seeming contention a conflict or difference whose terms never come clear.

The Muddled Middle

In the middle—what I have called the muddled middle—exist a still more luckless number who take their major terms of reference from neither party or perhaps, in still more degenerate terms, from both. These are they who, roughly, having been abandoned, bereft of significant parents, teachers, doctors, gurus, have abandoned themselves, and who, in their misery, seek mere relief or, in their boredom, mere kicks. Perhaps the fact that they seek even these indicates that they have not totally abandoned themselves, even as, perhaps, they have not been totally abandoned.

They take their terms from the technologist-physicians in that, without any appreciable feel for or sense of themselves or the world, they seek simply to impose on their minds and bodies—treated virtually as alien objects outside which they, like the physicians, stand —other states (often *any* other state) by almost any means, mechanically viewed and mechanically used. They take their terms from the quasi- or proto-religious or mystical, insofar as they seek to break out of the straitjacket of present consciousness toward some unknown which they sense must be better, insofar as they attempt to decondition themselves at any price—sickness or death, if necessary—to find some freedom, some new perspective if not some new vision.

They also derive their terms from neither party, insofar as they forsake all the prudential considerations represented by physicians, and at the same time mistake the pursuit of momentary pleasures for the search for bliss represented by the quasi- and proto-mystics. The result is catastrophic fragmentation of persons never too well put together, anyway. It is exhibited in quantitatively thinned and qualitatively impoverished social relations, kicks—literally self-assaults—in place of joy at least glimpsed and moved toward, and unwanted and pointless sicknesses and hungers of body and soul. These interact in a dialectic of destruction that is a model of devolution of person and world.

I do not doubt that the number of available drugs is going to increase till we possess and have widespread knowledge about substances possibly helpful in inducing or sustaining or altering or eliminating almost any state of the body/mind. The drug manufacturers, on one side, proceed apace in permuting and combining almost all possible chemical substances; and the amateurs, on their side, search as well nature's herbarium, tribal practice and lore, the mushrooms and barks and shoots and leaves and flowers that properly treated—physically and ceremonially—yield or might yield this or that catalyst or foundation for this or that transformation, momentary or enduring.

No one will deny that these are powerful agents and reagents. No one will deny that power is dangerous, and promising, and that, either way, it beckons. The vision of such substances let loose at random chills every imagination. And since what we see as preview is sufficient horror (though also hope), all stand in the status of sorcerer's apprentices—as we stand before so much else—wondering what to do with the powers we have, unprepared for them, let loose.

Drugs, Crime, and War

The power of the substances, evidently, even at this early stage, is sufficient to organize a whole criminal industry, and force a large segment of society into crime both in its employment of the drugs—crime merely by definition—and in the activities necessary to procure the drugs at prohibition-engendered, fantastic prices. By the same token, as already indicated, a vast symbiotic control, cure, propaganda, and punishment industry, with a budget likely soon to rival the military one, has been built up; a snoop and spy system, developed and spread wide and deep; dogs forced into detection and your friendly policeman into dawn raids and no-knock warrants; the courts clogged; humane judges violated in their consciences; trust relations between parents and children, teachers and pupils, and even friends and peers, infected with mutual suspicion. All this and more has been rapidly brought into being and launched on a course of unlimited growth. But the same materials, on the other side, have originated a whole new culture, new perceptions, new sensitivities between persons and sensibilities within them, a vast opening toward those intimations for the lack of acquaintance with which Western culture and civilization appear to be suffocating and dying in the excesses of their own unreasonable worship and service of an irrational "rationality," that is, a consciousness narrowed almost to mere calculation, cast always in means/ends terms that terminate in no reasonably desirable or mutually related ends.

What is being played out around, or focused upon, the "drug problem"—as with the other problems mentioned and, indeed, now, nearly all problems—is the civilizational crisis itself. Someone, at a conference I recently attended, spoke of Western man's "rational fatigue." But more than fatigue, more than subjective exhaustion, is at stake. Rationality, defined as it has been since Descartes, has run itself out, and the persons and the society which deified it are in moral peril if not in their terminal sickness or death throes.

The concentration camps, the international balance of terror, Herman Kahn's unthinkable thinking of the unthinkable, free-fire zones and biocide, the thousand and one My Lais that are not incidents in but are the essence of the Vietnam War, and the Vietnams more surely than tomorrow yet to come—all these and their like are not aberrations from but perfect expressions of the mentality of rationalism which, originating in modern times in the West, bids fair now to engulf and sink the world. And at the level personally apprehended, the growing emptiness, alienation, anxiety or apathy, goal-fragmentation or goallessness, impersonalization and depersonalization, disenchantment and disillusionment, despair or, beyond despair, anaesthesia, speak for the same phenomenon.

The Civilizational Crisis

I do not think we can cope with or cure the drug problem in the small or in the large—indeed, I do not think we can do other than make very bad matters very much worse—unless we are ready, first, to recognize the civilizational crisis, and then do or let others do something sufficient about it. The more we attempt to exert control over drug use or abuse—both responses, most generally, to control gone insane in the culture—the more we add to the control structure that is itself the essential cause of the essential problem. Our very way of framing the problem, and indeed the perceptions and misperceptions of man and life that permit us to frame it that way—even before we "respond"—so offend the sensibilities that are sought in and sometimes seemingly furthered by at least some drugs, that we have with the users no common universe of discourse. We have no way so to enter their lives that we might know better forms to enhance them than the ones they, perhaps too cavalierly and casually, employ. If we add, or permit our official agents to add, the crimes of spying and lying to the sin of being uncomprehending and the fault of being incomprehensible, we must expect at best to be ignored as irrelevant and at worst to be viewed and treated as enemy.

I do not doubt for a moment—nor do most of those I know who have stayed close enough to the phenomena to be credible witnesses—that many have passed by means of drugs (in many cases, later, dropped) to states of awareness, to insights, to modalities of being, to apparent conversions, which one must conclude could have been reached by them in no other way. These transformations seem to me, on my best intuition, all-important steps in the several developments of those who have undergone them and, potentially, in the evolution of society. I do not hold—but then neither, after the phase or event, do most of the users—that drugs are the best way, but that, for many in our society at the time, they were the only way.

The Deep-grained Error at the Root

All this may seem cold comfort even to those who watch from afar the horrors of the bodily-psychic diseases, the disintegration, diminution, addiction, destruction of self and others, that careless use of these powerful compounds brings with it. And to those close or involved, the horrors are almost sufficient to explain, though not to excuse, the hysteria in high places, the forceful, wrongly directed acts committed in badly aimed remedy in law. I agonize, probably, as much as any but the worst-placed victims. But I will give no one the comfort of confirming him in error, especially when the consequence of the error is the very victimization he deplores. The error is in the way we view the problem, and the connected problems, and, indeed, life; and that error is so deep-grained in our several beings and in our society's core enterprises and missions that something like a conversion experience or a long, laborious course of personal and social reconstruction is required for its eradication. We—at least the official and conventional we—are so sunk in our ignorance that we think we have nothing to learn from those who stumble in a different dark but at least seek and sometimes glimpse a different light.

What is called for is, I fear, unlikely to be forthcoming: a credible body of elders or sages or adepts or wise men, manifesting in their lives that expanded and enlarged and heightened and deepened conscience and consciousness, reached by means other than substantial, and expressing itself in a way of being and acting that recommends itself on its face to the searcher, justly imbues him with trust, and begins and promises to continue to inspire him in a way that he senses is fulfilling at once to himself and his mission, given his thus-to-be-discovered nature, in his thus-to-be-illuminated world.

No less than this will do us much good in the matter of drugs— or education, or parenting, or social policy, for that matter—and probably nothing less will permit us, or our culture or civilization, to survive at all.

.13. The Revolution as a Trip: Symbol and Paradox

BARBARA G. MYERHOFF

AMONG THE special characteristics of symbols and rituals is their capacity to encompass ambiguity, contradiction, and paradox, as has been demonstrated so well by Claude Lévi-Strauss,[1] Clifford Geertz,[2] and especially Victor Turner.[3] The conflicts and disorderly arrangements handled by ritual and symbol may issue from many sources—for example, internal inconsistencies within an ideological system, lack of congruence between an ideology and the social system it purports to describe, justify, or interpret, or from ill-related structural features of a society. Through symbol and ritual, paradoxes are embraced and opposing elements fused so as to provide a sense of unity and order to those employing them, thus sparing the users any agonizing re-evaluations of their beliefs. Symbols and rituals serve as a screen through which reality is distorted in the service of a collective interpretation or myth.

[1]Claude Lévi-Strauss, *Structural Anthropology* (New York: Basic Books, 1963); "The Story of Asdiwal," in *The Structural Study of Myth and Totemism,* E. Leach, ed. (London: Tavistock, 1967).

[2]Clifford Geertz, "Ethos, World-view, and the Analysis of Sacred Symbols," *Antioch Review,* Winter, 1957–58; also "Religion as a Cultural System," in *Anthropological Approaches in the Study of Religion,* M. Banton, ed. (London: Tavistock, 1966).

[3]Victor Turner, *The Forest of Symbols: Aspects of Ndembu Ritual* (Ithaca: Cornell University Press, 1967); *The Drums of Affliction: A Study of Religious Processes Among the Ndembu of Zambia* (Oxford: Clarendon and the International African Institute, 1968); also, *The Ritual Process: Structure and Antistructure* (Chicago: Aldine, 1969).

251

FUNCTIONS OF SYMBOL AND RITUAL

Selective interpretation of reality and unification of paradox are the functions of symbol and ritual which are of particular concern here. In this paper, two paradoxes are singled out from the beliefs and actions of a small group of student political leaders involved in a university strike for a week during May, 1970. One of these paradoxes is the result of a contradiction within their ideology, and the other results from a conflict between the ideology and the external circumstances in which their actions occurred. In both cases, their rituals and symbols served well in providing them with a sense of the coherence and integrity of their ideology and allowing them to experience congruence between their beliefs and actions.

The events described here occurred on the campus of an American university which was large, privately funded, generally conservative, and without a pattern or history of political activism. In response to the Cambodian invasion, the slaying of the Kent State and Jackson State students, and the resultant student and faculty concern over these episodes, the university administration adopted a policy which, among other things, provided that for several days classes would be cancelled but the campus would not be closed. On the contrary, the university administration threw the campus open to students, parents, alumni, faculty, and others who were interested in "joining forces toward developing programs of positive, nonviolent actions addressed to the critical moral and political issues facing the nation."

The resulting actions of the students did not constitute a strike in the usual sense of a protest against the university administration. A great many students, the leaders in particular, had every intention of calling a strike but they had no opportunity to do so. Before classes could be boycotted or picketed, or buildings occupied to close the university in protest against the Cambodian-Kent-Jackson situation, the administration itself cancelled classes—a policy which created a peculiar situation for the student leaders, as will be seen. Nevertheless, the events of the following few days were generally construed and referred to as a "strike," a protest action by students against national domestic and international policies. Following this usage, I shall employ the term "strike" throughout this paper, though it should be understood in terms of these qualifications.

Other qualifications are necessary; this paper refers to a restricted, selective part of the ideas and actions of a very small, specialized group of students and does not take into account the actions and contributions of the many individuals and groups involved in the strike. The total matrix of events was extremely complex and the focus on the part played by one small group is clearly artificial, justifiable only for analytic purposes.

Turning now to this group, it should be made clear that, though it was very small, it was nevertheless highly influential and very important in shaping some of the events and providing the atmosphere which was so conspicuous during the strike. Entirely self-recruited, with varying degrees of prior political experience, the group was made up of about a dozen male Caucasians between eighteen and twenty-eight—undergraduates from several disciplines, generally middle- and upper-class in origin. They were highly visible, as a result of certain features of their ideology. Not merely long-hairs or hippies (that might be anyone these days), they were, as one informant put it, "counter-culture people—grubby, hairy, turned-on, hang-loose freaks," not derogatory terms in this context but ones which they used self-approvingly to emphasize and to describe their distinctive appearance.

These students drew their inspiration from the Yippie philosophy of Abbie Hoffman[4] and Jerry Rubin[5] and must be distinguished from the more disciplined, single-minded political activists associated with Students for a Democratic Society and the New Left, though there is always some overlap between hippies, Yippies, and activists. (The term "Yippie" is probably derived from the initials for the Youth International Party, which issued its first manifesto on January 16, 1967 through Liberation News Service, announcing the intention to hold a "Festival of Life" at the Democratic Convention in Chicago.) In their belief system, what they were into was not politics, properly speaking; in fact, several objected to being referred to as "political." If labels were necessary—and they weren't sure about that—then they wished to be known as "student spokesmen," rejecting even the term "leader."[6] This reflected the pronounced equalitarian, anti-elitist aspect of their ideology.

[4]Abbie Hoffman, *Revolution for the Hell of It* (New York: Dial Press, 1968); *Woodstock Nation* (New York: Random House, 1969).

[5]Jerry Rubin, *Do It!* (New York: Simon and Schuster, 1970).

[6]The term "leader" is used throughout this paper, with several other descriptive terms, for stylistic convenience and because the group served the latent function of providing leadership. Nevertheless, I would like to make it clear that the term is used by an outside observer and is not their own designation for themselves. As far as I was able to determine, they use no single term consistently to describe or identify themselves.

For them, politics connoted manipulations, self-aggrandizement, relentless goal-orientation, and "similar dehumanizing power trips." For their achievements to be worthwhile, they felt their actions had to issue from a consensus of beliefs and a shared set of value orientations rather than explicit programs and organization. Certainly coercion of any kind was unacceptable. They envisioned a broad-based movement with no clear division between leaders and followers, and a participatory democracy so complete that even delegation and representation were undesirable because they were "too removed from the people." Considerations of efficiency were not to be placed above opportunity for individualism and self-expression on the part of all those present on any occasion. Ideally, actions were to involve participants completely; more than merely volitional, they were to be joyous and spontaneous expressions of "where they were at." Delayed gratification and long-range planning were to be avoided and role playing was regarded as dehumanizing and false; people were expected to give their all, but always in their own way—to work night and day but hang loose at the same time. They felt they were in the midst of a revolution and that they were a new breed of revolutionary. In the words of a Yippie writer, their object was not merely political change, it was to "live the revolution."

The significance of this phrase lies in its suggestion of the dual nature of their objectives. They wished to alter power arrangements and social structures—this was the political aspect of their commitment to change. But at the same time they wished to introduce a very specific, all-embracing life style—and this can be called the cultural dimension of the revolution. In sum, "To end the war and change where people's heads are at." The political goals were clearly instrumental, the cultural were expressive; but neither was to be placed above the other, or to be given ideological or temporal priority, in their view. The leaders were considerably more specific about the life style which they advocated than about their political programs. The latter were highly eclectic, using issues and symbols from student movements all over the world as well as the nation, and the leaders were not always clear and in accord as to how to accomplish these enormous changes. In contrast, their ideas about life-style changes were a great deal more concrete; in fact, many or most of them had already succeeded, to some extent, in achieving these goals.

THE REVOLUTION AS FUN

An important part of their philosophy decreed that the revolution had to be fun. It was completely serious; nevertheless it was supposed to be antic, spontaneous, creative, outrageous, unpredictable, and aesthetic.[7] Distinctions between work and play were to be overcome, as were conventional dichotomies between art and life, leader and follower, emotion and reason. The grand goal, at its most abstract level, was contained in the phrase, "get it together." This referred not only to transcending the dichotomies mentioned, but also to manifesting this unity concretely by living together. Accordingly, communalization was one of the important objectives of these leaders and, in fact, there was great intensification of the activities of the established campus communes and several new ones were founded during this period. Communalization occurred in miniature as students and faculty were urged by leaders to spend nights and days together, living for a time in several offices and buildings which had been taken over as "liberated zones."

What the revolution really needed in this belief system was not leaders but "masters of ceremonies" or, as one fellow put it, "a head trip-master." Instead of programs and coordination, the head trip-master would help create a mood, an atmosphere, in which the revolution could be lived. In it, the drama could replace the lecture; the costume, the uniform, and guerrilla theater be used in lieu of forceful confrontation.[8] The ideal revolutionary was described by one young

[7]Huizinga also saw this relationship between creativity, beauty, fun, and play, and vaunted it no less than the Yippies. He laments the fact that play has been on the wane in our civilization since the eighteenth century and considers this a serious contributor to many of our present-day difficulties. Perhaps the Yippies may help us regain a more balanced approach to life by emphasizing the significance of play. S. N. Eisenstadt first pointed out the relevance of Huizinga's work for Yippie philosophy in a personal communication (Wisconsin, 1970). See Johan Huizinga, *Homo Ludens: A Study of the Play Element in Culture* (Boston: Beacon Press, 1950).

[8]"The ultimate debt of such fantasy and irrationalism is to surrealism," and is particularly manifest in the lyrics of popular songs, as pointed out by Birchall, among others. See Ian Birchall, "The Decline and Fall of British Rhythm and Blues," in *The Age of Rock: Sounds of the American Cultural Revolution*, Jonathan Eisen, ed. (New York: Vintage Books, 1969). Breton defines surrealism as "belief in the superior reality of . . . dream and the disinterested play of thought" (*ibid.*). The influence of surrealism, if it is such, may be traced to the Beatles or Bob Dylan's contributions to lyrics; or, of course, it may be a case of independent rediscovery of the value and significance of the non-rational thoughts caused by or reflected in the protracted use of psychedelic drugs.

man as a poet-warrior, representing the dual nature of the revolution: militant struggle and joyous creation. Like Weberian exemplary prophets, these leaders had actually begun to practice, model, and demonstrate this new life style. The symbol of the poet-warrior was extremely effective, precise, and useful. Even those who felt they themselves fell short of striking this dualistic stance at least knew someone else who did so successfully. The problem was always maintenance of balance—neither too fierce nor too effete. He must not let events deprive him of his complexity nor force a response that expressed only one aspect of himself. It was precisely this state of dynamic equilibrium between opposing responses which made the Yippie leaders so distinct.

How were these ideas, beliefs, visions, and symbols implemented? The leadership style of the student leaders faithfully reflected their beliefs, in many instances. The group passed around the responsibilities for the major activities during the week of the strike: chairing meetings, conducting rallies, giving statements to the communications media, and negotiating with university administrators. Until rather late in the week, they managed to avoid any explicit division of labor, specialization, or formal organization. When circumstances compelled them to form a corporate group, reluctantly they assembled an ad hoc strike committee of fifteen faculty members and students, internally undifferentiated, within which members operated quite autonomously. Under the general auspices of this committee, many small, highly specialized task committees were formed, representing enormously diverse goals. Each task committee reflected the highly specific interests of the members, and their relation to the strike was often tenuous at best. All shared a vague antiwar sentiment but often little else except the desire for change of one kind of another. The strike committee kept track of these numerous, proliferating, small groups but provided no centralization or coordination among them. The procedures were clearly congruent with their beliefs about appropriate leadership behavior. Strike committee and task committees alike "did their own thing," manifesting their own unique styles as well as goals.

The manner in which the strike leaders conducted their nightly town-hall meetings throughout the week also exemplified a deliberate attempt to implement their beliefs. At these meetings, the leaders placed themselves physically among the rest of those attending. All sat together on the floor. The use of microphone or stage was avoided except in those cases where the sheer size of the assembly made this impossible. One young man, in referring to this spatial manifestation of their ideals, said, "It was important that there be no front of the room." In status and power, all those present were undifferentiated participants; there was no "audience." Anyone who wished to do so, spoke, in any manner, on any subject, for as long as he desired, regardless of the issue at hand or considerations of agenda. The method was admittedly inefficient and cumbersome but the leaders were more than willing to pay this price. In discussing the advantage of this format, one of the leaders remarked, "Anyway, efficient is uptight."

It was the chairman's responsibility to stay cool, allow for spontaneous expression of feeling, and avoid polarization by discouraging the emergence of conspicuous factional interests. Given the diversity of opinion represented and the intensity of emotions, this was no easy task. At the close of a particularly long and rambling meeting, one leader requested everyone present to make a short summary statement. Someone spoke out on Women's Lib, another on racism, yet another on "gay" liberation, someone else on ending ROTC on campus, and so forth, reflecting the range of their diverse interests. After each speech, the chairman acknowledged the contribution with a rousing, "Right on!" All present joined him in the affirmation. No attempt was made to formulate priorities among these different positions, nor to coordinate them into a plan or program. It was assumed that everyone would look after his own interests in his own way, in concert with anyone who displayed a compatible style and purpose. Yet the meeting was deemed very satisfactory; everyone was left with a feeling of accord and unity. That no concrete action would issue from it did not make the meeting purposeless.

USE OF THE MASS MEDIA

Another aspect of these young people's ideology became evident in their tactics and strategy in interacting with the university administrators. Most interesting was their conception and use of the mass communications media. As they saw it, there was no meaningful distinction between image and reality. There was no revolution apart from people's perceptions of it. They saw themselves as powerless; indeed, neither they nor the strike had any existence at all without coverage. Lacking money, organization, or widespread general support, image manipulation was one of the few arenas in which they could compete with the university administration. The latter was acutely vulnerable to adverse publicity, in their evaluation. One leader stated, "The university, like any other big business, is out to sell a product—its image. That's their Achilles' heel." The university and the strike leaders, in a Hoffmanesque sense, vied with each other as to who, ultimately, would define the situation. The student leaders were concerned above all with demonstrating that the strike was a disruption of normal events, a dramatization of their conviction that a crisis was at hand. The university administration, on the other hand, attempted to cool the momentum of the strike, to absorb it as basically consisting of nothing more than "business as usual." The officials attempted to see to it that everything was occurring exactly according to their plan—in other words, that they were in control. The student leaders had to provide, in appearance or actuality, an impression of disequilibrium, unpredictability, and disorder, and to claim it was their strike, not an administration program.

Thus, when a very straight-looking professor came before the TV cameras to read an official announcement of the university policy in response to the Cambodia-Kent State-Jackson State events, the student leaders crowded him, conspicuously displaying their flamboyant attire—to lend the strike credibility in the eyes of the viewing audience which they wished to reach. Especially, they "wanted the kids watching to know that this was the freaks' strike."

The students understood full well the necessity for providing as much good copy to the media as possible. Their ideology called for actions that were antic, bizarre, original, unpredictable, and theatrical because these were fun and amusing, and so were intrinsically valued. But also, the leaders recognized that such actions, combined with their appearance, would get better coverage. They knew they were more visually interesting than their rivals, the university administration. "If we don't provide a good show, we won't get on the air, or even if we do, nobody will watch," said one student. To recruit potential supporters, to transmit information, to provide their own interpretation of events for themselves and others, to sharply define the differences between them and their opponents—these were among the student leaders' purposes which could be achieved by manipulation of their public presentations.

At every opportunity, the student leaders attempted to dramatize their separation from and opposition to the values and styles of the older generation, represented by faculty and university officials. Their point-by-point opposition to the way of life of their elders justifies considering them a contraculture in the sense used by Yinger.

I suggest the use of the term contraculture when the normative system of a group contains, as a primary element, a theme of conflict with the values of the total society. . . . In a contraculture . . . many of the values . . . are specifically contradictions in the value of the dominant culture.[9]

In this way, their utopian vision seems more reactive than innovative. Just as in some societies, the Lost Paradise is envisioned as exactly the reverse of the present life, so these young people are reversing the values of the older generation to arrive at the content of their own utopia. This is the reason that their life style itself, apart from any concrete political action, is perceived as so threatening to the dominant culture. Because the contraculture is a self-conscious rejection of the older generation, adhering to this way of life becomes a political and even revolutionary action in itself.

Clearly, the relations between these students and administrators is more than a manifestation of a generation gap. It is a genuine case of culture conflict. This was especially evident when student leaders seized opportunities to point up what they saw as the pervasive rigidity, impersonality, and humorlessness of the university bureaucracy. For example, much delight was aroused when students discovered that within a certain department, a number of low-ranking faculty members had been thwarted in their attempt to call a department meeting to discuss the crisis. Considerations of protocol had prevented these members from summoning their superiors to the proposed meeting. This episode, the students felt, illustrated precisely the most disdained features of the university's operations and they lost no opportunity to publicize the event. As one young man stated it, "While the world goes up in flames, and people are being destroyed and oppressed, these professors sit around and wrangle about their ranks and can't even get it together enough to have a meeting. Beautiful!"

[9]Milton J. Yinger, *Contraculture and Subculture: The Sociology of Subcultures*, D. D. Arnold, ed. (Berkeley, Calif.: Glendessary Press, 1970).

RITUALIZED SCENARIOS

The occasions of negotiations with the university administrators also provided examples of their tactics. The meetings were not new encounters. The same group of students and officials had confronted each other many times before. These interchanges were conspicuous for their ritualized character. Referred to as "scenarios" by the students, they were predictable in form and outcome. As such, scenarios represented an important and recurrent use of rituals employed in student/administration encounters. The students, and perhaps the administrators, too, did not expect any real change to come from these meetings, but they felt obliged to go through the motions. Both parties knew the rules, procedures, rhetoric, and roles associated with their respective positions and both knew their constituencies expected them to negotiate as a manifestation of their ultimate reasonableness and good will. But, in fact, the students did not accept the basic values and principles underlying the behavior of the administrators. They were knowledgeable about them but not basically in a state of consensus with them. The very term "scenario" indicated the predictable outcome of the discussions: no change would result.

The use of drama in public disputes where no change is expected to occur has been pointed out by Max Gluckman[10] and Victor Turner.[11] Typically, such drama is resorted to in static situations in which the disputants seek to establish their identity and their separation from each other, using stylized gestures, exalted rhetoric, and elaborate posturing of various kinds. A scenario is known in advance and is played out to publicize one's position and provide a polemic for the audience; it is not intended to bring results in terms of a rapprochement with the opposition. Those meetings which bring about genuine change are inevitably private and often secret.

The scenarios between student leaders and administrators were typical of many of the recent campus intergenerational encounters. The senior generation acknowledged the validity of the students' ultimate values (democracy, equality, individual responsibility, participation, and the like) but objected to their means (impolite) and the timetable (immediate implementation). The students ac-

[10]Max Gluckman, *Politics, Law, and Ritual in Tribal Society* (Chicago: Aldine, 1965).

[11]Turner, *Drums of Affliction.*

knowledged the administrators' problems and limitations (funds being cut off, trustees' conservatism, government pressures, community pressures, and so on) but insisted that where there was a will there would be a way. In these scenarios the student had the advantage of being able to point at the administration's inevitable failure to produce change as an indication of the intractability of the university machinery. That it was known that the meetings were futile from the start was conveniently overlooked. Instead, the students stressed their own ability to act, innovate, and carry out their desires immediately in contrast to the administrators' ponderous bureaucratic entanglements, which made rapid action impossible and prevented people from pursuing their most deeply held beliefs. This impasse was used to make a point about the life style of the older generation and had considerable political value in terms of the explicit ideology of the student leaders. Either the administrators didn't really believe in the fundamental values they allegedly shared with the students, and thus they were hypocrites, or they believed in them but were unable to act on them, in which case they were powerless or cowards or both. The students had a clear strategical advantage as a result of the social dramas which they called "scenarios."

A POLITICAL LOVE-IN

The most interesting, dramatic, and successful tactic employed by the students was the atmosphere they created during the week. They made the campus the site of a celebration of their generation. Acoustically and visually, they demarcated an area on which they enacted what they were and what they wanted life to be like, and showed what the campus looked, sounded, and felt like when they were running it. Sociologically, aesthetically, psychologically, and interpersonally, the main part of the campus was quite transformed. "It was more like a political love-in than a strike," said one girl. As a result of the "liberation" of the serigraphy facilities of the School of Art and Architecture, fanciful, brilliant posters adorned the inside and outside of many buildings. A sound truck in the middle of the campus blared rock music part of the day and every night. Guitars, sleeping bags, and free food were available everywhere for whoever had need of them. Dress was more extravagant than usual, and red armbands were ubiquitous. Inflatable plastic bubbles—huge, psychedelic structures—dotted the lawns, providing shade, shelter, and sleeping facilities. The tone was that of a youth festival, and merely walking across the campus was an exhilarating experience for most students. Political symbols were present, to be sure, reflected in the content of the leaflets, petitions, movies, teach-ins, rallies, buttons, and armbands, but the grim realities to which they referred did not establish the atmosphere which prevailed these few days.

The climactic and final event of the strike was a rock concert, estimated to have drawn a crowd larger than any ever assembled on the campus for a non-athletic event. The Woodstock mystique was deliberately re-evoked, with political overtones provided primarily by the lyrics of the songs. The musicians performed gratis and no one paid to enter after the first half hour, despite the original purpose of the concert, which was to raise funds to pay off strike committee debts. Even the most hardheaded and practical among the strike leaders agreed that it was more appropriate and necessary for the concert to be free than to raise funds, however desperately poor they were. Students and passers-by lolled about the grass, passed joints (marijuana) around, shared wine and fruit, romped and frolicked with their dogs and each other until well into the night.[12] The red armband was conspicuous at this event, as it had been all week. But now it was used for many purposes, as a dog leash, a napkin, a headband, a hankie, and even by several girls as a bra top. Of course, everyone knew that it signified great tragedies, but it became on this occasion a symbol of joy and solidarity as well. It was, in this context, a referent to that part of the revolution which was committed to spontaneity, irreverence, originality, and unpredictability. The student leaders had not managed to end the war by their efforts, but they had made some progress toward "changing where people's heads were at." They had mounted this and other unprecedented events at the university, and above all they had made the campus their own for a time. In this spirit, the armband symbolized their limited but undeniable success.

CONCLUSION

What are we to conclude from these ideas, actions, and events? In at least two areas, the student leaders had had to cope with intrac-

[12]At this point, as in many others, the cultural and the political components of the revolution fuse, as the ritual of "lighting up," being illegal, is as much a matter of politics as of life style. That no one was arrested on this occasion perhaps reflects the authorities' implicit or explicit realization of the hopelessness of curbing such widespread cultural innovations, in the name of politics.

table paradoxes. First, within their belief system, two opposing, equally valued themes are present: One, the political aspect of their revolutionary vision, may be called instrumental. The other, their cultural goal, represents expressive purposes.[13] The accomplishment of their political goals necessitates self-sacrifice, determination, delayed gratification, and rational, calculating, efficient organization. Yet these very qualities and actions are antithetical to the way life is to be lived in their view—spontaneously, openly, for the present, for its own sake, in unanalyzed, uncategorized, urgent subjectivity.[14]

The contradiction is a real one. The concept of "the revolution as a trip" is a genuine paradox and the dilemma faced by these young leaders was very difficult. Perhaps it was inevitable that one aspect of the dual revolution would be favored over the other. In this particular circumstance it was probably inevitable that the cultural emphasis become dominant. On this campus, at this time, the leaders had too little backing, their university following was too conservative, and they had too little political experience. And the administration was too clever, flexible, and invulnerable for them. "On the whole, they outclassed us," said one of the students in discussing the administrators. The students resolved this problem by

[13]This conflict is a recurrent one for all those espousing communal ideologies. As Turner points out, it is "the crucial difficulty of all utopians—that they have to produce life's necessities through work—in economists' jargon, to mobilize resources. To mobilize resources also means to mobilize people. This implies social organization . . . and entails the establishment, however transient, of orderly structural relations between man and man." (*The Ritual Process*, p. 135). Turner's essays on "communitas" and problems of its implementation are extremely lucid and helpful for anyone concerned with this problem (*ibid.*).

[14]Philip Slater sees this contradiction as between the activist on one hand, who is drawn to social commitment, and the drop-out or flower child on the other. The particular dilemma of those following Yippie ideology is the incorporation of both these value systems, and simultaneous and equal advocacy of them. The conflict between them is even more acute when taking place intrapsychically, as among Yippies, rather than interpersonally, between activists and flower children as Slater suggests. See *The Pursuit of Loneliness: American Culture at the Breaking Point* (Boston: Beacon Press, 1970). But if the conflict is endurable, the dualistic vision of the Yippies may resolve one of the ubiquitous problems faced by revolutionaries and radicals in general, as Slater makes clear: "If an activist devotes his life to altering the power structure, will he not become like old-culture adherents—utilitarian, invidious, scarcity-oriented, future-centered, and so on? Having made the world safe for flower people, will he be likely to relinquish it to them?" (p. 116). By being activists and flower children simultaneously, perhaps Yippies need not fear the temptation to relapse into old-culture means and values. Instead of having to turn power over to another group of people, they have only to let one side of their own ideology become more dominant.

using the strike to stress the cultural dimension of their revolution, dramatizing it, and declaring their identity as a generation with contracultural values as insistently and intensely as they could. Officially, the revolution was as political as it had ever been. Actually, it was the cultural program which was enacted consistently, but the defeat and abandonment of the political program was never acknowledged. The political symbols of the strike were employed consistently and always included references to what they regarded as egregious domestic and foreign policy and practice by government.

By favoring the cultural goals over the political, the students did the only thing they could do, given their limitations, but they did it so well, with such thoroughness and conviction, that it was not necessary to interpret their week's work as a failure.

There were other reasons, clearly, why this part of the revolution succeeded. The student leaders had a far more specific program concerning the cultural revolution and achieving it, than notion of how to bring about an altered political structure. Since many of them were already practicing the new life style, they knew full well how to implement it. And the sheer number of students who would join them in cultural activities was vastly greater than those willing to risk punitive actions by university administration or police in pursuit of political goals. It is, after all, more common and simpler to light up a "joint" and groove on the music than to occupy a building.

In pursuit of the goals of the cultural revolution, the students' shared rituals served them well. Young people from every quarter of the university, unknown to each other in terms of any background understanding and common interests save those of their generation, were able to communicate with each other fully and instantly through their rituals. Vast numbers of strangers knew very well all the meanings and actions of numerous rituals. (It might be said that this generation, as such, constitutes a subculture without ever having been a society or subsociety.) Lacking previous contact, they nevertheless have at their fingertips forms which unite them on any occasion. The use of shared ritual and its underlying meaning was never more apparent than in political meetings throughout the week. When the meetings floundered for various reasons, the leaders would often light up a "joint" and turn on the music; and, little by little, speechmaking would give way to rapping, anger to grooving, confusion to a sense of familiarity, solidarity, and shared meaning.

Tripping, rapping, turning on, "balling," grooving—all of them distinct rituals involving many of the most ubiquitous symbols of the generation, with the most general and powerful referents—drugs, music, costume, sex, play, and antipathy to the dominant culture and all its works. Immediately, strangers were knit together for a time. As Geertz puts it, "by their rituals, the fusion took place of the world as lived and the world as imagined, inducing a mood and motivation which confirms their construction of the world."[15]

The transition from the political to the cultural dimension in such meetings was subtle and gradual but distinct and frequent. By using these shared rituals and symbols, those involved were able to avoid the direct confrontation of the conflict inherent in their ideology. The same rituals and symbols served them in coping with the other paradox with which they lived during this time, that the strike was not their own doing at all. On the contrary, it had been given to them by the university administration—treacherously, in an attempt at co-option, in the opinion of many leaders. Rather than abandon their revolutionary purposes entirely, the leaders used the period of time which was given to them by official policy and shaped it into their own creation. This was their celebration of themselves and their oppositon to the way of life embodied by the administrators. And paradoxically, even ironically, the very enactment of such a way of life, as they demonstrated on the campus during that week, became a political act, as valid as any other program for change they could have mounted. By demonstrating the vitality, magnetism, freedom, and productivity of their chosen way of life, and their point-by-point opposition to that espoused and advocated by their elders, they made a political statement about what they regarded as the deadening and deadened alternatives being offered, and often insisted on, by their seniors.[16] The paradox was thus resolved and the cultural/expressive dimension fused with the instrumental/political.

The revolution, for those who became deeply involved in the strike, was indeed a trip. It was a journey to a new place, known

[15]Geertz, "Religion as a Cultural System."

[16]Slater (*op. cit.*) points out quite rightly that the flower children are far more radical than the militant activists, who always work more or less within the system, by its means if not for its goals. The political activists seek to change institutional structures while the hippies want to change motivational structures. Obviously, both are necessary, and the Yippies want to change both of these at the same time.

only to a particular generation, special and indescribable, incomprehensible and meaningless to outsiders or unbelievers. Sharing this journey convinced them that the new life which they envisioned was real, attainable, comprehensible, and beautiful. Their rituals were not sacred in the usual sense, and there were no supernatural referents for their symbols—though many were mystical—but there was a distinct parallel to religious ritual and symbol here, nevertheless. And in all religious ceremonies that "work," the feeling achieved was that those who took the trip together were set apart, had shared a unique and private bond. The mood attained was unmistakably religious—unquestioning, elevating, a shared affirmation of their interpretation of the meaning of life. The religious mood was not accomplished by a master theoretician. In fact, there had been no "head trip-master." But there were the strike leaders acting as masters-of-ceremonies, and they did succeed in mounting an impressive and fairly sustained presentation of a part of the shared beliefs of many members of their generation. The red armband, encompassing the joy and grief of the week, embraced the dualistic nature of their revolutionary goals and provided a unification of the opposing components of their world view for those to whom the symbol had meaning. For the others, those who had not taken the trip, the red armband as used, for example, during the rock concert—to stand for joy and grief at the same time—was a desecration, a perversion, a mystification, and a paradox. Their very lack of understanding confirmed the believers in their separateness, thus functioning as a boundary-maintaining mechanism.

And so the poet-warrior remained, for a time, clear as to who he was, who the enemy was, and who his comrades were. With a foot in two different planes, like a classical shaman, the poet-warrior bridges the real world and the world of man's fantasies, the world of grim, militant determination and struggle, and the world of whimsy, pleasure, and frivolity. The poet-warrior and the red armband provide order and a fusion of oppositions, and, like all good symbols, as Langer pointed out, "are truly man's most valuable property."[17]

[17]Suzanne Langer, *Philosophy in a New Key*, fourth edition (Cambridge, Mass.: Harvard University Press, 1960).

.14. The High School as a Focus of "Student Unrest"

EDGAR Z. FRIEDENBERG

FOR THE past four or five years, as conflicts on university campuses have become more widespread and intense, and have elicited increasing public concern, hostility, and repression, there has been a corresponding rise in tension and what is called "student unrest" in high schools. Corresponding, and related, but not analogous. There can be little doubt that the example of protest among college students, emphasized and overdetermined by the media and the response of public officials, has at least called the possibility of protest to the attention of public school students who would otherwise have gone on passively accepting their restricted status as pupils. But the circumstances of high school life, and the alternative roles available to people of high school age, are so different from those of college and, especially, graduate students—and graduate students have been pivotal in the movement—that neither the issues, the form, nor the prospects of rebellion in the high school are really comparable to apparently corresponding factors in college and universities.

The growth of "student unrest" in high school, indeed, is probably more comparable to growing unrest in prisons—a matter that was featured as front-page news in *The New York Times* of Sunday, November 15, 1970.[1] The factor common to revolt in all these instances appears to be a declining willingness to ascribe legitimacy to the governing authorities, whether they be deans, principals, or wardens, boards of trustees, school boards, or correctional officials. But

[1] Michael T. Kauffman, "Rising Protests and Lawsuits Shake Routines in Prisons," pp. 1, 79.

the situations of the inmates differ, as do the coercive resources available to the authorities and the students' prospects for escaping the institution or surviving within it after carrying through a revolt. And in the degree of their subjection, if not in their daily routines, high school students are more like prisoners than like college students. There is thus very much less that high school students can do by way of lawful protest without becoming subject to coercion by civil authorities. High school students who are younger than the lawful school-leaving age cannot drop out without becoming truants, and as such are subject to prosecution and confinement if they stay out of school. While the selective service system with the 2-S deferment has provided a comparable sanction for male college students, its effect was never so universal or its action so rapid as that of compulsory attendance laws. College students cannot be prosecuted even under the kind of court injunction now commonly granted university administrations unless their actions are held to disrupt the university's normal functions. But high school students cannot even stay away from school without courting harassment and prosecution. The fact that, however discontented they may be, they cannot lawfully leave school of course greatly diminishes their bargaining power, encourages officials to dismiss their complaints without remedy and—as in the case of prisoners—tends to force pupils into the courts as petitioners for relief from the constraints of the school.

DAYS IN COURT

The courts have proved something less than a perfect instrument for this purpose. Litigation is extremely costly, and is ordinarily available only to plaintiffs from relatively wealthy families who are willing to spend large sums in support of their demands. While the American Civil Liberties Union and its affiliates will undertake to plead an occasional case, the support of the parents is a necessary precondition to effective legal action; for, although under special circumstances an adult other than the parent may act as guardian for the limited purpose of filing the suit, most judges are sufficiently committed to the exercise of authority to hardly consider the case of a young plaintiff who was bucking both his parents and his school, even if there were established precedent for his legal position.

Furthermore, an appeal to the courts for relief from the practices of a school must usually involve a Constitutional question. The more important cases involving "student unrest" have been petitions under the Bill of Rights, against censorship or confiscation of student publications; regulations governing dress or the wearing of peace buttons or political insignia; or locker-searches without notice or warrant which result in disciplinary action or prosecution for possession of contraband—usually marijuana, or property that the student thinks of as borrowed and the school as stolen. Other constitutional issues arise over questions of due process: the right of students to be represented by counsel at administrative hearings that may result in suspension, expulsion, or compulsory transfer to a less desirable school; the right of access to one's own file and to have items deemed pejorative expunged from the record if they go beyond grades and official disciplinary actions to encompass value judgments as to the student's character and personality.

Generally speaking, the courts have been reluctant to interfere with the internal administration of any constituted body. It is usually easier to win an action for damages than to obtain a cease-and-desist order when the defendant occupies a position of recognized authority over the plaintiff, as schools, prison officials, and parents do over their wards. The rights of school officials to search the lockers or even the persons of pupils without warrant or probable cause has usually been sustained in the courts, as has the right—indeed, the responsibility— of school authorities to establish reasonable dress regulations. While state commissioners of education in more progressive states—notably, New York—have voluntarily issued orders forbidding schools to regulate dress more closely than required to maintain an atmosphere conducive to education, these orders are quite commonly flouted by school officials who are aware that they will not be enforced in communities in which there is little established respect for the dignity of students. Lawsuits seeking to restrict the scope of dress and hair regulations are usually fruitless;[2] petitions for court orders

[2]In a decision adverse to plaintiffs in a class action filed against the Principal of Cedartown High School, the Superintendent of Polk County (Georgia) Schools, and the Polk County Board of Education by "David Lindsey, a Minor, by his Mother and Next Friend, Mrs. Daphne Lindsey, on his behalf and on behalf of all those similarly situated" (Civil Action # 2243, United States District Court, Northern District of Georgia, Rome Division), U.S. District Judge Sidney O. Smith, Jr. ruled on October 26, 1970, in sustaining the suspension of David Lindsey from high school for excessively long hair:

If it is demonstrated that the rule relates to the efficient operation of the school, then it passes muster. If, on the other hand, it is merely the personal whim or preference of some administrator or

compelling the schools to readmit students suspended solely for dress or hair length have recently been rather more successful in the sense that the courts are sometimes willing to grant them, but tend to be ineffective since the schools often immediately re-suspend the pupil on similar grounds, without any apparent risk of a contempt citation.

In the areas of conduct specifically protected under the First Amendment, litigation has been more effective. The United States Supreme Court found for plaintiffs in a well-known case originating in the State of Iowa[3] in which high school pupils had been suspended for wearing armbands bearing peace insignia. The Court held such devices to be protected under the First Amendment as symbolic speech, but in its majority opinion specifically excluded dress regulations, as such, from its dictum. In a more recent case, a Connecticut state court has held that prior censorship of newspapers printed by students, or their exclusion from a school in which the distribution of other newspapers was permitted, violated the First Amendment, and ordered that such interference cease. But these decisions cannot be extended beyond immediate issues of freedom of speech to apply to other areas of conduct.

In a celebrated case some years ago, New York State Judge Constance Baker Motley held that a young Puerto Rican student whom the authorities in his school wanted to re-assign to a "600" school for

---

not enforced uniformly or not related in fact to school operation, it does not. The question is not whether the policy is wise or unwise, but whether under the evidence the rule reasonably relates to the problems of public education and attendant disciplinary needs. [E.g. *Brownlee vs. Bradley County, Tenn. Bd. of Ed.*, 311 F. Supp. 1360 (E.D. Tenn. 1970)].

In his *Conclusion of Law* in this Opinion, Judge Smith had noted:

The theory that grooming, at least insofar as hair styles are concerned, is an absolute First Amendment right is not without support. [*Breen v. Kahl*, 296 F. Supp. 702 (W. D. Wis. 1969), aff'd 419 F. 2nd 1034 (7th Cir. 1969); *Richards v. Thurston*, 304 F. Supp. 449 (D. Mass. 1969), aff'd 424 F. 2d 1281 (1st Cir. 1970).] Under this theory, the fact that one student's long hair causes others to be disorderly is of no consequence. If this view were universally accepted, there would be no hesitancy in ruling for the plaintiff. However, in this Circuit the argument that hair length is an absolute First Amendment right has been rejected. [*Ferrell v. Dallas Independent School District*, 261 F. Supp. 545 (W.D. Tex. 1966), aff'd 392 F. 2d 697 (5th Cir. 1968), cert. den 393 U.S. 856 (1968); *Davis v. Firment*, 269 F. Supp. 524 (E.D. La. 1967), aff'd 408 F. 2d 1085 (5th Cir. 1969); *Griffin v. Tatum*, 300 F. Supp. 60 (M.D. Ala. 1969), modified 425 F. 2d 201 (5th Cir. 1970); *Stephenson v. Wheeler County*, 306 F. Supp. 97 (S.D. Ga. 1969; aff'd 426 F. 2d 1154 (5th Cir. 1970). See also *Jackson et al. v. Dorrier et al.*, 424 F. 2d 213 (6th Cir. 1970).] Rather, the problem is viewed as a Fourteenth Amendment question and it must be determined whether the rule in question is "arbitrary, capricious, unreasonable, or discriminatory."

So it goes.

[3]*Tinker vs. Des Moines School District*, 393, U.S. 503 (1969).

troubled and troublesome children, had a right to be represented by counsel at the "guidance" hearing at which his educational destiny was to be decided, rejecting the contention of the school that the intrusion of a lawyer would interfere with its professional staff and that, since the proposed hearing was not punitive in character, no such right existed. Had Judge Motley not been reversed on the appeal of the New York City Board of Education, this would have been a landmark decision; it is worth mentioning now only because a few months ago, she rendered a similar verdict, even more sweeping in its implications, awarding money damages to a prisoner, Martin Sostre, on the basis of his having been subjected to cruel and unusual punishment including a long period of solitary confinement under appalling and inhumane conditions. This decision has been sustained.

There is, then, little basis for confidence that the courts will guard the liberties of high school students. What is more significant is that high school students and their parents should be compelled to have recourse to them, and over issues that would never have arisen had the schools been capable of a modicum of graciousness. That a boy or girl in Iowa or anywhere else should be obliged to travel the arduous and costly route of litigation to the Supreme Court of the United States in order to establish the right to attend school while wearing a peace armband passes belief. But it happened, and there are still many schools in which the decision would not be recognized nor the armband tolerated.

THE PREVALENCE OF HOSTILITY

It is hardly astonishing that the courts, as the fountainheads of "law and order," should be hostile to dissenting youth in America in 1970. No one, probably, expects otherwise. Colleges and universities have made generous use of the court injunction to stifle and severely punish the kind of mildly disruptive protest that has long been recognized as lawful in labor disputes. Police and National Guardsmen, when summoned to a campus to evict occupants of a building or quell a demonstration deemed disorderly, may beat or occasionally slay students with no apparent risk of prosecution. At Kent State University a court order forbidding any criticism of the action of the Grand Jury there, which indicted students and faculty thought to be sympathetic to demonstrating students while exonerating the guardsmen who slew four of them in May, 1970, remained in effect for several days. Indeed, when we think of a college or university student in court on any matter related to "student unrest" today, we assume him to be a defendant rather than a plaintiff.

High school students, too, are frequently "busted:" but when they are, unless summarily dealt with by the police, they usually go to juvenile court, there to be subjected to its dreadful informality, which is unhindered by most of the Constitutional safeguards afforded adult accused. They are denied the equal protection of the law Constitutionally guaranteed all other Americans, and cannot claim that protection as defendants. As plaintiffs, in actions initiated through their parents or other qualified adults, they may, however, claim such protection, for what it is worth when interpreted by the legal guardians of a community that is usually uptight and authoritarian. They appear, therefore, as plaintiffs if they appear at all.

The inherent hostility of society against dissenting students, whether in high school or college, is amply demonstrated by the phrase "student unrest." It is a curious phrase, which recalls the restless natives of an earlier imperialism—restless, presumably, because they *were* natives, inadequately civilized and hence unable to accept or be grateful for the advantages that might otherwise be lavished on them. The phrase "student unrest" is content-free: it refers to no specific source of grievance but rather identifies a prevalent pathology. It is the unrest that is the problem and that must be dealt with firmly and eradicated; there is no corresponding curiosity implied as to what the unrest is all about.

And except insofar as the unrest is a response to the hostility of a large society, it does not generally concern the same issues in high school as in college. That this is so may be inferred from the fact that the most serious conflicts involving college or university students have occurred on those campuses that are least like high schools—that have long been recognized as great universities and that have been relatively free from petty restraints on student conduct and life styles. On college and university campuses, moreover, serious conflicts have seldom arisen over strictly intramural issues, nor have such conflicts been contained within the university community. But serious conflict in universities rarely arises in the first instance from acts of aggressive hostility against students by faculty or administration.

Conflicts in high schools center much more on local grievances; they are more likely to be precipitated by specific administrative actions that students find offensive, and to be sustained by persistently oppressive administrative policies.

THE PAROCHIAL PUBLIC SCHOOL

But high schools are always local institutions, and usually parochial ones; they do not provide advisers to the federal government, seek funding for research in counterinsurgency, or graduate second lieutenants for the army. It is therefore seldom possible for high school students to link their grievances to any specific issue of national policy save one.

That one, of course, is the conduct of public education itself: its socializing function, and values and routines imposed by it as the price of access to a decent future; its role as the only institution in which the young may lawfully participate, and on the institution's own terms. Although the peer society in school, like the inmate society in prisons, undoubtedly affects the quality of daily life within it as much as or more than policies set by the authorities do, there is no public high school in which students possess any authority—as distinct from influence—and few in which they experience much autonomy. There are, in short, no effective formal channels through which students can express their will, and few areas in which they are free to make decisions that, for an adult, would be accepted by society as purely personal; whether to admit a teacher to one's locker or a guidance counselor to one's confidence; when, and from whom, to take a particular class; whether to take gym and, if so, how to dress for it; whom, as a club member, to invite as a speaker; where or how late to hold a dance or a party. Although each of these questions is affected, whether it arises in a high school or a college, by the resources and facilities available, which in turn reflect administrative policy, none would be thought any longer to fall within the arbitrary limits of authority of a college administrator. When infringements of such routine freedoms occur on a college campus, the administration usually is at some pains to justify its action as a special case that is not really a violation of an established area of student freedom at all.

In high school, the opposite is true. Not only do such freedoms not exisit as matters of right; when they are conceded in any particular case, the administration usually is careful to point out that it is "giving the kids the opportunity to learn how to use freedom" or "helping the kids to learn how to be responsible," or applying some other formula to make it clear that "freedom is a privilege and not a right." Thus, school officials attempt both to insure that their concession does not become a binding precedent and to reassure the public that they are not being permissive. When "student unrest" occurs in high school, then, it is in a relatively primitive form—sporadic, oriented to the particular event that aroused it, and lacking any rights established by law or custom which students may cite on their own behalf.

The protests of high school students might then have been expected to be more varied than those of college students, since they occur in response to a more random set of abuses. High schools, however, are governed by so nearly the same class mystique that they tend to make very similar ideological demands on their students. Frederick Wiseman's film *High School*, now three years old, might serve as a documentary portrayal of the social climate of most high schools in the country with students drawn primarily from the lower-middle or superordinate social classes. Those that draw their student body from slum or ghetto areas attempt to demand the same kinds of vocabulary, behavior, and patterns of achievement of their students as do schools whose students come from middle-class homes. Failing to achieve this, or worse yet, abandoning their ghetto students as incapable of learning, these administrators literally make prisons of their schools, and the corridors are patrolled and guarded by armed police.

TWO PATTERNS OF REVOLT

Whatever the social composition of the student body may be, the norms asserted by the high school are almost invariably those of a lower-middle-class bureaucracy seeking to control a captive "clientele." This is a very different situation from that faced by university administrators, whose practice must to some degree be influenced by traditions of independence of thought and inquiry, and even of personal conduct, asserted and sustained by the major professional organizations that influence the status of their institutions: the American Association of University Professors is not exactly militant, but it serves as a constant, if decreasingly relevant, reminder of "the way it spozed to be."[4] While these traditions have much less influence

---

[4] James Herndon's book of this title is probably the best and coolest account of how different "it spozed to be" in a predominantly black Oakland, California junior high school (New York: Simon & Schuster, 1968).

on the treatment of students than of faculty, the underlying pattern of values they embody is, though conventional, a liberal convention.

The high school, however, is threatened by two altogether different kinds of students. Fortunately—for the high school—they find it difficult to unite in opposition. Ghetto students are increasingly resistant both to the constraints and the empty rhetoric of the schools; and when they revolt, their revolt is much harder to put down than that of middle-class students, since they can seldom be tempted into the prescribed routines of protest, negotiation, punishment, and atonement—like the obedient practitioners of civil disobedience. Innocent of ideology, they just take over areas of school life and make them as nearly their own as the miserable facilities and capacity for petty harassment of the school permits; and the staff either lets them or puts them down with open police violence. With few shared values and no basis for mutual respect, there is nothing to play bureaucratic games with. If a politically active and well-organized ghetto community exists, the futility of this conflict may lead to demands for community control and a teaching staff and curriculum better adapted to the needs of the students. Otherwise, an equilibrium becomes established in which the school officials tolerate as much vandalism and truancy as may be needed to prevent their positions—already hollowed of any substance—from being directly threatened.[5]

It seems doubtful that "student unrest" in the colleges has done much to inspire, legitimate, or provide a model for that of ghetto high school students who, by and large, march to their own bongos. The discriminatory processes built into our society have kept the numbers of such students in our colleges and universities from so far achieving a critical mass. When more nearly open admissions policies do serve to augment their numbers substantially, I would predict that, finding themselves within reach of new economic goals and in the grip of new aspirations, they will, like other ethnic groups that have begun to "make it" seriously, become a very conservative rather than a disruptive force.

There have, it is true, been a number of conspicuous campus crises that were dominated by black students. Two of the most dramatic took place at the University of Wisconsin, Oshkosh, and at Cornell University. At Oshkosh, most of the black students, admitted under

[5]Miriam Wasserman's little-known but superb study, *The School Fix; NYC; USA* (New York: Outerbridge and Dienstfrey, 1970) is the most complete and thoroughgoing account of these and related processes of conflict, accommodation, and status assignment in contemporary urban schools.

less stringent admissions requirements to a campus and a community unaccustomed to a black presence, were dismissed when they attempted a relatively mild disruption of a university meeting. The much more celebrated and successful revolt of blacks at Cornell led ultimately to the resignation of several senior professors who were irked at what they regarded as President Perkins' capitulation, and to President Perkins' resignation as well. But the Wisconsin regents, who had apparently assumed that any black admitted to the university would humbly become cooperative out of sheer gratitude, revoked their new admissions policy—and its beneficiaries—when faced with a situation that most college administrators have learned to take in their stride under less novel and politically treacherous circumstances. And the Cornell students were not "disadvantaged;" they were—well, Cornell students—with the added necessity of establishing *machismo* under threat from white toughs on a campus on which fraternities still retain an atavistic degree of influence. Thus, the blacks were forced to deny some of their quite legitimate characteristics as middle-class academics in order to assume the revolutionary stance which had become almost obligatory for self-respecting blacks. But revolutionary blacks are a black elite who are likely to be swamped by the conventionally ambitious when much larger numbers of blacks gain access to the opportunity structure that the colleges provide.

Among white high school students, and their higher-status black colleagues, "student unrest" takes very different forms. As in colleges, it is primarily a middle- and upper-class pattern. Only college-bound young people, and those of their friends who adopt a similar life style, are likely to take school sufficiently seriously as a source of frustration to try to change it—and among these, only the college-bound who come from families in which the idea of education is familiar and specific enough for them to have internalized a set of norms by which to judge a school and find it seriously wanting.

This, again, tends to exclude those high school students whose interests are almost wholly absorbed by economic security or social mobility at a comparatively low level; not that they are likely to find the high school very satisfactory, but that they are unlikely to expect much more of education, anyhow. Their forms of rebellion are not directed primarily at the school and are not in turn defined by the school as serious problems; rather, they are seen as mischief, motor vehicle offenses, and, increasingly, "drug abuse." Schools are not threatened by behavior they define as mischievous; and customary techniques of discipline usually suffice to tame the college-bound and push the "pre-delinquent" either out of school or into forms of delinquency that bring him within the area of control of law enforcement officials. The category of "student unrest" is reserved for behavior that challenges the school routines and the values expressed in them.

School personnel are well aware that their basic responsibility in the eyes of the community is to socialize the young. Failures to transmit the formal curriculum are not merely tolerable but accepted as part of the normal set of contradictions we get ourselves into by giving lip-service to cultural and intellectual skills not really very much prized. But a failure to establish adherence to conventional forms of patriotic observance, or uncritical acceptance of authority and dedication to the accumulation of consumer goods, is not tolerable. Indeed, too much success in teaching students to read and to understand the world they live in would in itself constitute prima facie evidence of a failure in socialization, as evidenced by the fact that the sharpest students are nearly always the most unrestful. Consequently, the actions that constitute the most baneful forms of "student unrest" are those that call publicly into question the socialization of the student into acceptance of middle-American norms: the publication and distribution of "underground newspapers"—almost always superior in literary quality to anything procduced in conventional high school English composition classes;[6] demonstrating on behalf of antiwar or antipoverty measures, or attempts by students to actually seize control of student government.

There is no question but that such actions by high school students do indeed constitute threats to school officials—not merely as invasions of their previously unchallenged power to control but, more seriously, by mobilizing public opinion against them. Every victory for student autonomy in North America is attacked in the local press; the national media, split between their desire for the confidence of a mass audience and their tendency to identify with higher status, and hence more liberal, values, are less monolithic. The high school, like the university but in far greater degree, is caught in the essential hypocrisy that makes a mass, stratified democracy functional. It must assert what is indeed true—that all men are educable—while it

[6]Dianne Divoky, ed., *How Old Will You Be in 1984?* (New York: Avon, 1969) is a useful though inevitably dated anthology of a representative collection of pieces from "underground" high school newspapers current at the time.

strives to prevent most of them from becoming sufficiently cognizant of either their own intellectual resources or the dynamics of their society to insist on the dignity formally guaranteed them but deadly, should it be invoked, to the institutions that depend on their submission.

Colleges and universities, however, have enjoyed considerable room for maneuver because, since they have educated primarily students who were either already members of the ruling elite or bent upon acceptance into it, there seemed little risk that they would betray its interests. As a larger and larger proportion of all young people have been accepted into what are nominally colleges and universities, willingness to concede freedom of inquiry and expression to potentially unreliable ideological elements has sharply declined. But the norms protecting freedom of inquiry and expression, for what they're worth, persist. College students and professors in the United States may lose their appointments and damage their careers by what they say or publish; but they haven't yet been busted just for that, and their right of publication is so far acknowledged. For them, the crunch comes when they attempt to apply their values and insights to real life in the community.

In the high school, the crunch comes sooner—at the point where insight into self and society may be seen to dawn, and a sense of personal worth is linked to dawning social awareness. In a mass democracy, institutions of public education may be conceived of as having been installed to occupy the life space in which, if they were not there, education might occur. Rising "student unrest" in high schools suggests that they cannot altogether prevent it from occurring, although they can make life pretty tough for those students who are learning most.

Part III

Cross-Cultural Perspectives

.15. Students—A Marginal Elite in Politics

FRANK A. PINNER

THE THEORY of student movements—if there be one—does not suffer from a dearth of propositions; it rather suffers from propositional hypertrophy. Among the multitude of explanations being offered—psychological, sociological, economic, institutional, cultural—one or more will always serve to explain a given situation. Thus, we are able to explain everything and, consequently, nothing.

CHARACTERISTICS OF STUDENTS

When, during the last decade, student activism and, at times, violence became worldwide phenomena, social scientists set out to discover their "root and soil."[1] In the process, they rediscovered the prominent and often leading role that student movements had played in the distant and recent past, particularly in struggles of national liberation and unification and, less frequently, in other social upheavals. The question, then, was how to account for these political propensities, and it was only natural to look for some distinguishing characteristics of students which might motivate them to enter the public arena. The list of variables produced by Bakke five years ago is a good example of this approach. Although unwieldy because of its length, the list still constitutes only a fraction of all the variables proposed by one researcher or another.

The very fact that writers feel impelled to compile lists of vari-

[1] Wight Bakke, "Roots and Soil of Student Activism," *Comparative Education Review* 10 (1966): 163–74.

ables indicates that they do not deem any one or even a manageably small number of characteristics sufficient to account for observed behavior.[2] Clearly, they are in search of some typological concept, some syndrome, capable of doing the job. Yet, attempts at constructing such typologies are quite rare and, insofar as they exist, overly simplistic.[3]

In their eagerness to explain the predispositions of students, writers frequently fail to consider the specific social and political situations in which predispositions are activated.[4] But these situations should be identifiable. The rather limited range of issues which propel students into political life should give the analyst some indication of the particular space they occupy in history. Clearly, students *qua* students are rarely participants in the humdrum of politics—that is, in the gradual adjustments in the distribution of social costs and benefits and in the structures of authorities which are negotiated daily by professional politicians. Typically, student movements address themselves to larger questions: the unity or independence of their country, equality and inequality within the nation and among nations, and the legitimacy of authority. There are, of course, other issues, particularly the "intramural" or "intermural" problems relating to the curricula, the limited teaching resources, and the

[2]A notable exception is Lewis S. Feuer, who, by a judicious selection of episodes, manages to piece together a one-variable explanation of student movements, if not of all catastrophic events in history. See his *The Conflict of Generations* (New York: Basic Books, 1969). Feuer fails to consider the large number of studies which indicate that student radicals are typically the children of liberal parents and harbor no personal resentment against them. For a review of some of the relevant literature see Kenneth Keniston, "The Sources of Student Dissent," *Journal of Social Issues* 23 (1967): 117–21. Even in the case of China, a country with a Confucianist tradition which was challenged by the "family revolution," it is doubtful that political radicals were motivated by hatred of their elders. Compare Bruce D. Larkin, "China," in Donald K. Emmerson, ed., *Students and Politics in Developing Nations* (New York: Praeger, 1968).

[3]An example of such a typology is the one proposed by Michiya Shimbori, "The Sociology of a Student Movement—A Japanese Case Study," in Seymour Martin Lipset and Philip G. Altbach, eds., *Students in Revolt* (Boston: Houghton Mifflin, 1969), pp. 305–07. Shimbori suggests that types of student movements depend on the distances between government and people and university and people. It is not clear what types of student movements are supposed to correspond to the four possible combinations of long and short distances.

[4]An attempt to place a student movement into its political context is Belden Fields, *Student Politics in France* (New York: Basic Books, 1970). However, the author is more concerned with the internal viability of a student organization than with its role in the political process.

governance of academic institutions.[5] But it is rather remarkable that these problems typically come to the surface only when the other, more momentous issues of national and international policy are also salient. Hence, it may not be entirely amiss to think of the "intra-mural" and "intermural" problems as side issues, cover issues, or overt expressions of some other, more latent, malaise.

In addition to levels of activism, an acceptable theory of student movements should address itself to the political direction of student activism. To be sure, few writers have been able to overlook the fairly obvious fact that students in fields leading to well-defined professional positions (medicine, agriculture, engineering, law) tend to be con-servative, while students of the humanities and social sciences tend to advocate social and political change. This is commonly seen to result from the greater uncertainty in role aspirations and expecta-tions among those obtaining a general education. But we have vir-tually no explanations for the changes in prevailing political trends in student activism.

Perhaps any attempt to establish the necessary and sufficient condi-tions of student activism and of its particular direction at a given time is overly ambitious. Perhaps all that can be expected of the researcher, given the present state of the art, is the identification of predisposing factors which will, from time to time, lead to some sort of overt political behavior. Even this more modest aim fails to be satisfied by the conventional listing of student attributes.

Some of these attributes clearly cannot be held responsible by themselves for student political behavior because they apply to a larger class of individuals. This is true of all variables relating either to the students' youth or to their intellectualism. Young people are often alleged to be more idealistic than adults, more impatient, more willing to accept high risks, and hence more prone to take vigorous action. To the extent that this is true—and we cannot be sure that it is, having only scant information about, say, the idealism of young working class Burmese, Italians, or, indeed, Americans—we should find a propensity toward activism not only among students but also among other young people. The same criticisms apply to various other types of psychological propositions. If political activ-ism somehow derives from young people's search for identity, then it would have to be demonstrated that this search is more intensive

[5]Shimbori, *The Sociology of a Student Movement*, pp. 287–301.

or more stressful among students than among young people of other classes, or that the acuity of the identity crisis has analogous political consequences among all young people. The same reasoning would apply to "generational conflict" as a condition of activism. Similarly, propositions which derive from the students' being intellectuals should apply not to students alone but to all intellectuals.

When status variables are pressed into service to explain student activism, the researcher has a variety of options—at least one for every occasion. He can argue that student attitudes are determined by the status of their parents—which is usually privileged in at least some degree—and that they will react by political action to any threat to that status. Or he can suggest that students are oriented to their future status, which may be different from that of their parents. If everything else fails, it is possible to assert that students suffer from status anxiety, either because their future is uncertain, if not bleak, or because of the tension between parental and future status. I myself have argued that students are typically concerned with their future, status-related roles; they will be propelled into political activism if role images are either "unavailable" or "unacceptable."[6] These two adjectives, particularly the latter, act as smoke screens to hide the absence of precise criteria for identifying the circumstances under which this mechanism will go into operation. Different explanations may, of course, be valid for different students, or for the same students at different times. The grab bag of status explanations will always yield some prize.[7]

A more sophisticated attempt to explain student movements considers the value or culture conflicts to which students are subject in their respective societies. This approach has at least the merit, unattainable in individual case studies, of placing the political activities of students into the social and political context.[8] In developing countries, Lipset points out, the culture and hence the values of the university are often alien to the indigenous culture. Further, there is a

[6]Frank A. Pinner, "Student Trade Unionism in France, Belgium and Holland: Anticipatory Socialization and Role-Seeking," *Sociology of Education* 37 (1964): 197.

[7]On this point, see the more detailed statement by Emmerson in his "Conclusion" in Emmerson, ed., *Students and Politics*, p. 396.

[8]Seymour Martin Lipset, "University Students and Politics in Underdeveloped Countries," *Comparative Education Review* 10 (1966): 138–42.

tension between the views of traditional and modern intellectuals and scholars. In authoritarian regimes, whether it be a tsarist or a communist, or fascist dictatorship, the libertarianism of any creative academic community comes into conflict with the restrictiveness of the political apparatus. Generational value conflicts occur not, as Feuer would have it, because the young aim to annihilate their progenitors, but because they take quite literally and push to their logical extremes the faiths they have inherited from their elders. It may be objected, as in the instance of the status variables, that there surely is one value conflict for every occasion. Still, while status problems of one kind or another affect many people in modern or developing societies—that is, societies exhibiting mobility and change—cultural value conflicts may well affect only certain groups in society, particularly elite groups.

The hypotheses about students just reviewed, particularly the last set, suggest two conclusions, one substantive and the other methodological. Substantively, the hypotheses—and the findings which support them—point to the social marginality of the student as an explanatory principle of high potential utility. Methodologically, we may find ourselves constrained to assume some principle whereby different social conditions and different social processes may, under varying conditions, yield the same results. In particular, processes of status change or of isolation within institutions, or cultural value conflict, or the very condition of youth, or some combination of several of these, may make students marginal within their societies.

Given this principle, it may be profitable to focus on the social type of the student in politics, irrespective of the particular social mechanisms that produce him. In the process of constructing such a type, we may discover that the students as political animals are but a species of a larger genus: that of marginal elites. I shall suggest that at least military leaderships and certain clerical groups—priests, monks, and the like—are part of the same genus. As a piece of suggestive historical evidence for this taxonomic kinship, I offer the well-known fact that many institutions of higher learning began as schools for the training of military officers or of the clergy, and that many still combine these functions with those of the modern university. Moreover, historically, the roles of scholar and soldier or of scholar and priest have frequently been combined or successively played by the same persons. Finally, a good portion of the history of universities, and even of societies, appears to have been occupied by the marital alliances and family quarrels among these three species. These are reasons enough to investigate their common characteristics.

MARGINAL ELITES

Marginal elites differ from other population groups in the following ways:

1. They are producers of collective goods, the need for which is most keenly felt by political and spiritual rulers. The military produce security from threats to the polity—of late, national security; the clergy produce religion, an important element of internal social cohesion; and students produce social intelligence, in the widest meaning of the word. In a sense, the members of marginal elites produce themselves by various processes of training which prepare them for the performance of their duties; military training, religious exercise, or study.

2. As producers of collective goods, members of marginal elites do not engage in exchange of goods or services with specific members of the community. To some extent, they always "live off the community," being supported either by taxes or by voluntary or quasi-voluntary contributions, the billeting of soldiers being a good example of the latter. This sets them apart from the "normal" life of the community, in which most relations are defined either by the duties and obligations assumed by superiors and inferiors, as in feudal systems, or by the values of the goods and services exchanged, as in modern societies.

3. The attainment of elite status is governed by processes of recruitment—including, in some instances, self-recruitment—and formal admission. It does not, essentially, depend on either tradition or achievement. While the latter two criteria may well determine an individual's status within his institution, it is simply membership in the institution that determines his status within society.

4. Members of marginal elites are often quartered together, physically separated from the rest of the community. Even if they do not occupy separate living complexes such as monasteries, barracks, dormitories, or largely segregated sections of town, they live away from their community of origin. They do not regard themselves as members of the community in which they live, nor are they so regarded by the community. Frequently they are deprived of normal sexual outlets with marriage partners, a circumstance which further

sets them apart from other citizens. (The criteria listed in this paragraph apply least to clergy of the Protestant denominations.)

5. They are given special privileges and immunities. Among these, the most striking are their subjection to a separate system of law and to the jurisdiction of a separate court system. The existence of separate systems of justice arose historically from the very segregation of military, clerical, and scholarly communities which, in Europe, existed outside the feudal caste system and in other countries as separate castes. It also derived from the desire of the supreme secular or spiritual rulers (emperor, pope, paramount chief, and the like) to protect his physical or spiritual forces from local encroachments. In the modern world, these privileges have gradually been disappearing, most slowly in the case of the military and most rapidly perhaps in the case of students. However, the continuing controversies everywhere concerning university or civil jurisdiction over students indicate that the issue of special privilege will persist as long as students form separate sub-communities.

THEIR CONTRADICTORY STANCES

Because of their social position, marginal elites tend to be motivated by the dual impulses of social distinctiveness and populism. In order to document their social identity, they tend to wear special dress (military uniforms, clerical or scholastic gowns, fraternity bands, hats, and insignia); and although in our egalitarian age the love of uniforms has tended to fade, even students are still recognizable, in most communities, by the style of their clothes. Both the desire to be different and the separateness of their sub-communities lead these elites to uncommon patterns of behavior, special social codes and, quite often, a flaunting of accepted community values. Indeed, marginal elites are, by virtue of their habitat and their primary allegiance to their own sub-community, "detribalized," "decommunalized," free of some of the bonds that constrain the established community citizenry.

But while maintaining their distinctiveness, particularly in relation to other social groups in the local community, marginal elites tend to exalt the importance of larger social and political entities, such as the nation, the church, or the race. Not only do they derive their sustenance from super-communal institutions; they must also, as producers of collective goods, help to maintain or even create the very collectivity that they conceive of serving, a polity, a nation, a race, a church. Hence, they are particularly attracted by ideologies of a populist type. These may range from conventional nationalism to racist chauvinism and from romantic beliefs of the Narodniki in peasant communalism to the current populist version of Marxism-Maoism.

Because of their social segregation—their sense of identity, and the ease with which communications can be established and maintained among groups living in relatively closed communities—marginal elites are easily mobilized for action. Together with the social position and the ideological predispositions of marginal elites, their high level of internal communication explains their sudden assumption of leadership roles at moments of political change.

Clearly, the image I have drawn of marginal elites is grossly exaggerated. It purposely overemphasizes the extent to which these groups are segregated from the rest of society. In the real world, degrees of segregation vary considerably. In a modern national state, the military may be a well-integrated part of the national bureaucracy. Modern clergy, more often than not, are deeply enmeshed in the network of social relations of the local community. And students, particularly those with clear professional career objectives, frequently espouse the attitudes and values appropriate to their future status. But the amount of segregation of marginal elites does vary from place to place and from time to time; and the greater the segregation, the more likely are the political consequences I have suggested.

Although the parallels are striking, it would clearly be dangerous to overestimate the similarities among the three marginal elite groups. For present purposes, it is particularly important to consider two main differences between students and other marginal elites: (1) although the military and the clerical communities typically have a well-defined hierarchical structure, the student community tends to be at best weakly organized; and (2) although the military and the clergy can wield social and political power, students have no power of their own. Given the relative permanence of their hierarchical organizations, the military and the churches can meaningfully enter the routine political process and negotiate with interest groups and political authorities. But student organizations tend to be loosely organized and lacking in continuity and consistency of aim. Consequently, their political effectiveness depends on (1) the derivative power they may have as members of the academic community, which may command public respect and whose alumni occupy important positions in society, and (2) their ability to enter into alliances with other groups. If both of these fail them, withdrawal from the public scene, harassing tactics, and terrorism remain the only alternatives.

Of these three resources, alliances appear to be by far the most effective. Where governments have fallen in the wake of student activities, this has almost invariably involved an alliance with the military.[9] The fall of Ngo Dinh Diem in Vietnam and the Irish independence movement are among the less frequent examples of alliances between the student movement and the church. But coalitions entered into by student movements are often short-lived and rarely outlast the outcome of a struggle, whether victory or defeat. Since the student movement is typically the weakest member of any coalition, it frequently finds itself deprived of the fruits of victory. For the same reasons, the students tend to become easy victims of repression when a coalition to which they belong has been defeated.

THE GERMAN CASE

The history of the German student movement offers an interesting illustration of typical changes in the relations between students and the military. Political alliances between student and military groups tended to emerge during periods when erosion of political authority occurred due to popular disaffection, manifest internal or external weakness, or both. Such alliances could be either "progressive" or "reactionary." But during periods of uncontested stability of the regime, both students and the military were part of the political elite and did not play independent political roles.

Prior to the Napoleonic wars, students and officers were rival elites, the former deriving their status from the prosperity of the urban bourgeoisie, the latter from their aristocratic upbringing and the prestige of their arms and command positions. Both were the protégés of the local ruler, or, as the commoner would have it, "our prince's privileged rabble."[10] Both carried side arms to document their social standing and their readiness to defend their "honor" at a moment's notice. Duels between students and officers were a com-

---

[9] Emmerson, *Students and Politics*, p. 390.

[10] Werner Klose, *Freiheit schreibt auf eure Fahnen—800 Jahre deutsche Studenten* (Oldenburg and Hamburg: Stalling, 1967), p. 127. Much of what follows has been borrowed from this excellent, if somewhat anecdotal, history of German student life.

mon occurrence, tolerated by both the military and the university authorities in spite of official prohibitions.

All this changed with the "national rising" which sealed the defeat of Napoleon. Once the French armies had been vanquished in Russia, students joined the armies of the German princes by the thousands, forming volunteer regiments of their own or submitting to the orders of the formerly hated officers and non-coms. Soldiering now became a romantic and even holy occupation, more meaningful than the pale imitation of life in classrooms and libraries.

Yet, the alliance of students and soldiers was of short duration. Once the external danger had subsided, the German princes lost interest in the students' nationalist fervor and soon came to see it as a danger to their regimes. The nationalistic students, meanwhile, attempted to consolidate their gains by founding the *Burschenschaft*, a new federation of fraternities extolling nationalism, military preparedness (*Wehrhaftigkeit*), and sexual purity. The new organizations were to replace both the aristocratic *Korps* and the *Landsmannschaften* (fraternities of students from the same region). They thought of themselves as patriotic, "freedom-loving"—a term suggesting a vague liberalism—and manly. Clearly, their insistence on the right to bear arms and to engage in dueling, together with growing demands among intellectuals for German unity and some form of constitutionalism, posed a threat to the German monarchies united in the Holy Alliance. The assassination of the writer Kotzebue by the superpatriotic student Carl Ludwig Sand in 1819 served as the pretext for the suppression of the *Burschenschaften* and other suspect organizations, and for the concerted persecution, under the guidance of Metternich, of "demagogues" throughout Central Europe.

The years of persecution saw a steady worsening of the relations between the students and liberal intellectuals on one side, and the military and police forces on the other. In 1833, after the revolutionary flare-up of 1830, fifty students briefly "occupied" the Frankfurt *Hauptwache* (military headquarters) as a signal of revolt. Once in control of the building, they did not know what to do with it; but the authorities responded with a monster investigation which eventually involved eighteen hundred suspects.[11]

[11]On the events of 1848 and the period preceding it, see also the excellent article by Edith H. Altbach, "Vanguard of Revolt: Students and Politics in Central Europe, 1815–48" in Seymour Martin Lipset and Philip G. Altbach, eds., *Students in Revolt*, pp. 451–74.

The years between 1830 and 1848 saw an intensification of anti-government feeling and activity, only a small part of which took specifically political forms. Through a variety of pranks and escapades, students expressed their disrespect for the governments of the various German princes, which had increasingly fallen into disrepute among many in the urban population, both bourgeois and working class, and also among small farmers. Some of the protest movements took the form of a multitude of new student fraternities, such as the *Turnerschaften* (gymnasts) and *Sängerschaften* (singing societies). Only a small minority among the students developed an interest in social problems and adopted egalitarian and Socialist ideas. Thus, the years preceding the revolution of 1848 saw an increase in the political and social concerns of a small minority of students, and the growth of a general disdain for established authority on the part of a great number of them.

In spite of the inadequacy of political preparation, the scattering of efforts, and the lack of ideological cohesion, students again assumed leading positions in the revolutionary movement once word of the Paris uprisings had reached the German states. The students of Göttingen formed a "commune" and called for arms. In Jena, students led a demonstration of several thousand townspeople and farmers. The students of Munich formed a revolutionary militia and forced the resignation of the king of Bavaria. In Vienna, the students formed an "academic legion" and forced the emperor to promise a constitution, freedom of the press, and a people's army. In Berlin, although the Prussian army retained military control, the continuing upheavals caused the king to withdraw the troops from Berlin, to promise a constitution, and to pledge his support for the national unification movement.

The failure of the movement of 1848 is often explained by the inability of intellectuals—the "professors' parliament" in Frankfurt and the student movement—to deal with the real issues of politics. This inability may well reflect the intellectuals' quite realistic fear that they might not be able to control the movement which they had been leading. Up to the revolution, "the people" had been, to them, a rather mythical concept which referred to the "German spirit" more than to real journeymen, shopkeepers, and laborers. In the minds of a majority of the students, "German" was an elite concept referring to the superiority of one's own kind and all too often to the inferiority of the Jews and the non-German subject populations of

Austria-Hungary and Prussia. The revolution, it turned out, did not remain the exclusive property of the intellectual elite; and the students could not be sure that they would be able to retain the leadership of the urban masses that had come into motion. The events of Berlin reflected these fears: as soon as the king had formally given in to the students' demands, they allied themselves with him and, substituting themselves for the regular army, turned their arms against the enraged populace of the capital.

During the second half of the nineteenth century and through the First World War, students remained part of the ruling elite and its military establishment. Politics, after 1848, increasingly became the business of political parties, which had no attraction for students. Instead, they affected a quasi-aristocratic life style in which fraternity life, with its elaborate ceremonials, its beer-drinking bouts, and its fencing and duelling, played a major role. And when war came, students by the thousands rushed enthusiastically into the bloodbath.

The apolitical patriotism of the prewar era turned into an aggressive and increasingly racist antirepublicanism during the Weimar years.[12] Whatever disillusionment the students may have suffered during the war, the revolution and the Spartacist uprisings of the first years of the Republic appeared even more threatening than war itself. At the request of Socialist ministers, the students once more took up arms to fight, within the regular army or in specially constituted militia formations, against revolutionary armies and governments. But they did this to save not the Republic but the "Fatherland" from threat of Bolshevism; and while consenting to save the Social-Democratic government, they insisted that the latter guarantee them "the traditional security of our social opportunities consistent with our educational level."[13] They feared, with some justification, that the end of the empire meant the end of the privileged position which academic youth had enjoyed in the past.

The ideological rationalization of these circumstances took the form of an ultra-nationalistic romanticism; all social and political ills were due to the disunity of the people fostered by communism, which had brought about the defeat of the emperor's victorious

---

[12]The Weimar period is carefully described in Hans Peter Bleuel and Ernst Klinnert, *Deutsche Studenten auf dem Weg ins Dritte Reiche* (Gütersloh: Sigbert Mohn, 1967).

[13]*Ibid.*, p. 67. Cited from a resolution of the student body of the University of Kiel.

armies. These ills were perpetuated by the political parties which represented particular interest groups rather than the people as a whole. From the point of view of the chauvinistic student, the only unifying element in society was the army, which, with considerable student support, and in violation of the Versailles treaty, prepared its own resurrection. The fraternities and other patriotic student organizations supported the "idea of military preparedness" (*Wehrhaftigkeit*), thus transferring their romantic notions of "honor" to the political field.

The Nazi movement posed a dilemma for the traditionalist students: they were in sympathy with its violent anti-Semitism, its bitter opposition to party government, and its militarism; but they were repelled by the Nazis' plebeian attitudes and behavior. Yet, in spite of years of maneuvering on the part of the *Korporationen*, bent on preserving their rituals and privileges, the end was inevitable: the entire student movement was absorbed by the Nazis. Toward the end of the Second World War, foci of resistance developed among the students, particularly those able to attend universities. After years of moral and intellectual degradation, they rediscovered the distinctiveness of the university as a community of scholars devoted to dispassionate study and humanistic values.

In a sense, the Nazi regime had accomplished what the Republic had failed to achieve: by putting political loyalty above all other social distinctions, it had had a leveling effect on society. Moreover, the loss of the eastern provinces deprived the former aristocracy of its economic and social base. Thus, the postwar student generation accepted the new regime; and the *Korporationen*, reconstituted in the late fifties through the efforts of their alumni, now resemble American fraternities more than the traditional *Korps* and *Burschenschaften*. There has been no new alliance with the military; if anything, the majority of German students is now antimilitaristic, partly in reaction to the Nazi experience and partly because the military are seen as the representatives of American predominance. As in other Western countries, the left-wing radicals who engaged in running battles with the "system" during the late sixties constituted a minority of the students. Yet they expressed in an extreme form the anti-authoritarian and antimilitaristic positions common to their generation. The distrust of political parties still exists, and it manifests itself in widespread sympathies with the notion of an "extra-parliamentary opposition" promoted by the left-wing groups.

HYPOTHESES

Although the danger of drawing generalizations from a single case must be recognized, it may be possible, by abstracting from the peculiarities of German culture and history, to derive hypotheses which can be tested elsewhere.

1. Marginal elites, of which students are one species, are caught in a dilemma between elitist and populist attitudes. They are impelled to protect their dictinctiveness and privilege while at the same time documenting their concern for the common man and the community or polity as a whole. Consequently, their level of activity will be high when either their own position or the integrity of society appears to be threatened.

2. Marginal elites perceive a threat to their own privilege when their economic security or social status is jeopardized or when their community (nation, polity, church) is either subjected to the control of an external power or torn by internal dissension or internecine warfare. They see such conditions as indications of the weakness of the government, which is expected to protect them as well as the integrity of the community. Under such circumstances, marginal elites move to substitute themselves or some coalition of which they are a part, for the existing institutional or governmental authorities.

3. Marginal elites are particularly receptive to ideologies emphasizing "unity," for acceptance of such ideologies by society implies a general consensus regarding the privileged position of the marginal elite and the continuity of the community which is the recipient of the collective goals produced by the elite.

4. Students differ from other marginal elites by being poorly organized and bereft of independent power resources. As a result, they are prone to enter into coalitions with other groups, particularly other marginal elites. Failing this, they are frequently driven to the use of terroristic devices.

5. The populist ideology leads students to identify with "the people." Depending on the current patterns of social alliances, such identifications take the form either of romantic idealizations of the common folk or of socialist beliefs in the power of the workers and the peasants. However, attempts to form alliances with these groups of the population usually fail, either because the students feel threatened in their elite position or because they meet with rejection on the part of "the people."

6. For the same reasons, students do not ordinarily enter into alliances with political parties. In addition, their ideology predisposes them to reject either party systems in general or some particular party system. Where students do have party connections, they are typically marginal to the organization and in opposition to the leadership.

7. More generally, students are not suitable members of interest group coalitions because they have no "stock in trade," that is, they have no control over resources that might be offered in exchange for the support of other groups. Consequently, they are more likely to ally themselves with other marginal elites, with whom they share certain ideological propensities. Such alliances, however, are rarely of long duration because the students, as the weakest partner in any coalition, tend to lose control of any movement with which they are associated.

It is clearly impossible to document, in a short paper, the general applicability of these propositions; only a few illustrative examples will be given below. For the time being, these propositions are hypotheses which further research may help to substantiate or reject. To the extent that they are true, detailed elaboration relating the levels of social and economic development to the elite structure of various countries is evidently needed.

The propensity of students to enter into alliances with the military when they feel threatened by the lower classes appears to be rather widespread. In Italy, socialism had been gathering considerable strength among young intellectuals toward the end of the nineteenth century, when the trade unions and socialist parties were securely controlled by intellectuals and genuine working class movements confined to a few industrial centers. As workers increasingly claimed their right to leading positions, the Socialist party experienced a loss of support among the intellectuals and students.[14] After the factory occupations following World War I, students entered into an alliance with the military and the Fascists. In Japan, on the other hand, where the labor movement remained weak until the end of World War II, students gave no active support to the militarist regime.

[14]Robert Michels, *Sozialismus und Faschismus in Italien* 1 (Munich: Meyer & Jessen, 1925), pp. 162–206. See also Guido Martinotti, "The Positive Marginality: Notes on Italian Students in Periods of Political Mobilization," in Seymour Martin Lipset and Philip G. Altbach, eds., *Students in Revolt*, pp. 167–201, for views rather similar to mine.

Although during the sixties, student movements in the developed countries have increasingly turned toward antimilitarism (probably as a reaction to American "imperialism"), the same has not been true in some of the developing countries, such as Ghana and Indonesia. In a historical survey, Altbach[15] has shown that in all Asian countries students have played either a leading role in, or given strong support to, independence movements. However, they become estranged from the new regime when party politics have taken over.

The theory of student movements as marginal elites clearly needs testing and possible modification. When more fully elaborated, it should be able to explain not only the positive cases, but the negative ones as well—for example, the absence of student activism. It is perhaps not too difficult to show, within the framework of this theory, why the political student groups of such Western countries as Great Britain and the Scandinavian states should have remained political debating clubs: there, political development had been rather smooth and military coups and religious upheavals did not occur. It is much less obvious why French students should have been absent from the political scene throughout the nineteenth and well into the twentieth centuries. Yet, for all its shortcomings, the theory I am proposing is worth exploring, for the mechanisms governing the alliance behavior of marginal elites may importantly contribute to our understanding of political change.

[15]Philip G. Altbach, "Student Movements in Historical Perspective: The Asian Case," *Youth and Society* 1 (1970), pp. 333–56.

.16. *Sources of Student Protest in France*

RAYMOND BOUDON

ONE OF the most unusual features of the French student protest in May, 1968 was its extensiveness. While in Germany, in the United States, or in Holland, student activism always involved a minority of students, it was almost impossible in May and June, 1968 to find a French student who was against what was called *le mouvement*.

Of course, in France as everywhere, the hard core of student activism is probably mainly composed of students who come from a high social class, and who are oriented more toward national or international politics than toward university problems. But, also as everywhere, this hard core represents a small minority, and the chief problem from a sociological viewpoint is to explain why the protest of this minority was enthusiastically adopted by a large majority of the students.

I shall ignore here the well-known fact of the high level of centralization which characterizes the French university system. This fact is, of course, not without importance. It explains at least in part why the student revolt, which started at Nanterre (an institution located in the west end of Paris) and at the Sorbonne, spread itself so easily and so quickly to practically all the academic institutions of the country. But it does not explain why the revolt involved practically all the students.

The hypothesis I shall try to defend here is that the student revolt in France was mainly due to the fact that the contradiction between the liberal, elitist orientation of the university and the rapid changes in the characteristics of the student body were probably more acute than in any other country. Because of the sharpness of this contradiction, the social situation of the French students in the sixties may be conceived of as radically different not only from that in other countries, but also from that of the prewar French students or even of the French students in earlier periods. I shall describe this new situation as one of anomie and marginality.

ADMISSION AND REJECTION PROCESSES

Let us start with the most obvious and best-known facts: both the rate of growth and the absolute number of students are high in France in comparison with the neighboring European countries. In 1957–58, there were 175,000 students, and in 1967–68, 500,000. In 1965, the ratio of the students entering university to their corresponding age group in the general population was about 18.8 percent against 11.7 percent in West Germany, 13.4 percent in the Netherlands, and 15.1 percent in Sweden.[1] In some countries, like Norway or Belgium, this ratio is close to the French one. But there, the absolute number of students is, of course, much smaller.

The French university, like most continental university systems, is characterized by the principle of free admission. The high school degree (*baccalauréat*) is the only requirement for entering the university. This led, at least until 1968, to an important and probably growing rate of dropouts. At any rate, even if we suppose this rate constant, the rapid growth of the student body implies that the absolute number of dropouts was substantially increasing.

A survey conducted at the Sorbonne, at the Faculty of Humanities, gives an idea of the importance of the number of dropouts.[2] After three years, the students who have successfully passed their exams get a degree called a *licence*. Here, for a small number of disciplines, are the proportions of the students who entered the Sorbonne in 1962 who, in 1966, had earned their *licence* degree. In classical literature, 47 percent; in philosophy, 41 percent; in geography, 37 percent. These disciplines provide the highest proportions. The lowest are: history, 26 percent; English language and literature, 26 percent; German language and literature, 25 percent; and sociology, 17

[1]Figures drawn from the official records published in *Informations statistiques* and from various OECD reports on the growth of education.

[2]Noëlle Bisseret, "La naissance et le diplôme: le processus de sélection au début des études universitaires," *Revue française de sociologie* 9 (1968 numéro spécial), pp. 185–207; and "La sélection à l'université et sa signification pour l'étude des rapports de dominance," *ibid.* 9 (octobre–decembre 1968), pp. 463–96.

percent. In absolute terms, of one hundred students who started their work in 1962, fifteen were graduated after three years, seventeen after four years, and twenty-four were still at the university, having fulfilled after four years only a part of the requirements which normally are fulfilled in three years.

On the whole, more than 40 percent of the students who entered the Sorbonne in 1962 had withdrawn by 1966 and only 30 percent were graduated.

Extrapolating from these figures to the whole system leads to the conclusion that while the French university was, and still is, characterized by free admission, it eliminates or provokes the withdrawal of a large and increasing number of students.

But this is only one side of the picture. The students who have earned their degree are exposed to a high rate of unemployment. In a prospective study published in 1965, Vermot-Gauchy held the view that in 1975 the French university system would deliver 65,000 *licence* degrees.[3] The number of new jobs theoretically demanding this level of competence would be approximately 45,000. But about 20,000 of these jobs would be given in priority to the minority of students trained in the highly selective *grandes écoles*, which give only advanced degrees. This would leave about 25,000 jobs for the 65,000 students with university training. The others would have to accept a job requiring a lower level of competence.

In psychology, Pierre Oléron in 1967 estimated that about 20 percent of the psychology students could reasonably hope to be employed in this discipline.[4]

Paradoxically enough, this matter of a high level of underemployment was rarely evoked during the events of May and June, 1968. At least publicly, the revolting students condemned the low rate of communication between teachers and students, the impersonality of the exams, the consumption-orientation of the social order, and so forth. To speak of underemployment was in some way taboo.[5] This may be explained by the fact that the issues of the revolt were created by the radical minority, stemming from middle-class families and, as such, relatively protected against this risk.

[3]Michel Vermot-Gauchy, *L'éducation nationale dans la France de demain* (Paris: SEDEIS, 1965).

[4]Pierre Oléron, "Données statistiques sur un échantillon d'étudiants en psychologie," *Bulletin de psychologie* 21 (octobre; 1967), pp. 1–4.

[5]Among the numerous collections of the different kinds of documents published by the students in May and June, 1968, see for instance: *Quelle université, quelle societé*? (Paris: Seuil, 1968).

The non-radical majority followed the radical leaders, but for reasons which had apparently nothing to do with the radical issues. Evidence for this may be found in the result of a survey conducted in September, 1968. When the students were asked what were, in their opinion, the causes of the May-June revolt, they quoted much more often the anxiety which they themselves felt in the face of unemployment than the more philosophical issues proposed by the radicals (see Table 1).[6]

Table 1.　Reasons for Student Revolt (1968) (in Percentages)

Students were asked to rank these reasons for the revolt, in order of importance.	Priorities		
	Most Important 1	2	Least Important 3
Anxiety about the probability of finding a job related to one's studies............................	56	33	8
Rejection of a consumption-oriented society	7	10	80
Unresponsiveness of the university to the needs of a modern society..	35	54	8

Note: The small percentages of answers with ex aequos were rejected.

We may draw two conclusions from this general analysis. The first one is that the liberalism of the free admission system, leading to a high level of exclusion and/or self-elimination after admission, gives rise to a high level of anxiety. This anxiety was expressed by one of the main issues of the May–June, 1968 revolt: abolition of exams. On the other hand, the students were aware that the university degrees represented in no way a guarantee against unemployment, so they were set in this paradoxical situation where they normally felt a great anxiety before exams whose social value was small and probably decreasing.

"BOURGEOIS" VERSUS LOWER-MIDDLE-CLASS UNIVERSITY

Anxiety before exams and competition for jobs are not sufficient to explain the explosion of the French university in 1968. More ac-

[6]Institut Français d'Opinion Publique "Sondage étudiants, septembre 1968," *Réalités* 254 (novembre 1968).

curately, it is possible to show that not only the growth of the student body but also the change in its social composition made out of the French university a contradictory and unstable system.

Roughly speaking, it is possible to associate with the recent history of the French university two ideal types. The first one was still living in the early fifties. The second one definitely replaced the latter in the early sixties.

Up to about 1950, the French university was characterized by a higher social-class composition. Children of businessmen and professionals represented 35 percent of the whole student body in 1939. In 1950, the proportion had hardly changed (33 percent). Children of clerks, shopkeepers, and craftsmen were very few and their proportion remained almost the same between the prewar decade and 1950. Children of workers and farmers were almost absent. Here again, the proportion is the same in 1939 and in 1950 (Table 2).[7]

Table 2.   Social Class Composition of the French Student Body (1939–60)

Father's Occupation	1939	1945	1950	1956	1960
Professional	188	180	174	118	125
Businessman	160	165	154	75	57
Civil servant*	257	250	281	286	283
Clerk	126	131	121	150	190
Craftsman or shopkeeper	38	47	51	125	122
Landowner	40	37	51	52	50
Worker	16	15	19	34	34
Farmer	9	7	8	8	7
Other	166	168	140	172	132
Total	1000	1000	999	1000	1000
N	52,014	81,205	192,003	135,197	174,150

*In France, teachers at all levels are civil servants, as are certain other professional workers.—Ed.

After 1950, this situation changed rapidly. Between 1950 and 1960, the proportion of children whose fathers were professionals fell from 17.4 percent to 12.5 percent, while the children whose fathers were clerks, shopkeepers, or craftmen rose from 17.2 percent to 31.2 percent. This amounts to saying that, roughly speaking, the ratio of the number of students coming from upper- and upper-middle-class families has been divided by about three in ten years.

[7]Drawn from *Informations statistiques* 32–33 (octobre–novembre 1961), p. 268.

This does not mean, of course, that the French university has reached a high level of democratization. The probability of entering the university is still much lower for a child from a lower-middle-class family than for one from a professional family, not to speak, of course, of a worker's child. But a small increment in the former probability may, given the fact that lower-middle-class families are much more numerous, change the composition of the student body in a drastic way.

This is probably what happened. The rate of university entrance, being already high among upper-class students, increased less here than among lower-middle-class students. This was sufficient to cause a considerable change in the social composition of the student body.

The above figures pertain to the 1960 situation. It is difficult to use more recent statistical data, because the occupational categories used in the official records were changed after this date, making a comparison with the previous period impossible. At any rate, it is reasonable to think that the trend observed between 1950 and 1960 may be extrapolated to the following period, so that it is fair to say that between the early fifties and the late sixties, when the revolt developed, the French university, which had been an elitist body, had become a lower-middle-class institution.

Ideologically, these remarks are not likely to have a great appeal. Sociologically, they are probably very important in explaining the May–June 1968 student revolt. Our contention is, indeed, that while the French academic institutions were well suited to an upper-class student body, they ceased to be adapted when the social characteristics of the student body had changed.

As long as the social recruitment of the university remained upper-class, the total absence of an orientation system did not matter. As the total number of students was relatively low, the competition for jobs was reduced. As the students came from upper-class origins, they could easily meet within their families people representing the occupational models to be followed by a young upper-class man or woman: lawyer, physician, engineer, teacher, and so forth. Moreover, these models were few. Most science and humanities students became teachers; the census of 1954 still shows, for instance, that half the science graduates were engaged in secondary and university teaching. A large proportion of students studied law and medicine, disciplines which led to socially highly valued occupations. Hence, for the lower-middle-class students an academic degree was a guarantee of employment, and for the upper-middle-class and upper-class students a guarantee of keeping the social rank provided by the family.

In short, the chief agency of social selection and orientation was the family itself. As regards the university, its role was limited to a kind of confirmation of the social ranking determined by the family system. An open-door system and an orientation process limited to the device of the *a posteriori* control through the exams was perfectly suited for this situation.

The other major feature of the "liberal university" was that it was more culture-centered than training centered. Here again, the limited number of students, the small number of the desirable occupational models, and the status-confirmation function of the university made possible and perhaps desirable the delay of the occupational training proper to the post-academic time span. It is hardly an exaggeration to say that these features characterized the French university during the nineteenth century and the first half of the twentieth century. The existential situation of the French student remained more or less stable until 1950. It is striking that among the academic reforms which have been undertaken both before and after the revolt of 1968, none has really tried to modify the basic principles of free admission and of the self-orientation of the students.

In May, 1968, the students strongly attacked the chief features of the liberal university. The "culture" on one side, the "exams" on the other side, were the chief targets of the protest. Of course, they did not propose to introduce a selective and positive orientation system. For sufficiently clear reasons, they requested only the abolishment of the negative selection system, the exams.

Why this protest? Because the harmony between the social and the academic system—the latter being characterized by a concentration on culture versus training and by merely negative selective mechanisms—had become outmoded both by the drastic change in the composition of the student body and by certain changes in the social system itself.

ANOMIE AND EXTRADETERMINATION

Some surveys show that the system of the "liberal university" is actually ill-suited for the lower-middle-class students and has ceased being adequate for the children of the social elites.

We shall use a study conducted in high schools of Bordeaux and its neighborhood to show that already, at the end of high school, lower-middle-class students see their own future as much more uncertain and harder to master than their school fellows from higher-class families.[8] The lower-middle-class students are more often unable to indicate the kind of occupation they would like to have. Whereas about 62 percent of the upper-class boys have precise desires as regards their future occupation, only 45 percent of the lower-middle-class high school students know the kind of job they would like to do. This is, of course, a consequence of the fact that the former are more likely to get advice from their families and to choose well-known and valued occupations.

Correlated with this difference regarding the occupational choice is a difference regarding anxiety. Lower-middle-class high school students feel more anxious (Table 3).

Table 3.   Anxiety of a Sample of High School Students in Relation to Social Status (in Percentages)

Social Status	Feeling No Anxiety	Feeling Anxiety	Don't Know
Lower	20.9	45.0	34.1
N	213.0	459.0	347.0
Higher...............	31.7	39.1	29.0
N	150.0	185.0	138.0

That this difference with regard to occupational-choice anxiety is due to the fact that lower-middle-class high school students are less supported by their families, both cognitively and emotionally, may be seen from the following table, where students have been ranked in four categories of social status. Quite clearly, lower-middle-class students perceive the influence of their families on themselves as much weaker than upper-class high school students (Table 4).

Complementarily, the former perceive the influence of the teachers as greater: about 15 percent of lower-middle-class students and 8 percent of upper-class students see this influence as strong.

Still more illuminating is the following result. The students who had already chosen an occupation were ranked according to the pres-

[8]Raymond Boudon and François Bourricaud, "Le choix professionnel des lycéens," mimeograph, convention Délégation Générale à la Recherche Scientifique et Technique, juillet 1968.

Table 4.   Perceived Influence of Family in Relation to Social Status Among High School Students (in Percentages)

Perceived Influence of Family	Social Status			
	Lower 1	2	3	Higher 4
Strong or moderate ..	37	38	43	61
Weak	63	62	57	39
N	248	192	244	179

tige of this occupation. If we cross-tabulate this variable with social status on the one hand and school achievement on the other, we notice that while upper-class pupils always choose a prestigious occupation, irrespective of their school achievement, such achievement exerts a great influence on the occupational choice of lower-middle-class students. Thus, more than 70 percent of upper-class pupils choose a prestigious occupation, whatever their school achievement is (Table 5). On the other hand, the proportion of lower-middle-class students choosing an occupation with high prestige rises from less than 30 percent to more than 60 percent as their quality of school achievement rises.

We may draw from these observations a number of conclusions

Table 5.   Prestige of Chosen Occupation in Relation to Social Status and School Achievement Among High School Students (in Percentages)

Prestige of Chosen Occupation	Social Status of Family								
	Lower			Medium			Upper		
	School Achievement			School Achievement			School Achievement		
	Low	Medium	High	Low	Medium	High	Low	Medium	High
Low......	27.5	16.0	8.0	14.5	8.5	9.0	11.0	10.5	8.5
Medium .	45.0	52.5	28.0	47.5	47.5	24.5	15.5	30.5	20.0
High	27.7	31.5	66.0	38.0	44.0	66.5	74.0	59.0	71.5
N	40.0	212.0	125.0	55.0	391.0	145.0	27.0	144.0	35.0
Distribution according to school achievement	14.5	76.5	19.0	11.0	79.5	9.0	13.0	70.0	17.0

which are directly relevant to our problem. First, while upper-middle-class students receive from their families strong psychological support, and perceive their future as predetermined more by the social status of their family than by their school performance, lower-middle-class students are less likely to be able to anticipate their future social position, and are much more dependent on the image of themselves the school system sends back to them. As a result, they show higher rates of both uncertainty and anxiety.

In short, this shows that for upper-class pupils, the main agency in the selection process remains, at least at the high school level, the family itself. By contrast, lower-middle-class pupils are exposed to a selection process where the school system plays the most important role.

This is the reason why, in the last years of high school (as line 1 of Table 5 shows), the distribution of pupils on school performance is the same whatever the social origin. Other surveys show, indeed, that in the earlier high school years, upper-class pupils have better performance.[9] But as the school system functions as a selection agency only for lower-middle-class pupils, they are the ones for whom academic selection counts.

We have now a more precise picture of the population entering the university. This population may roughly be divided into two parts: On the one side, we find a proportion of upper-class students, relatively less academically select, whose level of aspiration is fixed more by the social status of their family than by their aptitudes; and on the other side, a proportion of lower-middle-class students, more academically select, whose level of aspiration is highly dependent on the school and who, missing an effective family support, have no clear representation of what their future social position and occupation should be.

Let us suppose now that these two kinds of pupils enter a "liberal university" characterized by a rapid growth of both the number of students and the proportion of lower-middle-class students.

A first consequence of the less academically select character of the students, caught in rising competition, will be that these students will be exposed to social demotion and will notice at a certain point in

---

[9]See, for instance, Alain Girard and Paul Clerc, "Nouvelles données sur l'orientation scolaire au moment de l'entrée en sixiéme," *Population* 19 (octobre-décembre 1964): 829–64; Alfred Sauvy and Alain Girard, "Les diverses classes sociales devant l'enseignement," *Population* 20 (mars-avril 1965): 205-33.

their academic careers that they have to redefine their level of aspiration. While 53 percent of the lower-middle-class male students get the *licence* degree after four years, the corresponding figure is only 39 percent for upper-class students. The lower-middle-class students often have to earn money. As a matter of fact, a study conducted at the Sorbonne shows that when lower-middle-class students do not have to earn money during their studies, they achieve better. Moreover, the average age at which they enter the university is higher. Hence, although they are academically more select, they are exposed to a high rate of failure, and they experience these failures while they are generally too old to be able to face realistically the possibility of seeking another avenue to success.

For the upper-class student, a university degree is no longer a guarantee against social demotion. For the others, it is no longer a guarantee of social promotion. So, although the students represent still a small, privileged proportion of their age group, their situation appears to be more and more deteriorating in a society which stresses affluence.

Thus, the principles on which the "liberal university" rest lead to highly dysfunctional consequences. The complete lack of a positive orientation system was perfectly suited to a situation where most students, coming from the upper class, were efficiently oriented by their families. The conjunction of this orientation by the family and of a relative lack of competition gave the university a reduced role in the social selection process. Today—that is, progressively since 1960 —the situation has completely changed. The growth of the student body and the drastic change in its composition have led to the consequence that the university system now takes—probably against the will of a majority of the teachers—a dominant part in the social selection process. As this process works within the framework of the old institutions of the liberal university, it leads to easily traced psychological consequences.

Indeed, all the studies recently conducted in the French universities show that a high number of students have the feeling, first, that they have never really and freely chosen the kind of studies they are engaged in, that their choice is the consequence of a sequence of events over which they have no control; secondly, that they were not only ill-advised, but that they became conscious of this error too late to be able to correct it.

A study conducted with the psychology students at the Sorbonne gives illuminating results in this respect.[10] One question was: "If your choice had been completely free, which discipline or which occupation would you have chosen?" To this question, only 25 percent of the female students answered that they would have chosen psychology; whence it is possible to conclude that three out of four felt their orientation was determined from the outside. In addition, 30 percent among the first-year students and 19 percent among the third-year students answered that they would have chosen medicine. This shows that the negative feeling toward the pseudo-choice increases with time.

To summarize, admission at the university is no longer correlative, as Merton would say, of an anticipatory socialization process. The risk of failure, of unemployment, of social demotion is high. The student is no more a potential adult, able to anticipate with some accuracy his future social position and hence already belonging to the adult society, but a marginal man. This is due not only to the contradiction between the principles of the liberal university and the characteristics of the contemporary student body, but also to the fact that the dysfunctions of the liberal orientation system are increased by the rapid diversification of the occupational models following rapid technological change in the society as a whole. It is significant that most psychology students, for instance, explain their choice of this discipline because it appeared to them as a kind of weak equivalent of a socially much more identifiable goal, both as regards content and social valuation, that is, medicine.

Perhaps this latter factor explains the fact that in May and June, 1968, the climax of the revolt could be observed among students belonging to socially ill-defined disciplines, those who were training for half-professionalized occupations like psychology or sociology. Significantly enough, these disciplines are also those which show the highest rates of dropouts.

THE PRESENT SITUATION

Most of the hypothetical causes of the May–June, 1968 university crisis in France are common to continental counties. The Netherlands, Germany, Belgium, and Italy are also characterized by a free admission system inherited from the liberal, bourgeois university of the nineteenth century. But the absolute number of students is smaller

[10]Pierre Oléron, "Opinion d'étudiants en psychologie sur leurs études et leur future profession," *Bulletin de Psychologie* 20 (janvier 1967): 329–45.

in Belgium. In Germany, the relative number of students in proportion to their age group is smaller. This probably means, although it
is difficult to produce statistical evidence of this fact, that the composition of the student body is still closer to the "elitist" model. On
the other side, the federal organization of the German university
system made difficult the rapid nationwide extension of the revolt
which characterized the French protest of May–June, 1968.

In spite of these differences among countries, our contention is
that the dysfunctions of the liberal university we have tried to describe explain at least partly the student protest in all of continental
Europe.

These dysfunctions are emphasized by the fact that in comparison
with the United States or, to a certain extent, with the United King-
dom, there is little diversification of the academic institutions in
most of these countries. Thus, by and large, a student who fails has
no where else to go. In France, the creation of short-time university
institutions (technological institutes) is recent (1965). In 1968, an
almost negligible proportion of the students chose this way. Moreover, these institutions are still often perceived as second-rank institutions and their appeal cannot be compared to that of the regular
academic institutions. In contrast to the junior colleges in the United
States, their weight in the university system is still small, so that
they are not able to correct the dysfunctions of this system.

In 1968, a new law was voted by the Parliament which changed a
number of traditions in the organization of the French university
system. Students were given participation in the management of the
departments and of the universities. The universities were given more
autonomy and the Ministry of Education lost a part of its power to
the benefit of academic administration. But the principle of free admission was kept and the law remains quite vague on the problem of
building a system of positive orientation for the students. So it does
not seem that the actual causes of the revolt have been eradicated.

Nevertheless, the intensity of the student protest decreased suddenly after June, 1968. In 1969, it was limited to some institutions,
like Nanterre and the newly created "experimental university" or
Vincennes in the east end of Paris. Moreover, the protest took the
"classical" form of a periodical agitation on political issues led by
a radical minority, while the majority of the students seemed "uncommitted." In 1970, the radicals appeared to be still more isolated
and their interventions were more and more infrequent.

This is perhaps the proof that the rapid spread of the revolt in

1968 was due to an artificial conjunction between broad issues proposed by the radical minority and the diffuse dissatisfaction felt by the majority of the students with regard to the university system. Once more autonomy was given to the universities and more responsibility to the students, once the traditional examination system was replaced by a more flexible one, the main academic issues put forward by students in May–June, 1968 were satisfied.

But the causes of the revolt—causes, at least, in our interpretation—which could easily be translated into political issues remain, and are not likely to be eradicated very quickly. Moreover, these causes were probably only half-consciously perceived by the students. More accurately, they were perceived but transposed into issues like that of the abolishment of exams, of a condemnation of the "bourgeois culture," or into the utopian issue of a voluntary creation by the political authorities of a number of jobs corresponding to the number of students and to their qualifications.

The apparent weakness of the student protest in France after the climax of May–June, 1968 does not mean, we have tried to show, that the main problems have been solved by the school reform of September, 1968. As a matter of fact, the social marginality of the French students remains as high afterward as it was before, and is not likely to decrease very quickly. As regards the social expression of this marginality—overt revolt, retreat into specific cultural behavior—its form will depend, in the future as in the past, on the general social and political climate.

Part IV

References

.17. Selected References on Student Protest

KENNETH KENISTON and MICHAEL LERNER

A. EMPIRICAL STUDIES OF STUDENT ACTIVISTS

AIKEN, M., DEMERATH, N. J. III, and MARWELL, G. (1965). *Conscience and Confrontation.* East Lansing, Mich.: Christian Faith and Higher Education Institute.

AIKEN, M., DEMERATH, N. J. III, and MARWELL, G. (1971). *Dynamics of Idealism.* San Francisco: Jossey-Bass.

ASTIN, A. W. (1968). "Personal and environmental determinants of student activism," *Measurement and Evaluation in Guidance* (Fall), pp. 149–162.

ASTIN, A. W. (1970). "Some effects of campus protests on student attitudes," Washington, D.C.: American Council on Education.

ASTIN, H. S. (1969). "Self-perceptions of student activists as measured by the adjective check list," draft, Washington, D.C.: Bureau of Social Science Research.

ASTIN, H. S. (1970). "Profiles of students during the 1968–69 campus protest activities," draft, Washington, D.C.: Bureau of Social Science Research, October.

BAIRD, L. L. (1970). "Who protests: a study of student activists," in Foster and Long (G 1970).

BARTON, A. H. (1968). "The Columbia crisis: campus, Vietnam and the ghetto," *Public Opinion Quarterly* (Fall), 32:333–352.

BLOCK, J. H. (1968). "Rebellion re-examined: the role of identification and alienation," paper given at Foundations' Fund for Research in Psychiatry Conference "Adaptation to Change," Puerto Rico, June.

BLOCK, J. H., HAAN, N., and SMITH, M. B. (1969). "Socialization correlates of student activism," *Journal of Social Issues* (November), 25:143–177.

BRAUNGART, R. G. (1969). "Family status, socialization, and student politics: a multi-variate analysis," paper given at American Sociological Association, San Francisco, September 2.

BUREAU OF SOCIAL SCIENCE RESEARCH (1969). "Selected highlights of interview data on the campus unrest study," draft, Washington, D.C.

CHRISTIE, R. (1969). "Liberalism and radicalism," paper presented at American Psychological Association, Washington, D.C.

COLES, R. (1963). "Serpents and doves: non-violent youth in the south," in Erik Erikson (I 1963).

COLES, R. (1964). "Social struggle and weariness," *Psychiatry*, 27: 305–315.

COLES, R. (1967). "Psychiatric observations on students demonstrating for peace," *American Journal of Orthopsychiatry* (January), 37:107–111.

COLES, R. (1967). *Children of Crisis*. Boston: Little, Brown.

COWDRY, R. W., KENISTON, K., and CABIN, S. (1970). "The war and military obligation: private attitudes and public actions," *Journal of Personality*, 38, 4:525–549.

FISHMAN, J. R. and SOLOMON, F. (1964). "Youth and social action," *Journal of Social Issues*, 20:1–28.

FISHMAN, J. R. and SOLOMON, F. (n.d.). "Psychological observations on the student sit-in movement," *Proceedings of the Third World Congress of Psychiatry*, Toronto: University of Toronto/ McGill.

FLACKS, R. E. (1967). "The liberated generation: an exploration of the roots of student protest," *Journal of Social Issues*, 23:52–75.

FOSTER, J. and LONG, D. (1968). "The alienation of generations and status politics: alternative explanations of student political activism," in Roberta Sigel (I 1968).

FRANK, J. D. and NASH, E. H. (1965). "Commitment to peace work: a preliminary study of determinants and sustainers of behavior change," *American Journal of Orthopsychiatry* (January), 35:106–119.

FRANK, J. D. and SCHONFIELD, J. D. (1967). "Commitment to peace work II: a closer look at determiants," *American Journal of Orthopsychiatry* (January), 37:112–119.

FREEMAN, J. L. (1969). "Parents, it's not *all* your fault, but . . . ," *Journal of Personality*, 31:812–817.

GASTWIRTH, D. (1965). "Why students protest," unpublished paper, Yale University.

GAYLIN, W. (1970). *In the Service of Their Country: War Resisters in Prison*. New York: Grosset's Universal Library.

GOODMAN, J. (1968). "Alienation and commitment in contemporary America. Speculations from a study of student activists at the University of Michigan," Chicago, Ill.: University of Chicago, Department of Sociology, August.

HAAN, N., SMITH, M. B., and BLOCK, J. (1968). "Moral reasoning of young adults: political-social behavior, family backgrounds, and personality correlates," *Journal of Personality and Social Psychology* (November), 10:183–201.

HECKMAN, D. M. (1970). "World views and students who take risk for ethical conviction," unpublished Ph.D. thesis, Berkeley, Cal.: Graduate Theological Union.

HEIST, P (1965). "Intellect and commitment: the faces of discontent," in Western Interstate Commission for Higher Education and the Center for the Study of Higher Education (G 1965).

HEIST, P.(1966). "The dynamics of student discontent and protest," paper given at American Psychological Association, New York.

JANSEN, D. G., WINBORN, B. B., and MARTINSON, W. D. (1968). "Characteristics associated with campus socio-political action leadership," *Journal of Counseling Psychology* (November), 15:552–562.

KAHN, R. M. and BOWERS, W. J. (1970). "The social context of the rank-and-file student activist: a test of four hypotheses," *Sociology of Education* (Winter), 43:38–55.

KATZ, J. (1967). "The student activists: rights, needs, and powers of undergraduates," Stanford: Institute for the Study of Human Problems.

KENISTON, K. (1968). *Young Radicals: Notes on Committed Youth*. New York: Harcourt, Brace and World.

KERPELMAN, L. C. (1969). "Student political activism and ideology: comparative characteristics of activists and non-activists," *Journal of Counseling Psychology*, 16:8–13.

KERPELMAN, L. C. (1970). "Student activism and ideology in higher education institutions," final report Project No. 8–A–028, Office of Education, Bureau of Research, University of Massachusetts, Department of Psychology, March.

KORNHAUSER, W. (1967). "Alienation and participation in the mass university," paper given at American OrthoPsychiatric Association, Washington, D.C.

KROUT, M. H. and SANGER, R. (1939). "Personality development in radicals," *Sociometry*, 2:31–46.

LA GAIPA, J. J. (1969). "Student power and dogmatism," *Journal of Psychology*, 73:201–207.

LEVITT, M. (1967). "Negro student rebellion against parental political beliefs," *Social Forces* (March), 45:438–440.

LYONNS, G. (1965). "The police car demonstration: a survey of participants," in Lipset and Wolin (C 1965).

McCORMACK, T. H. (1950). "The motivation of radicals," *American Journal of Sociology* (July), 56:17–24.

MOCK, K. (1968). "The potential activist and his perception of the university," Berkeley, Cal.: Center for the Study of Higher Education.

OLSEN, M. E. (1968). "Perceived legitimacy of social protest actions," *Social Problems* (Winter), 15:297–310.

ORBELL, J. (1967). "Protest participation among southern negro college students," *American Political Science Review* (June), 61:446–456.

PAULUS, G. (1968). "A multivariate analysis study of student activist leaders, student government leaders, and non-activists," in Peterson (E 1968).

PIERCE, R. A. (1969). "Personality styles of student activists," Rochester, New York: University of Rochester.

PINARD, N., KIRK J., and VON ESCHEN, D. (1969). "Processes of recruitment in the sit-in movement," *Public Opinion Quarterly* (Fall), 33:355–359.

PINKNEY, A. (1969). *The Committed: White Activists in the Civil Rights Movement.* New Haven: College and University Preses.

ROSENHAN, D. (1968). "The natural socialization of altruistic autonomy," in Macaulay and Berkowitz (I 1969).

ROSENHAN, D. (1969). "Some origins of concern for others," in Mussen, Langer, and Covington (I 1969).

SCHEDLER, P. (1966). "Parental attitudes and political activism of college students," master's thesis, Chicago, Ill.: University of Chicago.

SCHNEIDER, P. (1966). "A study of members of SDS and YD at Harvard," bachelor's thesis, Wellesley College.

SEARLES, R. and WILLIAMS, J. A. Jr. (1962). "Negro college students' participation in sit-ins," *Social Forces* (March), 40:215–220.

SMITH, M. B. (1969). "Morality and student protest," in Smith (E 1969).

SMITH, M. B. (1969). "The crisis on the campus," in Smith (E 1969).

SMITH, M. B., HAAN, N., and BLOCK, J. (1970). "Social-psychological aspects of student activism," *Youth and Society*, Vol. 1, no. 3.

SOLOMON, F. and FISHMAN, J. R. (1963). "Perspectives on the student sit-in movement," *American Journal of Orthopsychiatry*, 33: 873–874.

SOLOMON, F. and FISHMAN, J. R. (1964). "Youth and social action II: action and identity formation in the first student sit-in demonstration," *Journal of Social Issues* (April), 20: 36–45.

SOLOMON, F. and FISHMAN, J. R. (1964). "The psychosocial meaning of non-violence in student civil rights activity," *Psychiatry* (May), 27:91–99.

SOLOMON, F. and FISHMAN, J. R. (1964). "Youth and peace: a psychosocial study of student peace demonstrators in Washington, D.C." *Journal of Social Issues* (October), 20:54–73.

SOLOMON, F., WALKER, W. L., O'CONNOR, G., and FISHMAN, J. (1965). "Civil rights activity and reduction in crime among negroes," *Archives of General Psychiatry* (March), 12:227–236.

SOMERS, R. H. (1965). "The mainsprings of the rebellion: a survey of Berkeley students in November 1964," in Lipset and Wolin (C 1965).

SOMERS, R. H. (1969). "The Berkeley campus in the twilight of the Free Speech Movement: hope or futility?" in McEvoy and Miller (G 1969).

TESSLAR, M. A. and HEDLUND, R. D. (1970). "Students aren't crazies," *The New Republic* (September 12), pp. 17–18.

THOMAS, L. E. (1968). "Family congruence on political orientations in politically active parents and their college-age children," doctoral thesis, Committee on Human Development, Chicago, Ill.: University of Chicago.

WAINERMAN, C. H. (1967). "Intellect and dissent: a survey of Cornell students," *Cornell Journal of Social Relations* (Spring), 2:101–122.

WATTS, W. A. and WHITTAKER, D. (1966). "Some socio-psychological differences between highly committed members of the Free Speech Movement and the student population at Berkeley," *Applied Behavioral Science*, 2:41–62.

WATTS, W. A. and WHITTAKER, D. (1968). "Profile of a non-conformist youth culture: a study of the Berkeley non-students," *Sociology and Education* (Spring), 41:179–200.

WATTS, W. A., LYNCH, S., and WHITTAKER, D. (1969). "Alienation and activism in today's college-age youth: socialization patterns and current family relationships," *Journal of Counseling Psychology* (January), 16:1–7.

WESTBY, D. and BRAUNGART, R. (1966). "Class and politics in the family backgrounds of student political activists," *American Sociological Review* (October), 31:690–692.

WESTBY, D. and BRAUNGART, R. (1968). "The alienation of generations and status politics: alternative explanations of student political activism," in Sigel (I 1968).

WESTBY, D. and BRAUNGART, R. (1970). "Activists and the history of the future," in Foster and Long (G 1970).

WINBORN B. B. and JANSEN, D. G. (1967). "Personality characteristics of campus socio-political action leaders," *Journal of Counseling Psychology*, 14:509–513.

B. EMPIRICAL STUDIES OF INSTITUTIONS

ASTIN, A. W. (1968). "Personal and environmental determinants of student activism," *Measurement and Evaluation in Guidance* (Fall), pp. 149–162.

ASTIN, A. W. (1970a). "Campus disruption, 1968–1969: an analysis of causal factors," in Korten, Cook and Lacey (I 1970).

ASTIN, A. W. (1970b). "Determinants of student activism," in Foster and Long (G 1970).

ASTIN, A. W. (1970c). "Campus unrest, 1969–70." Washington, D.C.: American Council on Education.

ASTIN, A. W. and BAYER, A. E. (1970). "Antecedents and consequents of disruptive campus protest," *Measurement and Evaluation in Guidance* (forthcoming).

ASTIN, H. S. (1970). "The interviewing experience: a survey of interviewers who participated in the study of campus unrest," *BSSR Research Report*, Washington, D.C.: Bureau of Social Science Research.

BAYER, A. E. and ASTIN, A. W. (1969). "Violence and disruption on the U.S. campus, 1968–1969," *Educational Record* (Fall), 337–350.

BAYER, A. E., ASTIN, A. W., and BORUCH, R. F. (1970). "Social issues and protest activity: recent student trends," Washington, D.C.: Office of Research, American Council on Education, Vol. 5, no. 2.

BISCONTI, A. S. (1970). "Events in protest: preliminary findings in the analysis of 103 protests based on campus newspaper reports," Washington, D.C.: American Council on Education.

DUNLAP, R (1970). "A comment on 'Multiversity, university size, university quality and student protest: an empirical study,'" *American Sociological Review* (June), 35:3:525–528.

FOSTER, J. and LONG D. (1970). "The dynamics of institutional response," in Foster and Long (G 1970).

HASSENGER, R. (1970. "Protest and the Catholic colleges," in Foster and Long (G 1970).

HODGKINSON, H. (1970). "Student protest—an institutional and national profile," *The Record—Teachers College* (Spring), 71: 537–555.

LEVINE, M. and NAISBITT, J. (1970). *Right On*. New York: Bantam Books.

LONG, D. (1970). "Black protest," in Foster and Long (G 1970).

LONG, D. and FOSTER, J. (1970). "Levels of protest," in Foster and Long (G 1970).

PETERSON, R. E. (1966). *The Scope of Organized Student Protest in 1964–1965*. Princeton, N.J.: Educational Testing Service.

PETERSON, R. E. (1968). *The Scope of Organized Student Protest in 1967–1968*. Princeton, N.J.: Educational Testing Service.

PETERSON, R. E. (1970). "The scope of organized student protest," in Foster and Long (G 1970).

PETERSON, R. E. (1971). *May, 1970*. New York: McGraw-Hill.

SASAJIMA, M., DAVIS, J. A., and PETERSON, R. E. (1968). "Organized student protest and institutional climate," *American Educational Research Journal* (May), pp. 291–304.

SCOTT, J. W. and EL-ASSAL, M. (1969). "Multiversity, university size, university quality and student protest: an empirical study," *American Sociological Review* (October), 34:702–709.

URBAN RESEARCH CORPORATION (1970a). *Student Protests, 1969. Summary.* Chicago, Ill.

URBAN RESEARCH CORPORATION (1970b). *Legislative Response to Student Protest.* Chicago, Ill.

URBAN RESEARCH CORPORATION (1970c). "Continuing revolt on campus," *Urban Crisis Monitor* (March 27), 3:13:16–43.

URBAN RESEARCH CORPORATION (1970d). *On Strike . . . Shut it Down!* A report on the first national student strike in U.S. history. Chicago, Ill., May.

URBAN RESEARCH CORPORATION (1970e). "Special issue on student protests," *Urban Crisis Monitor* (June 5), 3:23:2–54.

VOLKWEIN, J. F. (1968). "Research summary: relationship of college student protest and participation in policy-making to institutional characteristics," summary of his Ph.D. thesis for the Department of Sociology, Cornell University.

WILLIAMSON, E. G. and COWAN, J. L. (1966). *The American Student's Freedom of Expression: A Research Appraisal.* Minneapolis, Minn.: The University of Minnesota Press.

C. SELECTED STUDIES OF SPECIFIC PROTESTS

1. Berkeley.

DRAPER, H. (1965). *Berkeley, The New Student Revolt.* New York: Grove.

KATOPE, C. G. and ZOLBROD, P. G., eds. (1966). *Beyond Berkeley: A Source Book in Student Values.* New York: World Publishing.

LIPSET, S. M. and WOLIN, S. S., eds. (1965). *The Berkeley Student Revolt.* Garden City, N.Y.: Doubleday.

LUNSFORD, T. (1965). *The "Free Speech" Crises at Berkeley, 1964–65: Some Issues for Social and Legal Research.* Berkeley, Cal.: University of California, Center for Research and Development in Higher Education, December.

MILLER, M. and GILMORE, S., eds. (1965). *Revolution at Berkeley.* New York: Dell.

2. Columbia.

AVORN, J. L. ET AL. (1969). *Up Against the Ivy Wall.* New York: Atheneum.

THE COX COMMISSION (1968). Fact-finding commission appointed to investigate the disturbances at Columbia University in April and May, 1968. *Crisis at Columbia.* New York: Vintage.

3. Harvard.

EICHEL, L. E., JOST, K. W., LUSKIN, R. D., and NEUSTADT, R. M. (1970). *The Harvard Strike.* Boston: Houghton Mifflin.
KELMAN, S. (1970. *Push Comes to Shove.* Boston: Houghton Mifflin.
ZORZA, R. (1970). *The Right to Say "We."* New Yorker: Praeger.

4. Collections, other protests.

ANONYMOUS (1969). "The sit-in: a chronology," *University of Chicago Magazine* (March–April), 61: 39–47.
FOSTER, J., LONG, D., ET AL. (1970). "Part III. Scenes of conflict: seven case studies," in Foster and Long (G 1970).
HERSEY, J. (1970). *Letter to the Alumni.* New York: A. Knopf.
KENISTON, K. (1970). "New Haven notebook: May Day weekend at Yale," *New Leader* (June 22), pp. 10–17.
McEVOY, J. and MILLER, A. (1969). "Part One—The Scene: Analytic case studies of campus disorders," in McEvoy and Miller (G 1969).

D. STUDIES OF FACULTY ROLE IN CAMPUS UNREST

BAYER, A. E. (1970a). *College and University Faculty: A Statistical Description.* Washington, D.C.: American Council on Education, Research Report Vol. 5, No. 5.
BAYER, A. E. (1970b). "Institutional correlates of faculty support of campus unrest," Washington: American Council on Education (November 20).
BORUCH, R. F. (1969). *The Faculty Role in Campus Unrest.* Washington, D.C.: Office of Research, American Council on Education, Research Report, Vol. 4, no. 5, September.
KELMAN, H. D. (1966). "Notes on faculty activism," *Letter to Michigan Alumni.*
LADD, E. C. Jr. (1969). "Professors and political petitions," *Science* (March 28), 163:1424–1430.
LIPSET, S. M. (1970). "The politics of academia," in Nichols (G 1970).

LIPSET, S. M. (1971). "Faculty and students: allied and in conflict," in Lipset and Schaflander (G 1971).

MORGAN, W. R. (1970). "Faculty mediation in campus conflict," in Foster and Long (G 1970).

NOLL, C. E. and ROSSI, P. H. (1966). "General social and economic attitudes of college and university faculty members," Chicago: National Opinion Research Center, November.

SCHUMAN, H. and LAUMANN, E. O. (1967). "Do most professors support the war?" *Trans-action* (November), p. 34.

SPEIGEL, J. P. (1968). "The group psychology of campus disorders: a transactional approach," mimeo, Brandeis University, Lemberg Center for the Study of Violence.

E. SUMMARIES OF RESEARCH STUDIES

ALTBACH, P. G. (1967). "Students and politics," in Lipset (G 1967).

ALTBACH, P. G. (1968). "Student activism and academic research: action and reaction," in Altbach (G 1968).

BAY, C. (1967). "Political and apolitical students: facts in search of theory," *Journal of Social Issues,* 23:76–91.

BLOCK, J., HAAN, N., and SMITH, M. B. (1968). "Activism and apathy in contemporary adolescents," in Adams (I 1968).

FLACKS, R. (1970a). "Social and cultural meanings of student revolt," in Sampson and Korn (G 1970).

FLACKS, R. (1970b). "Who protests: the social bases of the student movement," in Foster and Long (G 1970).

FOSTER, J. (1970). "Student protest: what is known, what is said," in Foster and Long (G 1970).

KENISTON, K. (1967). "The sources of student dissent," *Journal of Social Issues,* 23:108–137.

KENISTON, K. (1969). "Notes on young radicals," *Change* (November-December), pp. 25–33.

KENISTON, K. (1970). "What's bugging the students," *Educational Record* (May), 51:2:116–129.

LIPSET, S. M. (1966). "Student opposition in the United States," *Government and Opposition,* 1:351–374.

LIPSET, S. M. (1968). "The activists: a profile," *Public Interest* (Fall), pp. 39–61.

LIPSET, S. M. (1971). "The sources of student activism," in Lipset and Schaflander (G 1971).

LIPSET, S. M. and ALTBACH, P. G. (1967). "Student politics and higher education in the United States," in Lipset (G 1967).

MATTHEWS, D. and PROTHRO, J. (1969). "Negro students and the protest movement," McEvoy and Miller (G 1969).

PETERSON, R. E. (1968). "The student Left in American higher education," *Daedalus* (Winter), 97:293–317.

SAMPSON, E. E. (1968). "Student activism and a decade of protest," *Journal of Social Issues* (July), 23:3:1–33.

SMITH, M. B. (1969). *Social Psychology and Human Values.* Chicago, Ill.: Aldine.

TRENT, J. W. and CRAISE, J. L. (1967). "Commitment and conformity in the American college," *Journal of Social Issues* (July), 23: 34–51.

F. HISTORICAL STUDIES

ALTBACH, P. G. and PETERSON, P. M. (1971). "Before Berkeley: historical perspectives on American student activism," this volume, chapter 1.

EHLE, J. (1965). *The Free Men.* New York: Harper and Row.

GARSON, G. D. (1970). "The ideology of the new student Left," in Foster and Long (G 1970).

HOROWITZ, D. (1962). *Student.* New York: Ballantine Books.

LIPSET, S. M. (1971). "The historical background," in Lipset and Schaflander (G 1971).

McCORD, W. M. (1965). *Mississippi: The Long Hot Summer.* New York: Norton.

OBEAR, F. W. (1970). "Student activism in the sixties," in Foster and Long (G 1970).

O'BRIEN, J. (1971). "The growth of the student Left in the 1960's," *The Annals of The American Academy of Political and Social Science* (May), 395:15–25.

SHOBEN, E. J. Jr., WERDELL, P., and LONG, D. (1970). "Radical student organizations," in Foster and Long (G 1970).

SUTHERLAND, E., ed. (1966). *Letters from Mississippi.* New York: Signet Books.

ZINN, H. (1965). *SNCC: The New Abolitionists.* Boston: Beacon.

G. ANTHOLOGIES AND REPORTS ON ACTIVISM AND UNREST

ALTBACH, P. G. (1968). *Student Politics and Higher Education in the United States: A Select Bibliography.* St. Louis, Mo.: United Ministries in Higher Education, and Cambridge, Mass.: Center for International Affairs, Harvard University.

BELL, D. and KRISTOL, I., eds. (1969). *Confrontation.* New York: Basic Books.

CARNEGIE COMMISSION on HIGHER EDUCATION. (1970). *Campus Unrest: Discontent, Dissent, Disruption.* New York: McGraw-Hill.

COHEN, M. and HALE, D., eds. (1967). *The New Student Left. An Anthology.* Boston: Beacon Press.

FOSTER, J. and LONG, D., eds. (1970). *Protest! Student Activism in America.* New York: William Morrow.

JACOBS, P. and LANDAU, S., eds. (1966). *The New Radicals. A Report with Documents.* New York: Vintage.

KOPKIND, A., ed. (1966). *Thoughts on Young Radicals.* New York: New Republic, Harrison-Blaine.

LIPSET, S. M. (1967). *Student Politics.* New York: Basic Books.

LIPSET, S. M. and ALTBACH, P. G., eds. (1969). *Students in Revolt.* Boston: Houghton Mifflin.

LIPSET, S. M. and SCHAFLANDER, G. (1971). *Passion and Politics.* Boston: Little, Brown.

LUCE, P. A. (1966). *The New Left.* New York: David McKay.

MCEVOY, J. and MILLER, A., eds. (1969). *Black Power and Student Rebellion.* Belmont, Cal.: Wadsworth.

NEWFIELD, J. (1966). *A Prophetic Minority.* New York: Signet Books.

NICHOLS, D. C., ed. (1970). *Perspectives on Campus Tensions.* Washington, D.C.: American Council on Education.

PRESIDENT'S COMMISSION ON CAMPUS UNREST (1970). *Report*, Washington, D.C., published in *The Chronicle of Higher Education* (October), 5:2: 1–24.

SAMPSON, E. E. and KORN, H. A. eds. (1970). *Student Activism and Protest.* San Francisco: Jossey-Bass.

SKOLNICK, J. H. (1966). *The Politics of Protest.* New York: Ballantine Books.

SPECIAL COMMITTEE ON CAMPUS TENSIONS. (1970). *Campus Tensions: Analysis and Recommendations.* Washington, D.C.: American Council on Education.

WESTERN INTERSTATE COMMISSION FOR HIGHER EDUCATION AND THE CENTER FOR THE STUDY OF HIGHER EDUCATION. (1965). *Order and Freedom on the Campus.*

H. SELECTED INTERPRETIVE WORKS

BELL, D. (1969). "Columbia and the new Left," in Bell and Kristol (G 1969).

BETTELHEIM, B. (1969). "Obsolete youth," *Encounter*, 23:3:29–42.

BRZEZINKSI, Z. K. (1970). *Between Two Ages: America's Role in the Technetronic Era.* New York: Viking.

FEUER, L. (1969). *The Conflict of Generations.* New York: Basic Books.

FLACKS, R. (1970). "The revolt of the young intelligentsia: revolutionary class-consciousness in post-scarcity America," in Miller and Aya (I 1970).

JENCKS, C. (1967). "Limits of the new Left," *New Republic* (October 21).

REICH, C. (1970). *The Greening of America.* New York: Random House.

ROSZAK, T. (1969). *The Making of a Counter-Culture.* New York: Doubleday.

SLATER, P. E. (1970). *The Pursuit of Loneliness.* Boston: Beacon Press.

I. OTHERS

ADAMS, J. F., ed. (1968). *Understanding Adolescence: Current Developments in Adolescent Psychology.* Boston: Allyn and Bacon.

ERIKSON, E. H. and ERIKSON, K. T. (1957). "The confirmation of the delinquent," *Chicago Review*, 10:15–23.

FOSTER, J. (1970). "The trustees and protest," in Foster and Long (G 1970).

GREELEY, A. M. (1970). "Malice in wonderland," *Change* (September-October), 2:32–38.

HARTNETT, R. T. (1969). *College and University Trustees, Their Backgrounds, Roles and Educational Attitudes.* Princeton, N.J.: Educational Testing Service.

KORTEN, F. F., COOK, S. W., and LACEY, J. I., eds. (1970). *Psychology and the Problems of Society.* Washington, D.C.: American Psychological Association.

LERNER, M. (1969). "Respectable bigotry," *American Scholar* (Fall).

LIPSET, S. M. (1969). "The possible political effects of student activism," *Social Science Information*, 8:7–29.

MACAULAY, J. and BERKOWITZ, L., eds. (1968). *Altruism and Helping*. New York: Academic Press.

MCKIBBEN, W. (1970). "The benefits and burdens of higher education," draft paper prepared for the Carnegie Commission on Higher Education, June.

MILLER, N. and AYA, R. (1970). *Revolution Reconsidered*. New York: Free Press.

MOYNIHAN, D. P. (1970). "Elite land," *Psychology Today* (September), 4:35–37.

MUSSEN, P., LANGER, J., and COVINGTON, M., eds. (1969). *Trends and Issues in Developmental Psychiatry*. New York: Holt, Rinehart and Winston.

NORTH AMERICAN CONGRESS ON LATIN AMERICA. (1968). *Who Rules Columbia*. New York: NACLA.

SCHRAG, P. (1970). "Covering the academic fires," *Change* (July-August), 2:4:10–13.

SIGEL, R., ed. (1968). *Learning About Politics: Studies in Political Socialization*. New York: Random House.

SPAETH, J. L. (1969). "Public reactions to college student protests," *Sociology of Education*, 42:199–206.

STERN, G. (1966). "Myth and reality in the American college," AAUP Bulletin (Winter), pp. 408–414.

TRENT, J. W. and MEDSKER, L. (1968). *Beyond High School. A Psychosociological Study of 10,000 High School Graduates*. San Francisco: Jossey-Bass.

WISCONSIN SURVEY RESEARCH LABORATORY (1966). "Some student reactions to 'depersonalization' at the University of Wisconsin," mimeo, Madison, Wis.: University of Wisconsin (January).

WISCONSIN SURVEY RESEARCH LABORATORY (1970). "Student views on the Vietnam war: 1969," mimeo, Madison, Wis.: University of Wisconsin (May).

ZIEBARTH, E. W. (1970). "Trustees in the academic revolution," in Nichols (G 1970).